ENVISIONING REAL UTOPIAS

ENVISIONING REAL UTOPIAS

ERIK OLIN WRIGHT

VERSO
London • New York

First published by Verso 2010
© Erik Olin Wright 2010

7 9 10 8 6

Verso
UK: 6 Meard Street, London W1F 0EG
US: 20 Jay Street, Suite 1010, Brooklyn, NY 11201
www.versobooks.com

Verso is the imprint of New Left Books

ISBN-13: 978-1-84467-618-7 (hbk)
ISBN-13: 978-1-84467-617-0 (pbk)

British Library Cataloguing in Publication Data
A catalogue record for this book is available from the British Library

Library of Congress Cataloging-in-Publication Data
A catalog record for this book is available from the Library of Congress

Typeset in Sabon by Hewer Text UK Ltd, Edinburgh
Printed and bound by CPI Group (UK) Ltd, Croydon, CR0 4YY

To my daughters, Jenny and Becky

CONTENTS

PREFACE

In 1970, facing the draft during the Vietnam War, I attended the Thomas Starr King School for the Ministry, a Unitarian-Universalist seminary in Berkeley, California. Students studying in seminaries were given a draft deferment and so seminary enrollments rose dramatically in the late 1960s. As part of my studies, I organized a student-run seminar called "Utopia and Revolution." For ten weeks I met with a dozen or so other students from the various seminaries in the Berkeley Graduate Theological Union to discuss the principles and prospects for the revolutionary transformation of American society and the rest of the world. We were young and earnest, animated by the idealism of the civil rights movement and the anti-war movement and by the countercultural currents opposed to competitive individualism and consumerism. We discussed the prospects for the revolutionary overthrow of American capitalism and the ramifications of the "dictatorship of the proletariat," as well as the potential for a countercultural subversion of existing structures of power and domination through living alternative ways of life.

In order to facilitate our discussions in that seminar, I recorded the sessions and typed up transcripts each week to give to each of the participants. In the first session we discussed what each of us meant by "Utopia." Towards the end of the discussion I suggested the following:

> It would be undesirable, I think, for the task of constructing an image of utopia, as we are doing, to be seen as an attempt to find definitive institutional answers to various problems. We can perhaps determine what kinds of social institutions *negate* our goals and which kind of institutions seem to at least move towards those goals, but it would be impossible to come up with detailed plans of actual institutions which would fully embody all of our ideals. Our real task is to try to think of institutions which themselves are capable of dynamic change, of

responding to the needs of the people and evolving accordingly, rather than of institutions which are so perfect that they need no further change.

In due course the system of conscripting young men into the army changed to a draft lottery and I got a good number, so in 1971 I was able to begin my graduate studies in Sociology at the University of California, Berkeley.

For the next two decades my work revolved around the problem of reconstructing Marxism, particularly its theoretical framework for the analysis of classes. The problem of socialism and alternatives to capitalism surfaced from time to time, but was not the central focus of my research and writing.

I returned to the theme of utopia and emancipatory transformation in 1992. The Berlin Wall had fallen, the Soviet Union disintegrated. Neoliberalism and market fundamentalism dominated government policies in capitalist democracies. With the demise and discrediting of the centrally planned economies, many people believed that capitalism and liberal democracy were the only possible future for humanity. The "end of history" was announced.[1]

This is the context in which I began the Real Utopias Project in the early 1990s as an attempt at deepening serious discussion of alternatives to existing structures of power, privilege and inequality. The idea of the project was to focus on specific proposals for the fundamental redesign of different arenas of social institutions rather than on either general, abstract formulations of grand designs, or on small immediately attainable reforms of existing practices. This is a tricky kind of discussion to pursue rigorously. It is much easier to talk about concrete ways of tinkering with existing arrangements than it is to formulate plausible radical reconstructions. Marx was right that detailed blueprints of alternative designs are often pointless exercises in fantasy. What I and my collaborators in the Real Utopias Project wanted to achieve was a clear elaboration of workable institutional principles that could inform emancipatory alternatives to the existing world. This falls between a discussion simply of the moral values that motivate the enterprise and the fine-grained details of institutional characteristics.

---

1 Francis Fukuyama, *The End of History and the Last Man* (New York: The Free Press, 1992).

By 2003 four books had been published from the Project (two more have appeared since then) and it seemed like a good time to step back from specific proposals and try to embed the Project in a larger framework of analysis.[2] At the same time I began work with Michael Burawoy on a book project, so far not completed, which we called *Sociological Marxism*. We had written a joint paper with this title for a handbook of sociological theory and thought it would be a good idea to expand that piece into a book-length manuscript.[3] The core argument of the original paper was that the most robust and enduring aspect of the Marxist tradition was its class analysis, and that around class analysis it was possible to construct a wide-ranging sociological Marxism. In the projected book we planned to trace the historical roots of sociological Marxism in the Marxist tradition, for which Burawoy would take major responsibility, and to elaborate more thoroughly its theoretical foundations, for which I would have the principal responsibility. I began writing a draft of my part of the manuscript in which the concluding chapters were an elaboration of the idea of envisioning real utopias. As it turned out, Burawoy got elected President of the American Sociological Association and embarked on a new line of thinking and writing on the theme of "public sociology," so our joint book project was sidelined. He encouraged me to take those final chapters and use them as the core of a separate book, which eventually became *Envisioning Real Utopias*.

In the fall of 2004 I presented an initial version of the core argument of the book, written as a paper, "Taking the 'Social' in Socialism Seriously," at the annual meetings of the American Sociological Association and the Society for the Advancement

---

2   The six books in the Real Utopias Project are: *Associations and Democracy*, by Joshua Cohen and Joel Rogers (London: Verso, 1995); *Equal Shares: Making Market Socialism Work*, by John Roemer (London: Verso, 1996); *Recasting Egalitarianism: New Rules for Equity and Accountability in Markets, Communities and States*, by Samuel Bowles and Herbert Gintis (London: Verso, 1999); *Deepening Democracy: Innovations in Empowered Participatory Governance*, by Archon Fung and Erik Olin Wright (London: Verso, 2003); *Redesigning Distribution: Basic Income and Stakeholder Grants as Cornerstones of a More Egalitarian Capitalism*, by Bruce Ackerman, Anne Alstott and Philippe Van Parijs (London: Verso, 2007); *Gender Equality: Transforming Family Divisions of Labor*, by Janet Gornick and Marcia Meyers (London: Verso, 2009).
3   Michael Burawoy and Erik Olin Wright, "Sociological Marxism," in Jonathan Turner (ed.), *Handbook of Sociological Theory* (New York: Kluwer Academic/Plenum Publishers, 2001).

of Socio-Economics. It seemed well received at both conferences. Then I presented the paper at the meeting of the Analytical Marxism Group, a group of academics that had been meeting almost annually since around 1980 to discuss each other's work.[4] They did not like the paper very much, especially my effort at differentiating types of economic systems in terms of the particular form of power that was "dominant" within the organization of the economy. We had a long, intense (and somewhat frustrating) discussion of the problem of defining "dominance" of particular elements in a complex structure of relations. No one had any particularly constructive suggestions, and I left the gathering a bit demoralized.

On further thought in the months following the meeting I decided that while the analytical problem raised in the discussion was a real one, it did not seriously undermine the central substantive thrust of my approach to the problem (these issues will be discussed in chapter 5), and so I returned to the paper and gave it a thorough reworking in 2005. The result, which lays out the core ideas that are more fully elaborated in this book, was eventually published in *New Left Review* in 2006.[5]

By spring of 2005 I felt that I had a defensible core argument, but was not sure about how ambitious I wanted the book to be. Should it basically be a modest elaboration of the *NLR* piece? Should I try to embed the specific arguments around envisioning real utopias in a broader agenda of emancipatory social theory? Should I directly engage Marxism both to establish the location of my argument within the Marxist tradition and to specify the ways

---

4 The Analytical Marxism Group was begun to discuss central themes in Marxist theory, especially the concept of exploitation. In the course of the early 1980s the members of the group developed a distinctive style for exploring Marxism, which was eventually dubbed "Analytical Marxism." I was invited to participate in the group in 1981. Other members of the group (not all of whom were there from the start) include G.A. Cohen, John Roemer, Hillel Steiner, Sam Bowles, Josh Cohen, Robert van der Veen, Philippe Van Parijs, and Robert Brenner. Adam Przeworski and Jon Elster were members of the group in the 1980s but had left by the time I presented this work. For a collection of writings by members of this circle, see John Roemer (ed.), *Analytical Marxism* (Cambridge: Cambridge University Press, 1985).

5 When submitted to *New Left Review* the paper still had the title "Taking the 'Social' in Socialism Seriously," but the editors of the journal said that they did not like long, wordy titles, and changed it to "Compass Points: Towards a Socialist Alternative," which played off a metaphor I used in the paper. While I still much preferred the original title, I acquiesced to their editorial judgment.

in which it departs from aspects of that tradition? I decided that the best way for me to resolve such issues was to begin publicly discussing the ideas in the book as widely as possible by accepting invitations to give visiting lectures whenever they came in. This would enable me both to refine the arguments themselves through a dialogic process and to get a better sense of how useful it would be to expand the agenda of the book itself.

So, I began what eventually became four years of traveling around the world giving lectures, seminars, workshops, and, in a few places, extended lecture series, on the book manuscript at universities, conferences, and other venues. I never anticipated that I would in the end give over 50 talks in 18 countries:

2005: University of Arizona; University of Umea, Sweden (four lectures); Charles University, Prague; Seminar at the Czech Parliament, Prague; University of Trento, Italy; Croatian Sociological Association, Zagreb; University of Zagreb; Conference on Moral Economy, University of Lancaster; School of Social Ecology, U.C. Irvine; School of Social Justice, University College, Dublin.

2006: Department of Sociology, Princeton University; Conference on Hegel, Marx, and Psychoanalysis, Sarajevo, Bosnia; London School of Economics; University of California, Berkeley (six lectures); Midwest Social Forum, Milwaukee; University of Toronto.

2007: NYU (four lectures); Columbia University; Haverford College; Wheaton College; Tohoku University, Sendai, Japan; Kyushu University, Fukuoka, Japan; Kwansei Gakuin University, Osaka, Japan; Kyoto University; University of Tokyo; University of Buenos Aires, Argentina; Universidad Diego Portales, Santiago, Chile; Renmin University, Beijing; Tsinghua University, Beijing; Chinese Academy of Social Sciences, Beijing; Sun-Yat Sen University, Guangzhou; Nanjing University; Fudan University, Shanghai; Witwatersrand University, Johannesburg, South Africa (four lectures); University of Johannesburg, Johannesburg; COSATU leadership workshop, Johannesburg; University of California, Berkeley (series of eight lectures and seminars); University of Trondheim, Norway (three lectures); Middle Eastern Technical University, Ankara (four lectures); Bogazici University, Istanbul; University of Minnesota.

2008: University of Barcelona; University of Milan; University of Sienna; University of the Basque Country, Bilbao, Spain; Sciences Po, Paris; Colegio de Mexico, Mexico City; Lancaster University.

One might have thought that eventually there would be significant diminishing intellectual returns from giving such a large
number of talks. But this really was not the case. Each wave of
presentations and discussions occurred in the context of recent
revisions and new formulations, and some of the most important refinements were triggered by discussions very late in this
process.[6] At these talks I took careful notes of the discussions, and
at some of them I recorded the discussions and prepared written
transcripts.[7] From these notes, written during the four years of
discussions, I accumulated an inventory of problems, unresolved
issues, and possible revisions. I more or less continuously revised
the manuscript, posting the most current draft of chapters on the
web. Often when I gave lectures some of the participants had
read some of the pieces of the book-in-progress and had prepared
comments in advance.

In planning such far-flung lecture trips in such different parts
of the world I had anticipated getting sharply different reactions
in different places. Surely the questions people would pose in
China would be different from those asked in Norway. The most
striking fact of my discussions in these venues, however, was the
commonality of issues raised, the commonality of criticisms and
concerns, and also the commonality of the general enthusiasm
for the agenda I laid out. Everywhere people seemed to appre-
ciate the institutional pluralism of the conception of socialism I
proposed and the moral vision of social justice I defended, but
also, everywhere, people were skeptical about the possibilities of
social power rooted in civil society providing a basis for transcending capitalism, especially under conditions of globalization.
Of course, there was considerable self-selection on the part of
my audiences: the people who were most likely to show up at
a lecture called "Envisioning Real Utopias" would be critics of
existing institutions and already positively disposed to thinking
about emancipatory alternatives. Still, it was reassuring to me
that with a few interesting exceptions people were receptive both
to the idea of placing democracy and social power at the center
of the problem of transforming capitalism into an emancipatory

---

6 For example, to anticipate some of the discussion in chapter 5, two "pathways
of social empowerment" were added after my visit to Barcelona in May of 2008.

7 Some of the transcripts of the discussions of the book manuscript in these
lectures and seminars, and some of the audio recordings as well, are available on
my website: http://www.ssc.wisc.edu/~wright.

alternative, and to exploring the institutionally heterogeneous ways in which this could be realized in practice. I felt that I was part of a global conversation on the dilemmas of our time, and even if many people remained unconvinced about the feasibility of real utopias, the analysis I laid out nevertheless resonated.

In the spaces between all of this travel, I taught a PhD level seminar on real utopias at the University of Wisconsin in 2005 and 2008. In the spring semester of 2008 I organized this seminar around the existing draft of the book—students read and commented on one chapter each week. The seminar also involved a weekly video-conference connection with a group of sociology students at the University of Buenos Aires who had attended my lectures there in May of 2007 and wanted to participate in the Wisconsin seminar.[8] At the end of the semester the students from Argentina came to Madison for a two-day mini-conference on "Envisioning Real Utopias" with the students from Wisconsin and a few from Berkeley, NYU, and Minnesota who had also been involved in the lectures and seminars I had given at their universities. The final consolidation and revision of the book came in the immediate aftermath of this intensive and (for me anyway) extraordinarily productive seminar.

It is very hard in a process like this to know exactly where all of the new ideas and refinements came from. The most accurate description is that they came out of the extended dialogue in which I was so vigorously engaged. Of course, it is always true that ideas are social products, not just the result of individual imagination springing from interior reflection. But in the case of this book, the ideas are not simply a social product, but a collective product generated by the collaboration of hundreds of people around the world with whom I have discussed its arguments. I am deeply grateful to the many people who came to these discussions and contributed their thoughts to the collaborative process of developing the ideas in this book.

I worry about thanking specific people, since I am sure that I will leave off someone whose skepticism, poignant comment or suggestion has played an important role in pushing the arguments of the book forward. Still, there are some specific people that I must acknowledge: Michael Burawoy has been both my most

---

8   Audio recordings of most of the weekly discussions in this seminar, along with student comments and my responses, are available online at: http://www. ssc.wisc.edu/~wright.

consistent critic and one of my two most consistent supporters. He is relentlessly enthusiastic about the idea of real utopias, and equally relentlessly critical about many of the details of my analysis. He, more than anyone else, has emphasized the importance of the word "social" and it was through our discussions (especially on bike rides and hikes in Northern California) that the specific terminological convention of talking about the "social" in "socialism" emerged. My wife, Marcia Kahn Wright, has been the other most consistent supporter of this work and has not only continually refueled my commitment to the Real Utopias Project and tolerantly put up with the disruptions caused by my travel, but has substantively contributed important ideas to the book in our periodic late-night discussions of particular problems and themes. Harry Brighouse has become in recent years the person with whom I have discussed the problem of real utopias and its philosophical underpinnings the most. The specific elaboration of the concepts of social justice and human flourishing underpinning the normative foundations of this book owes much to our discussions. Two of my students, Gianpaolo Baiocchi and Amy Lang, did their doctoral dissertations on specific problems of real utopian institutional innovations, and I learned a tremendous amount from them about the fine-grained details of their cases and the implications these have for the broader problem of deepening democracy. My collaboration with Archon Fung in writing the anchoring essay of volume IV of the Real Utopias Project, *Deepening Democracy*, was of fundamental importance in helping me to understand why democracy is the core problem for transcending capitalism. My earlier work had emphasized the centrality of exploitation to capitalism, and of course exploitation is pivotal to the way capitalism works. But the central axis of transcending capitalism is democracy. Joel Rogers has been involved in various ways with the Real Utopias Project from the start. Indeed, he proposed the name on one of our weekly Sunday morning walks with my golden retriever in the early 1990s, as we were planning the conference on associational democracy that eventually became the basis for the first book in the project. My former student, Vivek Chibber, has repeatedly reminded me that class struggle and class politics must be at the core of the effort to transform and transcend capitalism even though he (I think) now reluctantly agrees with me that ruptural logics of class struggle are not very plausible in the world today. The members of the Analytical Marxism Group—G.A. Cohen, Philippe Van Parijs,

Sam Bowles, Josh Cohen, Hillel Steiner, Robert Brenner, John Roemer, and Robert van der Veen—might have been discouraging when I first presented the earliest version of the argument of this book to them in 2004, but in the end their reaction was certainly helpful in pushing the issues forward. More importantly, my understanding of philosophical ideas about equality and the conditions for its realization have developed largely through the quarter century of my discussions with the members of this group. Finally, I would like to thank the students in the graduate seminars at Berkeley and Wisconsin who read drafts of chapters of the book and wrote provocative interrogations for each discussion. Their willingness to raise sharp criticisms and express skepticism about many of my formulations has led to many revisions of the text and the addition of many footnotes in which I reply to objections which they raised in class.

A note on the audience for this book

I began writing this book with a broad, relatively popular audience in mind. I somehow hoped that I could deal seriously with these difficult theoretical and political matters and still make the book accessible and attractive to people not schooled in radical social theory or Marxism. As the book expanded and I encountered criticisms that I felt I needed to counter, it became clear to me that I was in practice engaged in a dialogue with a relatively sophisticated audience. One of the hallmarks of "academic" writing is responding to potential criticisms of one's arguments that will not have occurred to most readers. Still, I wanted the book at least to be readable by people not steeped in academic debates. I have tried to resolve this problem by placing in footnotes the discussions of many of the more academic refinements and responses to objections to the analysis. The main text itself can be read without looking at the footnotes.

There is one other tension concerning the hoped-for audience of the book. I want it to be relevant both to people whose intellectual and political coordinates are firmly anchored in the socialist left as well as to people broadly interested in the dilemmas and possibilities for a more just and humane world who do not see the Marxist tradition as a critical source of ideas or as an arena for debate. This is also a difficult divide to straddle. In engaging people sympathetic to Marxism around the problem of the radical transcendence of capitalism it is important to explore the issue of revolutionary transformation and the limitations in the traditional Marxist theory of history. People who feel no connection to the Marxist tradition are likely to see those discussions as being largely irrelevant. The use of the term "socialism" to describe the structural aspects of the emancipatory alternative to capitalism also reflects this tension: For people sympathetic to the Marxist tradition, my attempt at rethinking socialism in terms of social power and radical democracy connects with longstanding themes; to non-Marxists the term "socialism" may seem antiquated, and, in spite of my terminological protestations, to have too close a link to centralized statism.

This tension of writing both for people who identify in some way with Marxism and for those indifferent or hostile to Marxism is further exacerbated by my desire for the book to be relevant to people in different countries, where "Marxism" and "socialism" can carry very different connotations. In the United States the word "socialism" lies completely outside of mainstream political life, whereas in many European countries it is an umbrella label for progressive politics rooted in democratic egalitarian values.

I do not know if I have successfully navigated these problems of audience. My strategy is to try to write clearly, define all of the key concepts I use, and carefully present the steps in my arguments in a logical way that hopefully will make the text accessible to people both familiar and less familiar with this kind of discussion.

Madison, Wisconsin
July, 2009

INTRODUCTION:
WHY REAL UTOPIAS?[1]

There was a time, not so long ago, when both critics and defenders of capitalism believed that "another world was possible." It was generally called "socialism." While the right condemned socialism as violating individual rights to private property and unleashing monstrous forms of state oppression, and the left saw socialism as opening up new vistas of social equality, genuine freedom and the development of human potentials, both believed that a fundamental alternative to capitalism was possible.

Most people in the world today, especially in its economically developed regions, no longer believe in this possibility. Capitalism seems to them part of the natural order of things, and pessimism has replaced the optimism of the will that Gramsci once said would be essential if the world was to be transformed.

In this book I hope to contribute to rebuilding a sense of possibility for emancipatory social change by investigating the feasibility of radically different kinds of institutions and social relations that could potentially advance the democratic egalitarian goals historically associated with the idea of socialism. In part this investigation will be empirical, examining cases of institutional innovations that embody in one way or another emancipatory alternatives to the dominant forms of social organization. In part it will be more speculative, exploring theoretical proposals that have not yet been implemented but nevertheless are attentive to realistic problems of institutional design and social feasibility. The idea is to provide empirical and theoretical grounding for radical democratic egalitarian visions of an alternative social world.

---

1 Parts of this chapter appeared in the preface to the first volume in the Real Utopias Project, *Associations and Democracy*, by Joshua Cohen and Joel Rogers (London: Verso, 1995).

Four examples, which we will discuss in detail in later chapters, will give a sense of what this is all about:

1. Participatory city budgeting

In most cities in the world that are run by some form of elected government, city budgets are put together by the technical staff of the city's chief executive—usually a mayor. If the city also has an elected council, then this bureaucratically constructed budget is probably submitted to the council for modification and ratification. The basic shape of the budget is determined by the political agenda of the mayor and other dominant political forces working with economists, engineers, city planners, and other technocrats. That is the situation in the existing world.

Now, imagine the following alternative possible world: Instead of the city budget being formulated from the top down, suppose that the city is divided into a number of neighborhoods, and each neighborhood has a participatory budget assembly. Suppose also that there are a number of city-wide budget assemblies on various themes of interest to the entire municipality—cultural festivals, for example, or public transportation. The mandate for the participatory budget assemblies is to formulate concrete budget proposals, particularly for infrastructure projects of one sort or another, and submit them to a city-wide budget council. Any resident of the city can participate in the assemblies and vote on the proposals. They function rather like New England town meetings, except that they meet regularly over several months so that there is ample opportunity for proposals to be formulated and modified before being subjected to ratification. After ratifying these neighborhood and thematic budgets, the assemblies choose delegates to participate in the city-wide budget council for a few months until a coherent, consolidated city budget is adopted.

This model is in fact the reality in the city of Porto Alegre, Brazil. Before it was instituted in 1989 few people would have thought that a participatory budget could work in a relatively poor city of more than one and a half million people, in a country with weak democratic traditions, plagued by corruption and political patronage. It constitutes a form of direct, participatory democracy fundamentally at odds with the conventional way that social resources get allocated for alternative purposes in cities. We will discuss this case in some detail in chapter 6.

2. Wikipedia

Wikipedia is a large, free-wheeling internet encyclopedia. By mid-2009 it contained over 2.9 million English-language entries, making it the largest encyclopedia in the world. It is free to anyone on the planet who has access to the internet, which means that since the internet is now available in many libraries even in very poor countries, this vast store of information is potentially available without charge to anyone who needs it. In 2009, roughly 65 million people accessed Wikipedia monthly. The entries were composed by several hundred thousand unpaid volunteer editors. Any entry can be modified by an editor and those modifications modified in turn. While, as we will see in chapter 7, a variety of rules have evolved to deal with conflicts over content, Wikipedia has developed with an absolute minimum of monitoring and social control. And, to the surprise of most people, it is generally of fairly high quality. In a study reported in the journal *Nature*, in a selection of science topics the error rates in Wikipedia and the *Encyclopædia Britannica* were fairly similar.[2]

Wikipedia is a profoundly anti-capitalist way of producing and disseminating knowledge. It is based on the principle "to each according to need, from each according to ability." No one gets paid for editing, no one gets charged for access. It is egalitarian and produced on the basis of horizontal reciprocities rather than hierarchical control. In the year 2000, before Wikipedia was launched, no one—including its founders—would have thought possible what has now come to be.

3. The Mondragon worker-owned cooperatives

The prevailing wisdom among economists is that, in a market economy, employee-owned and managed firms are only viable under special conditions. They need to be small and the labor force within the firm needs to be fairly homogeneous. They may be able to fill niches in a capitalist economy, but they will not be able to produce sophisticated products with capital intensive technologies involving complex divisions of labor. High levels of complexity require hierarchical power relations and capitalist property relations.

---

2 See Jim Giles, "Special Report: Internet Encyclopaedias Go Head to Head," *Nature* 438 (2005), pp. 900–1.

Mondragon is a conglomerate of worker-owned cooperatives in the Basque region of Spain. It was founded in the 1950s during the Franco dictatorship and is now the 7th largest business group in Spain and the largest in the Basque region with more than 40,000 worker-owner members.[3] The conglomerate is made up of some 250 separate cooperative enterprises, each of which is employee-owned—there are no non-worker owners—producing a very wide range of goods and services: washing machines, auto-parts, banking, insurance, grocery stores. While, as we will see in chapter 7, it faces considerable challenges in the globalized market today, nevertheless the top management continues to be elected by the workers and major corporate decisions are made by a board of directors representing the members or by a general assembly of the members.

4. Unconditional basic income

The idea of an unconditional basic income (UBI) is quite simple: Every legal resident in a country receives a monthly living stipend sufficient to live above the "poverty line." Let's call this the "no frills culturally respectable standard of living." The grant is *unconditional* on the performance of any labor or other form of contribution, and it is *universal*—everyone receives the grant, rich and poor alike. Grants go to individuals, not families. Parents are the custodians of underage children's grants (which may be at a lower rate than the grants for adults).

Universalistic programs, like public education and health care, that provide services rather than cash, would continue alongside universal basic income, but with the latter in place, most other redistributive transfers would be eliminated—general welfare, family allowances, unemployment insurance, tax-based old age pensions—since the basic income grant would be sufficient to provide everyone with a decent subsistence. This means that in welfare systems that already provide generous antipoverty income support through a patchwork of specialized programs, the net increase in costs represented by universal unconditional basic income would not be large. Special needs subsidies of various sorts would continue—for example, for people with disabilities—but they would also be smaller than under current arrangements since

---

3   Mondragon Annual Report 2007, p. 3. Available at: http://www.mcc.es/ing/magnitudes/memoria2007.pdf.

the basic cost of living would be covered by the UBI. Minimum wage rules would be relaxed or eliminated since there would be little need to legally prohibit below-subsistence wages if all earnings, in effect, generated discretionary income. While everyone receives the grant as an unconditional right, most people at any given point in time would probably be net contributors since their taxes will rise by more than the basic income. Over time, however, most people will spend part of their lives as net beneficiaries and part of their lives as net contributors.

Unconditional basic income is a fundamental redesign of the system of income distribution. As we will see in detail in chapter 7, it has potentially profound ramifications for a democratic egalitarian transformation of capitalism: poverty is eliminated; the labor contract becomes more nearly voluntary since everyone has the option of exit; the power relations between workers and capitalists become less unequal, since workers, in effect, have an unconditional strike fund; the possibility of people forming cooperative associations to produce goods and services to serve human needs outside of the market increases since such activity no longer needs to provide the basic standard of living of participants.

No country has adopted an unconditional basic income, although the most generous welfare states have incomplete, fragmented versions and there has been one experimental pilot program for a basic income in a very poor country, Namibia.[4] It is a theoretical proposal which necessarily involves some speculation about its dynamic effects. It thus could turn out that a generous basic income, if implemented, would not be viable—it might self-destruct because of all sorts of perverse effects. But, as I will argue later, there are also good reasons to believe that it would work and that it could constitute one of the cornerstones of another possible world.

These are all examples of what I will call "real utopias." This may seem like a contradiction in terms. Utopias are fantasies, morally inspired designs for a humane world of peace and harmony unconstrained by realistic considerations of human psychology and social feasibility. Realists eschew such fantasies. What we need are hard-nosed proposals for pragmatically improving our

---

4 Claudia Haarmann, Dirk Haarmann, et al., "Making the Difference! The BIG in Namibia: Basic Income Grant Pilot Project Assessment Report, April 2009"; http://www.bignam.org.

institutions. Instead of indulging in utopian dreams we must accommodate ourselves to practical realities.

The idea of "real utopias" embraces this tension between dreams and practice. It is grounded in the belief that what is pragmatically possible is not fixed independently of our imaginations, but is itself shaped by our visions. Self-fulfilling prophecies are powerful forces in history, and while it may be naively optimistic to say "where there is a will there is a way," it is certainly true that without a "will" many "ways" become impossible. Nurturing clear-sighted understandings of what it would take to create social institutions free of oppression is part of creating a political will for radical social changes to reduce oppression. A vital belief in a utopian ideal may be necessary to motivate people to set off on the journey from the status quo in the first place, even though the likely actual destination may fall short of the utopian ideal. Yet, vague utopian fantasies may lead us astray, encouraging us to embark on trips that have no real destinations at all, or, worse still, which lead us towards some unforeseen abyss. Along with "where there is a will there is a way," the human struggle for emancipation confronts "the road to hell is paved with good intentions." What we need, then, is "real utopias": utopian ideals that are grounded in the real potentials of humanity, utopian destinations that have accessible waystations, utopian designs of institutions that can inform our practical tasks of navigating a world of imperfect conditions for social change.

The idea that social institutions can be rationally transformed in ways that enhance human well-being and happiness has a long and controversial history. On the one hand, radicals of diverse stripes have argued that social arrangements inherited from the past are not immutable facts of nature, but transformable human creations. Social institutions can be designed in ways that eliminate forms of oppression that thwart human aspirations towards living fulfilling and meaningful lives. The central task of emancipatory politics is to create such institutions.

On the other hand, conservatives have generally argued that grand designs for social reconstruction nearly always end in disaster. While contemporary social institutions may be far from perfect, they are generally serviceable. At least, it is argued, they provide the minimal conditions for social order and stable interactions. These institutions have evolved through a process of slow, incremental modification as people adapt social rules and practices to changing circumstances. The process is driven by trial and error much more than by conscious design, and by and large those institutions that have endured have done so because they have enduring virtues. This does not preclude institutional change, even deliberate institutional change, but it does mean that such change should be very cautious and incremental and should not include wholesale transformations of existing arrangements.

At the heart of these alternative perspectives is a disagreement about the relationship between the intended and unintended consequences of deliberate efforts at social change. The conservative critique of radical projects is not mainly that the emancipatory goals of radicals are morally indefensible—although some conservatives criticize the underlying values of such projects as well—but that the uncontrollable, and usually negative, unintended consequences of these efforts at massive social change inevitably swamp the intended consequences. Radicals and revolutionaries suffer from what Frederick Hayek termed the "fatal conceit"—the mistaken belief that through rational calculation and political will, society can be designed in ways that will significantly improve the human condition.[5] Incremental tinkering may not be inspiring, but it is the best we can do.

Of course, one can point out that many reforms favored by conservatives also have massive, destructive unintended consequences. The havoc created in many poor countries by World Bank structural adjustment programs would be an example. And furthermore, under certain circumstances conservatives themselves argue for radical, society-wide projects of institutional design, as in the catastrophic "shock therapy" strategy for transforming the command economy of the Soviet Union into free-market capitalism in the 1990s. Nevertheless, there is a certain apparent plausibility to the general claim by conservatives that the bigger the scale and scope of conscious projects of social change, the less likely it is that we will be able to predict ahead of time all of the ramifications of the changes involved.

Radicals on the left have generally rejected this vision of human possibility. Particularly in the Marxist tradition, radical intellectuals have insisted that wholesale redesign of social institutions is within the grasp of human beings. This does not mean, as Marx emphasized, that detailed institutional "blueprints" can be devised in advance of the opportunity to create an alternative. What can

---

5 Frederick A. Hayek, *The Fatal Conceit: The Errors of Socialism* (Chicago: University of Chicago Press, 1991).

be worked out are the core organizing principles of alternatives to existing institutions, the principles that would guide the pragmatic trial-and-error task of institution building. Of course, there will be unintended consequences of various sorts, but these can be dealt with as they arrive, "after the revolution." The crucial point is that unintended consequences need not pose a fatal threat to the emancipatory projects themselves.

Regardless of which of these stances seems most plausible, the *belief* in the possibility of radical alternatives to existing institutions has played an important role in contemporary political life. It is likely that the political space for social democratic reforms was, at least in part, expanded because more radical ruptures with capitalism were seen as possible, and that possibility in turn depended crucially on many people believing that radical ruptures were workable. The *belief* in the viability of revolutionary socialism, especially when backed by the grand historical experiments in the USSR and elsewhere, enhanced the *achievability* of reformist social democracy as a form of class compromise. The political conditions for progressive tinkering with social arrangements, therefore, may depend in significant ways on the presence of more radical visions of possible transformations. This does not mean, of course, that false beliefs about what is possible are to be supported simply because they are thought to have desirable consequences, but it does suggest that plausible visions of radical alternatives, with firm theoretical foundations, are an important condition for emancipatory social change.

We now live in a world in which these radical visions are often mocked rather than taken seriously. Along with the postmodernist rejection of "grand narratives," there is an ideological rejection of grand designs, even by many people still on the left of the political spectrum. This need not mean an abandonment of deeply egalitarian emancipatory values, but it does reflect a cynicism about the human capacity to realize those values on a substantial scale. This cynicism, in turn, weakens progressive political forces in general.

This book is an effort to counter such cynicism by elaborating a general framework for systematically exploring alternatives that embody the idea of "real utopia." We will begin in chapter 2 by embedding the specific problem of envisioning real utopias within a broader framework of "emancipatory social science." This framework is built around three tasks: diagnosis and critique; formulating alternatives; and elaborating strategies of transformation. These three tasks define the agendas of the three main parts of the book. Part I of the book (chapter 3) presents the basic diagnosis and critique of capitalism that animates the search for real utopian alternatives. Part II then discusses the problem of alternatives. Chapter 4 reviews the traditional Marxist approach to thinking about alternatives and shows why this approach is unsatisfactory. Chapter 5 elaborates an alternative strategy of analysis, anchored in the idea that socialism, as an alternative to capitalism, should be understood as a process of increasing social empowerment over state and economy. Chapters 6 and 7 explore a range of concrete proposals for institutional design in terms of this concept of social empowerment, the first of these chapters focusing on the problem of social empowerment and the state, and the second on the problem of social empowerment and the economy. Part III of the book turns to the problem of transformation—how to understand the process by which these real utopian alternatives could be brought about. Chapter 8 lays out the central elements of a theory of social transformation. Chapters 9 through 11 then examine three different broad strategies of emancipatory transformation—ruptural transformation (chapter 9), interstitial transformation (chapter 10), and symbiotic transformation (chapter 11). The book concludes with chapter 12, which distills the core arguments into seven key lessons.

THE TASKS OF EMANCIPATORY SOCIAL SCIENCE

Envisioning real utopias is a central component of a broader intellectual enterprise that can be called *emancipatory social science*. Emancipatory social science seeks to generate scientific knowledge relevant to the collective project of challenging various forms of human oppression. To call this a form of social *science*, rather than simply social criticism or social philosophy, recognizes the importance for this task of systematic scientific knowledge about how the world works. The word *emancipatory* identifies a central moral purpose in the production of knowledge—the elimination of oppression and the creation of the conditions for human flourishing.[1] And the word *social* implies the belief that human emancipation depends upon the transformation of the social world, not just the inner life of persons.

To fulfill this mission, any emancipatory social science faces three basic tasks: elaborating a systematic diagnosis and critique of the world as it exists; envisioning viable alternatives; and understanding the obstacles, possibilities, and dilemmas of transformation. In different times and places one or another of these may be more pressing than others, but all are necessary for a comprehensive emancipatory theory.

---

1 In a personal communication Steven Lukes noted that the word "emancipation" was originally connected to the struggle against slavery: the emancipation of slaves meant their freedom from bondage. More generally, the idea of emancipation was connected to liberal notions of freedom and achieving full liberal rights rather than socialist ideals of equality and social justice. In the twentieth century the left appropriated the term to refer to a broader vision of eliminating all forms of oppression, not just those involving coercive forms of denial of individual liberties. I am using the term in this broader sense.

DIAGNOSIS AND CRITIQUE

The starting point for building an emancipatory social science is identifying the ways in which existing social institutions and social structures systematically impose harms on people. It is not enough to show that people are suffering or that there are enormous inequalities in the extent to which people may live flourishing lives. A scientific emancipatory theory must show that the explanation for such suffering and inequality lies in specific properties of institutions and social structures. The first task of emancipatory social science, therefore, is the diagnosis and critique of the causal processes that generate these harms.

Diagnosis and critique are the aspects of emancipatory social science that have often generated the most systematic and developed empirical research. Consider feminism, for example. A great deal of feminist writing centers on the diagnosis of existing social relations, practices and institutions in terms of the ways in which they generate various forms of oppression of women. Studies of labor markets have emphasized such things as the sex-segregation of jobs, employment evaluation systems which denigrate job attributes associated with culturally defined feminine traits, discrimination in relation to promotion, institutional arrangements which place mothers at a disadvantage in employment, and so on. Feminist studies of culture demonstrate the ways in which a wide range of cultural practices in the media, education, literature, and other institutions have traditionally reinforced gender identities and stereotypes in ways that oppress women. And feminist studies of the state have examined the way in which state structures and policies have systematically reinforced the subordination of women and various forms of gender inequality. All this research is meant to show that gender inequality and domination are not simply the result of "natural" biological differences between men and women, but are rather generated by social structures, institutions, and practices. A similar set of observations could be made about empirical research inspired by the Marxist tradition of emancipatory theory, by theories of racial oppression, and by radical environmentalism. In each of these traditions much of the research done consists in documenting the harms generated by existing social structures and institutions, and attempting to identify the causal processes involved.

Diagnosis and critique are closely connected to questions of social justice and normative theory. To describe a social arrangement as generating "harms" is to infuse the analysis with a moral judgment.[2] Behind every emancipatory theory, therefore, there is an implicit theory of justice, some conception of what conditions would have to be met before the institutions of a society could be deemed just. Underlying the analysis in this book is what could be called a *radical democratic egalitarian* understanding of justice. It rests on two broad normative claims, one concerning the conditions for social justice and the other the conditions for political justice:

Social justice: *In a socially just society, all people would have broadly equal access to the necessary material and social means to live flourishing lives.*

Political justice: *In a politically just society, all people would have broadly equal access to the necessary means to partici-pate meaningfully in decisions about things which affect their lives. This includes both the freedom of individuals to make choices that affect their own lives as separate persons, and their capacity to participate in collective decisions which affect their lives as members of a broader community.*

Both of these claims are fraught with philosophical difficulty and controversy, and I will not attempt here to provide a fully elaborated defense. Nevertheless, it will be helpful to clarify the meaning and implications of these two principles and explain the grounds on which I believe they provide a foundation for the diagnosis and critique of social institutions.

---

2 It is, of course, possible for someone to agree that contemporary capitalism generates harms and human suffering and still also argue that this is not an injustice. One might believe, as many libertarians do, that people have the right to do what they want with their property even if alternative uses of their property would reduce human suffering. A consistent libertarian could accept the diagnosis that capitalism generates large deficits in human flourishing, and yet argue that it would be a violation of individual liberty and thus unjust to force people to use their property in ways other than of their choosing. Nevertheless, most people believe that when institutions generate systematic and pervasive harms in the lives of people, such institutions are likely also to be unjust. This of course still does not mean that people who acknowledge the injustice of capitalism will necessarily want to change it in any fundamental way, since there are other things besides justice which people care about.

1. Social justice

The conception of social justice which animates the critique of capitalism and the search for alternatives in this book revolves around three ideas: human flourishing; necessary material and social means; broadly equal access.

"Human flourishing" is a broad, multidimensional umbrella concept, covering a variety of aspects of human well-being.[3] It is like the idea of "health," which has both a restrictive meaning as the absence of diseases that interfere with ordinary bodily functioning, and an expansive meaning as robust physical vitality. The restrictive meaning of human flourishing concerns the absence of deficits that undermine ordinary human functioning. This includes things like hunger and other material deprivations, ill health, social isolation, and the psychological harms of social stigma. This is a heterogeneous list—some elements refer to bodily impairments, others to social and cultural impairments. But they all, through different mechanisms, undermine basic human functioning. A just society is one in which all people have unconditional access to the necessary means to flourish in this restrictive sense of the satisfaction of needs for basic human functioning.[4]

The expansive idea of flourishing refers to the various ways in which people are able to develop and exercise their talents and capacities, or, to use another expression, to realize their individual potentials. This does not imply that within each person there is some unique, latent, natural "essence" that will grow and become fully realized if only it is not blocked. The expansive idea of individual flourishing is not the equivalent of saying that within every acorn lies a mighty oak: that with proper soil, sun

---

3 Philosophers discussing egalitarian conceptions of social justice have used a variety of terms to identify the source of their moral concern: happiness, welfare, well-being, flourishing. There are advantages and disadvantages to each of these, and in practice it may not matter a great deal which is used to anchor a discussion of justice. I prefer "flourishing" because it suggests a broad idea of well-being and because many aspects of flourishing refer to objective properties, not just subjective states.

4 The restrictive sense of flourishing elaborated here corresponds closely to Amartya Sen's notion of "capabilities" and basic functioning. In his analysis, societies should be judged not on the basis of how much income they generate per capita, but on the extent to which they provide basic capabilities to all. See Amartya Sen, *Development as Freedom* (Oxford: Oxford University Press, 1999). See also Martha C. Nussbaum, *Women and Human Development: The Capabilities Approach* (Cambridge: Cambridge University Press, 2000) for an elaboration of the idea of flourishing as a core ideal of the good society.

and rain the oak will flourish and the potential within the acorn will be realized as the mature tree. Human talents and capacities are multidimensional; there are many possible lines of development, many different flourishing mature humans that can develop from the raw material of the infant. These capacities may be intellectual, artistic, physical, social, moral or spiritual. They involve creativity as well as mastery. A flourishing human life is one in which these talents and capacities develop.

The idea of human flourishing is neutral with respect to the various ways of life that can be constructed around particular ways of flourishing. There is no implication that intellectual capacities are more worthy of development than are physical or artistic or spiritual capacities, for example. There is also no supposition that in order to flourish human beings must develop all of their capacities: people have many different potentials, and it is impossible in general that all of these potentials can be realized, regardless of access to material and social means.[5]

Crucially, to develop and exercise these potentials requires material resources and appropriate social conditions. The importance of material resources for human flourishing is obvious. Certainly without things like adequate nutrition, housing, clothing, and personal security it is difficult for most people to flourish in either the restrictive or the expansive sense. But the development of intellectual,

---

5 The multidimensionality of the idea of flourishing also means that there is no bottom-line metric that would enable one to always say unambiguously something like "person X is flourishing more than person Y," since any given life is likely to combine flourishing and deficits along different dimensions. This is like the problem in talking about how healthy a person is in physical terms: one person has chronic back pain, another has asthma. Who is "healthier"? One can specify this question with respect to particular tasks and contexts and perhaps provide an answer—asthma does not impede the ordinary functioning of sitting at a desk and back pain does not impede the ordinary functioning of breathing on a smoggy day. But there is no way of rendering these two conditions commensurable on a one-dimensional healthiness scale in a way that would provide a simple answer to the question "who has greater health"? Nevertheless, in spite of this problem one can talk about the ways in which a given society promotes or impedes wellness, and it therefore is possible to use health-promotion as an evaluative criterion for institutions. Because of this multidimensional complexity, it is entirely possible that a given institutional arrangement promotes human flourishing in some respects and impedes it in others. This, in turn, may make it problematic to unequivocally proclaim that human flourishing would be enhanced by a particular change in institutions. This does not, however, mean that the idea of human flourishing is not an appropriate value for evaluating institutions. It just means that the evaluations may not always be simple and unequivocal.

physical, and social capacities requires much more than simple material necessities. It requires access to educational settings within which learning takes place and talents are cultivated, not just in childhood, but throughout life. It requires access to work settings where skills can be developed and exercised and activity is to a substantial extent self-directed. It requires communities which provide opportunities for active participation in civic affairs and cultural activities.

A just society is one in which everyone has broadly *equal access* to these conditions. "Equal access" is a criterion for equality that is similar to the idea of "equal opportunity." The difference is that equal opportunity would be satisfied by a fair lottery in which some people ended up with ample means to live a flourishing life and others lived in abject poverty so long as everyone had exactly the same chance of winning the lottery in the first place, whereas the "equal access" criterion is inconsistent with a lottery.[6]

Equal access does not imply that everyone should receive the same income or have identical material standards of living, both because the "necessary means" to flourish will vary across people and because some amount of inequality is consistent with everyone still having equal access to the *necessary* means to live flourishing lives.[7] Nor does the radical egalitarian view imply that everyone would in fact flourish in a just society, but simply that any failures to do so would not be due to inequalities in access to the necessary social and material resources that people need in order to flourish.

This conception of social justice does not simply concern class inequalities; it also condemns inequalities based on gender, race, physical disabilities, and any other morally irrelevant attribute

---

6 Equal opportunity is also associated with the idea of "starting gate equality," which suggests that so long as everyone has equal opportunity up until they are adults, then if some people squander their opportunities, their subsequent lack of access to the conditions to live a flourishing life would not constitute a failure of justice. "Equal access to the necessary social and material means to live a flourishing life" suggests that ideally people should have life-long access to the means to live a flourishing life. While there may be pragmatic constraints on this ideal, and of course there are complex issues bound up with incentives and "personal responsibility," the ideal remains that all human beings should have such access.

7 The point here is similar to the normative rule of "Fair Shares until everyone has enough; Fair Play for the surplus"; see William Ryan, *Equality* (New York: Pantheon Books, 1981), p. 9. "Enough" can either refer to the necessary means to securely satisfy basic needs (in which case it corresponds to what I have termed the restrictive sense of flourishing) or enough to live a flourishing life in the more expansive sense. The idea expressed is that once this condition is satisfied, "fair play" rather than fair shares should become the operative principle of justice.

which interferes with a person's access to the necessary material and social means to live a flourishing life. This is why the inclusion of *social* means is crucial, since disrespect, discrimination and social exclusion based on status attributes can constitute as serious impediments to flourishing as economic inequality. The radical egalitarian conception of social justice proposed here, therefore, includes what Nancy Fraser has called the politics of recognition as well as material distribution.[8]

While the conception of flourishing proposed here does not privilege particular ways of flourishing, it is not neutral with respect to those cultural conceptions of the "good life" which inherently deny some categories of people equal access to the conditions to flourish. A culture which designates some ethnic or racial or caste groups as unworthy of having access to the material and social means to develop their human capacities is unjust. This conception of social justice is also violated by cultures which insist that the highest form of flourishing for women is to be attentive wives serving the needs of their husbands and dedicated mothers raising children. Women can certainly flourish as dedicated mothers and attentive wives, but a culture which pressures women into these roles and restricts the ability of girls to develop other capacities and talents violates the principle of equal access to the material and social means to live a flourishing life. Such a culture supports an injustice by the standards proposed here.[9]

---

8 "Recognition" refers to the social practices through which people communicate mutual respect and validate their standing as moral equals within a society. See Nancy Fraser, "Rethinking Recognition," *New Left Review* 3 (2000). The issue of material distribution and moral recognition are, of course, interconnected, since the denial of respect ("misrecognition" and stigma) can reinforce material disadvantages, and class inequalities themselves also impose harms of disrespect. For a discussion of the interconnection of class and recognition, see Andrew Sayer, *The Moral Significance of Class* (Cambridge: Cambridge University Press, 2005).

9 The claim that some cultures systematically support certain forms of injustice is a particularly controversial aspect of the radical democratic egalitarian conception of justice being proposed here, for it implies a critique of the core values linked to certain cultures. Some people regard such critique as implying a Eurocentric or "Western" bias. I would argue that while it may historically be the case that the kinds of universalistic conceptions of human flourishing I am advocating are linked to Western culture, such universalism is not a uniquely Western trait, and a theory of justice linked to such universalism does not merely reflect the parochial perspective of Western individualism. Furthermore, by the standards I am defending here, Western cultures also, in certain key respects, support injustice, especially through the endorsement of coercively enforced

The radical egalitarian conception of social justice is not restricted to the nation state as the only appropriate social arena for egalitarianism. The principle that all people should have broadly equal access to the necessary social and material means to live flourishing lives applies to *all* people, and thus at its deepest level it is a global principle for humanity. It is unjust that a person born in Guatemala has much less access to the material and social conditions for living a flourishing life than a person born in Canada. As a tool for criticism, therefore, the egalitarian ideal can be directed at any social unit within which access to resources is structured through rules and powers. A family can be criticized as unjust when members have unequal access to the means to live flourishing lives available within the family; and global institutions can be criticized as unjust when they enforce rules which sustain such inequality on a global scale. In practical terms most discussions of social justice focus mainly on the problem of justice within the bounded social entities we call "nation states" since these are the social units within which political agency for social change remains largely concentrated, but this practical constraint does not define the core principle itself.[10]

It is, of course, not a simple matter to specify the institutional arrangements which would in practice satisfy this criterion for a just society. Any attempt to do so would have to contend with a range of difficult issues: How is the moral conviction about the just *distribution* of access to resources balanced against pragmatic considerations about *producing* the social and material means for flourishing? Some talents will contribute more than others to creating the social and material conditions for human flourishing. Should these kinds of talents be encouraged over others through the use of various kinds of incentives? And, if so, doesn't this violate the equal access idea? Some talents are more costly to develop than others, and since in the aggregate there is likely to be a budget constraint on the resources available for the development of talents, this may make it impossible to give everyone equal access to the necessary means to develop whatever talents they

---

private property rules and strong versions of competitive individualism.

10   It is important to be clear on this point: the moral universe for egalitarian ideals is global—humanity as a whole—but the struggles for these ideals are deeply shaped by the practical constraints of different arenas for agency.

might want to develop. Equal access to the means to flourish thus may not mean equal access to the necessary means to cultivate whatever talents one wants to cultivate. A full philosophical defense of the ideal of equal access to the conditions to live a flourishing life would have to contend with these, and other, problems. But whatever else is entailed by this ideal, it certainly implies access to the necessary means to satisfy basic needs for food, clothing, shelter, and health, as well as the means to develop and exercise some of one's talents and capacities and to be a full participant in the social life of the society in which one lives. We do not live in such a world.

2. Political justice

The second normative principle underlying the diagnosis and critique in this book concerns individual freedom and democracy. These two ideas are linked here because they both concern the power of people to make choices about things which affect their lives. This is the core principle: people should have as much control as possible over those decisions which affect their lives. "Freedom" is the power to make choices about one's own life; "democracy" is the power to participate in the effective control of collective choices that affect one's life as a member of the wider society. The democratic egalitarian principle of political justice is that all people should have equal access to the powers needed to make choices over their own lives and to participate in collective choices that affect them because of the society in which they live.

This egalitarian understanding of freedom recognizes the central liberal ideals of individual rights and autonomy, ideals which seek to minimize the extent to which individuals are subjected to external coercion. It differs from standard liberal formulations by also emphasizing the egalitarian principle that all people should have equal access to powers needed to make choices over their own lives and not simply be equally protected from coercion by others. This corresponds to what Philippe Van Parijs has called "*real* freedom for all."[11] Real freedom implies that people have actual capacities to make choices that matter to them, and this

---

11 Philippe Van Parijs, *Real Freedom for All* (Oxford: Oxford University Press, 1997).

requires that they have access to the basic resources needed for acting on their life plans.[12]

The democratic dimension of political justice concerns equal access to the political means necessary to participate in collective decisions over issues that affect one's life as a member of a society. This affirms not simply that in a democracy there should be formal political equality—all people should have equal legal access to the means of political participation—but that democracy needs to be empowered in ways which enable people to collectively control their common fate. Mostly, in contemporary society, people hold a fairly restrictive view of democracy. On the one hand, many issues of crucial public importance are not seen as legitimately subjected to democratic decision making. In particular, many economic decisions which have massive affects on our collective fate are seen as "private" matters to be made by executives and owners of large corporations. The demarcation between "public" and "private" is anchored in a relatively strong conception of private property which significantly insulates a wide range of decisions over economic resources and activities from intrusive democratic control. On the other hand, even for those issues which are seen as legitimate objects of public control, popular democratic empowerment is quite limited. Electoral politics are heavily dominated by elites, thus violating democratic principles of political equality, and other venues for popular participation are generally of largely symbolic character. Ordinary citizens have few opportunities for meaningfully exercising the democratic ideal of "rule by the people."

Radical democracy, in contrast, argues for an expansive understanding of democracy. The ideal of the political equality of all citizens requires strong institutional mechanisms for blocking the translation of private economic power into political power. The scope of democratic decision making is enlarged to all domains with important public consequences. And the arenas for empowered citizen participation extend beyond casting ballots in periodic elections.

Radical democracy is both an ideal in its own right—people should have the right to participate meaningfully in decisions

---

12 Egalitarian distributions of material resources thus have two distinct justifications: Social justice requires equal access to the necessary material means to live a flourishing life; political justice requires equal access to the necessary material means for real freedom. These two rationales for an egalitarian distribution of material resources are connected insofar as real freedom itself contributes to human flourishing.

which affect their lives—and an instrumental value—the realization of the radical egalitarian principle of social justice in terms
of human flourishing would be facilitated by radical democratic
institutions of political power. The combination of the radical
egalitarian view of social justice and the radical democratic view
of political power can be called *democratic egalitarianism*. This
defines the broad normative foundation for the diagnosis and
critique of existing institutions and the search for transformative
alternatives outlined in this book.

VIABLE ALTERNATIVES

The second task of emancipatory social science is to develop a
coherent, credible theory of the alternatives to existing institutions and social structures that would eliminate, or at least
significantly mitigate, the harms and injustices identified in the
diagnosis and critique. Social alternatives can be elaborated and
evaluated in terms of three different criteria: *desirability, viability,*
and *achievability*. As illustrated in Figure 2.1, these are nested in a
kind of hierarchy: not all desirable alternatives are viable, and not
all viable alternatives are achievable.

1. Desirability

The exploration of *desirable* alternatives, without the constraints
of viability or achievability, is the domain of utopian social
theory and much normative political philosophy. Typically such
discussions are institutionally very thin, the emphasis being on

FIGURE 2.1. *Three Criteria for Evaluating Social Alternatives*

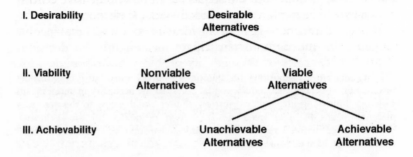

the enunciation of abstract principles rather than actual institutional designs. Thus, for example, the Marxist description of communism as a *classless society* governed by the principle "to each according to need, from each according to ability" is almost silent on the actual institutional arrangements which would make this principle operative. Liberal theories of justice similarly elaborate and defend the principles that should be embodied in the institutions of a just society without systematically exploring the problem of whether sustainable, robust institutions could actually be designed to apply those principles in the pure form in which they are formulated. These kinds of discussions are important, for they can contribute much to clarifying our values and strengthening our moral commitment to the arduous business of social change. But purely utopian thinking about alternatives may do relatively little to inform the practical task of institution building or to add credibility to challenges of existing institutions.

2. Viability

The study of *viable* alternatives asks of proposals for transforming existing social structures and institutions whether, if implemented, they would actually generate—in a sustainable, robust manner—the emancipatory consequences that motivated the proposal. A common objection to radical egalitarian proposals is: "sounds good on paper, but it will never work." The best-known example of this problem is comprehensive central planning, the classic form in which revolutionaries attempted to realize socialist principles. Socialists had sharp criticisms of the anarchy of the market and its destructive effects on society and believed that a rationally planned economy would improve people's lives. The institutional design that seemed to make this possible was centralized comprehensive planning. As it turned out, there are a range of "perverse" unintended consequences of comprehensive central planning which subvert its intended goals, both because of the information overload generated by complexity and because of a range of problems linked to incentives.

Another example of the viability problem is the proposal for a generous unconditional basic income, which we will discuss in chapter 6. Suppose everyone were given, with no conditions or restrictions whatsoever, a monthly stipend sufficient to live at a socially respectable standard of living. There are many reasons why, from the moral standpoint of radical egalitarian views of social justice, this could be seen as a desirable alternative to existing processes of economic distribution. Yet there are skeptics who argue that a generous basic income is not a viable alternative to the existing world: perhaps it would create perverse incentives and everyone would become couch potatoes; perhaps the tax rates would have to be so high that it would stifle economic activity; perhaps it would trigger such resentment towards people who lived entirely on the basic income from those who combined the basic income with labor market earnings, that an unconditional basic income could not be politically stable. These are the kinds of issues to be explored in the discussion of the viability of alternatives.

The viability of a specific institutional design for realizing emancipatory goals may, of course, depend heavily on historical context and various kinds of side conditions. For example, a generous unconditional basic income may be viable in a country in which there is a strong culturally rooted work ethic and sense of collective obligation—because in such a society there would be relatively few people who decide to consume the basic income without any reciprocal contribution—but may not be viable in a highly atomistic, selfish consumerist society. Or, a basic income could be viable in a society that over a long period had already developed a generous redistributive welfare state based on a patchwork of targeted programs, but not in a society with a miserly, limited welfare state. Discussions of viability, therefore, also include discussions of the contextual conditions-of-possibility for particular designs to work well.

The exploration of viable alternatives brackets the question of their practical achievability under existing social conditions. Some people might argue: what's the point of talking about some theoretically viable alternative if it is not strategically achievable? The response to the skeptic is this: there are so many uncertainties and contingencies about the future that we cannot possibly know now what the limits of achievable future alternatives really are. Think about the Soviet Union in 1987. No one thought that the collapse of the Soviet State and the consequent transition to capitalism would be achievable within a few years. Perhaps we can say something about what sorts of changes we can struggle for right now, what kinds of coalitions are possible and which are impossible under existing conditions, and what sorts of political strategies are likely to be effective or ineffective in the immediate future. But the further we look into the future, the less certain we can be about the limits on what is achievable.

Given this uncertainty about the future, there are two reasons why it is important to have as clear-headed an understanding as possible of the range of viable alternatives to the world in which we live, alternatives which, if implemented, would stand a good chance of being sustainable. First, developing such understanding now makes it more likely that, if in the future historical conditions expand the limits of achievable possibility, the social forces presently committed to emancipatory social change will be in a position to formulate practical strategies to implement an alternative. Viable alternatives are more likely to eventually become achievable alternatives if they are well thought out and understood. Second, the actual limits of what is achievable depend in part on the beliefs people hold about what sorts of alternatives are viable. This is a crucial point and fundamental to sociological understandings of the very idea of there being "limits of possibility" for social change: social limits of possibility are not independent of beliefs about those limits. When a physicist argues that there is a limit to the maximum speed at which things can travel, this is meant as an objective constraint operating independently of our beliefs about speed. Similarly, when a biologist argues that in the absence of certain conditions, life is impossible, this is a claim about objective constraints. Of course both the physicist and the biologist could be wrong, but the claims themselves are about real, untransgressable limits of possibility. Claims about social limits of possibility are different from these claims about physical and biological limits, for in the social case the beliefs people hold about limits systematically affect what is possible. Developing systematic, compelling accounts of viable alternatives to existing social structures and institutions of power and privilege, therefore, is one component of the social process through which the social limits on achievable alternatives can themselves be changed.

It is no easy matter to make a credible argument that "another world is possible." People are born into societies that are always already made. The rules of social life which they learn and internalize as they grow up seem natural. People are preoccupied with the tasks of daily life, with making a living, with coping with life's pains and enjoying life's pleasures. The idea that the social world could be deliberately changed in some fundamental way that would make life significantly better for most people seems pretty far-fetched, both because it is hard to imagine some dramatically better workable alternative and because it is hard to imagine how to successfully challenge existing institutions of power and privilege in order to create such an alternative. Thus, even if one accepts the diagnosis and critique of existing institutions, the most natural response for most people is probably a fatalistic sense that there is not much that could be done to really change things.

Such fatalism poses a serious problem for people committed to challenging the injustices and harms of the existing social world, since fatalism and cynicism about the prospects for emancipatory change reduce the prospects for such change. One strategy, of course, is to just not worry too much about having a scientifically credible argument about the possibilities for radical social change, but instead try to create an inspiring vision of a desirable alternative, grounded in anger at the injustices of the world in which we live and infused with hope and passion about human possibilities. At times, such charismatic wishful thinking has been a powerful force, contributing to the mobilization of people for struggle and sacrifice. But it is unlikely to form an adequate basis for transforming the world in ways that actually produce a sustainable emancipatory alternative. The history of human struggles for radical social change is filled with heroic victories over existing structures of oppression followed by the tragic construction of new forms of domination, oppression, and inequality. The second task of emancipatory social science, therefore, is to develop in as systematic a way as possible a scientifically grounded conception of viable alternative institutions.

3. Achievability

Developing coherent theories of *achievable* alternatives is the central task for the practical work of strategies for social change. This turns out to be a very difficult undertaking, both because views about achievability are vulnerable to "wishful thinking," and because of the high levels of contingency of conditions in the future which will affect the prospects of success of any long-term strategy.

As in the case of viability, achievability is not really a simple dichotomy between the achievable and the unachievable: different projects of institutional transformation have different prospects for ever being implemented. The probability that any given alternative to existing social structures and institutions could be implemented sometime in the future depends upon two kinds of processes. First, it depends upon the *consciously pursued strategies* and the *relative power* of social actors who support and oppose the alternative in question. Strategy matters because emancipatory alternatives are very unlikely to just "happen"; they can only come about because people work to implement them, and are able to overcome various obstacles and forms of opposition. The probability of ultimate success, then, depends upon the balance of power of contending social forces consciously attempting to implement or to resist emancipatory transformation. Second, the probability of any given alternative being implemented depends upon the trajectory over time of a wide range of *social structural conditions* that affect the possibilities of success of these strategies.[13] This trajectory of conditions is itself partially the result of the cumulative *unintended* effects of human action, but it is also the result of the conscious strategies of actors *to transform the conditions of their own actions*. The achievability of an alternative thus depends upon the extent to which it is possible to formulate coherent, compelling strategies which both help create the conditions for implementing alternatives in the future and have the potential to mobilize the necessary social forces to support the alternative when those conditions occur. Developing an understanding of these issues is the objective of the third general task of emancipatory social science: the theory of transformation.

TRANSFORMATION

The third task of emancipatory social science is elaborating a theory of social transformation. We can think of emancipatory

---

13 To quote (out of context) Marx's famous aphorism: "[people] make their own history, but they do not make it just as they please; they do not make it under circumstances chosen by themselves, but under circumstances directly encountered, given and transmitted from the past"; see Karl Marx, *The Eighteenth Brumaire of Louis Bonaparte* (New York: International Publishers, 1977), p. 97. The quotation is usually taken to mean that social structures impose constraints on human agency, but the actual context is about the mental conditions of action. The passage continues: "The tradition of all the dead generations weighs like a nightmare on the brain of the living. And just when they seem engaged in revolutionizing themselves and things, in creating something that has never yet existed, precisely in such periods of revolutionary crisis they anxiously conjure up the spirits from the past to their service and borrow from them names, battle cries and costumes in order to present the new scene of world history in this time-honored disguise and this borrowed language." Even though Marx's point was focused on these kinds of cultural constraints on transforming the world, the more general idea is that collective strategies encounter conditions which are not themselves directly amenable to strategic choice.

social science as a theory of a journey from the present to a possible future: the diagnosis and critique of society tells us why we want to leave the world in which we live; the theory of alternatives tells us where we want to go; and the theory of transformation tells us how to get from here to there—how to make viable alternatives achievable. A theory of transformation involves four central components:

1. A theory of social reproduction

A central proposition of all theories of social emancipation is that the structures and institutions that generate the forms of oppression and social harms identified in the diagnosis and critique of society do not continue to exist simply out of some law of social inertia; they require active mechanisms of social reproduction. This proposition is based on a counterfactual argument: since these structures and institutions impose real harms on people, in the absence of some such active process of social reproduction, the people harmed by the existing social arrangements would resist these harms and challenge these institutions in ways which would result in their transformation. The relative stability of oppressive structures and institutions, therefore, depends upon the existence of a variety of interconnected mechanisms of social reproduction which block or contain such a challenge. In order to transform those institutions, therefore, we must develop a scientific understanding of how this reproduction occurs.

2. A theory of the gaps and contradictions within the process of reproduction

If it were the case that the process of social reproduction was a completely coherent, pervasively integrated system, then there would be little scope for deliberate strategies of social transformation. Emancipatory change might still happen, but only as the outcome of unintended trajectories of change operating "behind the backs" of people. Some theories of society come close to affirming this kind of totalizing view of social reproduction: domination is so pervasive and coherent that all acts of apparent resistance merely serve to further stabilize the system of domination itself. Such theories may still embody a diagnosis and critique of society, but they ultimately reject the possibility of an emancipatory social science, for they provide no grounds for believing that effective struggles for emancipatory transformation are possible, and thus scientific knowledge cannot contribute to challenging forms of oppression.[14] An emancipatory theory of social transformation needs to examine the cracks in the edifice, the contradictions and gaps in the process of social reproduction, the ways in which social reproduction is prone to failures—in short, the various ways in which the process of social reproduction opens up spaces in which collective struggles for new possibilities are possible.

However, if we take seriously emancipatory social science as a form of *science*, not just *philosophical critique*, then we cannot assume *a priori* that sufficiently sharp contradictions of social reproduction exist to allow for effective emancipatory challenge. The *search* for contradictory processes that open spaces for emancipatory transformation is a central part of the agenda, but the *discovery* of such possibilities depends upon the progress of knowledge.

3. A theory of the underlying dynamics and trajectory of unintended social change

Emancipatory social science aspires to include not simply a sociological theory of social reproduction and social contradictions but also a systematic theory of the dynamic trajectory of *unintended* social change. In order to formulate compelling long-term projects of social transformation, it is obviously desirable to understand not simply the obstacles and openings for strategies in the present, but also how those obstacles and opportunities are likely to develop over time. This was the central thrust of the theory of history—historical materialism—in classical Marxism: it proposed a systematic, coherent account of the dynamic tendencies internal to capitalism which propelled it along a particular trajectory of unintended social change. This trajectory was not itself willed by anyone, it was not the result of a conscious project of generating this

---

14   The theoretical framework for analyzing power and domination elaborated by Michel Foucault sometimes comes very close to this view of totalizing, untransformable power relations. Resistance happens, but its transformative potential is denied. To a somewhat lesser extent, much of Pierre Bourdieu's work on social reproduction, with his emphasis on deeply engrained "habitus" (internalized dispositions), offers very little room for strategic challenge and transformation. Social change can happen, and perhaps this might be emancipatory in some historical moments where the match between internalized dispositions and social spaces is disrupted, but this is unlikely to be the result of collective projects of emancipatory transformation.

trajectory; it was the unintended by-product of the strategies of actors pursuing their goals within the existing structure of social relations. Historical materialism in effect proposed a broad-stroke history of the future. *Were* this theory adequate, it would be of enormous help in formulating long-term strategies for emancipatory transformation since it would give actors a sense of how the obstacles and opportunities for struggles were likely to evolve over time.

For reasons that will become clear in chapter 4, I do not believe that this classical theory of the immanent tendencies of social change is satisfactory, but neither do I believe that any compelling alternative has yet been developed. We may have a good scientific understanding of the mechanisms of social reproduction and their contradictions, but not of the immanent tendencies of social development generated by the interplay of reproduction, contradictions, and social action. The absence of a compelling theory of the dynamic trajectory of social change is thus a significant gap in emancipatory social science. It means that the formulation of robust projects of emancipatory social transformation necessarily must be formulated with relatively thin knowledge of the conditions likely to be faced in the future. This poses an interesting challenge: any plausible project of emancipatory transformation must adopt a long time-horizon, for the kinds of fundamental structural and institutional changes needed for creating a democratic egalitarian society cannot be achieved in the immediate future, and yet our capacity to generate scientifically credible knowledge about social conditions beyond the near future is very limited. There is thus a gap between the time-horizons of scientific theory and the time-horizons of transformative struggles.

4. A theory of collective actors, strategies, and struggles

In the end, if emancipatory visions of viable alternatives are to become the actual real utopias of achieved alternatives it will be the result of conscious strategies by people committed to democratic egalitarian values. The final central component of a theory of social transformation, therefore, is a theory of strategies of collective action and transformative struggle. The theory of social reproduction maps out the obstacles to social change we face. The theory of contradictions helps us understand the opportunities that exist in spite of those obstacles. A theory of the dynamic trajectory—if we had such a theory—would tell us how these obstacles and opportunities are likely to evolve over time. And the theory of transformative strategy helps us understand how we can collectively contend with the obstacles and take advantage of the opportunities to move us in the direction of social emancipation.

I: DIAGNOSIS AND CRITIQUE

3

WHAT'S SO BAD ABOUT CAPITALISM?

There is a great distance between the radical democratic egalitarian ideal and the social reality of the world in which we live. The dream of democratic egalitarians is to create the institutions needed to further the realization of that ideal. The first step in turning the dream into a practical ambition is to figure out what it is about the world in which we live that obstructs this realization. This diagnosis of the world of the actual provides the empirical context for exploring the world of the possible.

In this chapter we will focus on the problem of the ways the economic structures of capitalism violate the normative ideals of radical democratic egalitarianism. This is not to say that all the deficits identified by those ideals can be traced back to capitalist economic structures. Radical democratic egalitarianism is an encompassing moral conviction that challenges all social and cultural practices which generate inequalities in access to the material and social conditions for human flourishing, and challenges all obstructions to equal access to the conditions for real individual freedom and collectively empowered democracy. These include structures of power and privilege linked to gender, race, ethnicity, sexuality, nationality, and citizenship. The idea of envisioning real utopias, therefore, must ultimately include an account of institutional arrangements for robust egalitarianism in all of these dimensions. Nevertheless, since capitalism so pervasively and powerfully structures the prospects of establishing both egalitarian conditions for human flourishing and democratic empowerment, any radical democratic egalitarian project of social transformation must come to terms with the nature of capitalism and the prospects for its transformation. This is an especially urgent task at the beginning of the twenty-first century, since capitalism has become such a taken-for-granted form of economic structure. This is where we will begin.

DEFINING CAPITALISM: A BRIEF EXPOSITION

Capitalism is a particular way of organizing the economic activities of a society. It can be defined along two primary dimensions, in terms of the nature of its *class relations* and its central mechanisms of *economic coordination*.

Class relations are the social relations through which the means of production are owned and power is exercised over their use. In capitalism, the means of production are privately owned and their use is controlled by the owners or their surrogates. The means of production by themselves, of course, cannot produce anything; they have to be set in motion by human laboring activity of one sort or another. In capitalism, this labor is provided by workers who do not own the means of production and who, in order to acquire an income, are hired by capitalist firms to use the means of production. The fundamental class relation of capitalism, therefore, is the social relation between capitalists and workers.[1]

Economic coordination in capitalism is accomplished primarily through mechanisms of decentralized voluntary exchange by privately contracting parties—or what is generally called "free markets"—through which the prices and quantities of the goods and services produced are determined. Market coordination is conventionally contrasted with authoritative state coordination, in which the power of the state is used to command the allocations of resources for different purposes.[2] The famous metaphor

---

1   This is a highly simplified and abstract view of the class structure of capitalism in which there are only two class locations, workers and capitalists. While this is the core or fundamental class relation of capitalism, actual capitalist societies contain a variety of other kinds of class locations, particularly those loosely grouped under the heading "the middle class," that do not neatly fit into one or the other of these two polarized categories. For an extended discussion of the problem of combining the simple, abstract idea of a polarized class relation between capitalists and workers with the complexity of actual class structures, see Erik Olin Wright, *Class Counts* (Cambridge: Cambridge University Press, 1997), chapter 1. For a collection of alternative approaches to understanding class, see Erik Olin Wright (ed.), *Approaches to Class Analysis* (Cambridge: Cambridge University Press, 2005).

2   State and market are not exhaustive of mechanisms of economic coordination. As many economic sociologists have argued, coordination is also accomplished by associations, communities, and various kinds of social networks, including kinship networks. For a discussion of the issues of multiple processes of coordination, see Wolfgang Streeck, "Community, Market, State and Associations? The Prospective Contribution of Interest Governance to Social Order," in Wolfgang Streeck and

of "the invisible hand" captures the basic idea: individuals and firms, simply pursuing their own private interests, engage in bargaining and voluntary exchanges with other individuals and firms, and out of this uncoordinated set of micro-interactions comes an economic system that is more or less coordinated at the aggregate level.

The combination of these two features of capitalism—class relations defined by private ownership and propertyless workers, and coordination organized through decentralized market exchanges—generates the characteristic competitive drive for profits and capital accumulation of capitalist firms. Each firm, in order to survive over time, must compete successfully with other firms. Firms that innovate, lower their costs of production, and increase their productivity can undercut their rivals, increase their profits and thus expand at the expense of other firms. Each firm faces these competitive pressures, and thus in general all firms are forced to seek innovations of one sort or another in order to survive. The resulting relentless drive for profits generates the striking dynamism of capitalism relative to all earlier forms of economic organization.

Actual capitalist economies, of course, are much more complex than this. As economic sociologists stress, no capitalist economy could function effectively, or even survive, if it consisted exclusively of the institutions of private property and market competition. Many other institutional arrangements are needed to make capitalism actually work and are present in the social organization of all real capitalist economies. These institutional properties of real capitalist economies vary considerably over time and place. The result is a wide variety of real-world capitalisms, all of which differ from the abstract model of "pure" capitalism. Some capitalisms, for example, have strong, affirmative states which regulate many aspects of the market and empower workers in various ways to control certain aspects of the labor process. These are capitalist economies in which the "private" in "private ownership" has been partially eroded, and the voluntary exchange in markets is constrained by various institutional devices. In some capitalisms both firms and workers are organized into various kinds of collective associations that provide significant forms of coordination distinct from both market and state coordination.

Philippe C. Schmitter (eds), *Private Interest Government: Beyond Market and State* (Beverly Hills and London: Sage, 1985), pp. 1–29.

Trade associations, unions, chambers of commerce, and other kinds of association help constitute what some people have called "organized capitalism." Other capitalisms lack robust forms of collective association of this sort and operate in ways closer to the liberal market model. All varieties of capitalism also contain a significant domain of economic activity that occurs outside of both the market and state regulation, especially economic activities within households and kin networks, but also within broader social settings often referred to as "community."[3]

These variations are important; they matter for the lives of people within capitalist societies and for the dynamics of the economy. And, as we shall see in chapter 5, some of these variations can be understood as reducing the "capitalisticness" of the economy: some capitalist societies are in a meaningful sense less capitalistic than others.[4] Nevertheless, to the extent that these variations all retain the core elements of the institution of private property in the means of production and markets as the central mechanism of economic coordination, they remain varieties of capitalism.[5]

---

3 Household economic activities include all of the various activities that go under the rubric "housework." Community economic activity includes a wide range of informal work, ranging from babysitting exchanges among friends to volunteer service activities through churches. These are all "economic" insofar as they involve laboring activity to provide goods and services to satisfy human needs. For an extended discussion of such "noncommodified" forms of economic activity, see J. K. Gibson-Graham, *A Postcapitalist Politics* (Minneapolis: University of Minnesota Press, 2006), chapter 3.

4 There are two theoretically distinct forms of variation across capitalist economies: 1) *Types:* This includes things like variations in the degree of competitiveness of markets, the size of firms, the level of development of technology, the mix of different industrial sectors, the nature of the division of labor within the labor process, etc. 2) *Hybrids:* These are variations that come from the diverse ways in which capitalist and non-capitalist economic structures are combined and interpenetrate. This includes variations in the extent to which the state directly organizes production, the importance of household production, the role of cooperatives and other forms of collective property, the continuing presence of precapitalist economic forms, etc. This second form of variation is particularly important in understanding the problem of alternatives to capitalism. We will discuss this issue of hybrids at length in chapter 5.

5 There is a knotty theoretical problem which we will sidestep here: when you have an economic system that combines capitalist elements with various kinds of non-capitalist elements, what justifies still calling the system as a whole "capitalism"? How much non-capitalism is needed before the resulting hybrid is something entirely new rather than a hybrid form of capitalism as such? There are a variety of apparent answers to this question. One might say, for example, that the system remains capitalist so long as the capitalist elements are "the

ELEVEN CRITICISMS OF CAPITALISM

Capitalism is, for most people, simply taken for granted as part of the natural order of things. Particular behaviors by corporations or particular economic policies of the government might be the object of criticism, but capitalism itself is simply not the sort of thing that one criticizes. One of the central tasks for socialists, therefore, has always been to convince people that capitalism as such generates a range of undesirable consequences and that, as a result, one should at least entertain the idea that an alternative to capitalism might be desirable and possible.

The central criticisms of capitalism as an economic system can be organized into eleven basic propositions: *the point here is that it is eliminable*

1. *Capitalist class relations perpetuate eliminable forms of human suffering.*

2. *Capitalism blocks the universalization of conditions for expansive human flourishing.*

3. *Capitalism perpetuates eliminable deficits in individual freedom and autonomy.*

4. *Capitalism violates liberal egalitarian principles of social justice.*

5. *Capitalism is inefficient in certain crucial respects.*

6. *Capitalism has a systematic bias towards consumerism.*

7. *Capitalism is environmentally destructive.*

8. *Capitalist commodification threatens important broadly held values.*

9. *Capitalism, in a world of nation states, fuels militarism and imperialism.*

10. *Capitalism corrodes community.*

11. *Capitalism limits democracy.*

---

most important" or are "dominant." Or one might say that the system remains capitalist so long as the dynamics of social reproduction and development are "primarily" capitalist. These formulations capture an important intuition, but they all remain vague to the extent that words like "more" or "dominant" or "primarily" cannot be given precise quantitative meaning.

None of these criticisms is simple and straightforward, and certainly none of them is uncontroversial. They all involve a diagnosis of certain kinds of negative consequences that are hypothesized to be generated by the basic structure of capitalism as a system of production with class relations defined by private ownership and propertyless workers, and economic coordination organized through decentralized market exchanges. The propositions themselves do not indicate the extent to which these effects could be neutralized by creating counter-capitalist institutions inside of capitalist society. The diagnosis that these are harms generated by capitalism could be correct and it could also be true that they might be significantly ameliorated through various kinds of institutional changes that fall short of completely replacing capitalism. Headaches may be caused by stress, but the harm may be significantly reduced by aspirin. The problem of the transformations needed to remedy these harms is a theme on which we will focus in subsequent chapters. Here our objective is to diagnose the harms themselves and the specific mechanisms through which they are generated.

Two other preliminary comments: First, critics of capitalism are sometimes tempted to treat all of the serious problems and harms of the contemporary world—such as racism, sexism, war, religious fundamentalism, homophobia, and so on—as consequences of capitalism. This temptation should be resisted. Capitalism is not the root of all evils in the world today; there are other causal processes at work which fuel racism, ethno-nationalism, male domination, genocide, war, and other significant forms of oppression. Nevertheless, even in the case of those forms of oppression which capitalism may not itself generate, it may still be implicated by making the problems more difficult to overcome. Capitalism may not be the root cause of sexism, for example, but it could make it harder to overcome by failing to allocate sufficient resources to good quality, publicly provided childcare services. In the critique of capitalism, therefore, the critical task is to identify those harms which are directly generated by specifically capitalist mechanisms and to understand the ways in which capitalism may indirectly contribute to impeding the reduction of oppression.

Second, many of these eleven criticisms of capitalism can also be leveled against those economic systems in the twentieth century that were typically labeled "socialist," or what I will call in chapter 5 "statist." For example, one of the criticisms of capitalism (proposition 6) is that it is environmentally damaging, but we know that the authoritarian central planning apparatus of the statist economy in the Soviet Union also gave little weight to negative impacts on the environment. If the only possible alternative to capitalism were statism—an economic structure in which the means of production are owned and controlled by the state and coordinated through a centralized bureaucracy—then the critique of capitalism in these terms would lose some of its force. But, as I will argue in chapter 5, there is another alternative, a conception of socialism anchored in the idea of meaningful democratic control over both state and economy.[6] The central argument of this book is that an economy so structured enhances our collective capacity to mitigate the harms discussed in the eleven propositions below.

1. Capitalist class relations perpetuate eliminable forms of human suffering

Let us begin with a simple, indisputable observation: the world in which we live involves a juxtaposition of extraordinary productivity, affluence and enhanced opportunities for human creativity and fulfillment along with continuing human misery and thwarted human potential. This is true whether we look at the world as a whole, or just at the conditions of life of people within the most developed capitalist countries. There are many possible explanations for this situation. It is possible that poverty in the midst of plenty constitutes simply a sad fact of life: "the poor will always be with us." Alternatively, it might be a temporary state of affairs which further economic development will eradicate: capitalism, given enough time, especially if unfettered by state regulation, will eventually eradicate poverty. Or, perhaps, the suffering and lack of fulfillment are simply the fault of the individuals whose lives go badly: contemporary capitalism generates an abundance

---

6 In terms of environmental destruction, capitalism and statism suffer a similar deficit: a failure of broad public deliberation over the trade-offs between present consumption, economic growth, and environmental protection, and the absence of democratic mechanisms capable of translating public deliberation into effective public policy. If anything this deficit was worse in the authoritarian statist economies, since neither the state nor the economy was under democratic control. In capitalist countries with democratic states, even if the form of democracy is relatively thin, there is greater public space for deliberation on environmental issues and a political process for imposing some constraints on environmentally destructive practices of the economic system.

of opportunities which some people squander because they are too lazy or irresponsible or impulsive to take advantage of them. But it is also possible that the situation of poverty existing in the midst of plenty is a symptom of certain fundamental properties of the socioeconomic system. This is the central claim of the socialist critique of capitalism: *capitalism systematically generates unnecessary human suffering*—"unnecessary" in the specific sense that with an appropriate change in socioeconomic relations these deficits could be eliminated. The harshest anti-capitalist rhetoric denouncing capitalism in terms of oppression and exploitation centers on this theme.

To many people it will seem odd, perhaps even absurd, to indict capitalism as a pivotal source of poverty in contemporary society. The "free market" and profit-seeking entrepreneurialism are continually touted as the source of technological progress, economic growth, and increasing prosperity. While social problems and human suffering certainly continue to exist in affluent capitalist societies, the argument goes, these cannot be attributed to capitalism as such, but rather to other social processes that just happen to coexist with capitalism in capitalist society. If 20 percent of children in the United States live in poverty at the beginning of the twenty-first century this is because of family breakdown, or cultural deficits in poor communities, or ill-considered public policies creating welfare dependency and poverty traps, or a poorly designed educational system which fails to prepare people for rapidly changing labor markets. The persistence of poverty is not due to anything connected to the capitalist nature of the economic system as such. True, the free market may generate economic inequality, but it also generates economic growth, and as defenders of capitalist institutions are fond of saying, "a rising tide lifts all boats." Why should anyone care about inequality if it has the consequence of improving the lot of the poor in the long run? And besides, all alternatives to capitalism create even more problems. Look at the fate of the state-run economies in the Soviet Union and elsewhere: capitalism won out because it was so much more efficient and able to provide a rising standard of living for most people, not to mention the fact that capitalism tends to support more individual freedom and political democracy than its alternatives.

It is certainly the case, if one takes a long-term view of the matter, that capitalism has generated dramatic technological and scientific progress over the last two centuries or so, which has resulted in improved nutrition, reduced illness, and increased life-expectancy for a significant proportion of the population in many places on earth. What is especially relevant to our discussion is that these improvements are not simply concentrated in some privileged class or stratum, but have diffused quite broadly, including, more recently, to significant parts of the developing world. While this progress cannot be attributed exclusively to capitalism as such—state action has played an important role in public health, for example—capitalism has been central to the process. This fact—that capitalism is a growth machine and that growth can have significant positive effects on the living standards of large numbers of people—is one of the reasons capitalism remains such a robust social order.

The claim in this first proposition, however, is *not* that capitalism has not in certain ways contributed to a reduction of human suffering relative to *prior* states of the world, but that relative to *possible* states of the world it perpetuates eliminable sources of suffering. This implies a counterfactual—that in the world today significant reductions in human suffering would be possible with appropriate non-capitalist institutions in place. This counterfactual is not shown to be false simply by citing the empirical observation that improvements in material conditions have occurred under existing capitalism. The claim is that these improvements fall far short of what is possible.

What then is the argument behind the claim that capitalism has an inherent tendency to perpetuate eliminable suffering? Three mechanisms are especially important here: exploitation; the uncontrolled negative social externalities of technological change; and competition under capitalist conditions.

Exploitation

Capitalism confers economic power on a category of people—owners of capital—who have an active economic interest in keeping large segments of the population in an economically vulnerable and dependent position. Here is the argument:

Capitalism is an economic system driven by the never-ending pursuit of profits. This is not primarily a question of the personal greed of individual capitalists—although a culture of profit-maximizing undoubtedly reinforces the single-minded pursuit of self-interest that looks very much like "greed." Rather, it is a result of the dynamics of capitalist competition and the pressures on firms to continually attempt to improve profits or else risk decline.

A pivotal aspect of the pursuit of profits by capitalist firms centers on the laboring activity of employees. Capitalist firms hire workers to use the means of production to produce the goods and services which the capitalist firm then sells. The difference between the total costs of producing those goods and services and the price at which they are sold constitutes the profits of the firm. In order to maximize profits, such firms face a double problem with respect to labor: on the one hand, hiring labor is a cost that takes the form of wages and capitalists want to keep these costs (like all production costs) as low as possible. The lower the wage costs, the higher the profits, all other things being equal. On the other hand, capitalists want workers to work as hard and as diligently as possible, since the more effort workers expend, the more will be produced at a given level of wages. The more produced for a given level of costs, the higher the profits.[7] The economic interests of capitalists—the profits they command—therefore depend upon extracting as much labor effort from workers at as little cost as possible. This, roughly, is what is meant by "exploitation."[8]

Of course, individual capitalists cannot unilaterally set wages nor unilaterally determine the intensity of work, both because

---

7 These two objectives—getting workers to work as hard as possible while paying them as little as possible—are in some tension, since how hard workers work is in part affected by how much they are paid. This is true for two principal reasons: workers who are better paid are more likely to feel a sense of obligation to their employers and thus work harder, and workers who are better paid have a greater stake in their job and more to lose if they are fired, and thus work more diligently. Although they do not explicitly use the term "exploitation" in their analysis, these issues are brilliantly explored in an essay on the nature of work incentives by Samuel Bowles and Herbert Gintis, "Contested Exchange: New Microfoundations for the Political Economy of Capitalism," *Politics and Society* 18 (1990), pp. 165–222.

8 Exploitation is a controversial concept when applied to the analysis of capitalism. In neoclassical economics exploitation can only happen in capitalism if there is some form of coercion operating in market relations that forces workers to sell their labor for less than its competitive market price. Some sociologists (for example, Aage B. Sørenson, "Toward a Sounder Basis for Class Analysis," *American Journal of Sociology* 105: 6 [2000], pp. 1523–58) have adopted a variant of this neoclassical economics notion by defining exploitation as a "rent" connected to various forms of "social closure." For an extended discussion of the issues involved in defining exploitation, see Wright, *Class Counts*, chapter 1, and G. A. Cohen, "The Labour Theory of Value and the Concept of Exploitation," in G. A. Cohen, *History, Labour and Freedom* (Oxford: Oxford University Press, 1989).

they are constrained by labor market conditions and because they face various forms of resistance by workers. In order to maximize profits, therefore, capitalists also have an interest in maintaining labor market conditions which both ensure ample supplies of labor and which undercut the capacity of workers to resist pressures to intensify labor effort. In particular, capitalists have an interest in there being large numbers of workers competing for jobs, which will tend to drive down wages, as well as there being sufficiently high levels of unemployment to make workers anxious about the prospects of losing their jobs. In other words, capitalists have a strong interest in increasing the vulnerability of workers.

Technological change

Technological change within the process of production is an inherent tendency of capitalist competition, since it is one of the key ways capitalists increase productivity in their efforts to sustain profits. In and of itself, increasing productivity is a good thing, since it means fewer inputs are needed to produce a given level of output. This is one of the great achievements of capitalism, emphasized by all defenders of this way of organizing economic activity.

So, what is the problem? The problem is that technological change continually renders skills obsolete, destroys jobs, and displaces workers, and this imposes great hardship on people. But, defenders of capitalism will reply, technological change also creates demands for new skills and new jobs, and on average this has led to a long term upgrading of the quality of jobs and wages in the economy. Far from perpetuating elim- inable poverty, the argument goes, technological change makes possible a dramatic reduction of poverty. The problem with this reply is that capitalism as an economic system does not itself contain any mechanism for moving people with outmoded skills and limited job opportunities into expanding jobs which require new skills. The task of providing new skills and new jobs for displaced workers is a very demanding one: many such workers are relatively old and capitalist firms have little incen- tive to invest in the human capital of older workers; the new job opportunities are often geographically distant from where displaced workers live and the cost of social dislocation in moving to such jobs is considerable; and capitalist firms are often hesitant to provide effective training for workers of any age with inadequate skills, since such newly trained workers would be free to move their human capital to other firms. Thus while it is true that technological change within capitalism often generates higher productivity jobs requiring new skills, and at least some of these new jobs may be better paid than the jobs that have been destroyed, the process of job destruction and creation generates a continual flow of displaced people, many of whom are unable to take advantage of any new opportunities. Technological change produces marginalization as well as new opportunities, and—*in the absence of some countervailing non-capitalist process*—marginalization generates poverty. This is inherent in the logic of capitalism, and in the absence of non-capitalist institutions, such marginalization perpetuates human suffering.

Profit-maximizing competition

Technological change is a specific example of a broader dynamic in capitalist economies: the ways in which profit-maximizing competition among firms destroys jobs and displaces workers. It is a commonplace observation of contemporary discussions of free trade and global capitalism that capitalist firms often move their production to lower-wage economies in order to cut costs and increase profits. This may not be due to technological change or technical efficiency, but simply because of the wage differentials between different places. In the course of such movement of capital, jobs are destroyed and workers marginalized. For all sorts of reasons capital is much more mobile than people: people have roots in communities which make it very costly to move; there are often legal barriers to movement across international boundaries; and even within national boundaries, displaced workers may lack the information and resources needed to move to new jobs. The result is that even if capitalist competition and weakly regulated capital markets stimulate economic growth, they leave in their wake displaced workers, especially when markets are organized globally.

Taken together, these three processes—exploitation, negative social externalities of technological change, profit-maximizing competition—mean that while capitalism is an engine of economic growth, it also inherently generates vulnerability, poverty, deprivation, and marginalization. These processes are especially salient when capitalism is viewed as a global system. On the one hand, the global movements of capital and extensions of capitalist exploitation, technological change, and profit-maximizing competition to the less developed regions of the world have in some cases contributed to rapid economic growth and development, most strikingly in the late twentieth century and early twenty-first century in China and India.[9] On the other hand, these same processes have also produced deep and devastating forms of marginalization and desperate poverty in various parts of the world.

In principle, of course, the fruits of growth could be distributed in ways that improved everyone's material welfare. It is unquestionably the case that capitalism has generated sufficient material wealth in the world today so that even with no further economic growth no person would have to be poor in the developed capitalist countries, and basic needs could be met for everyone even in poor third-world countries. However, there is no mechanism *internal to capitalism itself* to generate the redistribution needed to produce these effects, either within the rich countries or globally. For the rising tide to indeed raise *all* boats, counter-capitalist institutions must be created capable of neutralizing the destructive impact of capitalism on the lives of many people. It is precisely because capitalism creates the potential to eliminate material deprivation, but cannot itself fully actualize that potential, that it can be indicted for perpetuating eliminable forms of human suffering.

2. Capitalism blocks the universalization of conditions for expansive human flourishing

When socialists, especially those anchored in the Marxist tradition, criticize capitalism, a litany of harms is usually invoked: poverty, blighted lives, unnecessary toil, blocked opportunities, oppression, and perhaps more theoretically complex ideas like alienation and exploitation. However, when the vision of an alternative to capitalism is sketched, the image is not simply that of a consumer paradise without poverty or material deprivation, but rather a social order in which individuals thrive, where their talents and creative potentials are nurtured and freely exercised

---

9 Marx, in fact, celebrated this aspect of capitalist expansion to the far corners of the world on the grounds that it was necessary for the modernization of less developed regions. Imperialism was the necessary process for generating a truly global capitalism, which in turn for Marx was the necessary condition for transcending capitalism. See Bill Warren, *Imperialism: Pioneer of Capitalism* (London: Verso, 1980).

to the fullest extent. The elimination of material deprivation and poverty are, of course, essential conditions for the full realization and exercise of human potentials, but it is that realization which lies at the core of the emancipatory ideal for socialists. This, then, is what I mean by the expansive sense of "human flourishing": the realization and exercise of the talents and potentials of individuals.

The second criticism of capitalism asserts that while capitalism may have significantly contributed to enlarging the potential for human flourishing, especially through the enormous advances in human productivity it has generated, and while it certainly has created conditions under which a segment of the population has access to the conditions to live flourishing lives, it nevertheless blocks the extension of those conditions to all people even within developed capitalist countries, not to mention the rest of the world. Three issues are especially salient here: first, the large inequalities generated by capitalism in access to the material conditions for living flourishing lives; second, inequalities in access to interesting and challenging work; and third, the destructive effects on the possibilities of flourishing generated by hyper-competition.

Material inequality and flourishing

The relationship between markets and inequality is complicated. On the one hand, markets and competition have certain equality-promoting effects: capitalist markets create conditions for a certain real degree of class mobility compared to earlier societies, and this means that a person's location within the system of economic inequality is less determined by birth than in earlier forms of class society. Rags-to-riches sagas are real, if relatively rare, events, and are facilitated by open, competitive markets. A vibrant market economy is also generally corrosive of various forms of non-economic status inequality, such as those based on gender, race, ethnicity, and religion, at least insofar as competitive labor markets create incentives for employers to seek out talent regardless of such "ascriptive" attributes. To the extent that capitalism has contributed to the destruction of such ascriptive discrimination, it has advanced the process of universalizing the conditions for human flourishing.[10]

---

10 Both Karl Marx and Max Weber saw the impact of capitalism on such

But markets are also powerful engines for generating inequalities. Market competition produces winners and losers, and since there are strong tendencies for the effects of winning and losing to be cumulative within individual lives and to have an impact on the next generation, in the absence of countervailing mechanisms inequalities in the market will tend to intensify over time. Some of these inequalities are the result of factors at least partially under the control of individuals. In particular, people make decisions about how to allocate their time and resources when they make different kinds of investments, including investments in the acquisition of human capital (skills and knowledge), and thus even if everyone started out with the same human and financial endowments, over time inequalities would emerge reflecting the different preferences and efforts of actors. But much of the inequality generated by markets is simply the result of chance rather than hard work and foresight. A worker can responsibly invest in education and training only to be confronted with outmoded skills and much-reduced employment prospects at some point in the future. Even if this does not result in absolute poverty, it can result in a greatly diminished capacity for individuals to exercise their talents. Firms can go bankrupt, and employees lose their jobs, not because of poor planning and bad business practices, but because of market shocks over which no one has control. Rather than being robust mechanisms for rewarding "merit," markets often function much more like brutal lotteries.

The large economic inequalities generated by markets mean that, in the absence of some countervailing non-market distributive mechanism, the material means for living a flourishing life will be very unevenly distributed both across the population within countries and across the regions of global capitalism. In an obvious way this has especially serious consequences for children, where material inequalities can severely constrain access to the conditions for developing their human potentials. But this is not just a problem for the early years of life. The idea of "flourishing" includes not just the development of

"ascriptive" status inequalities—status inequalities linked to attributes of birth—as being one of its virtues. Marx, in the *Communist Manifesto*, sees such traditional forms of status as "melting into air" under the assault of capitalism, and Weber sees the dynamism of capitalist markets destroying rigid status orders. For a discussion of this similarity in Marx and Weber, see Erik Olin Wright, "The Shadow of Exploitation in Weber's Class Analysis," *American Sociological Review* 67: 6 (2002), pp. 832–53.

human intellectual, psychological and social capacities during childhood, but also the lifelong opportunity to exercise those capacities, and to develop new capacities as life circumstances change. Capitalist markets generate large inequalities in the realistic opportunities for such lifelong development and exercise of talents and capacities.

Work

It has no incentive to create meaningful work

Beyond the question of economic rewards for labor market activity, capitalism generates very large disparities in access to interesting and challenging work. The incentive of capitalist employers is to design jobs in such a way that they can extract the maximum effort from workers at the lowest cost. Frequently—although not invariably—this is accomplished by adopting technologies which reduce the skill levels required to do the job, routinize the principal tasks, and simplify the monitoring requirements of the work. To be sure, it is also the case that technical change can open up demands for new kinds of highly skilled workers, and some of these jobs also involve considerable problem-solving and opportunities for creativity. The problem is that the supply of such challenging jobs by capitalist firms is not determined by the needs of people for settings in which to do interesting work, but by the profitability of such jobs for the firm, and there is no reason in general for profitability to be maximized by creating meaningful, interesting, and challenging work for employees. What is more, when meaningful, interesting jobs are created in response to new technologies and conditions, if they require scarce skills and are thus highly paid, capitalist competition in general generates ongoing pressures to routinize the tasks associated with such jobs as much as possible in order to reduce the costs associated with hiring highly skilled employees.[11] The result is that in capitalist economies most people for most of their work lives face job opportunities which offer

---

11   There is thus a kind of cyclical process at work here: technical change often creates demands for high-skilled workers for new kinds of jobs; over time subsequent innovation is directed towards routinizing those jobs to remove the necessity for so many high-skilled workers. A good example of this is the trajectory over time of the job of computer programmer. In the 1960s this was an extremely skilled job requiring a great deal of education. By the early twenty-first century, with the tremendous growth in the importance of computers, many of the tasks of computer programming have been reduced to routine work that can be accomplished with relatively little training.

how taken for granted it is   we do not want to work

meager opportunities at best for creativity and challenge, and this obstructs human flourishing.

Destructive competition

The relationship between competition and human flourishing is a complex one. On the one hand, competition—trying to be better than others—is one of those social processes that push people to make the investments of time, energy, and resources needed to develop their talents. This is not to say that the only motivation for developing one's talents is the desire to be better than others; people are also motivated by the sense of accomplishment and fulfillment that comes from the mastery of skills and from the challenges of exercising those skills once they are developed. Still, competition is a powerful force for rewarding people for successfully developing their talents, and thus a certain degree of competition undoubtedly stimulates human flourishing. On the other hand, competition underwrites a culture of accomplishment which evaluates people only in terms of their *relative* standing compared to others. Achievement is defined not as the realization of one's potential but as winning, as being better than other people. In the most intense versions of such competition—what Robert Frank and Philip Cook call "winner-take-all" competitions—there is only one winner at the top who receives virtually all of the prizes; everyone else loses.[12] Such intense competition has potentially negative consequences for human flourishing. Most obviously, in winner-take-all competitions, once one realizes that one does not have a realistic chance of winning, it is very easy to become discouraged and give up altogether. More broadly, within systems of intense competition, most people will be relative "failures." The resulting loss of self-esteem and self-confidence undermines the psychological conditions for flourishing. Furthermore, since in capitalism the allocation of resources to facilitate the development of talents is viewed primarily as an economic investment, and investments are evaluated in terms of their expected economic returns, there will be a strong tendency for resources for the cultivation of talents to become highly concentrated among the most talented. In a market, after all, it would be a bad investment to devote lots of resources to developing the talents of the less talented, and thus there will be

---

12   Robert H. Frank and Philip J. Cook, *The Winner-Take-All Society: Why the Few at the Top Get So Much More Than the Rest of Us* (New York: Penguin, 1996).

a tendency for people with ordinary talents to generally have less access to the means of developing their talents. This too obstructs the universalization of human flourishing.[13]

Competition as such has thus both positive and negative effects on the universalization of conditions for human flourishing. The net affect is likely to be a function of the intensity of competition and the extent to which competition is balanced with other mechanisms that facilitate flourishing. The more an economy is organized on a purely capitalist basis, in which market competition and private ownership dictate the allocation of resources to different tasks, the less likely it is that this balance will be achieved.

3. Capitalism perpetuates eliminable deficits in individual freedom and autonomy

If there is one value that defenders of capitalism claim it achieves to the highest possible extent, it is individual freedom and autonomy. "Freedom to choose," rooted in strong individual property rights, is, as Milton Friedman has argued, the central moral virtue claimed for capitalism.[14] Capitalism generates stores filled with countless varieties of products, and consumers are free to buy whatever they want subject only to their budgetary constraints. Investors are free to choose where to invest. Workers are free to quit jobs. All exchanges in the market are voluntary. Individual freedom of choice certainly seems to be at the very heart of how capitalism works.

This market and property based freedom of choice is not an illusion, but neither does it amount to a complete account of the relationship of individual freedom and autonomy to capitalism. There are two reasons why capitalism significantly obstructs, rather than fully realizes, this ideal. First, the relations of domination within capitalist workplaces constitute pervasive restrictions on individual autonomy and self-direction. At the core of the

---

13   There is also a tendency in winner-take-all markets for people to over-invest in the development of certain kinds of talents because of an unrealistic expectation of the likely returns. This is most poignantly the case in the over-investment of time and energy in developing athletic skills, especially among boys in poor central city neighborhoods. For a discussion of overinvestment in sports, see Frank and Cook, *The Winner-Take-All Society*.

14   Milton Friedman and Rose Friedman, *Free to Choose* (New York: Harcourt, 1980), and Milton Friedman, *Capitalism and Freedom* (Chicago: University of Chicago Press, 1962).

institution of private property is the power of owners to decide how their property is to be used. In the context of capitalist firms this is the basis for conferring authority on owners to direct the actions of their employees. An essential part of the employment contract is the agreement of employees to do what they are told.[15] This may, of course, still allow for some degree of self-direction within work, both because as a practical matter employers may be unable to effectively monitor every aspect of employee behavior, and because in some labor processes the employer may grant the employee considerable autonomy. Nevertheless, for most workers in most capitalist workplaces, individual freedom and self-direction are quite curtailed. This lack of autonomy and freedom within the world of work is an important part of what has been called "alienation" in the critique of capitalism.

One response to this by defenders of capitalism is to argue that if workers do not like what they are told to do, they are free to quit. They are thus not really being dominated since they continually submit voluntarily to the authority of their boss. The freedom of individuals to quit their jobs, however, provides only an illusory escape from such domination since without ownership of means of production or access to basic necessities of life, workers must seek work in capitalist firms or state organizations, and in all of these they must surrender autonomy.

The second way in which capitalism undermines the ideal of individual freedom and autonomy centers on the massive inequalities of wealth and income which capitalism generates. As Philippe Van Parijs has forcefully argued, such inequalities imply that there is a significant inequality in "real freedom" across persons. "Real freedom" consists in the effective capacity of individuals to act on their life plans, to be in a position to actually make the choices which matter to them.[16] Large inequalities of wealth and income

---

15 In an important book on the meaning of democracy, Robert Dahl has argued that there is no logical reason why rights to private ownership confer rights to dictatorial power over employees. Just as we have abolished slavery even in cases where a person might want to voluntarily enter into a contract to be a slave, we could prohibit people from giving up their right to autonomy within the employment contract of capitalist firms. See Robert A. Dahl, *A Preface to Economic Democracy* (Berkeley and Los Angeles: University of California Press, 1985).

16 Philippe Van Parijs, *Real Freedom for All* (Oxford: Oxford University Press, 1997). Van Parijs emphasizes the ways in which the distribution of income generates inequalities in real freedom. For a discussion of how the vast inequalities in the distribution of wealth also curtail the freedom of most people, see Bruce Ackerman and Anne Alstott, *The Stakeholder Society* (New Haven: Yale

mean some people have much greater freedom in this sense than do others. While it is certainly true that relative to previous forms of society capitalism enhances individual autonomy and freedom, it also erects barriers to the full realization of this value.

4. Capitalism violates liberal egalitarian principles of social justice

Liberal egalitarian conceptions of justice revolve around the idea of *equality of opportunity*.[17] Basically the idea is that a system of distribution is just if it is the case that all inequalities are the result of a combination of individual choice and what is called "option luck." Option luck is like a freely chosen lottery—a person knows the risks and probabilities of success in advance and then decides to gamble. If they win, they are rich. If they lose, they have nothing to complain about. This is contrasted with "brute luck." These are risks over which one has no control, and therefore for which one bears no moral responsibility. The "genetic lottery" which determines a person's underlying genetic endowments is the most often discussed example, but most illnesses and accidents would also have this character. For the liberal egalitarian, people must be compensated for any deficits in their opportunities or welfare that occur because of brute luck, but they do not need any compensation for the consequences of option luck. Once full compensation for brute luck has been made, then everyone effectively has the same opportunity, and all remaining inequalities are the result of choices for which a person has moral responsibility.

Capitalism is fundamentally incompatible with this strong notion of equality of opportunity. The private accumulation of wealth and the large disparities in earnings in capitalism give some people inherent, unfair advantages over others. This is particularly the case with respect to children. The huge inequalities in the material conditions under which children grow up violates principles of equality of opportunity, both because it gives some children great advantages in the acquisition of human capital and because it gives some young adults access to large amounts of capital while others have none. Thus, even apart from the complex

University Press, 2000).

17 Liberal egalitarians share with liberals an emphasis on individual choice and liberty in their conceptions of justice, but they differ in how demanding they are when specifying the conditions under which individual choices can be seen as generating just outcomes.

problem of how to compensate people for "bad brute luck" in the genetic lottery, so long as there is inheritance of private wealth, and so long as investments in children's human capital is strongly linked to inequalities in parental resources, equality of opportunity will be a fiction. Capitalism, since it necessarily generates such inequalities in the conditions of life for children, is thus incompatible with equality of opportunity.[18]

Capitalism also violates ordinary liberal ideals of justice, not just the strong views of equality of opportunity of liberal egalitarians. One of the core ideas of liberal notions of justice is that, in the pursuit of one's self-interest, it is unjust to impose unchosen burdens on others. This is why theft is illegitimate: stealing coercively imposes a cost on the victim. The private profit-maximizing logic of capitalism means that capitalist firms have an inherent tendency to try to displace costs onto others: all things being equal, profits will be higher if some of the costs of production are born by people other than the owners, i.e. if unchosen burdens are imposed on others. The classic example is pollution: it is generally cheaper for capitalist firms to dump waste products in the environment than to pay the costs of preventing the pollution. But such pollution imposes costs on others—in the form of such things as increased health costs, environmental clean-up costs, and the degraded aesthetics of the environment. Such instances of costs displaced onto others are called "negative externalities." They are not just a form of economic inefficiency—although they are that as well as we will see in proposition 5 below—but also of injustice.

A defender of capitalism can reply that if all property rights were fully specified and fully enforced, then there would be no "negative externalities." In a world of fully specified property rights, complete contracts, and perfect information, then in order for a capitalist firm to impose their pollution costs on me it would have to purchase permission from me. I could, if I wanted to, sell my personal right to breathe clean air for a price. Capitalist firms would then decide whether it was cheaper to prevent the

---

18 The argument here is not simply that existing capitalisms are imperfect because they have failed to correct for inequalities of opportunities. The argument is that they could not in principle fully compensate for such inequalities without ceasing to be capitalist. This means that an honest defender of capitalism would have to admit that capitalism necessarily violates meaningful equality of opportunity, and in this way is inherently unjust, but that it is desirable in other respects, and these other respects are sufficiently salient that on balance capitalism should be supported.

pollution or to pay these costs. If the firm decides to pollute the air this would simply be a voluntary exchange between those who breathe the pollution and the firm. The same idea could apply to all other kinds of negative externalities: the decline in the value of homes when a large firm moves production to a new location; the unpleasant noise generated by airplane traffic; and so on. So the argument goes.

This kind of comprehensive specification of property rights and the creation of complete markets in which those rights can be exchanged is impossible for many reasons. The information conditions which would be needed to make such markets work are impossible to achieve. Even if a rough approximation were achieved, the transaction costs of actually executing these exchanges would be monumental. But even more fundamentally, since many of the negative externalities of profit-maximizing behaviors are imposed on future generations, the actual people who bear the unchosen burdens cannot be party to any "voluntary exchange." There is simply no way that future generations can participate in a market bargaining process where the costs to them of resource depletion generated by profit-maximizing markets are given a price to be paid by resources users today.

Of course, this issue of the *intergenerational* injustice of imposing negative externalities on future generations will be a problem for any economic system in which there are long-term consequences of present production and consumption decisions. The question is whether the problem is worse in some economic systems relative to others. Because of the ways in which capitalism promotes narrow self-interest, shortens time-horizons, and organizes economic decisions through decentralized markets, such problems of the injustice of intergenerational negative externalities are particularly intense. While an economic system in which broad investment choices were subjected to democratic control would not guarantee that the interests of future generations were adequately met, at least in such a system the balancing of present and future interests could be a central issue of deliberation rather than simply the result of the atomized private choices of self-interested individuals.

5. Capitalism is inefficient in certain crucial respects

If the ideals of freedom and autonomy are thought to be the central moral virtues of capitalism, efficiency is generally thought to be its core practical virtue. Whatever one might think about the enduring inequalities of capitalism and its injustices, at least it is supposed to promote efficiency. It "delivers the goods." The market and competition, the argument goes, impose a severe discipline on firms in ways which promote both static efficiency and dynamic efficiency.

Static efficiency (sometimes also called "allocative efficiency") refers to the efficiency in the allocations of resources to produce different sorts of things. Capitalism promotes allocative efficiency through the standard mechanism of supply and demand in markets where prices are determined through competition and decentralized decision making. The story is familiar: if the supply of some good falls below the demand for that good, prices will be bid up, which means that the producers of that good will in general make extra profits (since they can sell their goods at higher prices without their costs per item proportionately increasing). This higher than average level of profits leads to an increase in production of the product in short supply, and thus resources are reallocated from less profitable activities. This reallocation continues until the price of the good falls as the demand is met.

Dynamic efficiency refers to technological and organizational innovation that increases productivity over time. This has already been discussed in conjunction with proposition 1 above: Under the threat that other capitalist firms will innovate and lower costs (or innovate and improve quality), each firm feels the pressure to innovate in order to maintain profits. Of course, devoting time, resources, and human energy to innovation is risky, since much of this effort will not issue in useful results. But it is also risky to refrain from seeking innovation, since if other firms innovate, then in the long run a firm's viability in its market will decline. Competitive pressure thus tends to stimulate innovation, and this increases efficiency in the sense that gradually fewer inputs are needed to produce the same output.

These are indeed sources of efficiency in capitalism. In these respects, compared to earlier forms of economic organization as well as to centralized authoritarian state-organized production, capitalism seems to be more efficient. This does not mean, however, that capitalism does not itself contain certain important sources of inefficiency. Whether or not on balance capitalism is more or less efficient than the alternatives thus becomes a difficult empirical question, since all of these forms of efficiency and inefficiency would have to be included in the equation, not just efficiency defined within the narrow metric of the market.

Six sources of inefficiency in capitalism are especially important: the underproduction of public goods; the under-pricing of natural resources; negative externalities; monitoring and enforcing market contracts; pathologies of intellectual property rights; and the costs of inequality.

Public goods

For well-understood reasons, acknowledged by defenders of capitalism as well as its critics, capitalism inherently generates significant deficits in the production of public goods. The notion of public goods refers to a wide range of things satisfying two conditions: that it is very difficult to exclude anyone from consuming them when they are produced, and that one person's consumption of the good does not reduce another person's consumption. Clean air and national defense are conventional examples. Knowledge is another example: one person's consumption of knowledge does not reduce the stock of knowledge, and once knowledge is produced it is pretty hard to prevent people from consuming it. Capitalist markets do not do well in providing for public goods, since it is hard to capture profits when you cannot easily exclude people from consuming the thing you have produced. And, since many public goods are important both for the quality of life and for economic productivity, it is inefficient to rely on markets to produce them.

At first glance it might seem that public goods constitute a fairly narrow category of things. In fact they are quite broad. One way of thinking of them is in terms of the idea of "positive externalities." A positive externality is some positive side-effect of producing something. Consider public transportation, for which there are many positive externalities—for example, energy conservation, reduced traffic congestion, and lower pollution. These are all valuable positive side-effects that can be viewed as public goods, but they are non-marketable: an urban transit company cannot charge people for the reduced healthcare costs or the less frequent repainting of houses resulting from the lower air pollution generated by public transportation. These are benefits experienced by a much broader group of people than those who buy travel tickets. If a public transportation company is organized in a capitalist manner, it will have to charge ticket prices that enable it to cover all of the direct costs of producing the service. If it received payment for all of the positive externalities generated by its service, then the ticket price for individual rides could be vastly lowered (since those prices would not have to cover the full cost of the transportation), but there is no mechanism within markets for public transportation to charge people for these positive externalities. As a result, the ticket prices for individual rides have to be much higher than they should be from an overall efficiency standpoint, and as a result of the higher ticket price there will be lower demand for public transportation, hence less will be provided, and the positive externalities will be reduced.[19] This is economically inefficient.

The same kind of argument about positive externalities can be made about education, public health services, and even things like the arts and sports. In each of these cases there are positive externalities for the society in general that reach beyond the people directly consuming the service: it is better to live in a society of educated people than of uneducated people; it is better to live in a society in which vaccinations are freely available, even if one is not vaccinated; it is better to live in a society with lots of arts activities, even if one does not directly consume them; it is better to live in a society with extensive recreational activities for youth even if one is not young. If this is correct, then it is economically inefficient to rely on capitalism and the market to produce these things.

Under-pricing and over-consumption of natural resources

In standard economic theory, in a competitive market the price of things closely reflects the costs of producing them. This is seen as efficient because it means that the prices are sending the right signals to producers and investors. If the prices are significantly above the costs of producing something, this means that investors in those products will be earning extra profits, and this will send a signal to producers to increase production; if the prices

---

19 These positive externalities of public transportation are one of the main justifications for public subsidies for public transit systems, but typically these subsidies are relatively small and transit systems are expected to cover nearly all of the operating costs of producing the service through user fees. This is economically irrational. It could easily be the case that if all of the positive externalities of public transportation were taken into consideration (including the positive externalities for future generations), then full subsidization with free public transportation for the riders would be the most efficient way of pricing the service.

are below the costs of producing, then this means that people are losing money, and this sends a signal that less should be invested and produced.

This standard argument of efficient market signals generated by the costs of production interacting with supply and demand breaks down in a crucial way with respect to the extraction and processing of nonrenewable natural resources. The problem basically lies with the time-horizons in which people experience the "costs of production" and therefore interpret the signals generated by prices. We know that sometime in the future the costs of production of fossil fuels will be vastly higher than they are today because of the depletion of the resource. If these future higher costs of production were part of the calculation of profitability today, then it would be clear that current prices are not covering these costs. Production would accordingly be reduced until prices rose sufficiently to cover these future higher costs. The market, however, is incapable of imposing these long-term costs on present production. The result is under-pricing of nonrenewable natural resources and thus their overexploitation. This is an inefficient use of these resources over the long term.

In some cases this same mechanism also affects renewable resources. This happens when the short-term costs of production are such that a resource is exploited at a faster rate than it can be renewed. The classic example here is the rapid depletion of large fishing stocks. Fish in the ocean are certainly a renewable natural resource so long as the rate at which fish are caught does not exceed the capacity of the fishing stock to reproduce itself. With modern technology, however, the direct costs of catching fish are so low that the price of fish in the market leads to under-pricing and thus over-consumption. Because of the time-horizons in which the market imposes costs on producers, there is no way that a capitalist market itself can solve this problem.[20] Again, this leads to a grossly inefficient allocation of resources.

---

20 This, of course, does not mean that there is no solution to the depletion of fisheries, but simply that the solution requires a violation of market principles and capitalist competition, although not necessarily the complete abolition of market processes. When an aggregate quota is set for fishing, for example, one could still have capitalist firms bidding competitively over the right to particular quotas. The imposition of the quota is done through a non-market, non-capitalist mechanism—typically authoritatively by the state—but the allocation of rights within a quota could be organized on a market basis.

Negative externalities

We have already discussed negative externalities in terms of liberal notions of justice. Negative externalities are also a source of inefficiency in the allocation of resources. Again, an efficient allocation of resources in a market only occurs when producers experience monetary costs that reflect the true costs of production, because only in this situation will the demand for these products send the right signal to producers. The problem in capitalist economies is that capitalist firms have a strong incentive to displace as much of their costs onto other people as possible, since this increases their ability to compete in the market. As already noted, pollution is the classic example: from a strictly profit-maximizing point of view it would be irrational for capitalist firms not to dump waste material into the environment if they can get away with it. The same can be said about expensive health and safety measures that might affect the workers in the firm in the long term. Unless unhealthy conditions have an effect on costs of production, there is an incentive for profit-maximizing firms to avoid these costs.

These considerations are not just theoretical arguments. In contemporary discussions of pollution control and occupational health and safety, corporations constantly complain that the regulations on such matters make them less competitive. Firms in developing countries, the complaint goes, are not subjected to these regulations and thus face lower costs of production and so can sell their products at lower prices. What this actually means is that the unregulated producers are able to impose costs on others. It could well be that the complaining corporations are correct that they will go out of business unless regulations are relaxed, but this simply means that capitalist market competition, under these conditions, forces inefficiency in the allocation of resources.

Capitalism itself cannot solve such problems; they are an intrinsic consequence of private profit-driven economic decisions. This does not mean, of course, that in capitalist societies nothing can be done about negative externalities. The widespread attempts at state regulation of capitalist production are precisely a way of counteracting negative externalities by trying to prevent firms from displacing costs onto others. The state-regulatory mechanisms, however, always have the character of eroding the strictly private property rights associated with capitalism: some of those rights, such as the right to decide how much waste to dump into the environment, become public, rather than private.

Monitoring and enforcing market contracts and private property

A fourth source of inefficiency in capitalism centers on the costs associated with enforcing market-based contracts. At the center of market exchanges is the problem of contracts—voluntary agreements to exchange property rights of various sorts. Contracts are not self-enforcing, and there are a range of costs associated with the monitoring and enforcement of these agreements. The more resources have to be devoted to this task, the less are available to actually produce the goods and services exchanged in the market. This is inefficient in the sense that these resources are not being used to produce anything but simply to prevent cheating.

The massive amount of money spent on lawyers and litigation over such things as contract disputes, civil suits, enforcement of intellectual property rights, and challenges to government regulations of corporations are obvious examples of ways in which capitalist property rights generate efficiency losses. Such expenditures of resources may be entirely rational given the stakes in the disputes, and they may be necessary for production to take place under capitalist conditions, but nevertheless they deflect resources from directly productive activities.

The efficiency problems generated by contract enforcement, however, go beyond issues of litigation. They also affect the mundane operation of contractual relations. Two examples will illustrate the scope of this problem: the costs associated with supervising employees within the labor process, and the enormous paperwork costs of paying for medical care through a system of decentralized private insurance.

The employment contract involves an exchange of a wage for a certain amount of work. The problem is that while a worker can formally agree to perform this laboring activity, it is impossible for the worker to actually give up real control over the expenditure of effort to someone else. Since people are not robots, they always retain some measure of control over their activities. Because, in general, employers want workers to work harder than the workers themselves would like to, this means that employers face a problem in actually extracting effective effort from employees. The solution to this problem is some combination of threats for shirking (especially the threat of being fired), incentives for good performance (especially job ladders and pay increases), and supervision to monitor employee performance and enforce the sanctions.[21]

Of course, potentials for shirking exist in any cooperative activity. The specific class relations of capitalism, however, intensify this problem, since workers within the labor process are not themselves owners of the firm in which they work. If they were, for example in the form of a worker-owned co-op, then their individual interests would be much more strongly aligned with those of the firm in which they worked, and fewer resources would have to be devoted to the tasks of social control.[22] Since in general workers would work harder and with less monitoring when they own the means of production, the heavy social control apparatus of capitalist production is a source of inefficiency.

A second example of efficiency problems linked to enforcing contracts in capitalist markets concerns healthcare. In the United States healthcare is paid through a variety of mechanisms: some organized by the state, some by individuals paying doctors on a fee-for-service basis, and some through private insurance organized on capitalist profit-maximizing principles. Doctors, clinics, and hospitals have to hire many people to process insurance forms and keep track of co-payments from patients; insurance companies have to hire people to monitor claims and evaluate the risk profiles of potential purchasers of insurance; and of course patients have to spend considerable time and energy keeping track of the many confusing and incomprehensible bills. In Canada, in contrast, virtually all medical bills are paid for by the state in a system appropriately termed "single-payer." The Canadian government sets fees for different services in

---

21 For a discussion of the economic logic of the problem of extracting labor effort from workers, see Bowles and Gintis, "Contested Exchange," and Michael Burawoy and Erik Olin Wright, "Coercion and Consent in Contested Exchange," *Politics and Society* 18:2 (1990), pp. 251–66.

22 The claim here is that although there will still be issues of free-riding even in cooperative enterprises, the costs of solving the problem will be less since workers will engage in more consistent mutual supervision by virtue of the greater stakes in the collective enterprise. Cooperative ownership by workers also underwrites a different set of moral norms about labor effort, which also reduce monitoring costs. These issues are extensively discussed in volume III of the Real Utopias Project: Samuel Bowles and Herb Gintis, *Recasting Egalitarianism: New Rules for Communities, States and Markets* (London: Verso, 1998). For a somewhat skeptical view of the general efficiency gains from cooperative ownership, see Henry Hansmann, *The Ownership of Enterprise* (Cambridge, MA: Harvard University Press, 1996).

a bargaining process with physicians and health organizations. The physicians submit all bills to a single place for reimbursement. One measure of the efficiency losses directly connected to the problem of enforcing private insurance contracts is the proportion of total medical costs absorbed in paperwork and administration associated with payment in the two systems. In 1999, healthcare administrative costs in the US amounted to 31 percent of healthcare expenditures but only 16.7 percent in Canada. What are called "overhead costs" within total administrative costs come to almost 12 percent of private insurance company spending on health in the US, but only about 1.3 percent of spending in the Canadian system.[23] While not all administrative costs are connected to contract issues, much of the difference between the Canadian and US administrative costs is connected to the complexities of monitoring and payment connected to the market. The simplified Canadian system of resource allocation and accounting is much more efficient than the US one based on capitalist property relations.

Intellectual property rights

Intellectual property rights include a variety of legal rules that prevent people from having free access to the use of various kinds of knowledge and information: patents restrict the use of inventions; copyrights prevent the duplication of intellectual products and artistic creations; trademarks protect the use of brand names. The justification for these forms of private property rights is that without them there would be little incentive to produce inventions, intellectual products, or artistic creations. Inventions require the investment of time, energy, and resources in research and development, much of it quite risky. Intellectual products like books and artworks also require much time and effort, and sometimes financial investment as well. Unless the people who make these investments know in advance that if the products turn out to be valuable they will have rights to the economic returns on the products, they will not bother making the investments in the first place.

This certainly seems like a plausible argument. It turns out, however, that there is very little empirical evidence to support the

23   These figures are reported in Steffie Woolhandler, Terry Campbell, and David U. Himmelstein, "Costs of Health Care Administration in the United States and Canada," *The New England Journal of Medicine* 349 (2003), pp. 768–75.

claim.[24] There are three major issues here. First, while intellectual property rights may provide incentives, they also impede the diffusion of information and use of new ideas to generate further advances. The net effect of patents and copyrights on invention, creativity, and intellectual production therefore depends upon the relative magnitude of these two opposing forces—the positive impact of incentives and the negative impact of impediments to use and diffusion. There is no reason to assume that the former generally outweighs the latter.

Second, the defenders of intellectual property rights assume that the only reliable incentive for creativity and invention is monetary reward, but this is simply not the case. A great deal of research and development is done in publicly financed projects in universities and other research settings. Scientists are driven by a range of motives other than monetary rewards: prestige, curiosity, solving problems for the sake of humanity. Most artists and writers, even the most dedicated, do not receive large financial rewards from their work and yet they persist because of their commitments to aesthetic values and a need to express themselves. This is not to say that financial reward plays no role, and certainly if producers of intellectual products receive no financial rewards for their creative work it may be difficult for them to continue. But for many—perhaps most—people engaged in creative intellectual activities, monetary incentives protected by intellectual property rights are of secondary importance.

Third, it may also be the case that the emphasis on monetary incentives and the strong protection of intellectual property actually undermines some of the other motivations that are important for innovation and creativity. There is good empirical research demonstrating that monetary incentives can undermine altruistic motivations for cooperation, thus having the net effect of reducing cooperation.[25] This could also affect scientific and artistic

---

24 For a thorough discussion of why patents do not, in general, promote innovation, see Michele Boldrin and David Levine, *Against Intellectual Monopoly* (Cambridge: Cambridge University Press, 2007).

25 The issue here is the extent to which altruistic or other moral motivations for cooperation are complementary to selfish motivations. Two motivations are complementary when the presence of one does not undermine the effectiveness of the other. If this is the case, then in a situation where people are motivated to cooperate for moral reasons, they will be even more motivated if monetary incentives are added. If, on the other hand, the motivations are substitutes or are contradictory, then adding monetary incentives reduces the force of motivations rooted in moral commitments. For a discussion of the problem of how self-interested motives can crowd out more altruistic motives, see Sam Bowles,

creativity: the presence of strong financial rewards for commercially profitable creative efforts may undermine the motivation to pursue more free-wheeling artistic work and scientific research.

While it may be true that some limited protection of intellectual property rights is needed for incentive purposes—for example, to insure proper attribution of authorship—the strong regime of private property in intellectual products that characterizes capitalism probably on balance fetters innovation and creativity. What has come to be called the "open source" movement in information technology is a practical demonstration of this. The open source movement is best known for the development of the Linux computer operating system. There is no patent or copyright on the source code for Linux. It has been created by thousands of programmers cooperating and contributing new codes and ideas to its development. By most accounts this has resulted in an operating system that is technologically superior to its main rival, the PC operating system developed by Microsoft.

The costs of inequality

Many defenses of capitalism argue that there is a trade-off between equality and efficiency: the redistribution needed to move towards greater equality, the argument goes, undermines the incentives to work hard and invest, thus ultimately reducing economic efficiency. Like the argument about intellectual property rights, this argument may seem intuitively plausible, but empirical research on the question has not been able to establish a direct relation between the levels of inequality in a country and rates of economic growth, productivity growth, or any other aggregate measure of efficiency.[26] As in the case of intellectual property rights, the issue here is that there are a number of important reasons why inequality beyond some level undermines efficiency, and these negative effects may swamp whatever positive incentive effects are connected to inequality. First, high levels of inequality, particularly when associated with marginalization

"Policies Designed for Self-Interested Citizens May Undermine 'The Moral Sentiments': Evidence from Economic Experiments," *Science* 320: 5883 (2008), pp. 1605–9.

26 See Lane Kenworthy, "Equality and Efficiency: The Illusory Tradeoff," *European Journal of Political Research* 27: 2 (2006), pp. 225–54, and *Egalitarian Capitalism: Jobs, Incomes, and Growth in Affluent Countries* (New York: Russell Sage Foundation, 2007), chapter 4.

at the bottom, generate social conflict and social disorder. Police, guards, courts, prisons, not to mention the direct costs of crime itself, are all costs of inequality. Second, even apart from the costs of social disorder, high levels of inequality erode social solidarity, a sense that "we are all in the same boat together." Solidarity is an important source of efficient cooperation—cooperation that does not require large payments and surveillance to elicit effort and responsibility. Third, and perhaps most crucially for the questions of efficiency, high levels of inequality imply a huge waste of human talents and resources. Steven Jay Gould, the eminent evolutionary biologist, put it this way: "I am somehow less interested in the weight and convolutions of Einstein's brain than in the near certainty that people of equal talent have lived and died in cotton fields and sweatshops."[27] High levels of inequality mean, necessarily, inequalities in access to the material means to develop talents and human potentials. This is massively wasteful.

Most of these problems of economic inefficiency are not unique to capitalism. In any developed, complex industrial economy with high levels of interdependency there will be a problem of potential negative externalities and temptations to overexploit natural resources. Shirking and other forms of opportunistic behavior are issues in any form of economic organization. There will always be difficult issues of combining material incentives and intrinsic motivations for creativity and innovation. So, the criticism of capitalism in terms of these sources of inefficiency is not that they are unique to capitalism, but rather they are likely to be especially intense and difficult to counteract in capitalism by virtue of the centrality of private, profit-seeking motivations in the operation of the capitalist market and the conflictual character of capitalist class relations.

6. Capitalism has a systematic bias towards consumerism[28]

One of the virtues of capitalism is that it contains a core dynamic which tends to increase productivity over time. When productivity increases, there are two sorts of things that in principle can happen: we could produce the same amount of things with fewer

27 Stephen Jay Gould, "Wide Hats and Narrow Minds," in *The Panda's Thumb* (New York: W.W. Norton, 1980), p. 151.
28 The discussion of this proposition draws heavily from two books by Juliet Schor: *The Overworked American: The Unexpected Decline of Leisure* (New York: Basic Books, 1992) and *The Overspent American: Upscaling, Downshifting and the New Consumer* (New York: Basic Books, 1998).

inputs, or we could produce more things with the same amount of inputs. The criticism of capitalism is that it contains a systematic bias towards turning increases in productivity into increased consumption rather than increased "free time." There are times, of course, when the best way of improving the conditions of life of people is to increase output. When an economy does not produce enough to provide adequate nutrition, housing and other amenities for people, economic growth in the sense of an increase in total output would generally be a good thing. But when a society is already extremely rich there is no longer any intrinsic reason why growth in aggregate consumption is desirable.

The dynamics of capitalist profit-driven market competition impose strong pressure on capitalist economies to grow in total output, not just in productivity. Profits are made from selling goods and services. The more a capitalist firm sells, the higher the profits. Capitalist firms are therefore constantly attempting to increase their production and their sales. Enormous resources are devoted to this specific task, most clearly in the form of advertising and marketing strategies, but also in terms of government policies that systematically facilitate expansion of output. In the aggregate, this creates a strong trajectory of growth biased towards increased production. Since this implies a dynamic ever-increasing consumption supported by cultural forms which emphasize the ways in which increased consumption brings individual satisfaction, this bias is appropriately called "consumerism."

This output bias is enshrined in the standard way in which "growth rates" are reported: the growth in the gross national product or gross domestic product is evaluated in terms of market prices. In such a calculation, free time is given zero value (because it is not sold on the market), and thus a process of economic growth in which productivity was turned into more time would be viewed as stagnation, and a country in which people worked shorter work weeks and had longer vacations than another country with similar levels of productivity would be viewed as a "poorer" country.

A defender of capitalism might reply to the criticism of consumerism by arguing that the basic reason capitalism generates growth in output instead of growth in leisure is because this is what people want. Consumerism simply reflects the real preferences of people for more stuff. It is arrogant for left-wing intellectuals to disparage the consumption preferences of ordinary people. If people really preferred leisure to more consumption, then they would work less hard.

This reply rests on three incorrect assumptions about the conditions under which people make choices between leisure, work, and consumption. First, the claim that consumerism simply reflects what people really want assumes that the preferences of people for consumption and leisure are formed in an autonomous manner, unaffected by the strategies of capitalist firms. This is an implausible assumption. What people feel they need in order to live well is heavily shaped by cultural messages and socially diffused expectations. To imagine that preferences for consumption are formed autonomously is to claim that advertising, marketing and the promotion of consumerist lifestyles in the mass media have no effects on people.

Second, the claim that people would work less hard if they really wanted to assumes that there are no significant institutional impediments to people freely choosing the balance between work and leisure in their lives. This is simply not the case; there are significant obstacles other than individual consumerist preference which prevent people from freely choosing the balance between work, consumption, and "free time." Many capitalist firms prefer to hire fewer workers for longer hours than to hire more workers for fewer hours since in many jobs there are fixed overhead costs of employment per worker. Some of these are the result of the rules governing the employment contract over things like fringe benefits and payroll taxes, but some of the fixed overhead costs of production are intrinsic to various production processes. These would include the costs of formal training, the costs of acquiring tacit knowledge of workplaces, the costs of building social capital within workplaces (i.e. the development of networks and smooth communication among participants in the labor process). All of these mean that it is generally cheaper to hire one worker for 40 hours than two for 20 hours, and this creates disincentives for employers to allow employees to freely choose the number of hours they want to work (or, equivalently, it leads employers to impose a severe wage and fringe benefit penalty on reductions in working hours, making the trade-off between work and leisure much more costly for workers).

Third, the argument that consumerism is simply a preference (rather than a systematic bias) assumes that if large numbers of people were to choose a much less consumerist lifestyle, this would not have significant disruptive macroeconomic effects of the sort which would eventually make anti-consumerism itself unsustainable. If somehow it were to come to pass that large numbers of people in a capitalist society were able to resist the preferences shaped by consumerist culture and opt for "voluntary simplicity" with lower consumption and much more leisure time, this would precipitate a severe economic crisis, for if demand in the market were to significantly decline, the profits of many capitalist firms would collapse. In the absence of an expanding market, competition among firms would become much more intense since any firm's gain would be another firm's loss, and, more broadly, social conflicts would intensify. For these reasons, the state in capitalist economies would adopt policies to counteract anti-consumerist movements if they were to gain sufficient strength to have a significant impact on the market.

The state's role in promoting the consumption bias inherent in capitalist economies is particularly sharply revealed in times of economic crisis. In an economic downturn, governments attempt to "stimulate" the economy by, in various ways, encouraging people to consume more by reducing taxes, by reducing interest rates so borrowing is cheaper or, in some cases, by directly giving people more money to spend. In the severe economic crisis that began in 2008, economists warned that not only was consumption declining because of rising unemployment, but people were beginning to save more and this would only make matters worse. In order to get the economy back on track it was essential that people start spending more, saving less. Reinvigorating mass consumerism is a condition for reinvigorating capitalism.

This bias towards consumerism is a problem, of course, only if there are negative consequences of ever-increasing consumption. Four issues are especially important here: First, as discussed in proposition 7 below, consumerism is environmentally damaging. Second, many people in highly productive societies feel enormous "time binds" in their lives. Time scarcity is a continual source of stress, but the cultural pressures and institutional arrangements that accompany consumerism make it difficult for people individually to solve these problems. Third, a good case can be made that capitalist consumerism leads to less fulfilling and meaningful lives than do less manically consumption-oriented ways of life. Certainly research on happiness indicates that once a person has a comfortable standard of living, increased income and consumption do not lead to increased life satisfaction and happiness.[29]

---

29 For a review of research on the link between economic standing and happiness, see Richard Layard, *Happiness* (New York: Penguin, 2005).

People find meaning and happiness through their connections with other people, through their engagement in interesting work and activities, and through their participation in communities, much more than through lavish consumption. Consumerism as a cultural model for living a good life, therefore, hinders human flourishing. Finally, even if one takes a culturally relativist stance on the good life and argues that consumerism is just as good a way of life as less consumerist alternatives, it is still the case that capitalism is not neutral with respect to this choice, but erects systematic obstacles to less consumption-oriented ways of life. It is this bias, rather than consumerism per se, that is the central problem.

7. Capitalism is environmentally destructive

Capitalism significantly contributes to environmental problems in three principal ways. Each of these has been discussed under other propositions above, but the issue of environmental destruction is sufficiently important that it is worth reiterating them.

First, the systematic pressure on profit-maximizing firms to generate negative externalities means that in the absence of some strong countervailing mechanism, capitalist firms will ignore environmental costs. This is a stronger claim than a simple argument about the rational action of individuals with selfish motives. Individuals may litter the environment by throwing a can out of a car window because this is a low-cost way of disposing of a can and they are indifferent to its negative impact on others, but it is not the case that there are strong pressures on individuals to act this way. Capitalist firms face competitive pressures to reduce costs, and externalizing those costs onto the environment is a good strategy for doing this. This pressure cannot be countered by the market itself; it requires some form of non-capitalist intervention either by the state or by organized social forces.

Second, nonrenewable natural resources are systematically under-priced in the market since their value to people in the future is not registered in the dynamics of supply and demand in the present. The result is that actors in capitalist markets over-consume these resources. Capitalist markets are inherently organized around relatively short time-horizons, and thus the only way that the value to future generations of these resources can be taken into account in decisions about present uses is through the imposition of constraints on capitalism, again, by the state or by organized social forces.

Finally, the strong bias towards consumerism in the dynamics of capitalist markets has dire ecological consequences. In principle productivity growth could be quite beneficial for the environment, since this means that fewer inputs are needed to produce a given output. However, the bias generated by capitalist competition towards the expansion of markets and the consumption of ever-greater quantities of things means that productivity growth is, in general, translated into more production and higher consumption standards within capitalism. Particularly if we look at this issue in global terms, where economic growth in parts of the developing world fuels consumerism as a worldwide phenomenon, it is hard to imagine how this could be ecologically sustainable. This does not mean that consumption standards in poor countries shouldn't rise. By any standard of social justice, this is desirable. But it does imply that an economic system that fosters escalating consumerism in already rich countries and blocks any long-term plan to constrain consumption growth in these countries is environmentally destructive on a global level.

8. Capitalist commodification threatens important broadly held values

The word "commodification" refers to the process by which new spheres of human activity become organized through markets. Historically this has mainly involved the shift in production from the household, where goods and services were produced for the direct consumption of family members, to production by capitalist firms for the market; but in the contemporary period commodification also refers to the shift of production from the state to the capitalist market.[30] The classic example of the commodification of household production is food: there was a time in which most people grew most of their own food, processed it for storage, and transformed it into meals. By the twentieth century most people in developed capitalist societies purchased all food ingredients in

---

30 The extensive "privatization" of state services—including such things as public utilities like water and electricity, public transportation, health services, and even such core state services as welfare agencies, prisons, and public education— are examples of partial commodification, since in these cases the provision of the services typically remain fairly heavily regulated by public power.

the market, but still transformed these inputs into meals within the home. Increasingly, since the closing decades of the twentieth century, the food purchased in the market came closer and closer to a final meal—frozen pizzas, microwave meals, etc.—and fully commodified meals in restaurants became an increasingly important part of food consumption for most people in developed capitalist economies.

Markets may be an economically efficient way of organizing the production and distribution of many things, yet most people feel that there are certain aspects of human activity which should not be organized by markets even if it would be "efficient" in a technical economic sense to do so. Virtually everyone, except for a few extreme libertarians, believes that it would be wrong to create a capitalist market for the production and adoption of babies.[31] Even if it were the case that the exchanges on such a market were entirely voluntary, the idea of turning a baby into a commodity with a market price and selling the baby to the highest bidder is seen by most people as a monstrous violation of the moral value of human beings. Most people also object to a market in voluntary slaves—that is, a market in which you are allowed to sell yourself voluntarily into slavery. And most people object to markets in most body parts and organs, whether the organs come from live donors as in the case of things like kidneys and corneas, or from deceased donors, as in the case of hearts.[32] In part, this is because of the belief that such markets would inevitably prey on the vulnerabilities of the poor and lead to many

---

31 Some libertarians argue that a market for the production and adoption of babies would improve the lives of everyone involved: poor women would have their income substantially raised; prospective adoptive couples would find it easier to get babies; the babies would live better lives; and there would be fewer abortions. Since everyone would gain from the exchange, the argument goes, why prohibit it? Furthermore, some strong libertarians argue that parents have a kind of property right in their children, and thus they should have the right to sell this property just like any other property. For a defense of these kinds of positions, see Murray Rothbart, *The Ethics of Liberty* (New York: NYU Press, 1998), chapter 14.

32 There is less consensus about the desirability of markets in renewable body parts, most notably in the case of blood. Many people feel there is nothing wrong in having for-profit commercial blood donation firms. Research on blood donation, however, generally shows that both the quality and quantity of blood acquired through market mechanisms is lower than in well-organized non-market systems that rely on (and reinforce) altruism. See Jane Piliavin and Peter Callero, *Giving Blood: The Development of an Altruistic Identity* (Baltimore: Johns Hopkins University Press, 1991) and Kieran Healy, *Last Best Gifts: Altruism and the Market for Human Blood and Organs* (Chicago: University of Chicago Press, 2006).

types of abuse, but also it is because of wariness in reducing the human body to the status of a commodity with a market price attached to it. So, even in highly commodified capitalist societies, most people believe that there are moral limits to the domains in which capitalist markets should be allowed to organize our activities. Human beings should not be treated like commodities.

If commodification threatened important moral values only in a few special cases, then the critique of capitalism in these terms would be relatively limited. This is not, however, the case. On closer inspection there is a fairly broad range of activities for which commodification raises salient moral issues. Consider the following examples:

Childcare

Children require labor-intensive care. This can be provided through a variety of social organizations: the family, state-organized childcare services, various kinds of community-based childcare, or for-profit market-based childcare organized by capitalist firms. The market solution to this problem does not mean that all for-profit childcare will be of poor quality and harmful to the well-being of children. What it means is that the quality of the care will often be a function of the capacity of parents to pay. Capitalist firms providing childcare services will be organized around the objective of maximizing profits, and meeting the needs of children will matter only to the extent that it contributes to this goal. In order to maximize profits, firms will have strong incentives to seek low-cost labor for the staff of childcare centers, especially for those servicing poor families. The training of care-givers will be low, and the staffing ratios suboptimal in most centers. Parents with lots of resources and a capacity to obtain good information about the quality of providers will be able to purchase good quality childcare, but many families will not.

For strong defenders of the market, this sharp differentiation in quality of childcare is not a problem. After all, the reasoning goes, poor quality market-provided childcare may still be better than no childcare services at all, and in any case the parents can choose to provide the childcare at home if they prefer.[33] It is only

---

33 Milton Friedman, in *Capitalism and Freedom*, makes a similar argument for doctors: It would be desirable to eliminate official licensing of doctors since this would make lower-cost medical services available to the poor. Official licensing of doctors is simply a way to create a monopoly of services by certified doctors.

because it involves an overall improvement in their situation that they choose the poor quality market-based childcare over higher quality family-provided care. If anyone is devaluing the needs of children in this process, it is the parents, for it is they who decide the balance of trade-offs between on the one hand buying substandard care on the market and earning more income from their jobs and, on the other, providing their own childcare and earning less. The capitalist childcare firms in the market merely respond to their preferences.

This defense ignores the ways in which it is precisely the capitalist character of the economy that imposes these trade-offs on people. Other systems of organizing the provision of care-giving services would create other trade-offs—between providing good quality childcare services for everyone and having lower taxes, for example—but they would not inherently impose the choice between higher earnings and poor quality childcare on poor parents. In any case, whether one believes that the morally accountable agent for the devaluation of the needs of children is the consumer (parents) or the capitalist firm, the fact remains that a market-based for-profit organization of childcare services will have this effect.

These problems in the quality of childcare services can, of course, be moderated by state licensing, quality standards and monitoring, but to the extent that these are effective, they interfere with the functioning of the market, restrict the operation of the rights of private property, and thus render the provision of the service less purely capitalistic. If such regulation retains the underlying capitalist market structure of production, it will, necessarily, have the effect of raising the costs of such services and pricing poor families out of the market unless some other non-market mechanisms are introduced, such as cost-subsidies from the state. This too moves the provision away from a purely commodified form. The important point here is that so long as non-family childcare services are provided strictly through the capitalist market, there will be a strong tendency for the commodification of childcare to contribute to the devaluation of the needs of children.

Without official certification there would be private quality-rating services, and consumers could then decide whether they wanted high-priced doctors with high-quality private certification, or cheaper alternatives.

Product safety

One of the issues that any producer for the market must deal
with is the safety to the consumer of the things they produce and
sell. This is especially salient in certain domains of production,
such as food or transportation. Generally, improving the safety
of a product increases its cost, at least when safety requires more
expensive designs or rigorous quality controls. The question then
becomes this: under conditions of competitive capitalist markets,
how do profit-maximizing firms make choices about the costs and
benefits of improved safety?

This is an issue about which we have good empirical evidence.
One of the most notorious cases was the decision over the fuel
tank safety of the Ford Pinto in the 1970s. Here is the basic
story, based on internal memos from the Ford Corporation as
analyzed by Mark Dowie:[34] The Ford Pinto had a design flaw in
its fuel tanks which made it prone to explosion in certain kinds
of accidents. Once this flaw was discovered, the company had to
decide whether it was cost-effective to fix the problem or, alternatively, to pay the costs of settlements of civil suits resulting from
injury and death caused by the defect. To make this cost-benefit
analysis, the Ford Motor Company calculated what, from their
point of view, was the value of each life lost in such accidents.
They calculated this primarily on the basis of the future income
lost because of death, which in 1971 (in their estimate) came to
around $200,000. The cost of recalling all Pintos and fixing the
problem came to about $11 per car. With these numbers, what
should Ford do? The retrofitting would cost Ford about $137
million—$11 for each of the 12.5 million vehicles on the road.
Roughly 180 people died every year because of the defect. The
total "benefit" of the repair to the Ford Motor Company, therefore, came to only about $36 million (180 x $200,000). Even
if the court settlements got considerably higher, the company
executives figured it was cheaper to be sued in court and pay out
to victims than pay for the repairs, so they didn't do the repairs.

This kind of calculation makes perfect sense in a profit-
maximizing capitalist market. The only way to "rationally" figure
out the cost-benefit trade-off here was to estimate the "market
value" of a human life. This virtual commodification of life then

---

34 This account is based on research by Mark Dowie reported in his essay
"Pinto Madness," *Mother Jones*, September/October 1977.

makes it possible to weigh costs and benefits from the point of view of the profit-maximization strategy of the firm. Of course, it will always be the case that in assessing risks and allocating resources some kind of calculation of costs and benefits has to be done, since you cannot do everything and scarce resources ultimately have to be allocated. The issue here is that capitalist markets reduce this problem to the question of *what is most profitable to capitalist firms* and this is corrosive of human values.

The arts

Many people regard the arts as a vitally important domain of human activity for exploring life, meaning, and beauty. Of course, artists and performers of all sorts have often been prepared to make considerable personal economic sacrifices in order to participate vigorously in the arts, and much arts activity takes place outside of the discipline of the capitalist market. But still, the arts do need financial resources to thrive: drama needs theaters; symphonies need concert halls; and all performers and artists need to eat. If the main source of such funding is from the capitalist market, then the autonomy and vitality of the arts are threatened. Many theaters face enormous pressures to produce only those plays that will be a "commercial success," rather than plays that are controversial, innovative, or less accessible. Musicians are hampered by the commercial imperatives of "record deals." Writers find it difficult to publish novels when profit-maximizing strategies of publishers become oriented to producing "blockbusters." A fully commodified market for the arts thus threatens the core values of human artistic activity. This is one of the central reasons why in most countries there is substantial public subsidy of the arts. It is also why the wealthy subsidize through philanthropy the kinds of arts they like to consume—opera, art museums, symphonies. They realize that if these organizations had to rely strictly on commercial success through the sale of tickets to the consumers of the performances they would not be able to survive.

Religion and spirituality

Religion and spirituality grapple with some of the deepest issues people confront: death, life, purpose, ultimate meaning. All religions see these issues as transcending the mundane world of economic activity; religion is valued because of its importance in helping people come to terms with these matters. The distinctive value of religion is continually threatened by commodification. A notorious example, decried by many religious Christians, is the commercialization of Christmas. But perhaps even more profoundly, the commodification of churches themselves—turning churches into profit-maximizing sellers of religion—threatens religious values.

These examples are not meant to suggest that it is always inappropriate to use market criteria and market rationality in making decisions about the allocation of resources. The argument is simply that for many important economic decisions, the logic of the market needs to be balanced with other values, and for certain kinds of allocations, market criteria should be largely marginalized. This is a complex task because of the heterogeneity of different values that come into play in many contexts. The kind of dialogue and deliberation required to navigate these problems is impossible when commodification is regarded as the universally best solution to the problem of economic provision, and when the specific form of rational calculation of costs and benefits embodied in the market is taken as a universal paradigm for making choices. This is precisely the discipline imposed by capitalism.

9. Capitalism, in a world of nation states, fuels militarism and imperialism

As I will use the terms here, both militarism and imperialism refer to the properties and strategies of states. *Militarism* refers to the development of military power beyond a level needed for narrow defensive purposes. A highly militaristic state is one in which military personnel, beliefs, and values permeate the state, subordinating state policy to military priorities. Examples would include Japan in the 1930s and the United States since the mid twentieth century. In the US, military priorities dominate the budget of the national state, military spending plays a pivotal role in the relationship between the state and economy, and military values and perspectives permeate foreign policy. These patterns may have intensified in the first decade of the twenty-first century, but they have characterized the US state since the 1950s. *Imperialism* refers to strategies of states in which states use political and military power for purposes of economic domination outside of the state's immediate territorial jurisdiction.[35] The political and military power used may involve territorial conquest or overthrow of regimes, but it may also involve "softer" forms of power like international loans and foreign aid so long as such transfers reinforce economic dependencies. The central idea is that imperialism is a political-economic system in which state power is used internationally to support global forms of economic exploitation and domination.

Imperialism and militarism are obviously connected, since military power is one of the central forms of power deployed to extend and defend global forms of imperialist economic relations. Nevertheless, it is useful to distinguish these since militarism is not simply in the service of economic objectives but is also shaped by geopolitical dynamics,[36] and economic imperialism does not rely only on military power.

Defined in this way, militarism and imperialism are hardly unique to capitalism. Feudal states were centrally organized around military power and forms of subordination anchored in military command, and the imperial domination of territories for purposes of exploiting human and natural resources has occurred since the earliest city-states were formed. So capitalism as such does not create militarism and imperialism. Nevertheless, capitalism does, in specific ways, fuel both imperialism and militarism and shape their distinctive character in the world today.

Imperialism has accompanied capitalism from its beginnings. At the core of a capitalist economy is the search for markets and profits, and frequently this involves extending markets to new places and seeking sources of profits globally. Sometimes this kind of global market-making and capitalist expansion takes place through purely

---

35 The word "imperialism" is sometimes used to refer to the strategies of empires in which a state conquers and subordinates other parts of the world, either in the form of colonies or as components of an expanded multi-national state. At other times it is used to refer to global economic systems in which capitalist corporations from the developed capitalist world economically dominate economic activities and capital accumulation in other parts of the world. I am using the term to describe a particular intersection of the strategies of states and economic domination across territories.

36 By "geopolitical dynamics" I mean dynamics that are generated by rivalries among states in an inter-state system. These rivalries are fueled by a variety of processes, some of which may be economic and closely tied to capitalism, but which also include ideological and cultural forces. Nationalism as an ideological and cultural process, for example, can animate drives for state formation and conflicts between states which contribute to militarism in ways distinct from economically grounded imperialism.

economic means: merchants extend their trade networks, find new supplies of particular commodities and new outlets for profitable investment across long distances. But frequently such global expansion of capitalism has been backed by military power.

A variety of different forces historically have come into play in linking economic expansion with military force. The use of military power to expand and defend markets can be a way of excluding rival capitalist classes from those markets. This was particularly important in the era of mercantilism and colonialism where large capitalist trading companies were closely connected to states which enforced monopolies on their trading activities. The use of military power can also play a pivotal role in overcoming resistance to capitalist penetration, as was the case in the imperialist wars against China in the nineteenth century. In the second half of the twentieth century military power played an important role in preserving the possibilities for capital accumulation on a global scale by attempting to repress anti-capitalist revolutionary movements and policies in various parts of the world, both through direct military intervention and through a variety of forms of indirect intervention.[37]

In addition to militarism being fueled by capitalism because of its link to imperialism, militarism is also connected deeply to capitalism through the economic importance of military spending. This is particularly central in the US where military spending plays a critical role in the capitalist economy and underwrites the profits of many large corporations, but even in countries with a less militarized state such as Sweden, the production of military hardware can be a very profitable sector of capitalist production. While it would be an exaggeration to argue that the direct interest of capitalist firms in military spending explains militarism, the economic importance of military spending creates significant, powerful constituencies who oppose demilitarization.

---

37 The use of military force by the developed capitalist countries, especially the United States, against anti-capitalist movements in the Third World was politically framed in terms of containing the Soviet Union and China as geopolitical threats to US security. While it was undoubtedly the case that there was a geopolitical dynamic of conflict in play in this period, it was also the case that US military interventions—whether in the form of direct US military involvement as in Vietnam or indirect involvement in supporting military coups in Iran, Guatemala, Chile and many other places—was a response to various kinds of threats to global capitalist economic structures in these places.

10. Capitalism corrodes community

"Community" is one of those flexible terms in social and political discussions which are used in a wide variety of ways for different purposes. Here I will define the idea of community quite broadly as any social unit within which people are concerned about the well-being of other people and feel solidarity and obligations towards others. A "community" need not be a small geographical locale like a neighborhood, but often communities are geographically rooted, since such deep attachments and commitments are often built on direct, face-to-face interactions. One can also talk about the *degree* of community in a particular social setting, since reciprocity, solidarity, mutual concern and caring can vary in intensity and durability. A strong community is one in which these mutual obligations run very deep; a weak community is one in which they are less demanding and more easily disrupted.

Community as a moral ideal refers to the value of such solidarity, reciprocity, mutual concern, and mutual caring. Access to community in this sense is one aspect of the social conditions for human flourishing. But community is not just a question of what defines a good society in a moral sense; it is also an instrumental question of how best to solve a deep, inherent practical problem for human beings: we can only survive, and above all, thrive, if we cooperate with each other. Cooperation can be built on a foundation of pure self-interest, but such cooperation is more fragile and requires more sanctions and monitoring than cooperation that grows out of a sense of reciprocity, obligation, and solidarity. So, even if one does not especially value mutual caring and mutual concern as a moral ideal, one can still acknowledge that community is instrumentally valuable in lowering the costs of social cooperation.[38]

Capitalism, as a system of organizing economic activity, has an intensely contradictory relation to community as a way of organizing social cooperation. On the one hand, capitalism presupposes at least weak forms of community, since some degree of mutual

---

38 The claim that a sense of community lowers the cost of cooperation can be clarified through the familiar story of the "free-rider" problem in collective action. A free-rider problem occurs when it is possible to personally benefit from some collective action without incurring the costs that come from participating in the collective action. In a world in which people are exclusively motivated by self-interest it is usually fairly costly to block such free riding, since it requires a fair amount of coercion or special incentives. When people are motivated by a sense of community—shared obligations, reciprocity, mutual caring, etc.—then free riding becomes a less pressing issue.

obligation is essential for market exchanges and contracts to be possible. Emile Durkheim referred to this as the "noncontractual basis of contract."[39] Polanyi emphasizes the ways in which markets would destroy society if they were not constrained by effective communal institutions.[40] On the other hand, capitalism undermines community. Two considerations are especially important here: first, the ways in which markets foster motivations antithetical to community, and second, the way capitalism generates inequalities that undermine broad social solidarity.

The central motivations built into capitalist markets are deeply antagonistic to the principles of community. G. A. Cohen explains this antagonism brilliantly in his essay "Back to Socialist Basics":

> I mean here by 'community' the anti-market principle according to which I serve you not because of what I can get out of doing so but because you need my service. This is anti-market because the market motivates productive contribution not on the basis of commitment to one's fellow human beings and a desire to serve them while being served *by* them, but on the basis of impersonal cash reward. The immediate motive to productive activity in a market society is typically some mixture of greed and fear . . . In greed, other people are seen as possible sources of enrichment, and in fear they are seen as threats. These are horrible ways of seeing other people, however much we have become habituated and inured to them, as a result of centuries of capitalist development.[41]

The market cultivates dispositions in people that sharply contradict the kinds of motivations needed for strong community. This does not mean, of course, that community and market cannot coexist: there is no sociological law that states that societies cannot exist with deeply contradictory principles at work. But it does mean that in capitalism a large domain of important social interaction is dominated by motives antithetical to community and thus in order to strengthen community one has to struggle against the pervasive presence of markets and market thinking. The scope of community, therefore, tends to be narrowed to the level of personal relations and local settings rather than extended to broader circles of social interaction.

---

39   Emile Durkheim, *The Division of Labor* (New York: The Free Press, 1947).
40   Karl Polanyi, *The Great Transformation: The Political and Economic Origins of Our Time* (Boston: Beacon Press, 2001).
41   G. A. Cohen, "Back to Socialist Basics," *New Left Review* 207 (September–October 1994), p. 9.

Capitalism also undermines community through the ways in which it fosters economic inequality, particularly given the underlying mechanisms of exploitation within capitalist class relations. In an exploitative relation, the exploiting category has active interests in maintaining the vulnerability and deprivations of the exploited category. This generates antagonisms of interests that undermine the sense of shared fate and mutual generosity.

Marx thought that this fracturing of social solidarity within capitalist society would be counterbalanced by the deepening of solidarity within the exploited class. He believed that the dynamics of capitalism would generate increasing interdependency and homogeneity of conditions among the broad mass of workers, and that that interdependency and homogeneity would generate an increasing sense of solidarity. The community of workers, then, would be the basis for the eventual transformation of capitalism into a community of all people. Unfortunately, the dynamics of capitalism have not generated this radical homogeneity of class situation, but have instead produced ever more complex forms of economic inequality and intensified forms of labor market competition. Instead of a tendency towards ever wider solidarity among the mass of non-capitalists, capitalism has generated ever narrower circles of niche solidarity among people with unequal, segmented opportunities in the market. Community is thus narrowed and fractured both because of the inherent principles of greed and fear that drive competition, and because of the structure of inequality which results from that competition.

11. Capitalism limits democracy

Defenders of capitalism often argue that capitalism is an essential condition for democracy. The best-known statement of this thesis comes from Milton Friedman's capitalist manifesto, *Capitalism and Freedom*. The great virtue of capitalism, Friedman argues, is that it prevents a unitary concentration of power by institutionally separating economic power from state power. Capitalism thus underwrites a social order with competing elites, and this facilitates both individual freedom and democratic political competition. To be sure, capitalism does not guarantee democracy; there are many examples of authoritarian states in capitalist societies. Capitalism is thus a necessary, but not sufficient, condition for democracy. But it is a crucial necessary condition, Friedman argues, and when combined with economic development (which capitalism also generates), eventually makes democracy almost inevitable.

Even if one rejects the strong version of Friedman's argument—that without capitalism, democracy is impossible—there is no doubt that capitalism under conditions of high levels of economic development is strongly associated with democratic forms of the state. As Adam Przeworski has shown, in 100 percent of cases (so far), in no capitalist society in which the per capita income is above about $6,000 (in 1985 "purchasing power parity" dollars) has a democratic government ever turned into a dictatorship.[42] Nevertheless, if we take the idea of democracy as "rule by the people" seriously, there are three important ways in which capitalism limits democracy.

First, by definition, "private" ownership of means of production means that significant domains which have broad collective effects are simply removed from collective decision making. While the boundaries between the aspects of property rights that are considered private and the aspects that are subjected to public control are periodically contested, in capitalist society the presumption is that decisions over property are private matters and only in special circumstances can public bodies legitimately encroach on them.

If it were the case that the private decisions of owners of capitalist firms had no significant consequences for the well-being of people not party to the decisions, then this would not constitute an important limit on democracy. The idea of democracy is that people should collectively make decisions over those matters which affect their collective fate, not that all uses of resources in a society should be made through collective-democratic processes. The key issue, then, is that the private decisions made by the owners of capitalist firms often have massive collective consequences both for employees and for people not directly employed in the firm, and thus the exclusion of such decisions from public deliberation and control reduces democracy. A society in which there are meaningful forms of workers' democratic control within firms, as well as external democratic public controls, is a more democratic society than one which lacks these institutional arrangements. Of course, as defenders of capitalism argue, there may be reasons for the exclusion of non-owners from such decisions, either on the grounds of

---

42 Adam Przeworski, "Self-enforcing Democracy," in Donald Wittman and Barry Weingast (eds), *Oxford Handbook of Political Economy* (New York: Oxford University Press, 2006).

economic efficiency or on the grounds that people have the right to dispose of "their" property as they see fit, even if this has large consequences for others, but these considerations do not change the fact that capitalist property rights reduce democracy.[43]

Second, even apart from the direct effects of the exclusion of democratic bodies from control over the allocation of investments, the inability of democratic bodies to control the flows and movement of capital undermines the ability of democracy to set collective priorities even over those activities which capitalist firms themselves do not directly organize. The ability of communities to decide how best to provide public education or childcare or police and fire services, for example, is reduced by the fact that the local tax base depends upon private investment, and the amount of that investment is under private control. The democratic collectivity has very limited power to ask the question: how should we allocate *the aggregate social surplus* to different priorities—economic growth, individual consumption, public amenities, publicly supported care-giving, the arts, the police, etc. The issue here is not simply that many of these decisions are made outside of democratic deliberation, but that because investments are made privately, the threat of disinvestment heavily constrains all other allocative decisions within democratic bodies, even over those things in which capitalists do not make investments.[44]

---

43 A defender of capitalism who also believes in the value of democracy can defend capitalism against this critique in three ways: 1. Restricted democracy is the only stable form of democracy. While on paper it would be nice for people to have broad democratic control over the full range of things which affect their collective fate, this is just not possible. Any attempt at building such institutions will fail. 2. An expansive democracy is possible and it could be stable, but it would result in undesirable losses in efficiency. The optimal trade-off between these two values—efficiency and democracy—requires removing basic investment decisions from direct democratic control. 3. There are two values which clash here: the moral right people have to dispose of their property as they wish, and the right of people to collective control decisions that affect their collective fate. For a variety of reasons elaborated by libertarians, the first of these has lexical priority of the second (i.e. it must be fully met before the second value comes into play).

44 The threat of disinvestment has been identified by many writers as the pivotal form of structural power of capital within a capitalist democracy. This dependency of the state on private investment is identified by Göran Therborn as one of the key characteristics that renders it a "capitalist state." Charles Lindblom identifies it as the essential reason the state is forced to worry about creating a favorable "business climate." Joshua Cohen and Joel Rogers identify it as the core of the "demand constraint" on democratic politics: people can only effectively demand those things which are compatible with ongoing capitalist investment. In all of these analyses democracy is limited by the power of capital.

Third, the high concentrations of wealth and economic power generated by capitalist dynamics subvert principles of democratic political equality. Political equality means that there are no morally irrelevant attributes—such as race, gender, religious affiliation, wealth, income, and so on—generating inequalities in the opportunity of people to participate effectively in democratic politics and influence political decisions. This does not mean that every person in fact has an equal influence on political outcomes. Someone who is seen as trustworthy and honest and capable of expressing ideas clearly and persuasively may have factually more influence on a political process than someone who lacks these attributes. These, however, are attributes morally relevant to public deliberation over collective decisions. The key to political equality is that morally irrelevant attributes should not generate inequalities in political power. Capitalism violates this condition. While the violation of political equality may be more severe in the United States than in most other developed capitalist countries, the wealthy and those who occupy powerful positions in the economy invariably have a disproportionate influence on political outcomes in all capitalist societies. There are many mechanisms in play here. Wealthy people have a much greater ability to contribute to political campaigns. Powerful people in corporations are embedded in social networks which give them access to policy makers in government, and are in a position to fund lobbyists to influence both politicians and bureaucratic officials. They have greater influence on the media, especially the private capitalist media, and through this are able to influence public opinion. While one-person-one-vote in electoral competition is a critical form of political equality, its efficacy in insuring broad political equality in capitalist democracies is severely undermined by the deep interconnections between political and economic power within capitalism.

These eleven propositions define what is wrong with capitalism from a radical egalitarian, democratic, normative standpoint. If it could be shown that these propositions are false in the sense that capitalism, left to its own devices, would in time remedy all of these harms, then the impulse to articulate the parameters of

See Göran Therborn, *What Does the Ruling Class Do When it Rules?* (London: Verso, 1980); Charles E. Lindblom, *Politics and Markets: The World's Political Economic Systems* (New York: Basic Books, 1977); Joshua Cohen and Joel Rogers, *On Democracy* (New York: Penguin, 1982).

an emancipatory alternative to capitalism would be significantly undercut. But given our current state of knowledge about the inherent properties and dynamics of capitalism, this seems quite implausible. If this judgment is correct, then any serious effort to ameliorate these harms must ultimately confront capitalism itself.

This immediately poses two serious problems. First, what is the alternative to capitalism? Unless one believes that a viable alternative which would actually reduce these harms is possible, what would be the point in challenging capitalism itself? Second, how do we challenge the power relations and institutions of the existing society in order to create this alternative? How do we get from here to there? The rest of this book will explore a way of thinking about these questions.

II: ALTERNATIVES

4

THINKING ABOUT ALTERNATIVES TO CAPITALISM

In this chapter we will explore the logic of two broad strategies for constructing the foundations of a theory of emancipatory social alternatives. The first was initially elaborated by Karl Marx, in what is historically by far the most important approach to the problem. Even though Marxist perspectives on social change are now out of favor with critics of capitalism, the Marxist tradition still stands as the most ambitious attempt to construct a scientific theory of alternatives to capitalism, and it is important to understand the logic and the limitations of its approach. We will begin by briefly sketching its central elements, before turning to a discussion of certain ways in which Marx's strategy is unsatisfactory. The chapter concludes by explaining the central logic of an alternative, which will then be elaborated upon further in chapter 5.

MARX'S THEORY OF ALTERNATIVES TO CAPITALISM: THE THEORY OF HISTORICAL TRAJECTORY

Marx had an intellectually brilliant, if ultimately unsatisfactory, solution to the problem of specifying an alternative to capitalism in a credible way. Rather than develop a systematic theoretical model to demonstrate the possibility of a viable emancipatory alternative, he proposed a theory of the long-term *impossibility of capitalism*. His arguments are familiar: because of its inner dynamics and contradictions, capitalism has a tendency to destroy its own conditions of possibility. This is a deterministic theory: in the long run capitalism will become an impossible social order, so *some* alternative will of necessity have to occur. The trick is then to make a credible case that a democratic egalitarian organization of economy and society is a plausible form of such an alternative.

Here is where Marx's theory becomes especially elegant, for the contradictions which propel capitalism along its trajectory of self-erosion also create an historical agent—the working class—which has both an interest in creating a democratic egalitarian society and an increasing capacity to translate that interest into action. Given all of these elements, Marx's actual theory of socialism itself involves a kind of pragmatist faith in the principle "where there is a will there is a way," grounded in a spirit of experimental problem-solving by creative solidaristic workers.

Let us look at these arguments more closely. They can be distilled into five core theses.

Thesis 1. *The long-term non-sustainability of capitalism thesis*
In the long run capitalism is an unsustainable economic system. Its internal dynamics ("laws of motion") systematically undermine the conditions of its own reproducibility, thus making capitalism progressively more and more fragile and, eventually, unsustainable.

This is a proposition about the long-term trajectory of capitalist development. It is a prediction about the future, indeed a very strong prediction: the trajectory of capitalist development will culminate in the demise of capitalism itself. Capitalism is an historically specific form of economic organization that came into being as a result of the internal dynamics of the previous form of economy and that will eventually cease to exist. Capitalism is an integrated system, not just an assemblage of parts, and it thus contains coherent mechanisms for its own reproduction. But it is a specific kind of system—a system containing dynamic contradictions which, over time, undermine these mechanisms of reproduction, eventually making the system unsustainable. The claim here is not simply that capitalism, as a human construction, *can* be transformed into something else through deliberate human initiative. Rather, the claim is that capitalism *will* be transformed into something else because of its inherent contradictions. This proposition does not itself imply that capitalism will be replaced by something better from the point of view of human welfare, just that its self-destructive dynamics ensure that it will be a historically time-limited form of economy.

This prediction is based on four principal empirical trends Marx observed in the nineteenth century, combined with a theoretical argument about the underlying mechanisms which generate these trends. The empirical trends are these: First, in the course of capitalist development the level of productivity increases enormously, particularly due to gains from the increasing capital intensity of production. Second, capitalism expands relentlessly in a double sense: more and more domains of production are commodified and organized by capitalist firms, and capitalist markets extend to ever-wider reaches of the world. Capitalism thus develops both intensively and extensively, deepening its penetration of society and extending its reach geographically. Third, capitalist development tends to increase the concentration and centralization of capital: over time capitalist firms become larger and larger, and the percentage of production in the market controlled by those large firms steadily increases. This means that not only does the world become ever increasingly organized through capitalist markets, but these markets become ever increasingly dominated by giant firms. Fourth, the economic crises that periodically disrupt capitalist markets and production tend to become more serious and prolonged as capitalism develops. This final observation is linked to the first three: as a broad generalization, the more developed the forces of production are, the more comprehensive the market in a capitalist economy will be; and the more that market is dominated by giant corporations, the more severe its economic crises will be when they occur.

These are the general empirical observations Marx made in the third quarter of the nineteenth century. In order to make a scientific projection of these trends into the future it was necessary to identify the underlying causal processes which were generating them. It was by doing so that Marx was able to make his strong predictions about the history of capitalism's future.[1] Much of his great work, Capital, is devoted to elaborating these underlying causal processes, which collectively constitute the "laws of motion" of capitalism. The crucial component of this analysis for our purposes is what Marx called the "law of the falling tendency of the rate of profit." This is meant to designate a set of interconnected causal processes which generate a systematic tendency for the aggregate rate of profit in a capitalist economy to decline over time. It is this element in Marx's overall theory that most

---

1 This is basically the same logic used today in computer forecasting for things like global warming: You begin with a series of observable historical trends up to the present and then propose models of causal processes thought to generate these trends which effectively replicate the observed trajectory. This, along with assumptions about the behavior of various parameters, enables a range of predictions about the trajectory into the future using computer simulations.

directly bears on the question of the progressive intensification of crises in capitalism over time and thus on the long-term instability of the system.

The theoretical elaboration of this law is quite complex, involving technical details of the labor theory of value among other things.[2] I will not attempt to provide a systematic exposition of the theoretical foundations of Marx's analysis here, but the gist of the argument for the falling rate of profit is this: There are two different kinds of processes at work in generating economic crises in capitalism. First, there are periodic rises and falls in the rate of profit which generate what we now call business cycles. There are many factors that contribute to these, but mostly they can be subsumed under the heading "the anarchy of the market," including, for example, the tendency of capitalist firms to produce more than the market can absorb ("overproduction"), or the tendency of capitalists to push the wages of their workers down in order to reduce costs, thus depressing demand in the market ("under-consumption"). These are processes closely related to the economic crisis mechanisms later identified by Keynes in the twentieth century.

Second, Marx postulated a long-term causal process which gradually reduces the average rate of profit in a capitalist economy across business cycles. This long-term mechanism, Marx argued, is linked to the rising capital intensity of capitalist production. The key idea is that aggregate profits in capitalism depend upon the production of an economic *surplus*—that is, producing more than is required to simply reproduce the inputs used up in production, both the labor inputs and the non-labor inputs (raw materials, means of production, etc.). The monetary value of this surplus is what we call "profits." The rate of profit, then, is the ratio between the value of this surplus product and the value of all of the inputs used in production. Why should this ratio decline over time? Marx's answer relies on the technical details of the labor theory of value. Roughly the argument is that the value of all products is determined by the amount of labor time embodied in their production (thus the *labor* theory of value). Since, according to the labor theory of value, only labor creates value, the value of the surplus—called "surplus value"—thus depends upon how

---

2   There are many expositions of the law of the falling tendency of the rate of profit. For an explanation of the law that explicitly links this to an account of the long-term trajectory of capitalist crises, see Erik Olin Wright, *Class, Crisis and the State* (London: Verso, 1978), chapter 3.

much labor is performed in producing the surplus. As capital intensity increases, the amount of new labor used in production relative to the amount of means of production and raw materials declines. In a sense the surplus-value-generating-intensity of production declines even though overall productivity increases. Since with increasing capital intensity the ratio of surplus value to the value of all inputs will tend to decline, the monetary rate of profit—which is determined by this labor value ratio—will also decline. Because competition among firms forces each individual firm to innovate in the process of production, and since Marx believed these innovations would tend to raise the capital intensity of production over time, there is therefore a long-term tendency for the rate of profit to decline.[3]

This long-term decline in the aggregate rate of profit in a capitalist economy means that over time the episodic crises that occur from things like overproduction and under-consumption will become more and more serious; the troughs of depressions will be deeper, and the peaks of expansion lower. The declining long-term rate of profit, in effect, reduces the room for maneuver within the system: small cyclical declines will push more firms into bankruptcy and it will be harder to regenerate the conditions for profitable capital accumulation. At the limit, as the long-term rate of profit approaches zero, capitalism would become so unstable as to be unsustainable.

Thesis 2. *The intensification of anti-capitalist class struggle thesis*
The dynamics of capitalist development systematically tend (a) to increase the proportion of the population—the working class—whose interests are pervasively hurt by capitalism, and at the same time, (b) to increase the collective capacity of the working class to challenge capitalism. The result is an intensification of class struggle directed against capitalism.

Thesis 1 is a proposition about the structural tendencies of capitalist development. Thesis 2 is a proposition about agency. It postulates that capitalism produces a collective actor with both an

---

3 Marx and subsequent Marxist-inspired political economists also argue that there are various counter-tendencies to this process. Still, as indicated by the decision to call the falling rate of profit the "tendency" and these other things "counter-tendencies," Marx saw these countervailing factors as secondary and incapable, in the long term, of completely negating the principal tendency.

interest in challenging capitalism and the capacity to do so. To use a metaphor popular in the Marxist tradition, capitalism produces its own gravediggers.

The first part of this proposition concerns the creation of the working class, generally referred to as the process of *proletarianization*. Proletarianization involves two kinds of social change. First there is the process through which an increasing proportion of the population is brought into the capitalist employment relation and thus subjected to capitalist exploitation. This involves the large-scale destruction of various kinds of non-capitalist types of work, most notably, in Marx's time, small-holder self-employed agricultural workers and other kinds of "petty bourgeois" self-employed producers. More recently this aspect of proletarianization has centered on the entry of married women into the paid labor force. Second, there is the process through which the autonomy and skills of workers within capitalist employment are reduced through the process of work routinization and "deskilling." Taken together, these two processes of social change mean that over time the size of the working class increases as does the homogeneity of working conditions.

Proletarianization by itself, however, would not be enough to generate the intensification of anti-capitalist class struggle postulated in thesis 2, since the intensity of social conflict depends not only on the intensity of opposing interests but also, crucially, on the capacity of people to engage in collective actions in pursuit of those interests. Grievances are never sufficient to explain overt conflicts, since it is often the case that people lack the capacity to act on their grievances. The second part of thesis 2 suggests that the dynamics of capitalist development also tend to solve this problem. In particular, the growth of large work sites as a result of increasing capital intensity and the increasing scale of production means that the physical concentration of workers increases, which facilitates the communication and coordination needed for collective action. The increasing homogenization of working conditions also means that cleavages of interests based on skill differences among workers decline, and the destruction of the petty bourgeoisie and small firms means that the prospects for individual escape from the working class are reduced, thus increasing the sense of sharing a common fate. If these trends were to continue, the clarion call "workers of the world unite—you have nothing to lose but your chains and a world to win" would increasingly make sense to a growing number of people.

Thesis 3. *The revolutionary transformation thesis*
Since capitalism becomes increasingly precarious as an economic system (thesis 1), while the principal class arrayed against capitalism becomes increasingly large and capable of challenging it (thesis 2), eventually these oppositional social forces will become sufficiently strong, and capitalism itself sufficiently weak, that the institutions designed to protect capitalism will no longer be able to prevent it from being overthrown.

In Marxist theory, capitalist society is more than just a capitalist economy. It also contains an array of institutions which, among other things, function to protect capitalism from various kinds of threats. In the classical idiom of Marxism these institutions are referred to as the "superstructure." Of particular importance in this regard are the state—which helps to reproduce capitalism through a variety of mechanisms, particularly the use of force to protect property rights and repress organized challenges to capitalism—and ideological and cultural institutions, which help to reproduce capitalism by shaping ideas, values, and beliefs.

Now, it could be the case that these institutions are potentially so robust and powerful that they would reproduce capitalism even when it became completely stagnant and moribund. There are two principal reasons why Marxists have felt that this is an unlikely outcome. First, it takes resources to run the state and the machinery of ideology effectively, and those resources come out of the social surplus. If capitalism is in more or less continual and deepening economic crisis because of the collapse of the rate of profit, it will become increasingly difficult to fund these "social overhead" costs. The fiscal crisis of the state is one symptom of this. Second, if capitalism ceases to "deliver the goods" and becomes mired in endless crisis—which is what thesis 1 argues is its fate in the long run—then it would become increasingly difficult to maintain the solid allegiance of the rank-and-file personnel of the state. One aspect of the intensification of class struggle (thesis 2) is the emergence of an anti-capitalist political leadership offering a vision of an alternative to capitalism—socialism—which becomes increasingly attractive to many people not firmly in the working class, including much of the personnel of the state, once capitalism ceases to provide a credible vision for the future. Once the capitalist economic base can no longer adequately fund the state, and the personnel in the state no longer consistently defend it, a successful political assault on the state becomes possible.[4] And once this has occurred, then the rapid construction of a new economic structure becomes possible.

Marx was relatively vague about the actual process through which this destruction of the political superstructure of capitalism would occur. Typically Marxists have envisioned it as involving a violent revolution which "smashes" the capitalist state and forces a relatively abrupt rupture in the basic organizing principles of both the economy and the state. The assumption was that the resistance of the capitalist class to any fundamental transformation of capitalism would be sufficiently strong, and the cohesion of the capitalist state would remain sufficiently intact, that a peaceful, democratic transformation would simply not be possible. Any attempt along these lines would culminate in violent state repression—the capitalist class and the state would simply refuse to play by the rules—and thus in practice the only viable strategy for challenging the basic structure of capitalism would be a violent overthrow of the state. This, however, is not an essential part of the theory itself, but an historically contingent prediction. The fundamental argument is that once capitalism becomes a moribund economic system, the superstructural institutions of capitalism will no longer be able to effectively reproduce it in face of an intensified class struggle for its radical transformation.

One of the implications of thesis 3 is that the actual historical timing of the "end of capitalism" does not simply depend upon the laws of motion of capitalism which propel it towards self-destruction. It also depends upon the collective actions of class-based social forces, and the development of the collective power of these forces will be affected by a myriad of contingent historical factors. While the long-term stagnation and crisis of the capitalist economy creates the opportunity for its transformation, the transformation itself is still the result of collective struggles against capitalism and the state. In this sense the actual destiny of capitalism is not really "collapse" but "overthrow": within the logic of the theory, the revolutionary challengers to capitalism

---

4 In the absence of a theory of the long-run stagnation of capitalism there would be little reason to believe that the capacity of the state to reproduce capitalism would necessarily decline. The existence of periodic cyclical crises, unless they have a tendency to become more severe over time, would not be sufficient to weaken the superstructure in a decisive way. This is why the theory of the falling tendency of the rate of profit is so important to Marx's theory of the future of capitalism.

are likely to succeed well before capitalism reaches the point of complete economic disintegration.

There is much debate in the history of Marxism over the question of whether or not Marx believed the overthrow of capitalism was "inevitable". What he certainly believed was inevitable was, first, that capitalism would become a moribund, stagnant, crisis-ridden social order and that over time this would render it increasingly vulnerable to collective challenge, and second, that the potential for a collective agent to emerge that was capable of challenging capitalism would increase in the long run. This collective agent still needs a collective will and organization, and this requires leadership and revolutionary ideas. Still, Marx is saying something much stronger than simply that the demise of capitalism is a possibility sometime in the future; he predicts that eventually this will happen.

Thesis 4. *The transition to socialism thesis*
Given the ultimate non-sustainability of capitalism (thesis 1), and the interests and capacities of the social actors arrayed against capitalism (thesis 2), in the aftermath of the destruction of the capitalist state and capitalism through intensified class struggle (thesis 3), socialism, defined as a society in which the system of production is collectively owned and controlled through egalitarian democratic institutions, is capitalism's most likely successor since the collectively organized working class will be in the best position to ensure that its interests are embodied in the new post-capitalist institutions.

Strictly speaking, theses 1–3 merely provide a basis for the prediction that capitalism will eventually come to an end, but they do not provide systematic grounds for predicting the properties of the alternative that will replace it. Nevertheless, Marx, and subsequent thinkers within the Marxist tradition, had an optimistic view of the prospects for post-capitalist society being organized in line with radically egalitarian and democratic principles.

There were three main reasons for this optimism. First, capitalism raises the level of productivity enormously, which means that in a post-capitalist society scarcity in a broad sense will have been largely overcome. This makes a more egalitarian distribution easier to sustain, but also liberates enormous amounts of time for people to take on the collective responsibility of democratically running the economy. Second, capitalist development generates large mega-corporations which already constitute a kind of quasi-"social" property since they are actually run by representatives of the owners rather than the owners themselves. This makes the transition to a more fully democratic system of control easier than would have been the case in earlier forms of capitalism. Finally—and most crucially—in order to overthrow capitalism the working class has to become a coherent, powerful, and organized political force. This means that it is in the position to construct the kind of egalitarian and democratic institutions that best embody the interests of workers.

Of course, being in a politically powerful position and having an interest in the egalitarian and democratic organization of the economy does not prove that in practice it is actually possible to construct such institutions in a stable and sustainable way. Marx provided only the slightest of hints about what socialist institutions would look like: socialism would replace private ownership of the means of production by some collective form of owner-ship (although the precise meaning of this idea remained vague), and the market would be replaced by some form of comprehen-sive planning—although again almost nothing was said about the mechanics of such planning, how it would work, and why we should believe it was sustainable.[5] In a few places, most notably in his famous analysis of the Paris Commune, Marx provides empir-ical evidence that a vibrant form of democratic, egalitarian power has occurred for a limited time under special circumstances, but this hardly provides a strong case for the claim that such collective organization could sustainably build the institutions to organize a complex, modern economy in a democratic egalitarian manner. Basically, in the end, the theory relies on a combination of "where there is a will there is a way" and "necessity is the parent of invention": workers would be empowered through their collec-tive political organization, and the actual process of constructing these new institutions would proceed in a creative, trial-and-error, democratic experimentalist manner. In effect this means that Marx proposed a highly deterministic theory of the demise of capitalism and a relatively voluntaristic theory of the construction of its alternative.[6]

---

5   For a good discussion of the limited elements of Marx's vision of socialism, see Geoff Hodgson, *Economics and Utopia: Why the Learning Economy is Not the End of History* (London: Routledge: 1999), chapter 2.
6   Marx's determinism here does not imply a rejection of human agency.

Thesis 5. *The communism destination thesis*
The dynamics of socialist development gradually lead to a strengthening of community solidarity and a progressive erosion of material inequalities so that eventually classes and the state will "wither away," resulting in the emergence of a communist society organized around the distributional principle "to each according to need, from each according to ability."

This final thesis can be considered a utopian affirmation of the normative ideal of radical egalitarianism. While it is plausible that community solidarity would increase and material inequality decline in a socialist economy (defined in the general manner of thesis 4), there really is no sustained argument for why in such a society the state would wither away to the point where social order would be ensured entirely through voluntary cooperation and reciprocity, with no coercive authority and no binding rules. The sociological idea underlying such a claim must be (more or less) that only class inequality generates robust forms of conflict and anti-social self-interest, so that once class inequality disappears there would no longer be any need for coercion to play a role in social reproduction. This does not seem a plausible claim, and certainly Marx does not provide any systematic defense of it. As a result, it seems best to regard the communism destination thesis as a regulative ideal, as a moral vision to guide our actions rather than an actual claim about the future trajectory of social change.

Taken together, these five theses constitute a powerful and elegant argument for the viability of a radical egalitarian, democratic alternative to capitalism. If one can convincingly show that capitalism ultimately destroys itself and that therefore some alternative will have to occur, and furthermore that in conjunction with the demise of capitalism a powerful collective actor will emerge with an interest in constructing a democratic

---

The strong prediction Marx makes that capitalism destroys itself is possible precisely because human beings are conscious actors capable of rational and creative actions. The theory is deterministic because the consequences of these strategies and actions have a predictable cumulative effect on the sustainability of capitalism. For a discussion of this deep relationship between agency and determinism, see G. A. Cohen, "Historical Inevitability and Revolutionary Agency," chapter 4 in *History, Labour and Freedom: Themes From Marx* (Oxford, Clarendon Press: 1988).

egalitarian alternative, then it is not too much of a leap of faith to believe that such institutions could be created in a pragmatic manner.

INADEQUACIES IN MARX'S THEORY
OF CAPITALISM'S FUTURE

While there is much in the Marxist tradition of social theory that is of great value—particularly its critique of capitalism and the conceptual framework of its analysis of class—its theory of historical trajectory has a number of serious weaknesses.[7] Four problems undermine the adequacy of the traditional Marxist theory for building a theory of alternatives to capitalism: crisis tendencies within capitalism do not appear to have an inherent tendency to become ever more intense over time; class structures have become more complex over time, rather than simplified through a process of homogenizing proletarianization; the collective capacity of the working class to challenge structures of capitalist power seems to decline within mature capitalist societies; ruptural strategies of social transformation, even if they were capable of overthrowing the capitalist state, do not seem to provide a sociopolitical setting for sustained democratic experimentalism. Since each of these themes has been extensively treated in contemporary discussions of Marxism and social change, I will only briefly review the core arguments here.

The theory of crisis intensification

The thesis that the crisis tendencies of capitalism will have a systematic tendency to intensify over time is critical to the whole argument, for this is the basis for the idea that the contradictions of capitalism ultimately destroy its own conditions of existence. If the most we can say is that capitalism will have a tendency to periodic economic

---

7 It is useful to distinguish between what might be called "sociological Marxism," anchored in the Marxist analysis of class and the critique of capitalism, and the Marxist theory of history (sometimes also called "historical materialism"), anchored in the theory of capitalist dynamics and historical trajectory. While the latter, I believe, is no longer defensible as it stands, the former remains a highly productive framework for critical theory and research and an essential component of emancipatory social science. For a discussion of sociological Marxism, see Michael Burawoy and Erik Olin Wright, "Sociological Marxism," in Jonathan

crises of greater or lesser severity, but there is no overall tendency of intensification of disruptions to capital accumulation, then we no longer have grounds for the idea that capitalism becomes progressively more fragile over time. And without this trajectory towards a self-destructive future, capitalism would not have the property of becoming more vulnerable to collective challenge from anticapitalist social forces. One can still hold the view that a severe and prolonged capitalist crisis, *if* it were to occur, might provide an historical "window of opportunity" for radical social transformation, but this is much weaker than a prediction about the increasing likelihood of such crises over time.

There are a number of reasons to be skeptical of the self-destruction thesis. First, while capitalism certainly contains a variety of processes which tend to produce periodic economic disruptions, Marx, and many subsequent Marxists, underestimated the extent to which state interventions can significantly moderate these tendencies. The result is that there does not appear to be any consistent tendency for economic disruptions to get worse over time. Second, while the rate of profit may be lower in the later stages of capitalist development than in earlier ones, there does not appear to be any long-term tendency for it to continue to decline within mature capitalist economies. Third, on more theoretical grounds, the conceptual foundations of the "law of the falling tendency of the rate of profit" are quite problematic. Most fundamentally, the labor theory of value on which this law is based has been criticized even by economists broadly sympathetic to the normative and explanatory goals of Marxism. While the idea of labor as the source of value may be a useful device for illustrating the idea of the exploitation of labor, there is no persuasive reason for believing that labor and labor alone causally generates value. Marx certainly provided no sustained defense of this assumption, and neither have contemporary discussions resulted in a convincing case.[8] If the labor theory of

---

Turner (ed.), *Handbook of Sociological Theory* (New York: Kluwer Academic/ Plenum Publishers, 2001). For a discussion of the Marxist tradition as revolving around three clusters of problems—class analysis and the critique of capitalism, a normative vision of socialism, and the theory of history—see Erik Olin Wright, *Interrogating Inequality* (London: Verso, 1994), chapter 11.

8 The labor theory of value was a broadly accepted tool of economic analysis in Marx's time and thus he perhaps did not feel the need for a sustained defense. When Marx does comment on the grounds for the belief that labor is the basis of value his argument is quite simple: we observe qualitatively different things

value is rejected, then the argument that increasing capital intensity reduces the rate of profit no longer holds.[9]

Now, in light of these considerations it might be possible to
construct some new theory of the self-destructive trajectory of
capitalism. One idea in present discussions is that the heightened
globalization of capitalism at the beginning of the twenty-first
century severely undermines the capacity of the state to moderate
crisis tendencies, since the geographical scope of market processes
is no longer under the regulatory reach of state intervention. This
could, conceivably, mean that economic crises in the future will
be significantly more intense than in the late twentieth century
since no effective global crisis-management institutions are likely
to develop. The financial crisis that began in 2008 may signal this
new process of intensification.

A second idea is that the environmental destruction generated by capitalist growth will ultimately destroy the ecological
conditions of existence of capitalism. A third suggestion is that
the shift from an industrial economy to a service economy, and,
perhaps, to a "knowledge economy," means that in the future it
will be more and more difficult for owners of capital to dominate
economic activity. Intellectual property is inherently more difficult

---

exchanging in fixed ratios in the market—X pounds of steel are the same as Y
tubes of toothpaste. How can such qualitatively different things be reduced to
relative quantities? They must, Marx reasoned, have some quantitative substance
in common. Labor time expended in their production, he then argued, is the
only common quantitative substance. But this claim is simply wrong. Steel and
toothpaste also share the property that they are produced with a certain number
of calories of energy, for example. One could on this basis construct an energy
theory of value, along with an account of the relationship between profits and
surplus energy value. More generally, the value of commodities should be thought
of as determined by the amount of scarce resources of all sorts that are embodied
in their production, not just labor. For a discussion of the labor theory of value
relevant to these issues, see Ian Steedman, *Marx after Sraffa* (London: New Left
Books, 1977).

9 Furthermore, even if one accepts the central intuitions of the labor theory
of value, the specific argument postulated by Marx for the tendency for the
falling rate of profit is not persuasive. The pivotal idea in the theory is that rising
capital intensity (referred to in this context as the "rising organic composition
of capital") will have the unintended effect in the aggregate of lowering the rate
of profit. But once capitalist production is already highly mechanized there is
no longer any reason to believe that capital intensity will continue to rise with
subsequent innovation. A good example is the replacement of mechanical adding
machines with hand calculators. This is not simply a "counter-tendency": there
is no inherent directionality to the capital intensity of technical change in the
process of production once capital intensity has reached a certain point.

to monopolize than physical capital. Particularly with the advent of new information technologies it is simply too easy for people to subvert private property rights in information and knowledge. Furthermore, the production of knowledge and information is most efficiently done as a collaborative, cooperative social activity, and thus the imposition of capitalist property rights on this process increasingly acts as a "fetter" on the further development of these forces of production. As a result, in the long run, capitalism will become more and more vulnerable to the challenge of non-capitalist ways of organizing the production and distribution of information and knowledge.

Any or all of these factors could mean that the long-term trajectory of capitalism will culminate in its self-destruction. The arguments, however, remain speculative and underdeveloped, and for the moment it does not appear that there is good reason to believe that the internal contradictions of capitalism render it, in the long run, an unsustainable economic structure. Capitalism may be *undesirable* for all the reasons outlined in chapter 3, while still being *reproducible*. This does not imply, it must be stressed, that capitalism is untransformable: even if its internal dynamics do not generate a trajectory towards self-destruction it could still be transformed through collective action. But such collective action will not necessarily be abetted by the increasing fragility of capitalism.

The theory of proletarianization

The second major problem with the classical Marxist theory of the destiny of capitalism centers on the theory of proletarianization. While it is certainly true that the course of capitalist development has incorporated an increasing proportion of the labor force into capitalist employment relations, in the developed capitalist world this has not resulted in a process of intensified proletarianization and class homogenization but rather in a trajectory of increasing complexity of class structures. A number of broad trends are worth noting.

First, there is the development and expansion of what I have called "contradictory locations within class relations."[10] Class

---

10 For extended discussions of the problem of complexity of locations within class structures, see Erik Olin Wright, *Classes* (London: Verso, 1985), *The Debate on Classes*, (London: Verso, 1989), and *Class Counts* (Cambridge: Cambridge

locations are the specific places occupied by individuals within a class structure. Working-class locations and capitalist-class locations are the two fundamental positions determined by the class relations of capitalism. But many locations in the class structure do not fall neatly into these two basic positions. In particular, class locations like those of managers and supervisors have the relational properties of both capitalists and workers and thus occupy "contradictory locations." Professionals and highly skilled technical workers also occupy contradictory locations through their control over credentials. Somewhat less than half of the labor force in most developed capitalist countries occupies such contradictory locations.[11]

Second, after a very long period of decline, in many capitalist countries there has been a marked growth of self-employment and small employers. To be sure, many of these small firms and independent self-employed persons are subordinated in various ways to large corporations, but nevertheless they are quite distinct from the working class.

Third, while wealth has in recent years become more concentrated within at least some capitalist countries (most notably the United States), it is also the case that there has been a wider diffusion of stock ownership—an increasing proportion of the population have some corporate investments, either in the form of direct investments in stocks or in contributory pension funds. While this is far from creating anything like "the ownership society" or a "people's capitalism," it nevertheless adds complexity to the class structure of capitalism.

Fourth, with the large-scale entry of women into the labor force the ways in which many individuals are linked to class structures have become more complex than in the past, since in two-earner households family members are linked to the class structure through two jobs, not just one. The result is that significant numbers of people live in what can be termed "cross-class households," households in which the paid employment of husbands and wives are in different class locations.[12]

Finally, there is increasing stratification within the working

---

University Press, 1997).

11 See Wright, *Class Counts*, chapters 2 and 3.

12 In the 1980s—the period for which I have solid data on this question—approximately 15% of the adult population lived in cross-class households in the United States.

class in many developed capitalist countries. After a long period in which inequality in earnings among wage earners declined, such inequality sharply increased in the last quarter of the twentieth century. Added to this, in some countries—most notably in the US—there has been a fairly sharp polarization in the patterns of job growth since the early 1990s: jobs have expanded very rapidly at the top and bottom of the wage structure, but not in the middle.[13] The working class, however it is defined, has become more internally differentiated rather than more homogeneous.

None of these forms of complexity in class relations mean that class is of declining importance in people's lives, or that class structures are becoming less capitalist in any fundamental way. They simply mean that the structural transformations predicted by the intensification of class struggle thesis have not occurred.

The theory of class capacity

The second component of the intensification of anti-capitalist class struggle thesis in classical Marxist theory concerns the increasing capacity of the working class to challenge capitalism. This capacity has had, if anything, a tendency to decline within developed capitalist societies. Partially this is the result of the increasing heterogeneity of interests among employees, both because of complexity of the class structure and stratification within the working class itself. Such heterogeneity makes the task of building solidarity and forming stable political coalitions more difficult. But the weakness of system-challenging class capacity also reflects ways in which capitalist democracies have offered people real opportunities to organize for significant improvement in their conditions of life *within* the constraints of capitalism. In taking advantage of these opportunities, one of the central constraints imposed by the state has been abandoning any attempt at revolutionary organization and mobilization. The resulting "class compromises"—in the form of the labor movement and the welfare state—have enabled workers to make real gains. While these gains have certainly been somewhat eroded in the last decades of the twentieth century, nevertheless they remain sufficiently strong to obstruct anti-system solidarities. Given the

---

13   For a detailed examination of these trends in job growth, see Erik Olin Wright and Rachel Dwyer, "Patterns of Job Expansion and Contraction in the United States, 1960s–1990s," *Socioeconomic Review* 1 (2003), pp. 289–325.

robustness of capitalism and the strength of the institutions that reproduce it, at least in mature capitalist democracies, such class compromises are probably still a credible course of action for working-class organizations. In any case, in no developed capitalist society has the working class developed a collective capacity to challenge the foundations of capitalist power.

The theory of ruptural transformation

While there are no examples of successful revolutionary challenges to capitalism in developed capitalist countries (and virtually no examples even of significant but unsuccessful challenges), revolutionary challenges to capitalism have occurred in less developed capitalist societies, and in a few cases socialist revolutionaries have succeeded in gaining power. States have been overthrown and revolutionary regimes at least symbolically committed to socialism installed. These attempts at ruptural transformation, however, have never been able to sustain an extended process of democratic experimentalist institution-building. The "where there is a will there is a way" theory of constructing alternative, emancipatory institutions depends upon the active, creative empowered participation of ordinary people in a process of democratic deliberation and institution-building. While there have been brief episodes of such egalitarian democratic participation within attempts at the revolutionary transformations of capitalism, such episodes have always been short-lived and relatively isolated.

Perhaps the failure of sustained democratic experimentalism in the aftermath of revolutions was because revolutionary regimes always faced extreme pressure, both economic and military, from powerful capitalist countries, and felt a great urgency to consolidate power and build institutions of sufficient strength to withstand that pressure. Since democratic experimentalism is inevitably a messy process which depends heavily on an ability to learn from one's mistakes over time, it is understandable that revolutionary regimes might have felt they could not wait for this to work. Or perhaps the problem was mainly the low level of economic development of the economies within which revolutionary movements succeeded in seizing political power. Classical Marxism certainly never imagined that a transformation of capitalism into a democratic egalitarian alternative would be possible unless capitalism had already generated very high levels of productivity. But it may also be that the concentrated forms of political power, organization, and violence needed to successfully produce a revolutionary rupture in existing institutions are themselves incompatible with those forms of participatory practice needed for meaningful democratic experimentalism in the construction of new emancipatory institutions. Revolutionary parties may in certain circumstances be effective "organizational weapons" for toppling capitalist states, but they appear to be extremely ineffective means for constructing a democratic egalitarian alternative. As a result, the empirical cases we have of ruptures with capitalism have resulted in authoritarian state-bureaucratic forms of economic organization rather than anything approaching a democratic-egalitarian alternative to capitalism.

TOWARDS AN ALTERNATIVE FORMULATION OF THE PROBLEM

The classical Marxist theory of alternatives to capitalism is deeply anchored in a deterministic theory concerning key properties of the trajectory of capitalism: by predicting the basic contours of the future of capitalism Marx hoped to contribute to the realization of an emancipatory alternative beyond capitalism. In the absence of a compelling dynamic theory of the destiny of capitalism, an alternative strategy is to shift our efforts from building a theory of dynamic *trajectory* to building a theory of structural *possibility*. Let me explain this contrast. A theory of dynamic trajectory attempts to predict certain features of the future course of social change on the basis of an understanding of causal mechanisms that push society in a particular direction. By charting certain developments which we know *will* happen (assuming the theory is accurate), such a theory helps define the conditions for exploring things which *can* happen. Capitalism will (eventually) destroy itself, so socialism could be the alternative. A theory of structural possibility, in contrast, attempts not to predict the course of development over time, but simply to chart the range of possibilities for institutional changes under different social conditions.

The strongest version of a theory of structural possibility would be like having a comprehensive road map before embarking on a journey. The road map would show you all the possible destinations from your current location, and all the alternative routes that will take you to each. A really good map would inform you about the road conditions on the different routes, indicating which require all-terrain vehicles and which might be either temporarily or permanently impassable (at least until some better mode of transportation is invented). With such a map the only question you face in actually making a trip to a particular destination is whether or not you have the proper vehicle for the journey. It may turn out, of course, that you are unable to divert sufficient resources to the purchase of the required vehicle to get to the most desirable destination, but at least you would have a realistic understanding of this constraint before leaving for the trip and could therefore change your plans.

Alas, there is no map, and no existing social theory is sufficiently powerful to even begin to construct such a comprehensive representation of possible social destinations, possible futures. It may well be that such a theory is impossible in principle—the process of social change is too complex and too deeply affected by contingent concatenations of causal processes to be represented in the form of detailed maps of possible futures. In any case, we don't have any such map available. And yet we want to leave the place where we are because of its harms and injustices. What is to be done?

Instead of the metaphor of a road map guiding us to a known destination, perhaps the best we can do is to think of the project of emancipatory social change as a voyage of exploration. We leave the well-known world with a compass that shows us the direction we want to go, and an odometer which tells us how far from our point of departure we have traveled, but without a map which lays out the entire route from the point of departure to the final destination. This has perils, of course: we may encounter chasms we cannot cross, unforeseen obstacles which force us to move in a direction we had not planned. We may have to backtrack and try a new route. There will be moments when we reach high ground, with clear views towards the horizon, and this will greatly facilitate our navigation for a while. But at other times we must pick our way through confusing terrain and dense forests with little ability to see where we are going. Perhaps with technologies we invent along the way we can create some artificial high ground and see somewhat into the distance. And, in the end, we may discover that there are absolute limits to how far we can move in the hoped-for direction. While we cannot know in advance how far we can go, we can know if we are moving in the right direction.

This approach to thinking about emancipatory alternatives retains a strong normative vision of life beyond capitalism, but acknowledges the limitations of our scientific knowledge of the real possibilities of transcending capitalism. But note that this is not the same as embracing the false certainty that there exist untransgressable limits for constructing a radical democratic egalitarian alternative. The absence of solid scientific knowledge concerning the limits of possibility applies both to the prospects for radical alternatives and to the sustainability of capitalism.

The key to embarking on a journey of exploration and discovery is the usefulness of our navigational device. We need to construct what might be called a *socialist compass*: the principles which tell us if we are moving in the right direction. This will be the task of the next chapter.

THE SOCIALIST COMPASS

In the absence of a comprehensive institutional design for a radical democratic egalitarian alternative to capitalism what we need to work out are principles of institutional innovation and change which will tell us whether we are at least moving in the right direction. In this chapter we will explore one way of doing this. I will begin by interrogating the meaning of the word "social" in socialism. This will enable us to define an abstract ideal-type contrast between three ways of organizing power over the economy: capitalism, statism, and socialism. On the basis of this contrast I will then specify the navigational principles of the socialist compass.

what's this

TAKING THE "SOCIAL" IN SOCIALISM SERIOUSLY

Both social democracy and socialism contain the word "social." Generally, the notion of the social is invoked in a loose and ill-defined way, often used to suggest a political program committed to the broad welfare of society rather than the narrow interests of particular elites. Sometimes, especially in more radical versions of socialist discourse, "social ownership" is invoked as a contrast to "private ownership," but in practice this has generally been collapsed into state ownership, so that the term "social" itself ends up doing relatively little analytical work in the elaboration of the political program.

In this chapter I will argue that the idea of the "social" in socialism can be usefully employed to identify a cluster of principles and visions of change that help differentiate socialism more precisely both from capitalism and what could be called a purely statist response to capitalism. This, in turn, will suggest a way of thinking about principles of transformation that may be used to guide challenges to capitalism.

Most discussions of socialism develop the concept in terms

- public ownership

of a binary contrast with capitalism. The standard strategy is to begin with a discussion of different ways of organizing production and from this to define capitalism as a distinctive type of "mode of production" or "economic structure"—an economic structure within which the means of production are privately owned, workers must thus sell their labor power in order to obtain their livelihoods, and production is oriented towards profit-maximization through exchange on the market. Socialism is then defined in terms of the negation of one or more of these conditions. Since the pivot of the concept of capitalism is the *private* ownership of the means of production, this has generally meant that socialism is understood as requiring *public* ownership of one form or another, most typically through the institutional device of state ownership.

precise def of capitalism

Here I will elaborate an alternative approach to specifying the concept of socialism in which it is contrasted with two alternative forms of economic structure: *capitalism* and *statism*. Capitalism, statism, and socialism can be thought of as alternative ways of organizing the power relations through which economic resources are allocated, controlled, and used. To explain what this means I will first need to clarify a number of key concepts: 1) power; 2) ownership; and 3) the state, the economy, and civil society understood as three broad domains of social interaction and power. Second, I will develop a conceptual typology of capitalism, statism, and socialism as types of economic structures based on different configurations of ownership and power linked to these three domains. Third, I will explain how this typology of economic structures helps us draw a conceptual map of the empirical variability of the macro-structures of economic systems. This will provide us with the conceptual vocabulary required to elaborate our socialist compass of pathways to social empowerment.

CLARIFICATIONS OF A CONCEPTUAL VOCABULARY

Power

Power is one of the most perpetually contested concepts in social theory. Here I want to stress the simple idea of power as the *capacity* of actors to accomplish things in the world. The expression "accomplish things in the world" is a very general, all-encompassing idea. It is meant to capture the idea of producing effects in the world without specifying in advance any particular kind of effects: to be powerful is to be able to produce significant effects with respect to some kind of goal or purpose. This formulation is broader, for example, than saying that power is the capacity to realize one's interests. This definition has both an *instrumental* and a *structural* dimension: it is instrumental in that it focuses on the capacities people use to accomplish things in the world; it is structural in that the effectiveness of these capacities depends upon the social structural conditions under which people act.[1] The power of capitalists, for example, depends both upon their wealth and upon a social structure within which this wealth can be deployed in particular ways. Owning a factory is a source of power only if there also exists a labor force separated from the means of subsistence which must rely on a labor market in order to earn a living, and a set of state institutions that enforce contracts and protect property rights. The simple ownership of this economic resource only becomes a source of real power under appropriate social conditions.

Understood in this way, power need not be a zero-sum phenomenon: increasing the capacity of one person or group to accomplish things need not necessarily imply reducing the capacity of others. Nor does this concept of power inherently imply "domination" in the sense of one actor being able to control the actions of other actors even over their objections: a group of people effectively cooperating to accomplish some task can be said to be exercising power with respect to this task even if no coercion is involved in forging the cooperation. A well-organized smoothly cooperating group is more powerful than a fractious, disorganized group: it has greater capacity to accomplish things. Still, given the character of social relations and conflicting interests, effective

---

1   Sometimes in social theory a sharp contrast is drawn between *instrumental* and *structural* notions of power. For example, Steven Lukes, in his justly celebrated book *Power: A Radical View* (Basingstoke: Palgrave Macmillan, 2005) defines three faces of power, the third of which is the power to have one's interests secured by the social organization of society without one's conscious action. This suggests a meaning of power that generates effects independently of the agency of people. Nicos Poulantzas, following Louis Althusser, goes further in rejecting entirely the instrumental notion of power, arguing that it is just an effect of structural conditions. Here I am adopting a use of the distinction between structural and instrumental power that emphasizes their interaction. This is similar to the treatment of power by Alex Callinicos, in his *Making History* (Leiden: Brill, 2004), in which he argues that structures are a dimension of power insofar as they enable actors to wield power resources in various ways.

power in many social contexts does involve domination. Power *to* often depends upon power *over*.

With this definition of power, one of the ways in which its forms can be differentiated is in terms of the underlying social basis for the capacity to generate effects in the world. In the present context we will distinguish three important forms of power: *economic power*, based on the control over economic resources; *state power*, based on control over rule making and rule enforcing capacity over territory; and what I will call *social power*, based on the capacity to mobilize people for voluntary collective actions of various sorts. Using slogans, we can say that there are three ways of getting people to do things: you can *bribe* them; you can *force* them; you can *convince* them. These correspond to the exercise of economic power, state power, and social power.[2] And as we shall see, these are closely linked to the distinctions between capitalism, statism, and socialism.

Ownership

*who own
what is owned
what can be done to the owned thing*

"Ownership" is a multidimensional idea involving a bundle of different kinds of enforceable rights (i.e. effective powers) over things. Ownership varies along three dimensions:

1. The *agents* of ownership: who is the holder of the ownership rights. There are many possible kinds of social agents that can be owners—individuals, families, organizations, states, and perhaps some more abstract entity such as "society" or even "humanity."

2. The *objects* of ownership: what sorts of things can be owned and what sorts cannot be owned. There was a time in the United States, for example, when people could be owned by other people in the form of slaves. This is no longer the case. Some kinds of things may be owned by certain kinds of agents but not others. For example, in some economies land is owned in common by all people, whereas in others it can be owned by individuals. In the United States today certain kinds of weapons can be owned by the state but not by individuals or other organizations.

3. The *rights* of ownership: what sorts of rights are entailed by ownership. Ownership rights include things like the right to use something in different sorts of ways, the right to destroy it, the

---

2 Because social power is rooted in voluntary association, and voluntary association is intimately connected to persuasion and communication, social power is also closely linked to what might be termed ideological or cultural power.

right to sell it or give it away, the right to let other people use it, and the right to the income generated by its use.

The problem of ownership is especially complex since different kinds of ownership rights may be distributed across different kinds of agents in different ways for different objects of ownership. Consider, for example, the common notion that in capitalism the means of production are *privately* owned. The means of production are a particular object of ownership. To say that they are privately owned means that individuals and organizations outside of the state (such as corporations and nonprofit organizations) have the right to make various kinds of decisions about the means of production without interference by the state and other non-owners. In practice, however, the actual ownership relations over the means of production in all capitalist economies are more complex than this since the effective power over many aspects of the use of machines, buildings, land, raw materials, and so forth have been removed from the private owners and are held by the state. Owners of firms, for example, are restricted in how they can use their means of production because of health and safety requirements. They cannot freely contract with a worker to ignore these requirements, and thus in this specific respect they are not full owners of the machine; some of the rights of ownership have been taken over by the state. Capitalists do not even have full property rights in the flow of net income (profits) generated by the use of their means of production since the state imposes various forms of taxation on that income. In effect, the profits that are generated by the use of means of production are divided between a public entity—the state—and the private owners.[3]

Because of this complexity of the allocation of specific property rights within the bundle we call "ownership," it is not always a simple task to identify who "owns" the means of production— different rights are assigned to different actors. The issue is further complicated by the well-known distinction between "ownership" and "control" in many economic contexts. Large capitalist corporations are owned by shareowners, but the actual control over the operation of the firms is in the hands of managers and executives. Formally the top executives are hired by the owners, typically through the intermediary of a board of directors, and

3   This, of course, is why libertarians say "taxation is theft": in their view, since private ownership should entail full property rights, the state's appropriation of part of the profits is simply a form of stealing.

thus executives and the managers below them whom they hire are officially simply the agents of the "real" owners. In practice it may be quite difficult for the owners to effectively monitor and control the actions of these managerial agents. This poses potentially serious problems for owners since the business strategies which may be optimal for the managers may not always be the same as for the owners (thus the famous "principal/agent problem" of economic theory). To overcome this problem a range of institutional mechanisms have been devised in an attempt to align more tightly the interests of managers and shareowners: career ladders are a way of potentially increasing the loyalty of managers to the firm, and stock options for executives are often seen as a way of increasing the coordination of interests of top managers and owners. In any case, it cannot be taken for granted that the formal owners of the means of production have effective power over production itself.

In the present context we are concerned with the problem of ownership primarily because of the ways in which it bears on understanding how different kinds of economic systems work. For this purpose, of particular importance are ownership rights to *transfer property rights* (which in the case of private ownership means the right to sell or give away what one owns and buy what other people own) and rights to *control the use and allocation of the surplus* (i.e. the net income generated by the use of the means of production). Even in highly regulated capitalist economies in which many of the powers of private ownership have been taken away from individuals and firms, private owners retain the right to buy and sell property for which they have rights to the net income generated by use of the property. This is a crucial dimension of ownership because it determines the allocation of the social surplus to alternative forms of investment, and thus the directions of economic change over time.

Throughout this book I will use the term "ownership" mainly in this narrower sense of the right to transfer property and the rights over the surplus, and use the terms "power" and "control" to describe the effective capacity to direct the use of the means of production. In these terms we will distinguish capitalism, statism, and socialism both in terms of the kind of power that is deployed over economic activities (economic power, state power, and social power) and in terms of the nature of ownership of the means of production (private ownership, state ownership, and social ownership).

The ideas of *private ownership* and *state ownership* of the means of production are familiar: private ownership means that individuals and groups of individuals have legally enforceable rights to buy and sell income-generating property; state ownership means that the state directly retains rights over the disposition of means of production and the net income which it generates. But what does "social ownership" mean? This is both less familiar and less clear. Social ownership of the means of production means that income-generating property is owned in common by everyone in a "society," and thus everyone has the collective right to the net income generated by the use of those means of production and the collective right to dispose of the property which generates this income. This need not imply that the net income is simply divided up equally among everyone, although that could be one expression of the principle of common ownership. Common ownership means that people collectively have the right to decide on the purposes to which the means of production are put and on the allocation of the social surplus—the net income generated by the use of means of production—and this is consistent with a wide range of actual allocations.

The term "society" in this definition does not mean a nation state or country. Rather, it refers to any social unit within which people engage in interdependent economic activity which uses means of production and generates some kind of product. In Israel the traditional kibbutzim would constitute an example of social ownership: all of the means of production in the kibbutz were owned in common by all members of the community who collectively controlled the use of the surplus generated by the use of those means of production. Worker cooperatives also can constitute an example of social ownership, depending upon the specific ways in which the property rights of the cooperative are organized. It is thus possible for an economic structure to consist of units characterized by social ownership as well as private ownership and state ownership.

This way of thinking about social ownership means that we can talk about the *depth*, *breadth*, and *inclusiveness* of social ownership. The *depth* of social ownership refers to the extent to which particular means of production are effectively under social control rather than private or state control. Just as private ownership varies in the array of rights linked to particular means of production that are exercised privately, so too social ownership can vary in the range of rights under effective social control.

The *breadth* of social ownership refers to the range of economic activities that are characterized by social ownership. At one extreme is the kibbutz in the period in which it was organized most profoundly along egalitarian, communal lines, in which there was virtually no private property. *Inclusiveness* refers to the range of people included under the idea of "people engaged in interdependent economic activities." This can be understood quite restrictively as those persons directly using particular means of production, or much more broadly as all people whose lives are affected by the use of those means of production, or what are sometimes called the "stakeholders" in the means of production.[4]

The lines of demarcation among these three forms of ownership are not always clear. If the state is controlled in a deeply democratic manner, then state ownership may become very much like a specific form of social ownership. In a democratic society does the state own the national parks or do "the people" own the parks? If individual members of a producer co-op are assigned individual shares in the cooperative—which they can sell and which give them individually differentiated claims on the net income of the economic activity—then the social ownership of the cooperative may begin to look much more like a form of private ownership. If in an otherwise capitalist economy the state imposes restrictions on the transfer of property rights (for example, export controls over flows of capital) and regulates the allocations surplus for different kinds of investments, then private ownership can begin to look more like state ownership.

---

4 The term "stakeholders" is used in contrast with the term "shareowners." Shareowners are the set of people with private property rights in the means of production. Stakeholders are all those with a "stake" in the means of production because their lives are affected by how those means of production are used. The idea that social ownership of specific means of production should extend to all stakeholders is the principle most consistent with the normative ideals of radical democratic egalitarianism discussed in chapter 1. Recall that the democratic egalitarian principle of political justice is that all people should have equal access to the means necessary to participate in decisions which affect their lives as individuals and as members as communities. This corresponds to the expansive notion of social ownership in which all "stakeholders" have ownership rights. This leaves open the question of how those rights should be allocated across different categories of stakeholders (since different people have different stakes) and how the principle of stakeholder rights should be balanced with pragmatic questions concerning the effective exercise of those rights.

Three domains of power and interaction: the state, the economy, and civil society

Efforts at formulating rigorous, foundational definitions of the economy, the state, and civil society as domains of social interaction and power quickly run into all sorts of conceptual difficulties.[5] Should the "economy," for example, include all activities in which goods and services are produced, or only those that are mediated by the market? Should preparing a meal in the home be considered part of the "economy"? Should taking care of one's own children be viewed as part of the economy, or only childcare services produced outside the home? Should the economy be defined by the *functions* it fulfills within a "social system" (e.g., the function of "adaptation," as in Talcott Parson's schema), by the *motives* of actors engaged in various activities (e.g., utility maximization under conditions of scarcity, as in neoclassical economics), by the *means* that actors use to pursue their goals (e.g., the use of money and other resources to satisfy interests), or by some other factor? Perhaps we should distinguish "economic *activity*" from "*the* economy"—the former can take place within any domain of social life, while the latter refers to a more specialized arena of activity within which economic activities are dominant. But then, what does "dominant" really mean?

To nail down these kinds of issues is an arduous matter and would, I believe, deflect us from our main task here. So, for present purposes I will define these three domains of social interaction in relatively conventional ways, bracketing these deeper problems of conceptualization:

The state is the cluster of institutions, more or less coherently organized, which imposes binding rules and regulations over a

---

5   Most attempts at formulating broad frameworks for building macro-sociological theory invoke elusive categories like "domains" or "spheres" or "arenas" or "levels" or "subsystems" of social interaction. None of these terms is entirely satisfactory. They mostly evoke spatial metaphors that are misleading. In talking about the economy and civil society as spheres of social interaction I do not mean to suggest that civil society stops at the workplace and the economy begins once you enter. Civil society is made up of voluntary associations (including loose associations like social networks) and these occur within the organizations of the economy as well as those of "society." All such terms are based on the loose idea that societies can, in some sense, be thought of as "systems" with distinguishable "parts" or "dimensions," and that a central task of social analysis is to figure out what the salient parts are and how are they connected.

territory. Max Weber defined the state as an organization which effectively monopolizes the legitimate use of force over a territory.[6] I prefer Michael Mann's alternative emphasis on the state as the organization with an administrative capacity to impose binding rules and regulations over territories.[7] The legitimate use of force is one of the key ways this is accomplished, but it is not necessarily the most important way. *State power* is then defined as the effective capacity to impose rules and regulate social relations over territory, a capacity which depends on such things as information and communications infrastructure, the ideological commitments of citizens to obey rules and commands, the level of discipline of administrative officials, the practical effectiveness of the regulations to solve problems, as well as the monopoly over the legitimate use of coercion.

The economy is the sphere of social activity in which people interact to produce and distribute goods and services. In capitalism this activity involves privately owned firms in which production and distribution is mediated by market exchange. *Economic power* is based on the kinds of economically relevant resources different categories of social actors control and deploy within these interactions of production and distribution.

Civil society is the sphere of social interaction in which people voluntarily form associations of different sorts for various purposes.[8] Some of these associations have the character of formal organizations with well-defined memberships and objectives. Clubs, political parties, labor unions, churches, and neighborhood associations would be examples. Others are looser associations, in the limiting case more like social networks than bounded organizations. The idea of a "community," when it means something more than simply the aggregation of individuals

---

6   Max Weber, "Politics as a Vocation," in Hans Gerth and C. Wright Mills (eds), *From Max Weber* (New York: Oxford University Press, 1946).

7   Michael Mann, *The Sources of Social Power*, Volume I (Cambridge: Cambridge University Press, 1986).

8   The term "voluntary" in this formulation is, like many of the concepts used in this discussion, fraught with difficulties. It is meant to highlight a contrast with what can be called "compulsory" associations, especially the state. In many contexts there are all sorts of social pressures and constraints which shape the desire and ability of people to participate in associational life, and thus the strictly "voluntary" quality of such associations may be problematic. Churches often have this character, particularly in social settings where there are significant sanctions for not belonging to a church. The voluntariness of participation in associations is thus a variable.

living in a place, can also be viewed as a kind informal association within civil society. *Power in civil society* depends on capacities for collective action through such voluntary association, and can accordingly be referred to as "associational power" or "social power."

The state, the economy, and civil society are all domains for extended social interaction, cooperation, and conflict among people, and each of them involves distinct sources of *power*. Actors within the economy have power by virtue of their ownership and control of economically relevant resources. Actors in the state have power by virtue of their control of rule making and rule enforcing capacity over territory, including coercive capacity. And actors in civil society have power by virtue of their ability to mobilize people for voluntary collective actions of various sorts.

A typology of economic structures: capitalism, statism, and socialism

We can now turn to the key problem: differentiating capitalism, statism, and socialism. One way of thinking about the variations in the types of economic structures that currently exist or could exist in the future is to think about *variations in the ways power rooted in the economy, the state, and civil society shapes the way economic resources are allocated, controlled and used.* Capitalism, statism, and socialism are differentiated, in these terms, on the basis of the form of ownership over means of production and the type of power that determines economic activities:

Capitalism is an economic structure within which the means of production are privately owned and the allocation and use of resources for different social purposes is accomplished through the exercise of economic power. Investments and the control of production are the result of the exercise of economic power by owners of capital.

Statism is an economic structure within which the means of production are owned by the state and the allocation and use of resources for different social purposes is accomplished through the exercise of state power. State officials control the investment process and production through some sort of state-administrative mechanism.

Socialism is an economic structure within which the means of production are socially owned and the allocation and use of resources for different social purposes is accomplished through the exercise of what can be termed "social power." "Social power" is power rooted in the capacity to mobilize people for cooperative, voluntary collective actions of various sorts in civil society. This implies that civil society should not be viewed simply as an arena of activity, sociability, and communication, but also of real power. Social power is contrasted with *economic power*, based on the ownership and control of economic resources, and *state power*, based on the control of rule making and rule enforcing capacity over territory. The idea of "democracy," in these terms, can be thought of as a specific way of linking social power and state power: in the ideal of democracy, state power is fully subordinated to and accountable to social power. The expression "rule by the people" does not really mean, "rule by the atomized aggregation of the separate individuals of the society taken as isolated persons," but rather, rule by the people collectively organized into associations in various ways: parties, communities, unions, etc. Democracy is thus, inherently, a deeply socialist principle. If "democracy" is the label for the subordination of state power to social power, "socialism" is the term for the subordination of economic power to social power.

It is important to be clear about the conceptual field being mapped here: these are all types of economic structures, but only in capitalism is it the case that economically based power plays the predominant role in determining the use of economic resources.[9] In statism and socialism a form of power distinct from the economy itself plays the dominant role in allocating economic resources for alternative uses. It is still the case, of course, that in capitalism state power and social power exist, but they do not play the central role in the direct allocation, control, and use of economic resources.

---

9   This special property of capitalism is something much remarked upon by Max Weber. He saw the decisive shift from pre-capitalist to capitalist society as lying in the institutional insulation of economic activity from non-economic forms of power and interference which was the essential organizational condition for the full "rationalization" of economic life. For a discussion of Weber's concept of rationalization as it bears on the class analysis of capitalism, see Erik Olin Wright, "The Shadow of Exploitation in Weber's Class Analysis," *American Sociological Review* 67 (2002), pp. 832–53.

This idea of a socialism rooted in social power is not the conventional way of understanding socialism. It differs from standard definitions in two principle ways. First, most definitions closely identify socialism with what I am calling statism. As Geoff Hodgson has forcefully argued, while Marx was generally quite vague about the institutional design of a socialist alternative to capitalism, in the few places where he discusses socialism it is clear that he envisioned a system of production and distribution controlled by the state.[10] Since Marx's time, state-centered socialism has been most strongly linked to the programs of communist parties, but until the end of the twentieth century most democratic socialist parties also linked the vision of socialism to state control over economic processes. In contrast to these traditional formulations, the concept of socialism being proposed here is grounded in the distinction between state power and social power, state ownership and social ownership.

The second way the proposed conceptualization of socialism differs from conventional understandings is that it does not say anything explicitly about markets. Particularly in the Marxist tradition, socialism has usually been treated as a non-market form of economic organization: socialism is a rationally planned economy contrasted to the anarchic character of the capitalist market economy. While from time to time there have been advocates of what is sometimes called "market socialism," in general socialism has been identified with planning (usually understood as centralized state planning) rather than markets. The definition of socialism offered here in terms of social ownership and social power does not preclude the possibility that markets could play a substantial role in coordinating the activities of socially owned and controlled enterprises.

To say that socialism is an economic structure within which the allocation and use of resources for different social purposes is accomplished through the exercise of "social power," defined as power rooted in civil society, leaves open the question of which sorts of associations in civil society are central to social empowerment and which are not. Traditionally socialists, especially those firmly anchored in the Marxist tradition, have understood this problem almost entirely in class terms, focusing especially on the importance of working-class associations for socialism. While it is the case that working-class organization is crucial for social empowerment over the economy, since class is so deeply linked to the ways people are

---

10   See Geoff Hodgson, *Economics and Utopia* (London: Routledge, 1999).

engaged in the process of production, social empowerment is a broader idea than simply working-class empowerment and includes a wide range of associations and collective actors not simply defined by their relationship to class structure. Socialism, understood in the way proposed here, is thus not equivalent to the working class controlling the means of production through its collective associations.[11] Rather, social empowerment over the economy means broad-based encompassing economic democracy.

Hybrids

In terms of these definitions, no actual living economy has ever been purely capitalist or statist or socialist, since it is never the case that the allocation, control, and use of economic resources is determined by a single form of power. Such pure cases live only in the fantasies (or nightmares) of theorists. *Totalitarianism* is a form of imaginary hyper-statism in which state power, unaccountable to civil society and unconstrained by economic power, comprehensively determines all aspects of both production and distribution. In a pure *libertarian capitalism* the state atrophies to a mere "night watchman state," serving only the purpose of enforcing property rights, and commercial activities penetrate into all corners of civil society, commodifying everything. The exercise of economic power would almost fully explain the allocation and use of resources. Citizens are atomized consumers who make individual choices in a market but exercise no collective power over the economy through association in civil society. *Communism*, as classically understood in Marxism, is a form of society in which the state has withered away and the economy is absorbed into civil society as the free, cooperative activity of associated individuals.

---

11   Even though I do not reduce socialism to working-class empowerment over the economy, working-class associations are still at the center of the conception of socialism proposed here for two reasons. First, as defined earlier, *social ownership* means ownership by "the set of people engaged in interdependent economic activity which uses the means of production and generates some kind of product." This means that associations representing workers will always be part of the exercise of ownership rights. Second, because they are directly engaged in production, the active cooperation of workers is essential for the effective exercise of social power over economic activity. If, in the future, socialism based on pervasive economic democracy actually occurs, there is likely to be considerable variability in the array of specific *non*-class associations that would play a central role in the realization of social power over the economy, but any possible socialism would have to include a central role for empowered working-class associations.

None of these pure forms could exist as stable, reproducible forms of social organization. The statist command economies, even in their most authoritarian forms, never completely eliminated informal social networks as a basis for cooperative social interaction which had real effects on economic activity outside of the direct control of the state, and the practical functioning of economic institutions was never fully subordinated to centralized command-and-control planning. Capitalism would be an unsustainable and chaotic social order if the state played the minimalist role specified in the libertarian fantasy, but it would also, as Polanyi argued, function much more erratically if civil society was absorbed into the economy as a fully commodified and atomized arena of social life.[12] Pure communism is also a utopian fantasy, since a complex society could not function without some sort of authoritative means of making and enforcing binding rules (a "state"). Feasible, sustainable forms of large-scale social organization, therefore, always involve some kind of reciprocal relations among these three domains of social interaction and power.

In practice, therefore, the concepts of capitalism, statism, and socialism should be thought of not simply as *all-or-nothing ideal types* of economic structures, but also as *variables*. The more the decisions made by actors exercising economic power determine the allocation and use of resources, the more capitalist an economic structure will be. The more power exercised through the state determines the allocation and use of resources, the more the society is statist. The more power rooted in civil society determines such allocations and uses, the more the society will be socialist.

Treating these concepts as varying in degree opens the possibility of complex mixed cases—*hybrids* in which an economy is capitalist in certain respects and in others statist or socialist.[13]

---

12   See Karl Polanyi, *The Great Transformation: The Political and Economic Origins of Our Time* (Boston: Beacon Press, 2001 [1944]) for the classic discussion of the necessity for markets to be embedded and constrained by society.

13   For a somewhat different conception of the hybrid nature of economic systems, see J. K. Gibson-Graham, *A Postcapitalist Politics* (Minneapolis: University of Minnesota Press, 2006). Gibson-Graham argues that all capitalist economies are really complex multi-form economies which include in addition to the capitalist economy and the state economy a wide range of other economic forms: the gift economy, the household economy, the informal economy, among others. Another interesting formulation of the problem of hybrids can be found in the writing of Colin Ward, the prominent English anarchist. Stuart White describes Ward's approach this way: "For Ward, society inevitably embodies a plurality of basic organizing techniques, including market, state and the anarchist

All existing capitalist societies contain significant elements of statism since states everywhere allocate part of the social surplus for various kinds of investments, especially in things like public infrastructure, defense and education. Furthermore, in all capitalist societies the state removes certain powers from holders of private property rights, for example when capitalist states impose rules on capitalist firms that regulate labels, product quality, or pollution. State power, rather than economic power, controls those specific aspects of production, and in these ways the economy is statist. Capitalist societies also always contain at least some socialist elements, at least through the ways collective actors in civil society influence the allocation of economic resources indirectly through their efforts to influence the state and capitalist corporations. The use of the simple, unmodified expression "capitalism" to describe an empirical case is thus shorthand for something like "a hybrid economic structure within which capitalism is the predominant way of organizing economic activity."[14]

This conception of hybrid economic structures opens up a very difficult set of questions about the nature of economic systems

---

technique of mutual aid: 'Every human society, except the most totalitarian of utopias or anti-utopias, is a plural society with large areas that are not in conformity with the officially imposed or declared values'." See Stuart White, "Making Anarchism Respectable? The Social Philosophy of Colin Ward," *Journal of Political Ideologies* 12: 1 (2007), p. 14, quoting from Colin Ward, *Anarchy in Action* (second edition, London: Freedom Press, 1982).

14   The concept of a *hybrid* economic structure is a specific instance of a style of social theory which can be called "combinatorial structuralism." The general idea is this: For a given domain of social inquiry one can propose a series of elementary structural forms. These are the building blocks of complexity: all concrete societies can then be analyzed in terms of different patterns of combination of these forms. These elementary structures are thus somewhat analogous to the elements in the periodic table of chemistry: all compounds are simply forms of combination of these ingredients. In analyzing economic structures I have proposed here a very simple "social chemistry": there are three elementary forms—capitalism, statism, and socialism. Actual societies, then, are formed through different ways of combining these. There may, of course, also be something akin to isotopes—different forms of each of the elements. There is capitalism consisting of small competitive firms and capitalism of large mega-corporations; capitalism in which capital accumulation is most dynamic in agriculture or in industry or in a variety of service sectors; capitalism with low capital intensity and high capital intensity; and so on. A fully developed combinatorial structuralism of economic forms would explore the diverse ways in which different kinds of elements as well as their variants can form configurations. Of particular importance would be identifying the ways in which some hybrids would be quite stable in the sense that the configuration could be reproduced over time, while others would be unstable and tend to break apart.

and how different principles and power relations get combined. In particular, there is the question of what precisely is meant by the claim that capitalism is "dominant" within a hybrid configuration.[15] The problem here is that there is no simple metric in terms of which we can measure and compare the relative weight of different forms of power. Thus while it may seem intuitively clear that in the United States today capitalism is "dominant"—and thus we can reasonably call the US economy "capitalist"—it is also the case that state power has a significant impact on the allocation of resources and the control over production and distribution in the US economy through the myriad ways in which it regulates economic activities and orders certain kinds of production (e.g., education, defense, and a significant amount of healthcare). If the state were to cease these economic activities, the American economy would collapse, and therefore the system "needs" its statist elements. The US economy is clearly an amalgam of capitalism and statism (and also, less clearly, of socialism), and while I believe that within this amalgam capitalism is dominant, it is not so clear how to measure such dominance.

I do not have a rigorous solution to this problem of precisely how to specify the dominance of one form of power within a configuration of power relations. The working solution I adopt involves a variety of the "functionalist" understanding of the problem: in the economies conventionally described as "capitalist" today, statist elements and socialist elements occupy spaces within functional limits established by capitalism. Attempts to move beyond those limits trigger a variety of negative consequences which tend to undermine the attempts themselves. This is a *functionalist* understanding of "dominance" since within the complex hybrid system of capitalist, statist, and socialist forms it is capitalism which establishes the principles of functional compatibility among the elements of the system and the conditions of system-disruption.

Two points of clarification are needed here. First, the limits in question are limits of functional *compatibility* in the sense that within these limits the statist and socialist elements of the hybrid are consistent with the reproduction of capitalism. This does not imply, however, that these non-capitalist elements always *positively*

---

15 This is very similar to the problem of "causal primacy": what does it mean to say that one cause is "more important" than another in a multi-causal system? For a discussion of this problem see Erik Olin Wright, Andrew Levine, and Elliott Sober, *Reconstructing Marxism: Essays on Explanation and the Theory of History* (London: Verso, 1992), chapter 7, "Causal Asymmetries."

contribute to the reproduction of capitalism. All that is being claimed here is that they are not systematically disruptive of capitalism, for if they were, this would trigger corrective measures. These limits of functional compatibility can sometimes be quite large, allowing for all sorts of variation and autonomy in statist and socialist elements, but they may also sometimes be quite narrow. Hybrids are, in these terms, *loosely coupled* systems rather than tightly integrated organic systems in which all parts must be finely articulated to all others in order for the system to function well. Second, the limits of functional compatibility operate within structures *in the present*; these limits are not oriented towards future states of the system. So long as existing practices of statist and socialist elements in the hybrid do not disrupt capital accumulation now, they are "functionally compatible." The system as such does not anticipate its own future states. This is one of the sources of "contradictions" in a system: practices which are perfectly compatible at one point in time (i.e. they do not disrupt capitalism) may generate cumulative effects which eventually are disruptive.

While this kind of functional reasoning about social systems is quite common, it turns out to be extremely difficult to provide clear theoretical criteria and empirical evidence about the limits of functional compatibility of the parts within a system. Indeed, the difficulty of specifying the limits of functional compatibility is at the center of many political struggles within capitalism: *claims* of incompatibility are one of the weapons pro-capitalist forces use to resist efforts to expand socialist and statist elements within the hybrid. The complexity of these structural configurations is such that there is always a great deal of ambiguity and uncertainty about functional interdependencies, and this opens up considerable space for ideologically driven battles over what is and is not compatible with a healthy capitalism. For the purposes of this book, however, I do not think it is necessary to resolve these issues. It is possible to analyze processes which strengthen and expand the socialist element in a hybrid structure and which thus move in the direction of socialism without being able to give criteria for the dominance of socialism or capitalism or statism. It is sufficient, for now, to be able to say that an economic structure is socialist to the extent that the economy is governed by the exercise of social power.

Although not framed in precisely the language of the present discussion, Marxists have traditionally assumed that within such hybrid forms, one type of economic structure (or "mode of production") would have to be unequivocally dominant in order for the society to be stable. The basic intuition here is that capitalism and socialism are incompatible since they serve opposing class interests, and thus a stable, balanced hybrid would be impossible. A society, in this view, requires some unifying principle rooted in a particular mode of production for social reproduction to effectively contain social contradictions and struggles. A capitalism–socialism hybrid in which both sources of power played a substantial role thus could not be a stable equilibrium: if such a balanced hybrid were to occur, then capitalist power over significant levels of economic resources would have an inherent tendency to erode the associational power of civil society over the economy to the point that capitalism would again become unequivocally dominant. It is important, however, not to feel too confident that one knows in advance everything that is possible "under heaven and earth," for there are always things that happen that are not, in advance, "dreamt of in our philosophy." In any case, in the discussion in this book I am not making any general assumptions about what sorts of hybrids would be stable or even possible.

THE SOCIALIST COMPASS: PATHWAYS TO SOCIAL EMPOWERMENT

To recapitulate the conceptual proposal: socialism can be contrasted to capitalism and statism in terms of the principal form of power that shapes economic activity—the production and distribution of goods and services. Specifically, the greater the degree of social empowerment over the ownership, use and control of economic resources and activities, the more we can describe an economy as socialist.

What does this actually mean in terms of institutional designs? For capitalism and statism, because of the rich examples of historically existing societies, we have a pretty good idea of the institutional arrangements which make these forms of economic structure possible. An economic structure built around private ownership of the means of production combined with relatively comprehensive markets is one in which economic power—the power of capital—plays the primary role in organizing production and allocating the social surplus to different investments. A centralized bureaucratic state that directly plans and organizes most large-scale economic activity, and which, through the apparatus of a political party, penetrates the associations of civil society, is an effective design for statism. But what about socialism? What sorts of institutional designs would enable power rooted in voluntary association in civil society to effectively control the production and distribution of goods and services? What does it mean to move in the direction of a society within which social empowerment is the central organizing principle of the economy?

As discussed in the previous chapter, our task here is not so much to propose blueprints for realizing the ideal of social empowerment over economic activity as to elaborate a set of principles which may tell us when we are moving in the right direction. This is the problem of specifying a socialist compass. The socialist compass has three principle directions anchored in each of the three forms of power discussed above:

1. Social empowerment over the way state power affects economic activity.

2. Social empowerment over the way economic power shapes economic activity.

3. Social empowerment directly over economic activity.

These three directions of social empowerment are connected to an array of linkages among the forms of power and the economy. These are illustrated in Figure 5.1.[16] The six arrows in this diagram represent the effects of power from one social domain on another and the effects of power directly on economic activities in the economy. These linkages can then be combined into a variety of different configurations through which social power—power rooted in civil society—affects the allocation of resources and the control of production and distribution in the economy. I will refer to these configurations as "pathways to social empowerment." In the rest of this chapter we will briefly discuss the character of seven of these pathways: statist socialism; social democratic statist regulation; associational democracy; social capitalism; cooperative market economy; social economy; and participatory socialism. In the next

----

16   This figure illustrates only the pathways through which social power operates; it is not meant to be a comprehensive map of all power relations over economic activity. A similar sort of map could be drawn for the pathways to statism, and the pathways of capitalist economic power.

FIGURE 5.1 *Linkings in the Pathways to Social Empowerment*

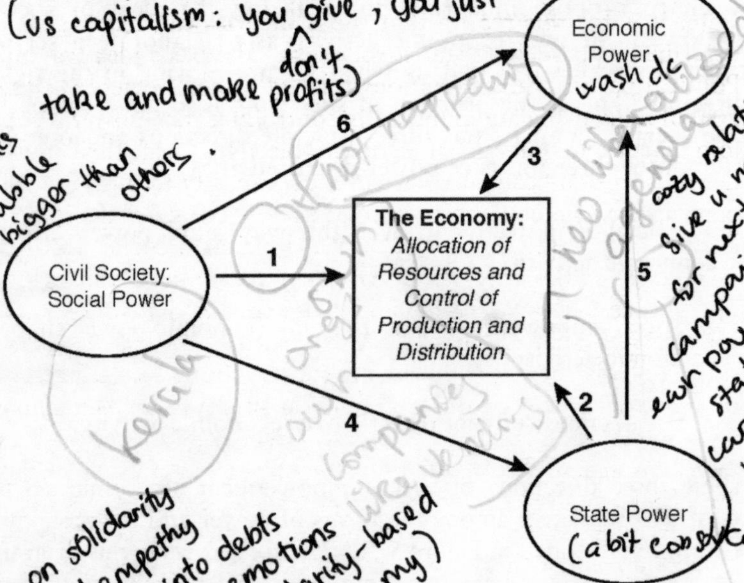
Economic Power
3
6
The Economy: Allocation of Resources and Control of Production and Distribution
1
Civil Society: Social Power
5
2
4
State Power

FIGURE OF THE INDIVIDUAL LINKAGES

1. Social economy: social provision of needs
2. State economy: state produced goods and services
3. Capitalist market economy
4. Democratic control over state power
5. State regulation of capitalist firms
6. Social participation in controlling economic power

two chapters we will examine a variety of specific proposals for real utopian institutional designs and see how they might contribute to social empowerment along these pathways.

1. Statist socialism

In traditional socialist theories, the essential route by which popular power—power rooted in associational activity of civil society—was translated into control over the economy was through the state. It is for this reason that those theories can reasonably be described as models of statist socialism. The basic idea was this: Political parties are associations formed in civil society with the goal of influencing and potentially controlling state power. People join parties in pursuit of certain objectives, and their power depends in significant ways upon their capacity to mobilize such participation for collective action of various sorts. So, if a socialist party is 1) deeply embedded in working-class social networks and communities and democratically accountable through an open process by which it politically represents the working class (or some broader coalition), and 2) controls the state, which in turn controls the economy, then one can argue—on a principle of transitivity-of-control—that in this situation an empowered civil society controls the economic system of production and distribution. This vision, diagramed in Figure 5.2, can be termed the classic model of *statist socialism*. Here, economic power as such is marginalized: it is not by virtue of the direct economic ownership and control over assets that people have power to organize production; it is by virtue of their collective political organization in civil society and their exercise of state power.

Statist socialism of this sort was at the heart of traditional Marxist ideas of revolutionary socialism. The idea—at least on paper—was that the party would be organically connected to the working class and effectively accountable to associated workers, and thus its control over the state would be a mechanism for civil society (understood in class terms) to control the state. Furthermore, revolutionary socialism envisioned a radical reorganization of the institutions of the state and economy—through organizational forms of participatory councils that in the case of the Russian Revolution came to be called "soviets"—in ways that would directly involve workers' associations in the exercise of power in both the state and production. These councils, if fully empowered in democratic ways and rooted in an autonomous civil society,

FIGURE 5.2 *Statist Socialism*

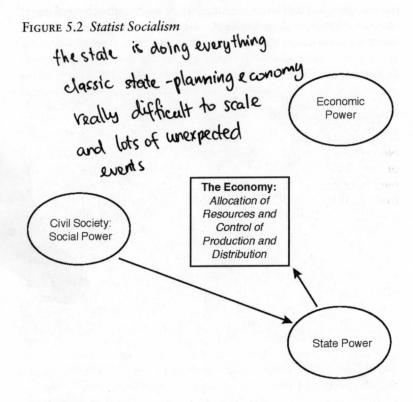

[handwritten annotation: the state is doing everything / classic state-planning economy / really difficult to scale / and lots of unexpected / events]

could be thought of as a mechanism for institutionalizing the ascendancy of social power. Again, the party was seen as pivotal to this process, since it would provide the leadership (play the "vanguard" role) for such a translation of associations in civil society into effective social power.

This is not, of course, how things turned out. Whether because of the inherent tendency of revolutionary party organizations to concentrate power at the top, or because of the terrible constraints of the historical circumstances of the Russian Revolution and its aftermath, whatever potential there was for the Communist Party to be subordinated to an autonomous civil society was destroyed in the course of the Russian Civil War and the early years of the revolution. By the time the new Soviet state had consolidated power and launched its concerted efforts at transforming the economy, the Party had become a mechanism of state domination, a vehicle for penetrating civil society and controlling economic organizations. The Soviet Union, therefore, became the archetype of *authoritarian statism* under the ideological banner of socialism, but not of a socialism rooted in democratic social empowerment. Subsequent successful revolutionary socialist parties, for all their differences, followed a broadly similar path, creating various forms of statism. The contrast between this reality and the theoretical model of a democratic statist socialism is illustrated in Figure 5.3.

Today, few socialists believe that comprehensive statist central planning is a viable structure for realizing socialist goals. Nevertheless, statist socialism remains an important component of any likely process of social empowerment. The state will remain central to the provision of a wide range of public goods, from health to education to public transportation. The central question for socialists, then, is the extent to which these aspects of state provision can effectively be brought under the control of a democratically empowered civil society. In capitalist societies, typically, these aspects of the provision of public goods by the state are only weakly subordinated to social power through the institutions of representative democracy. Because of the enormous influence of capitalist economic power on state policies, such public goods are often more geared to the needs of capital accumulation

FIGURE 5.3 *Theoretical Model and Historical Experience of Revolutionary Statist Socialism* the only thing running the economy is economic allocation

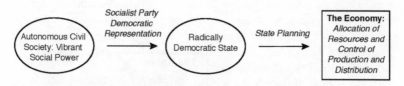

THEORETICAL MODEL OF DEMOCRATIC STATIST SOCIALISM

CHARACTERISTIC HISTORICAL OUTCOME OF REVOLUTIONARY STATIST SOCIALISM

than to social needs. Deepening the democratic quality of the state—linkage 4 in Figure 5.1—is thus the pivotal problem in relation to direct state provision of goods and services becoming a genuine pathway to social empowerment. In chapter 6 we will examine forms of participatory democracy that attempt to accomplish this.

2. Social democratic statist economic regulation

The second pathway for potential social empowerment centers on the ways in which the state constrains and regulates economic power (Figure 5.4). Even in the period of economic deregulation and the triumph of ideologies of the free market at the end of the twentieth century, the state remained deeply implicated in the regulation of production and distribution in ways that impinge on capitalist economic power. This includes a wide range of interventions: pollution control, workplace health and safety rules, product safety standards, skill credentialing in labor markets, minimum wages, and other labor market regulations. Any serious proposal

FIGURE 5.4 *Social Democratic Statist Economic Regulation*

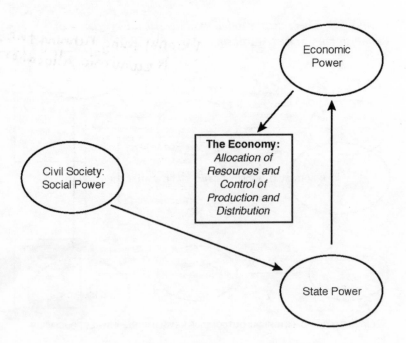

to contend with global warming would have to intensify such statist regulation of the use of economic power. All of these involve state power restricting certain powers of the owners of capital, and thereby affecting economic activities. To the extent that these forms of affirmative state intervention are themselves effectively subordinated to social power through democratic political processes, then this becomes a pathway to social empowerment.

Statist regulation of capitalist economic power, however, need not imply significant social empowerment. Again, the issue here is the extent and depth to which the regulatory activities of the state are genuine expressions of the democratic empowerment of civil society. In actual capitalist societies, much economic regulation is in fact more responsive to the needs and power of capital than to the needs and power generated within civil society. The result is a power configuration more like Figure 5.5 than 5.4: state power regulates capital but in ways that are systematically responsive to the power of capital itself.[17] The question, then, is the extent to which it is possible within

FIGURE 5.5 *Capitalist Statist Economic Regulation*

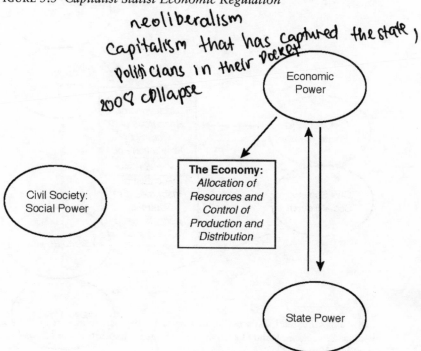

neoliberalism
Capitalism that has captured the state,
politicians in their pocket
2008 collapse

capitalist society to democratize state regulatory processes in ways which undercut the power of capital and enhance social power. One way of doing this is through what is sometimes called "associational democracy."

3. Associational democracy

Associational democracy encompasses a wide range of institutional devices through which collective associations in civil society directly participate in various kinds of governance activities, characteristically along with state agencies and business associations (Figure 5.6).[18] The most familiar is probably the tripartite neo-corporatist arrangements in some social democratic societies in which organized labor, associations of employers, and the state meet together to bargain over

FIGURE 5.6 *Associational Democracy*

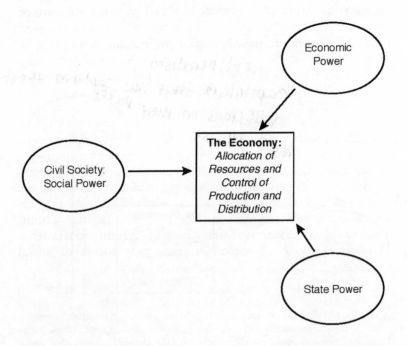

---

18   For an extended discussion of associative democracy as part of the Real Utopias Project, see Joshua Cohen and Joel Rogers, *Associations and Democracy* (London: Verso, 1995).

various kinds of economic regulations, especially those involved in labor market and employment relations. Associational democracy could be extended to many other domains, for example watershed councils which bring together civic associations, environmental groups, developers, and state agencies to regulate ecosystems, or health councils involving medical associations, community organizations, and public health officials to plan various aspects of healthcare. To the extent that the associations involved are internally democratic and representative of interests in civil society, and the decision-making process in which they are engaged is open and deliberative rather than heavily manipulated by elites and the state, then associative democracy constitutes a pathway to social empowerment.

4. Social capitalism

Economic power is power rooted in the direct control over the allocation, organization, and use of capital of various sorts. Secondary associations of civil society can, through a variety of mechanisms, directly affect the way such economic power is used (Figure 5.7). For example, unions often control large pension funds. These are generally governed by rules of fiduciary responsibility which severely limit the potential use of those funds for purposes other than providing secure pensions for the beneficiaries. But those rules could be changed, and unions could potentially exert power over corporations through the management of such funds. More ambitiously, as we will see in chapter 7, Robin Blackburn has proposed a new kind of pension fund, funded by a share-levy on corporations, which would enable a broader array of secondary associations in civil society to exert significant influence on the patterns of capital accumulation.[19] In Canada today, the union movement has created venture capital funds, controlled by labor, to provide equity to start-up firms that satisfy certain social criteria.

Historically one of the most important forms of social

---

19 Blackburn's proposal, as elaborated in "The Global Pension Crisis: from Gray Capitalism to Responsible Accumulation" (*Politics and Society* 34: 2 [2006], pp. 135–86), is modeled after the proposal by Rudolf Meidner in Sweden in the 1970s to introduce what were then called "wage earner funds" as a way of increasing union control over accumulation. The key idea is that corporations pay newly issued shares into these funds, not cash. This has the effect of gradually diluting private shareowner control over the total stock of corporations and enhancing the capacity of the associations (such as unions) which control these funds to shape corporate policy.

FIGURE 5.7 *Social Capitalism*

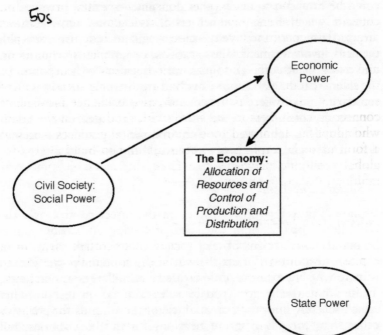

capitalism concerns the ways in which associations of workers
mobilize power in various ways to constrain the exercise
of economic power. This can occur in the form of ordinary
labor unions engaged in bargaining over pay and working
conditions—such bargaining constitutes a form of social power
which, if only in limited ways, affects the operation of economic
power. The co-determination rules in Germany, which mandate
worker representation on boards of directors of firms over a
certain size, modestly extends social power into the direct
governance of firms. Proposals to replace shareholder councils
with stakeholder councils for the control of corporate boards
of directors would be a more radical version. Or consider, for
example, the regulation of workplace health and safety. One
approach is for there to be a government regulatory agency
which sends inspectors to workplaces to monitor compliance
with the rules. Another is to empower workers' councils within
the workplace to monitor and enforce health and safety

conditions. The latter is an example of enhancing social power over economic power.

Social movements engaged in consumer-oriented pressure on corporations also represent a form of civil society empowerment directed at economic power. These would include, for example, the anti-sweatshop and labor standards movements centered on university campuses, and organized boycotts of corporations for selling products that do not conform to some socially salient standard.[20] Likewise, fair trade and equal exchange movements connecting consumers in the North with producers in the South who adopt fair labor and good environmental practices represent a form of social capitalism in their attempt to build alternative global economic networks free from the economic power of multinational corporations.

5. Cooperative market economy

A stand-alone fully worker-owned cooperative firm in a capitalist economy is a form of social capitalism: the egalitarian principle of one-person-one-vote of all members of the business means that the power relations within the firm are based on voluntary cooperation and persuasion, not the relative economic power of different people. Jointly the workers control through democratic means the economic power represented by the capital in the firm.

Most worker-owned cooperatives in the world today operate within markets organized along capitalist principles. This means that they face significant credit constraints in financial markets because of the reluctance of banks to lend to them, and they are vulnerable to market shocks and disruptions, just like ordinary capitalist firms. They are pretty much on their own.

The situation could potentially be quite different if worker-owned cooperatives were embedded within what might be called a cooperative market economy. A cooperative market economy (Figure 5.8) is one in which individual cooperative firms join together in larger associations of cooperatives—what might be termed a cooperative of cooperatives—which collectively

---

20   For a discussion of the limitations of civil-society-based movements for labor standards and the importance of such standards being backed by state power, see Gay Seidman, *Beyond the Boycott: Labor Rights, Human Rights and Transnational Activism* (New York: Russell Sage Foundation, 2008).

FIGURE 5.8 *Cooperative Market Economy*

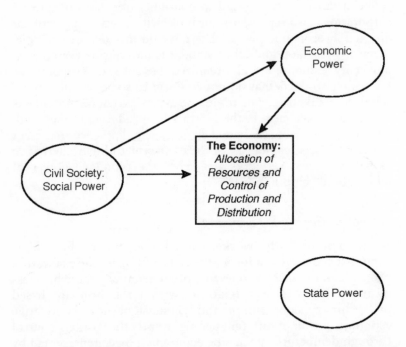

provide finance, training, problem-solving services, and other kinds of support for each other. The overarching cooperative in such a market stretches the social character of ownership within individual cooperative enterprises and moves it more towards a stakeholder model. In effect, the role of social power in directly organizing economic activity through this extended cooperative environment gains weight alongside the social capitalist pathway within the individual cooperative enterprises.

6. The social economy

The social economy is the pathway of social empowerment in which voluntary associations in civil society directly organize various aspects of economic activity, rather than simply shape the deployment of economic power (Figure 5.9). The "social economy" constitutes an alternative way of directly organizing economic activity that is distinct from capitalist market production, state organized production, and household production. Its hallmark is

FIGURE 5.9 *Social Economy*

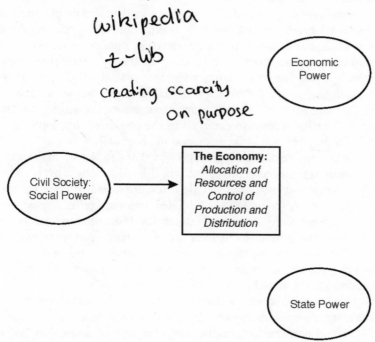

production organized by collectivities directly to satisfy human needs not subject to the discipline of profit-maximization or state-technocratic rationality.

This use of the term social economy is more restrictive than the definition generally adopted by self-described social economy activists. In Quebec, for example, where there is a strong social economy movement supporting the expansion of non-capitalist forms of economic activity, the term "social economy" is used as an encompassing idea that includes what I have called social capitalism and cooperative market economy and sometimes even capitalist firms that self-consciously adopt social objectives alongside conventional profit-seeking. This makes sense in the Quebec context where the word is used to foster broad coalitions and solidarities across the full spectrum of activities that fall outside of ordinary capitalist practices. In other places the term "social economy" is used to include all non-profit organizations, NGOs, and what is sometimes called the "third sector." In any case, all of these different uses of the term contain the specific pathway of social empowerment illustrated in Figure 5.9.[21]

A striking example of almost pure social economy production, discussed briefly in chapter 1, is Wikipedia. Wikipedia produces knowledge and disseminates information outside of markets and without state support. The funding of the infrastructure comes largely from donations from participants and supporters of the Wiki foundation. Technology-mediated social networks are the underlying form of this voluntary association, but stronger forms of association have also emerged in the course of development of Wikipedia. These will be discussed in chapter 7.

In capitalist societies the primary way that production in the social economy is financed is through charitable donations. This is one of the reasons that such activities are often organized by churches, but a variety of different kinds of NGOs also engage in a great deal of social economy activity. Habitat for Humanity would be an example: Using funds from a variety of sources—private donations, support from foundations, civic associations and government grants—the houses built by Habitat for Humanity depend heavily on community-based organization and volunteer activity.

The potential scope for the social economy could be enhanced if the state, through its capacity to tax, provided funding for socially organized non-market production. One way of doing this, as we will see in chapter 7, is through the institution of an unconditional basic income. By partially delinking income from employment earnings, an unconditional basic income would enable voluntary associations of all sorts to create new forms of meaningful and productive work in the social economy. But more targeted forms of government funding could also underwrite the social economy. This is already common in relation to the arts in many places in the world. Quebec has an extensive system of eldercare home services organized through nonprofit firms, and childcare services

---

21 When I presented this schema to a circle of academics and practitioners actively engaged in social economy projects in Quebec, they objected that the pathway in Figure 5.9 was too limited a specification of the social economy. Their practical work certainly includes many projects that would fall under what I have called social capitalism and the cooperative market economy. Their concern was that my more restrictive use of the term would create boundaries that might denigrate activities that were excluded from the social economy moniker. Labelling always has this danger. However, I do not think this is a real issue in the present context since the multiple pathways of social empowerment are viewed as complementary and synergetic rather than inherently antagonistic.

organized through parent-provider co-ops, which are partially subsidized through taxes in this way.

7. Participatory socialism: statist socialism with empowered participation

The final pathway to social empowerment combines the direct social participation characteristic of the social economy and statist socialism: the state and civil society jointly organize and control various kinds of production of goods and services. In participatory socialism the role of the state is more pervasive and direct than in the social economy. The state does not simply provide funding and set the parameters; it is also, in various ways, directly involved in the organization and production of the economic activity. On the other hand, participatory socialism is also different from statist socialism, for here social power plays a role not simply through the ordinary channels of democratic control of state policies, but directly inside the productive activities themselves.

The participatory budget process in Porto Alegre, Brazil, discussed briefly in chapter 1, is an instance of participatory socialism: citizens and associations in civil society not only hold the local state democratically accountable, but are also directly involved in the control of infrastructure projects formed through the municipal budget. Systems of workplace democracy and workers' co-management within state enterprises would also be a form of participatory socialism. So would public eduction when civil society is actively engaged in school governance.

One site where this already occurs in some places is in education. In Barcelona, Spain, some public elementary schools have been turned into what are called "learning communities" in which the governance of the school is substantially shifted to parents, teachers, and members of the community, and the function of the school shifts from narrowly teaching children to providing a broader range of learning activities for the community as a whole.[22] In the United States there is a long tradition of involvement of civic associations

22   For an analysis of the way the Spanish learning community schools can be viewed as a hybrid structure linking the state and civil society in the joint production of education, see Ramon Flecha, *Sharing Words* (Lanham, MD: Rowman and Littlefield, 2000). For a good ethnographic study of a specific learning community school see Montse Sánchez Aroca, "La Verneda-Sant Martí: A School Where People Dare to Dream," *Harvard Educational Review* 69: 3 (1999), pp. 320–57.

FIGURE 5.10 *Participatory Socialism*

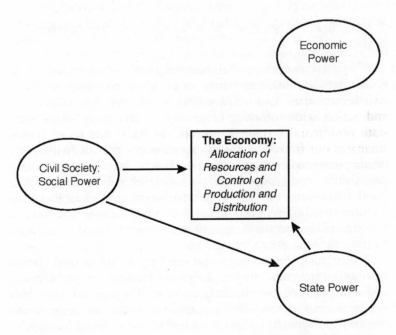

and parent-teacher associations in schools, although usually this falls far short of playing a decisive role in school governance.

CONCLUSION: THREE SKEPTICAL NOTES

Each of these seven pathways has, at its core, the idea of extensive and robust economic democracy through creating conditions in which social power, organized through the active participation and empowerment of ordinary people in civil society, exerts both direct and indirect democratic control over the economy. Taken individually, movement along one or another of these pathways might not pose much of a challenge to capitalism, but substantial movement along all of them taken together would constitute a fundamental transformation of capitalism's class relations and the structures of power and privilege rooted in them. Capitalism might still remain a component in the hybrid configuration of power relations governing economic activity, but it would be a subordinated capitalism heavily constrained within limits set by the deepened democratization of both state and economy. This would not automatically ensure that the radical democratic egalitarian ideals of social and political justice would be accomplished, but if we were somehow to successfully move along these pathways to such a hybrid form of social organization, we would be in a much better position to struggle for a radical democratic egalitarian vision of social and political justice.

Whether or not this potential can be actualized depends on three kinds of conditions. First, it depends upon the extent to which civil society itself is a vibrant domain of collective association and action with sufficient coherence to effectively shape both state power and economic power. The idea that social power emanates out from civil society presupposes that in civil society latent power exists that can potentially be translated into other domains of action. Second, effective social empowerment depends upon the presence of institutional mechanisms which facilitate the mobilization and deployment of social power along these routes. Social mobilization without institutional consolidation is unlikely to have durable effects on the overall configurations of power. And third, it depends upon the capacity of those institutional mechanisms to counter the deployment of power opposed to social empowerment. Above all, in the context of capitalist society, this means countering the power of capital as well as those aspects of state power opposed to initiatives and action from civil society.

There are good reasons to be skeptical about the prospects for each of these conditions.

Civil society and social power

To recapitulate the core idea of this chapter: Civil society is the site of a form of power with emancipatory potential—"social power"—rooted in the capacity of people to form associations to advance their collective goals. Socialism can then be defined as an economic structure in which social power in its multiple forms plays the dominant role in organizing economic activity, both directly, and indirectly through the ways social power shapes the exercise of both state power and economic power. This is the equivalent of arguing for the radical democratization of both state and economy, and this in turn requires an associationally rich civil society.

A skeptic can, with justification, reply: there is no reason to believe that the associations formed in civil society will be of the sort suitable for a pervasive democratization of control over the economy. There are two problems here. First, a vibrant civil society is precisely one with a multitude of heterogeneous associations, networks, and communities, built around different goals, with different kinds of members based on different sorts of solidarities. While this pluralistic heterogeneity may provide a context for a public sphere of debate and sociability, it does not seem like a promising basis for the kind of coherent power needed to effectively control the state or the economy. Second, the voluntary associations that comprise civil society include many nasty associations, based on exclusion, narrow interests, and the preservation of privilege. Voluntary associations include the Ku Klux Klan as well as the National Association for the Advancement of Colored People, associations to protect the exclusiveness of neighborhoods along racial and class lines as well as associations to promote community development and openness. Why should we believe that empowering such associations would contribute anything positive to ameliorating the harms of capitalism, let alone a broader vision of human emancipation?

The first of these two objections is one of the reasons why the conception of socialism proposed here is not the same as anarchism. An anarchist conception of transcending capitalism imagines a world in which the voluntarily coordinated collective action of people in civil society can spontaneously achieve sufficient coherence as to provide for social order and social reproduction without the necessity of a state. Socialism, in contrast, requires a state, a state with real power to institute and enforce the rules of the game and mechanisms of coordination without which the collective power from civil society would be unable to achieve the necessary integration to control either state or economy.

The second objection—that civil society contains many associations inconsistent with radical democratic egalitarian emancipatory ideals—is more troubling, for it opens the specter of a socialism rooted in exclusion and oppression. It is tempting to deal with this concern by somehow defining civil society as only consisting of benign associations that are consistent with socialist ideals of democratic egalitarianism; social empowerment would then be the empowerment of popular associations that were at least compatible with emancipatory goals.[23] Nasty socialism

---

23   There are some treatments of the concept of civil society that come close to defining it in terms of associations and social practices animated by universalistic, "civil" concerns. Exclusionary associations that are "anti-civil" are the enemies of civil society rather than components of it. See, for example, Jeffrey Alexander, *The Civil Sphere* (New York: Oxford University Press, 2006).

would be eliminated by fiat. I think this is an undesirable response. It is a bit like developing an argument for capitalism on the basis of theoretical arguments concerning incentives, risk-taking, and efficient markets and then responding to criticisms of the inevitable emergence of monopoly power by declaring "capitalism consists only of competitive firms incapable of dominating the market." If market-dominating powerful corporations emerge, then this is no longer "really capitalism." A better response is to admit that capitalism may indeed have a tendency to generate such concentrated forms of market power. If monopoly corporations seriously erode the alleged virtues of capitalism, then the response should be to propose institutional mechanisms, typically in the form of state regulations, which would counteract these effects. While these institutional devices have a contradictory character, since they violate some of the principles of capitalism (such as the sanctity of private property), a hybrid mix of capitalism and statism may be necessary in order to gain the virtues latent within a capitalist organization of economic structures.[24]

The issue of the existence of exclusionary associations in civil society poses, I think, an analogous challenge for an empowered civil society view of socialism. There is no guarantee that a society within which power rooted in civil society predominates would be one that upholds democratic egalitarian ideals. This, however, is not some unique problem for socialism; it is a characteristic of democratic institutions in general. As conservatives often point out, inherent in democracy is the potential for the tyranny of the majority, and yet in practice liberal democracies have been fairly successful at creating institutions that protect both individual rights and the interests of minorities. A socialist democracy rooted in social empowerment through associations in civil society would face similar challenges: how to devise institutional rules for the game of democratic deepening and associational empowerment which would foster the radical democratic egalitarian conception of emancipation. My assumption here is not that a socialism of social empowerment will inevitably successfully meet this challenge, but that moving along the pathways of social empowerment will provide a more

---

24   This is the standard way of arguing for the virtues of various forms of state-regulated capitalism: by countering the self-destructive aspects of capitalism, state regulation enables capitalism itself to contribute to human well-being, even if in so doing it makes capitalism less purely capitalistic.

favorable terrain on which to struggle for these ideals than does either capitalism or statism.

Institutional elaboration

The second source of skepticism centers on the problem of institutional mechanisms. It may be true that if we magically had the necessary institutions to translate power rooted in civil society into control over the state and economy then this would advance egalitarian and democratic values. But why should we believe that such institutions are possible? The arguments against such a possibility are familiar: Most people are too passive to care about any form of real empowerment. We need experts to make decisions about complex technical matters. Capitalist firms driven by the profit motive are needed for innovation and efficient investment. Only centralized, professionalized state apparatuses, relatively insulated from popular pressures and special interests, can properly regulate the economy in a technically efficient manner.

Responding to this sort of skepticism is the central aim of discussions of real utopias: exploring the viability of specific institutional designs that attempt to realize emancipatory values. In the next two chapters we will examine a range of such real utopian proposals to give more credibility to the idea that there are viable institutional arrangements that make movement on the pathways of social empowerment a plausible goal.

Achievability

The final source of skepticism is that even if there are imaginable institutional arrangements that would enhance social empowerment and contribute significantly to realizing democratic egalitarian ideals, it is impossible to create such institutions within capitalist society. Attempts at building such institutions in a serious way will inevitably provoke a backlash from elites whose power is rooted in the state and capitalist economy. Social empowerment will only be tolerated so long as it is not a threat to the basic power relations of capitalism. A serious movement along the pathways of social empowerment, therefore, will confront insurmountable obstacles, not because there are no viable institutional designs for a radical egalitarian democratic form of social empowerment, but because such efforts will be defeated by powerful actors whose interests would be threatened by any kind of socialism. You cannot build such institutions within a society in which capitalism remains the dominant form of social organization of economic power.

This is the critique posed by revolutionary socialists who argue that the power of capital and of the capitalist state has to be decisively broken in a system-level rupture in order for socialism to be possible. It could turn out that this argument is correct. If so, this almost certainly means that for the conceivable future socialism as an alternative to capitalism is simply not possible, either as a destination or as a direction of change. But these predictions may also be unduly pessimistic, reflecting an exaggerated sense of the power of capital and the capitalist class and an under-appreciation of the social spaces available for social innovation. These are issues we will explore in Part III on Transformations.

REAL UTOPIAS I: SOCIAL EMPOWERMENT AND THE STATE

In this chapter and the next we will explore a range of real utopian proposals that try to satisfy three main criteria: First, the institutional designs involved are *desirable* in terms of radical democratic egalitarian emancipatory ideals. Second, they constitute *viable* alternatives to existing arrangements (i.e. they are consistent with what we know about how institutions work and, if implemented, would not generate perverse unintended consequences which would either negate the desirable properties of the institution or make it unsustainable). Third, the proposals should contribute in some way to movement along the pathways of social empowerment outlined in the previous chapter. While social empowerment may not be a necessary condition for an institutional change to be worth pursuing, these are the kinds of changes that, cumulatively, have the potential of transcending capitalism.

A fourth criterion of considerable political importance will not be of central concern here: the *achievability* of the proposal. Some of the institutional proposals we will consider are certainly achievable in some form in the world today: some have been implemented in limited ways already and others are actively on the political agenda in certain places. Other ideas do not seem immediately achievable, but nevertheless it is not difficult to imagine circumstances in which they could become achievable if sufficient social forces mobilized around them. But at least some of the proposals discussed in this chapter and in the next seem fairly far-fetched politically, and are quite unlikely to be achievable in the form discussed. This is the case, for example, with the proposal formulated by John Roemer for equal-ownership market socialism discussed in chapter 7. Nevertheless, I believe that it is worth thinking about such apparently unachievable possibilities both because it is so difficult to predict what the political circumstances will be decades hence, and because exploring the logic of viable but (apparently) not achievable institutional designs can contribute to the future formulation of achievable innovations.

There are two strategies we will adopt for exploring real utopian designs and proposals. The first is empirical, focusing on concrete cases around the world which embody in different ways the principles of social empowerment elaborated in chapter 5. A full analysis of such empirical cases involves a number of tasks: first, establishing that indeed the case does embody processes of social empowerment; second, analyzing in as fine-grained a way as possible precisely how the institutional design in question actually works; third, distilling some general principles from the case that constitute elements of a more abstract institutional design; fourth, exploring the facilitating conditions that made the case possible; and, finally, revealing the contradictions, limits, and dilemmas faced by the real utopian design. A critical danger in this kind of analysis is that the study of such examples degenerates into propagandistic cheerleading. When radical critics of capitalism become desperate for empirical models that embody their aspirations, wishful thinking can triumph over sober assessments. The complementary danger, of course, is cynicism; there is great cachet among intellectuals in debunking naïve enthusiasm. What is needed, then, are accounts of empirical cases that are neither gullible nor cynical, but try to fully recognize the complexity and dilemmas as well as the real potentials of practical efforts at social empowerment.

The second strategy of analysis in these chapters is to propose purely theoretical models of new institutional designs that are not represented by any real world cases. This does not mean that such analyses cannot draw on empirical evidence of one sort or another, since in general there will be empirical phenomena that are relevant to understanding such proposals. But the core of the analysis concerns the elaboration of a logical structure based on explicit premises and theoretical arguments. Here too the critical task is to directly engage dilemmas, limits, and problems. The idea is for the models to be *real* utopian models, and we know in advance that the implementation of any such design will have unintended consequences. A fully elaborated theoretical analysis would try to explore these as well.

The set of proposals we will examine in these two chapters does not constitute a comprehensive project of institutional designs for socialism or some other encompassing alternative to existing social structures and institutions. Nor are these proposals meant to constitute an integrated political program for an anti-capitalist political party. While I do think that many elements of the institutional designs we will examine can and should be part of the political programs of socialist democratic egalitarianism, there remain many gaps and missing elements in what will be discussed. Since most of the pathways to social empowerment outlined in the previous chapter involve the state, we will begin here by examining proposals for real utopian institutional designs for deepening democracy in the state. The next chapter will examine designs for new economic institutions.

THREE INSTITUTIONAL FORMS OF DEMOCRACY[1]

The abstract idea of democracy as "rule by the people" is translated into actual systems of democratic governance through three primary institutional forms: direct democracy, representative democracy, and associational democracy:

Direct democracy. In direct democracy, ordinary citizens are directly involved in the activities of political governance. One form of this is what is sometimes called "plebiscitary democracy" in which citizens vote on various laws and policies. Another form would be the many ways in which citizens participate in public hearings and testimony over legislation in cities, or, more rarely, directly make decisions in town meetings.

Representative democracy. This is the most familiar institutional form for realizing democratic principles. In representative democracy the people rule through their representatives, typically chosen through competitive elections within territorial districts. In most democratic countries, this is by far the most important way by which ordinary people play some role in the exercise of political power.

Associational democracy. The third general form of democratic governance, associational democracy, is much less familiar to most people. In associational democracy, various kinds of collective organizations—like labor unions, business associations, or civic groups—are directly engaged in various aspects of political

---

1 Parts of this section are drawn directly from an unpublished paper written with Archon Fung, "Participation, Associations, and Representation in a Deeper Democracy" (2004).

decision making and governance. This can occur in many ways—through involvement in government commissions, through what is sometimes called "corporatism," through organizational representation on various kinds of regulatory agencies.

Each of these forms of democratic governance can be organized in ways that either deepen the quality of popular empowerment or that undercut rule by the people. For example, when electoral democracy relies mainly on the private financing of electoral campaigns, and particularly when there is a two-party system, this gives enormous influence to rich and powerful agents who are able to strongly influence the selection of viable candidates. Broad swathes of the electorate may retreat into private life, leaving the business of governing to a select class of anointed professionals.[2] On the other hand, certain kinds of public financing of elections, combined with systems of proportional representation and party organizations that are internally democratic, open up electoral competition to broader popular initiatives. When associations involved in democratic governance are themselves internally hierarchical and bureaucratic, when they represent only some interests in society and exclude the unassociated, when they are subordinated in various ways to elite interests, or when they are run by professionals and membership consists of little more than financial donation,[3] governance through secondary associations can become very undemocratic. On the other hand, when the associations are open and inclusive, and when their participation in governance involves empowered forms of bargaining and problem solving,

---

2 There is a current in political thought which defends thin forms of representative democracy. The classic defense is Joseph Schumpeter's treatment of "elite democracy" in *Capitalism, Socialism, and Democracy* (New York: Harper and Row, 1942). For contemporary proponents of thin democracy, see George Kateb, "The Moral Distinctiveness of Representative Democracy," *Ethics* 91 (1981), pp. 357–74; Richard Posner, *Law, Pragmatism, and Democracy* (Cambridge, MA: Harvard University Press, 2003); John R. Hibbing and Elizabeth Theiss-Morse, *Stealth Democracy: Americans' Beliefs about How Government Should Work* (New York: Cambridge University Press, 2002). For critique, see Archon Fung and Joshua Cohen, "Radical Democracy," *Swiss Journal of Political Science* 10: 4 (2004).

3 See Theda Skocpol, "Advocates Without Members: The Recent Transformation of American Civic Life," in Theda Skocpol and Morris P. Fiorina (eds), *Civic Engagement in American Democracy* (Washington, DC: Brookings and Russell Sage Foundation, 1999).

FIGURE 6.1 *Varieties of Democratic Governance*

The Degree of Democraticness

		Thin Democracy	Deep Democracy
	Representative Democracy	Elite-dominated electoral democracy	Robust egalitarian electoral democracy
Form of Democratic Rule	**Associational Democracy**	Bureaucratic corporatism	Democratic associational corporatism
	Direct Democracy	Plebiscitary elections	Empowered participatory governance

then associational democracy can deepen the accountability and effectiveness of public action. Finally, direct democracy can be very thin, as when citizens are simply given a yes/no vote on a referendum policy dictated by elites, or it can become a form of significant popular empowerment when it involves the devolution of real decision-making authority and resources to popular councils of various sorts. These various possibilities are illustrated in Figure 6.1.

All democracies involve some elements of each of these forms of governance. A radical, deep, egalitarian democracy is not one in which direct democracy entirely replaces representative democracy or associational democracy. Rather, the project of realizing emancipatory democratic ideals requires transforming each of these forms of governance in a more deeply democratic direction, and, importantly, articulating the ways in which each kind of democratic engagement can support and reinforce the others.

In what follows I will discuss institutional designs for deepening democracy for each of these kinds of democratic institutions. I will give particular attention to the problem of direct democracy since this is the institutional form of democratic governance that is generally considered the least tenable in the world today, but all three forms are important.

DIRECT DEMOCRACY: NEW FORMS OF
EMPOWERED PARTICIPATORY GOVERNANCE

There is a sense in which direct democracy most purely embodies the radical egalitarian democratic ideal, for it constitutes "rule by the people" in the most transparent way. The idea that people should have the power to participate in making decisions over matters which shape their collective fate evokes the idea of direct participation, not proxy participation. Both representative and associational democracy seem one step removed from "real" democracy; they are practical accommodations to intractable problems of scale, complexity, and time constraints that occur whenever the problem of collective fate and democratic decision making move beyond small scale, face-to-face communities. As a result, most people think that direct, participatory democracy is of little relevance for contemporary society.

I believe that there is much more scope for new forms of direct democracy that have the potential to contribute significantly to a broad reinvention of democracy and a movement along the pathways of social empowerment. In my work with Archon Fung we have called these new forms of direct democracy "empowered participatory governance," or EPG. To understand the logic of EPG we will first look in more detail at the celebrated example of innovative direct democracy that was discussed briefly in chapter 1—municipal participatory budgeting in Porto Alegre—and then examine the general principles of the EPG model.

An example: municipal participatory budgeting

The participatory budget in the city of Porto Alegre, a city of around one and a half million inhabitants in the southeast corner of Brazil, constitutes a move in the direction of robust direct democratic institutions.[4] This case provides the raw material for elaborating a set of general principles of institutional design for invigorating direct democracy. Since detailed descriptions of the

---

4 This case is at the center of volume IV of the Real Utopias Project: Archon Fung and Erik Olin Wright (eds), *Deepening Democracy: Institutional Innovations in Empowered Participatory Governance* (London: Verso, 2003). Part of the description in the following paragraphs is taken from pages 10–12 of that book.

Porto Alegre participatory budget are readily available, I will here sketch only the institutional design.[5]

The system of participatory budgeting was instituted by the Workers' Party (the PT), a left-wing socialist party that unexpectedly won the election for mayor in 1988 and adopted the participatory budget as a way of instituting a kind of "dual power" within city government.[6] Without going into details, the basic idea is that citizens meet in popular assemblies throughout the city to deliberate on how the city budget should be spent. Most of these assemblies are organized around geographical regions of the city; a few are organized around themes with a city-wide scope—like public transportation or culture. At the beginning of the budget cycle each year these assemblies meet in plenary sessions. City executives, administrators, representatives of community entities such as neighborhood associations, youth and sports clubs, and any interested inhabitant of the city attends these assemblies, but only residents of the region can vote in the regional assembly. Any city resident participating in a thematic assembly can vote in them. These assemblies are jointly coordinated by members of municipal government and by community delegates.

At this initial plenary assembly the results of the previous years' budget process are reviewed by representatives from the mayor's office. Also at this plenary assembly, delegates are chosen to meet in regional and thematic budget councils in order to formulate spending priorities. This is where the most intensely participatory work on the budget is done. These delegate meetings are held in neighborhoods throughout the region over a period of three months during which delegates meet with residents and representatives of secondary associations to hear proposals and consider a wide range of possible projects that the city might fund in the region. Typical projects include such things as street paving

---

5 For more detailed accounts, see, for example, Gianpaolo Baiocchi, *Militants and Citizens: The Politics of Participatory Democracy in Porto Alegre* (Stanford: Stanford University Press, 2005), and "Participation, Activism and Politics: The Porto Alegre Experiment," in Fung and Wright (eds), *Deepening Democracy*, pp. 45–76; and Boaventura de Sousa Santos, "Participatory Budgeting in Porto Alegre: Towards a Redistributive Democracy," *Politics and Society* 26: 4 (1998), pp. 461–510.

6 While the PT won the mayoral election in 1988, it did not win a majority of seats in the city council, which remained in the control of the traditional clientelist parties. The problem then was how to enact any meaningful progressive policies without controlling the city council. The PB was a central part of the solution—a kind of end run around the city council.

and repair, sewage construction and maintenance, daycare centers, public housing, and healthcare clinics. At the end of three months, these delegates report back to a second regional plenary assembly with a set of regional budget proposals (or, in the case of the city-wide thematic plenary assemblies, with budget proposals on the thematic issues). At this second plenary, proposals are ratified by a vote of people participating in the meeting, and two delegates and substitutes are elected to represent the assembly in a city-wide body called the Participatory Budgeting Council, which meets over the following several months to formulate an integrated city-wide budget from these regional and thematic budgetary proposals. It is mainly at this point that technical experts enter the process in a systematic way, making estimates of the costs of different projects and discussing technical constraints on various proposals. Since citizen representatives are in most cases non-professionals, city agencies offer courses and seminars on budgeting for council delegates as well as for interested participants from the regional assemblies. At the end of this process, the council submits a proposed budget to the mayor, who can either accept the budget or through veto remand it back to the council for revision. Once a budget has been agreed on by the mayor and the council, it is finally submitted to the regular city council for formal adoption. The whole process takes about six months and involves tens of thousands of city residents in active policy-making deliberations.

When the participatory budget was first introduced, it was conceived as a way for citizens as individuals to actively participate in core decision making in city governance. Over time, however, much of this participation became mediated by secondary associations in civil society. In particular, most of the people chosen within the plenary assemblies to serve as delegates in the regional and thematic budget councils are active participants in civil society associations of one sort or another. This means that the delegates are embedded in broader social networks and settings within which budget priorities are discussed, thus extending the social reach of the public deliberation on the issues. These connections of delegates to secondary associations also deepen the ways in which the participatory budget functions as a mechanism of social empowerment. Over time, therefore, the participatory budget has become a kind of amalgam of direct democracy and associative democracy.

Of course, in practice, this process is often messy, with many conflicts and glitches. There have been times when particular regional assemblies were captured by traditional clientelistic political leaders and attempts made to use the budget for patronage purposes.[7] In other instances the participatory assemblies failed to produce a coherent set of proposals. Still, taken as a whole, the participatory budget process has been an enormous success, both in terms of its claims as an experiment in deepening direct democracy and its effectiveness in the practical tasks of formulating city budgets.

A number of indicators suggest that this is a successful institutional experiment in deepening participatory democracy:

1. *There has been a massive shift in spending towards the poorest regions of the city.* As one would predict in a deliberative process where reasons and needs rather than power play the central role in allocations, the neediest parts of the city have gotten the most funding.

2. *Participation levels of citizens in the process have been high and sustained.* Although in recent years participation has declined significantly due to austerity budgets in Brazil (which meant there has been very little discretionary spending available for budgetary allocations at the urban level), throughout most of the history of the participatory budget somewhere around 8 percent of the adult population participated in at least one meeting in a typical budgetary cycle. Furthermore, active participation is not limited to highly educated people with lots of "cultural capital." Through his careful research on patterns of actual participation, Gianpaolo Baiocchi demonstrates that while the most disadvantaged and uneducated segments of the population are under-represented among both the participants at meetings and among elected delegates and councilors, it is not the case that the participatory budget process is dominated by educated elites.[8]

3. *There has been a clear thickening of civil society stimulated by the participatory process.* Often sociologists believe that the density of social networks and vitality of secondary associations

---

7   See Rebecca Abers, "From Clientelism to Cooperation: Participatory Policy and Civic Organizing in Porto Alegre, Brazil," *Politics and Society* 26: 4 (1998), pp. 511–37.
8   Baiocchi, "Participation, Activism and Politics: The Porto Alegre Experiment," p. 54

in civil society are largely the result of deep-rooted cultural and historical factors and not subject to rapid transformation. As Baiocchi richly shows, there has been a steady development of associational life in the city as groups form to better articulate their needs through the participatory budget process.

4. *Corruption has largely disappeared: this is a transparent, clean process.* The political opposition to the Workers' Party was unable to demonstrate any significant corruption in the process in the city of Porto Alegre, in spite of considerable efforts to do so. While there have been corruption scandals involving the Workers' Party at the national and state level, the Porto Alegre city government was free of such problems.

5. *The vote for the PT increased significantly over several electoral cycles within the city*, indicating that this process generated high levels of legitimation. Left parties elected in poor countries typically have quite short tenures in office: they raise expectations which they cannot fulfill and trigger concentrated opposition by right-wing political forces which leads to their defeat in fairly short order. In Porto Alegre the PT was able to increase and then sustain its electoral support over three electoral cycles—1992, 1996, and 2000. It was only in the context of scandals around the PT at higher levels of government, especially connected to the Lula presidency, that its local support declined in 2004 and it lost the mayoral election.

6. *There are some indications that tax compliance has increased among the middle class and affluent*, even though tax surveillance and enforcement has not really changed and the more affluent segments of Porto Alegre are not the principle beneficiaries of the participatory budget.[9] The problem of tax cheating is a universal issue in contemporary societies, but the non-payment of taxes is a particularly severe problem in places like Brazil with histories of corruption and bureaucratic incompetence in the machinery of tax surveillance. The increase in apparent compliance in Porto Alegre suggests that the enhanced democratic legitimacy and

---

9 The claim that tax compliance has improved was made to me by an economist in the Mayor's planning office in Porto Alegre and by several staff members involved in the participatory budgeting process. I have not seen any systematic research to verify this claim, so it should be treated cautiously.

transparency of the process may have begun to affect norms of civic responsibility and obligation.[10]

It is, of course, far from clear how widely this innovative experiment can be extended to other places, issues, contexts, or scales. But of course, in 1989 when this process was started by the PT in Porto Alegre, virtually no one would have imagined that it would work so effectively there either. The limits of possibility are not something about which we can have definitive knowledge before testing them. In any case, a wide range of other places are experimenting with various forms of participatory budgeting—in other cities in Brazil, in other Latin American countries, and in Europe—and preliminary research suggests that in at least some of these other cases the adaptations have been successful.[11]

General principles of institutional design: empowered participatory governance

Though the experience of Porto Alegre is remarkable, it offers lessons for democratic governance that extend beyond matters of municipal budgeting and beyond the particular political and cultural situation of Southern Brazil. The deep kinds of democratic engagement found in Porto Alegre can potentially be created in many different contexts, and generate similar kinds of benefits despite the differences of application. Empowered, participatory forms of direct democracy can increase the involvement and commitment of citizens in public life, make officials and

---

10 Margaret Levi, in *Of Rule and Revenue* (Berkeley: University of California Press, 1989), argues that high levels of tax compliance require two conditions to be met: first, most people believe it is a civic obligation to pay taxes because the funds raised are used for legitimate purposes, and, second, they believe most other people fulfill this obligation. Corruption by public officials erodes the first condition. This in turn increases the levels of tax cheating which erodes the second condition.

11 For a discussion of participatory budgeting in Europe, see Yves Sintomer, Carsten Herzberg, and Anja Rocke, "Participatory Budgeting in Europe: Potentials and Challenges," *International Journal of Urban and Regional Research* 32: 1 (2008), pp. 164–78. For a discussion of participatory budgeting in other Brazilian cities, see Leonardo Avritzer, "New Public Spheres in Brazil: Local Democracy and Deliberative Politics," *International Journal of Urban and Regional Research* 30: 3 (2006), pp. 623–37. For a discussion of cases elsewhere in Latin America, see Daniel Chavez and B. Goldfrank, *The Left in the City: Participatory Local Governments in Latin America* (London: Latin America Bureau, 2004).

politicians more accountable, improve the effectiveness of government, and make social policies more just.

On the basis of our research on Porto Alegre and several other cases, as well as our understanding of broader issues in the theory of democracy, Archon Fung and I have identified seven elements that characterize this kind of democratic process. The first six concern aspects of the internal design of EPG institutions; the seventh concerns an important aspect of the sociopolitical environment of such institutions which contributes to their robustness and stability.

1. Bottom-up empowered participation

The first design principle is perhaps the most obvious. In EPG many government decisions are determined through a process of popular participation. Ordinary people—perhaps as residents of neighborhoods or as consumers of government services, certainly as citizens of a democracy—should participate in the details of decisions that affect their lives. In EPG, this participation usually occurs in face-to-face meetings.

Now, public participation is nothing new in government. In EPG, however, participation is *empowered*, not simply *expressive* or *symbolic*. Participation in EPG institutions does not just give people a way of expressing their views on matters of public concern, but involves actual decision-making powers significantly involving direct participation. In the familiar institutions of representative democracy, ordinary citizens are involved in politics only to the extent that they choose decision makers—their representatives—through elections and voice their opinions through various channels of communication. The ideal of empowered participatory governance involves ordinary citizens directly in the deliberations and problem-solving processes through which decisions are made.

2. Pragmatic orientation

At the center of political decision making in EPG institutions is what might be termed a pragmatic orientation towards concrete problem solving. The idea is to bring people to the political table who share a common desire to accomplish certain concrete, practical goals even if they also have significant conflicts of interests outside of the immediate problem-solving agenda. The underlying assumption here is that if actors can for a time suspend their attachment to specific conceptions of their interests and get down to the practical issues of solving problems, then in the course of deliberation and experimentation their interests are likely to evolve along with their discovery of solutions to problems. While this may not result in a broad, general consensus, it can reduce the sharpness of antagonistic interests in ways that facilitate collaboration.[12]

This may mean that certain issues are "off the table" because they are not tractable to such a practical orientation, and this in turn may mean that the pragmatic orientation deflects political energy away from more radical challenges to inequalities of privilege and power. This can become a significant limitation of EPG. But the idea is that pragmatic solutions to real problems are often possible in spite of these broader conflicts and inequalities, and further that in the long run empowering people to deal with concrete problems can set the stage for more profound reconfigurations of power.

One common criticism of participatory democracy is that people are too apathetic, ignorant, or busy to participate. Evidence from empirical cases discussed in *Deepening Democracy*, however, suggests that when there are opportunities for people to become involved in decisions addressing practical problems that are deeply important to them, they do participate in substantial numbers. Poor people often participate more than wealthy ones when such opportunities are available.

3. Deliberation

The third principle addresses *how* decisions are made in EPG. In many political processes, decisions are determined according to the force of greater numbers—as when people vote according to their preferences or interests. In other contexts, for example government agencies and corporations, decisions are often made according to a hierarchy of expertise or status. In a conventional liberal democracy, the basic idea is that political decisions are the result of majority rule, where majorities are constructed through various complex processes of mobilizing support and bargaining. The bargaining involves compromises, through which conflicts of interest may be resolved, but the bottom line is that the majority rules by exercising power.

---

12 The importance of a pragmatic orientation has been stressed most systematically by Charles Sable in his various works on what he calls "democratic experimentalism." See in particular Michael C. Dorf and Charles F. Sabel, "A Constitution of Democratic Experimentalism," *Columbia Law Review* 98: 2 (1998).

In EPG, by contrast, participants make decisions as much as possible through deliberation. In the ideal, participants offer reasons, appealing to common interests or commonly held principles, to persuade one another of the proper course of action or problem-solving strategy. In EPG decisions are made in a way that allows a significant place for listening to and perhaps accepting alternative arguments and good reasons, rather than simply engaging in bargaining, strategic maneuvering, exchanges of favors, and so forth. In such deliberation, as social theorist Jürgen Habermas has written, the only force is the peculiar force of the better argument.

4. Devolution and decentralization

In order for bottom-up participation to be meaningful, it is essential that significant aspects of real decision-making power within the machinery of the state be devolved to local units of action such as neighborhood councils, local school councils, workplace councils, and so on. The people acting within these kinds of localized councils must be charged with devising and implementing solutions and be held accountable to performance criteria. The councils are not merely advisory bodies, but are rather endowed with substantial public authority to act on the results of their deliberation. Decision making is moved downward to the locus of problems as far as possible.

5. Recombinant decentralization

While the design principle of devolution and decentralization is familiar, the idea of "recombinant decentralization" is not. Usually discussions of governance structures draw a fairly sharp contrast between centralized and decentralized patterns of decision making. A distinctive feature of EPG, however, is a specific way of understanding the articulation of centralized and decentralized processes. Though basic decisions about means and ends are decentralized in EPG, there is a substantial role for central government and central authority as well. Local units do not operate as autonomous, atomized sites of decision making. Instead the institutional design involves linkages of accountability and communication that connect local units to muscular central power. These central offices—for instance the mayor's office or the headquarters of a police department or school system—can reinforce the quality of local democratic deliberation and problem solving in a variety of ways: by coordinating and distributing resources; by solving problems that local units cannot address by themselves; by rectifying pathological or incompetent decision making in failing groups; and by diffusing innovations and learning across boundaries.

Unlike ordinary bureaucratic, top-down, hierarchical models of organization, however, central authorities in EPG do not call the shots by developing plans and issuing orders for subordinates to execute. Instead, these central authorities *support* the problem-solving deliberations of more local, participatory entities and *hold them accountable* for operating in fair and effective ways.

Unlike more anarchist political models in which concerns for liberation lead to demands for *autonomous* decentralization, empowered participatory governance thus suggests new forms of *centrally coordinated decentralization* that reject both democratic centralism and strict decentralization as unworkable. The rigidity of the former leads it too often to disrespect local circumstances and intelligence and as a result it has a hard time learning from experience. Uncoordinated decentralization, on the other hand, isolates citizens into small units, surely a foolhardy measure for those who do not know how to solve a problem but suspect that others, somewhere else, do. Thus these reforms attempt to construct connections that spread information between local units and hold them accountable, and this requires a strong, effective center.

6. State-centered institutionalization

A sixth characteristic of institutional innovations like the participatory budget is that they are both deeply connected to formal institutions of state governance and involve significant transformations of those institutions. Many spontaneous activist efforts or projects led by non-governmental organizations or social movement groups share some of the characteristics of EPG. However, they seek to influence state outcomes through outside pressure, or sometimes to organize activities that operate parallel to official state programs. In both cases, they leave intact the basic institutions of state governance.

By contrast, EPG reforms attempt to remake official institutions. EPG experiments are authorized by the state to make substantial decisions, and, most crucially, they try to change the central procedures of power rather than merely attempt occasionally to influence what the state does. These transformations attempt to institutionalize the ongoing participation of ordinary citizens, most often in their role as consumers of public goods, in the direct determination of what those goods are and how they should be best provided.

This perpetual participation stands in contrast, for example, to the relatively brief democratic moments in both campaign-based social movements and electoral competitions in ordinary politics in which leaders/elites mobilize popular participation for specific outcomes. If popular pressure becomes sufficient to implement some favored policy or elected candidate, the moment of broad participation usually ends; subsequent legislation, policy making, and implementation then occurs in the largely isolated state sphere. In EPG the goal is to create durable institutions for the sustainable empowered participation of ordinary citizens in the activities of the state, rather than simply instigate episodic changes in state policy.

7. Countervailing power: the broader context of participatory empowerment

Many on the left would argue that EPG is impossible in most current societies because the differences of power—between workers and bosses, citizens and government officials, wealthy and poor citizens—are so great that fair deliberation is impossible. EPG institutions, from this perspective, are merely one additional arena in which the strong can dominate the weak. While I believe that the prospects for empowered participatory governance are not so dismal, I also believe that attempts at creating and consolidating institutions of empowered participation are very unlikely to be durable in the absence of what can be called *organized countervailing power* in the environment of such institutions. "Countervailing power" refers to a wide variety of processes that reduce—and perhaps even neutralize—the power advantages of ordinarily powerful groups and elites in the contexts of these governance institutions. Popular political parties, unions, and social movement organizations are the characteristic vehicles for such countervailing power. So, the argument here is this: empowered participatory governance requires some form of organized countervailing power in order to be sustained over time. If it is to work, it requires popular mobilization.

The most enthusiastic supporters of pragmatist approaches to invigorating democratic institutions through collaborative problem solving tend to minimize the importance of countervailing power. Michael Dorf and Charles Sable, for example, believe that the interests of actors are sufficiently underdetermined by their social positions so that once they are embedded in the ongoing process of democratic experimentalist problem solving their interests will evolve along with the solution to problems. Interests, therefore, are basically endogenous to the dynamics of problem-solving institutions rather than given exogenously by power relations within the society at large. This is how Dorf and Sable frame the problem:

> Facing urgent problems that none can solve alone and seeking methods of establishing joint accountability, parties will often prefer to explore a potential solution, even if they are unsure of its outcome, than to do nothing. . . . Once begun, pragmatic problem solving loosens the hold of interest by fitfully darting, as it were, beyond its reach, thereby discovering solutions bit by bit in the unfamiliar territory beyond the reach of bounded rationality and habitual calculations of advantage. Such discoveries beget others: The value to all of the current, partial innovation (measured as improvements in the performance of current problem-solving institutions) will likely be increased substantially by the next innovation, and (as in the case of learning by monitoring in firms) the continuous exchange of operating information among the collaborators will reduce the risk that any party can use the novel arrangements for self-dealing. In time, therefore, emerging solutions change what the actors do and how they rely on one another. Their very ideas of what is possible come to reflect these entanglements; 'self'-interest assumes as the starting point for subsequent calculations the surprises of practical deliberation that formerly confounded it. Thus, it is the very practical particularity of this deliberation—above all the novelty that results when diverse standpoints are brought to bear on unfamiliar alternatives—that advances the good of all participants.[13]

This extremely optimistic view of the plasticity of interests might be plausible if the persons engaged in the pragmatic problem-solving activities of democratic experimentalism were somehow insulated from the broader power relations of the society in which they lived. But this is simply not the case: pragmatic problem solving always occurs within social structures with powerful collective actors connected to pre-given interests continually interacting with people engaged in the problem-solving process. Unless

---

13   Dorf and Sabel, "A Constitution of Democratic Experimentalism," p. 322.

forms of countervailing power exist which can at least partially
blunt those intrusions, empowered participatory governance is
unlikely to generate solutions that sustainably advance the well-
being of subordinated groups.

New institutions of direct democracy containing these elements of
empowered participatory governance have the potential to significantly deepen the involvement of ordinary citizens in the exercise
of state power. Direct democracy, however, cannot be the only
pillar of a socially empowered democratic state. It is also essential
to formulate real utopian designs for representative democracy
and for associational democracy.

REPRESENTATIVE DEMOCRACY:
SKETCHES OF TWO PROPOSALS

More has been written about the problem of deepening and
revitalizing representative democracy than any other form of
democratic institution. The longstanding discussion in political
science about the relative merits of different electoral rules of
the game—such as single-member districts with plurality voting,
various forms of proportional representation, and instant runoff
elections—is basically about how alternative rules affect various
political values: representativeness of elected officials, efficiency,
stability, democracy, and pluralism. Debates over how best
to draw the boundaries of electoral districts are fundamentally
about the meaning of "representation" and "representativeness."
Similarly, the vigorous discussion, especially in the United States,
about campaign finance reform is primarily about the thinness of
representative democracy when private money plays such a pre-
eminent part in shaping electoral outcomes.

I will not review these relatively familiar discussions here, but
instead briefly sketch two recent proposals for enhancing the
democratic quality of representative democracy: egalitarian public
financing of politics, and randomly selected citizen assemblies.

Egalitarian public financing of electoral campaigns

Bruce Ackerman has proposed a novel institutional device which
potentially could have the consequence of both marginalizing
the role of wealth in electoral politics and creating a much more

deeply egalitarian form of financing politics in general, not just conventional electoral campaigns.[14] While the proposal was specifically designed to remedy the inadequacies of campaign financing in the United States under the very strong constraints of Supreme Court rulings that financial contributions to political campaigns constitute a form of "free speech," the general idea behind the Ackerman proposal is relevant to any political system in which citizens have unequal resources to contribute to political activity. The basic idea is simple: At the beginning of every year, every citizen would be given a special kind of debit card which Ackerman dubs a *patriot card*, but which I would prefer to call a *democracy card*. He proposes putting $50 on each card. In the US, with 220 million people above the age of eighteen, this would cost a total of roughly $11 billion per year. The funds on this card can be used exclusively for electoral campaigns: to contribute to a candidate for a specific electoral campaign or to a political party that participates in elections.[15] However—and this is the pivotal condition that makes this a radical egalitarian proposal—any candidate or party accepting funds from democracy cards cannot accept funds from *any* other source.[16] But why should candidates and parties opt for this restriction? Why not still court the fat cats and rely on private funding? There are two reasons for this: First, if the funding level of the democracy cards is sufficiently high, it will swamp other sources of funding. There will simply be much more money to be had through the democracy card "political market" for funding than in the private funding market, and since the two sources of funding cannot be mixed, most candidates will find it advantageous to raise funds from voters. Second, once the system is in place and becomes part of the normative order of political life, the use of private funding is itself likely to become a political issue. Candidates who rely on the democratic mechanism

---

14 Bruce Ackerman, *Voting With Dollars: A New Paradigm for Campaign Finance* (New Haven: Yale University Press, 2004).

15 While the democracy card proposal is specifically directed at financing elections, a modified version of the proposal could allow funds to be used for other forms of political action—for example, referenda, lobbying, or social movements. The central issue is that of creating a mechanism in which inequalities generated in the economic sphere are less easily translated into inequalities in financial resources for actors in the political sphere.

16 This prohibition on mixing private and public funding while allowing unlimited private funding for those who receive no public funds is what makes the democracy card consistent with the existing US Supreme Court rulings on the constitutional issues concerning restricting private spending on elections.

of seeking funding from equally endowed citizens will have a potent weapon to raise against candidates who seek funding from corporations and wealthy individuals.

The democracy card would set in motion a very different kind of electoral process. In effect, all elections would have essentially two phases: first, a phase in which candidates and parties attempt to recruit democracy card money from citizens, and second, a phase in which parties and candidates would use those funds in electoral competition. Of course, under current conditions electoral politics also have these two phases. Electoral campaigns in any democratic system require financial resources, so the question is whether the mechanisms available for providing these funds are consistent with democratic principles of political equality. Under the existing rules of the game, the first phase is a radically inegalitarian process: wealthy people and corporations are major players in the game of recruiting funding. What the system of democracy cards does is restore a strong notion of political equality to both phases of the electoral process. In addition to one-person-one-vote in the casting of ballots, there is now one-person-one-card in the funding of elections. The mechanism therefore provides public funding for electoral politics based on a radically egalitarian principle—each citizen has exactly the same capacity to contribute financially to political activity.

The actual mechanics of a democracy card system as elaborated by Ackerman has many other components. For example, one problem in such a system of election financing is how candidates can acquire the necessary funds to be able to campaign for democracy dollars in the first place. Ackerman proposes a mechanism by which candidates, after getting a certain number of signatures, can get initial direct public funding in the form of a campaign grant. This would provide the necessary start-up funding for the democracy-dollar recruiting phase of the electoral process. There would also need to be rules to prevent scams—situations in which a pseudo candidate recruits democracy dollars for personal consumption rather than electoral campaigns. One can also imagine additional rules by which some or all of a citizen's democracy dollars could be used to fund the non-electoral political activity of activist and lobbying groups. If the scope of funding targets for the cards was expanded, perhaps the amount in the card would also have to be increased. The rules might also have to vary under electoral systems in which parties play a bigger role than they do in the United States, and it might have to be modified in various ways to accommodate local as well as national politics. The key thing is that a well-designed system of public financing of electoral campaigns through a system of democracy cards would largely remove private money from the political process without ceding control over allocation of political financing to the state. It would thus deepen the political equality and efficacy of citizens. The state provides the funds, but citizens determine the allocations.

It might first appear that the democracy card proposal is really just a small, almost technical reform, mainly relevant to electoral systems deeply corrupted by the role of wealth in private campaign finance, as in the US. In many countries, lacking the peculiar constitutional rule that spending money is a form of free speech, there are sufficiently effective constraints on private funding that electoral democracy works reasonably well. A democracy card system might seem of little relevance in such cases. I think this is a mistake. While of course the details of a democracy card would need to vary depending on national context, creating an egalitarian mechanism through which individual citizens can contribute resources to political purposes would constitute a move towards greater political justice and deeper democracy in *all* capitalist democracies. The democracy card would contribute to a broad process of social empowerment in two primary ways. First, it would reduce one of the pathways through which economic power currently affects the use of state power. This would increase the potential for state power to be more fully subordinated to social power and thus be a more effective mechanism for the social control over economic processes. Second, by strengthening the sense of citizen equality and political capacity, the democracy card would encourage wider and deeper forms of citizen participation. Particularly if the idea was extended to a broader range of political activities than just elections, this could contribute to a more egalitarian structure of political associations in civil society which would enhance the prospects for social empowerment.[17]

---

17 Ackerman has a second proposal for institutional innovation which deals with another "democratic deficit" in contemporary liberal democracies: the lack of active citizen participation in public deliberation over political issues. An effective democracy depends upon informed citizens engaged in active deliberation over political issues, but such active involvement seems to be an increasingly marginal part of the lives of most citizens. To counter this problem, Ackerman proposes introducing a new holiday called "Deliberation Day" which would be held several weeks before national elections. This holiday

Random selection citizens' assemblies

The conventional way of understanding the idea of representative democracy is that representation is accomplished by citizens choosing political officials through elections to represent them in legislative and executive office. An alternative notion of representation would select political decision makers through some kind of random selection process. This is more or less how juries are selected in many countries, and it was how legislative bodies were selected in ancient Athens. The question, then, is whether such Random Selection Citizens' Assemblies (or Citizens' Assemblies for short) might be desirable and workable in the world today.

For certain situations, there are several potential advantages of a randomly selected assembly over an elected legislature. First, the members of such an assembly are ordinary citizens, not professional politicians. Their interests are thus likely to match more closely those of the population as a whole. Electoral processes inevitably generate what economists call principal-agent problems in the decision-making process: the elected representative is the agent of the citizens (the principal), but since their interests are not identical there is always the problem of the extent to which the agent will actually carry out the wishes of the principal. A randomly selected assembly directly empowers a subset of the principals and thus minimizes this problem.

Second, not only are the assembly members ordinary citizens, but with appropriate sampling techniques one can ensure that they are a fully representative sample of certain demographic characteristics. Elected legislatures are almost always male dominated; a Citizens' Assembly can, by design, be 50 percent women. Elected legislatures generally under-represent disadvantaged minorities. Again, a Citizens' Assembly can by design ensure such

---

would be devoted to organized, intensive public deliberation of the issues in play in the election. Citizens would be paid a reasonable amount—Ackerman proposes $150—to participate in an all-day event, held in convenient public venues such as public schools, at which a variety of activities would take place: nationally televised presentations by leading political figures; debates among local politicians; small group discussions; question-and-answer sessions with candidates. The objective would be both to raise the level of information acquired by the average voter, but even more importantly, to contribute to a shift in the norms of the political culture towards more active, public involvement of ordinary citizens in political discussion. For details, see Bruce Ackerman and James S. Fishkin, *Deliberation Day* (New Haven: Yale University Press, 2005).

representation—or perhaps even over-representation for certain purposes.

Third, *if* the Citizens' Assembly is capable of engaging in a genuine process of deliberation based on reason-giving and consensus-seeking, then the resulting decisions are more likely to reflect some kind of "general" interest of the citizens than the special interests of particular social forces with strong ties to politicians. In ordinary elected legislatures the problem of the relationship of the legislators to the citizens is not simply that the politicians have interests and preferences distinct from those of ordinary citizens, but that they are embedded in strong social networks and social milieus typically dominated by various types of elites. This is a particularly salient problem where lots of money is needed for electoral campaigns so that politicians are elected as much on the basis of one-dollar-one-vote as one-person-one-vote. But even apart from the money problem, social networks of professional politicians shape the kinds of deliberations that take place in legislatures. If, then, the decisions made by a Citizens' Assembly come out of a deeply deliberative, consensus-seeking process, the resulting decisions are more likely to reflect the "will of the people" than are decisions made by professional politicians.

This, of course, is a very big "if." There are many reasons to be skeptical about the likelihood of a deliberative process of consensus-formation occurring in Citizens' Assemblies. Objections run something like this: Members of the Citizens' Assembly will generally not be very well informed about the issues under discussion at the time they are chosen. Their initial views, therefore, will reflect the kinds of information disseminated by powerful interests through the general media. During the Assembly meetings new information will be presented by experts of various sorts, but most Assembly members will be ill-equipped to evaluate such information, to sift the good from the bad. They will generally not have the education needed for such evaluations, nor the professional experience to know what kind of information is trustworthy and what is not. The quality of decisions made by a democratic body depend not just on the process through which interests are clarified, but also on the quality of the information and the quality of information processing that links interests to decisions. However flawed the configuration of interests might be among professional politicians, at least they are equipped through their staff and party organizations, as well as generally through their own education and experience, to handle the information problems of decision making.

These are real issues and should not be dismissed lightly. Nevertheless, there is good evidence that given suitable conditions ordinary citizens are capable of assimilating large amounts of information, evaluating it in a reasonable manner, and using that information to make well-reasoned collective decisions. James Fishkin, a political scientist whose research centers on the possibilities for public deliberation of complex problems, has conducted a series of experiments in what he terms "deliberative polling." He describes the experiments this way:

> A random, representative sample is first polled on the targeted issues. After this baseline poll, members of the sample are invited to gather at a single place for a weekend in order to discuss the issues. Carefully balanced briefing materials are sent to the participants and are also made publicly available. The participants engage in dialogue with competing experts and political leaders based on questions they develop in small group discussions with trained moderators. Parts of the weekend events are broadcast on television, either live or in taped and edited form. After the deliberations, the sample is again asked the original questions. The resulting changes in opinion represent the conclusions the public would reach, if people had opportunity to become more informed and more engaged by the issues.[18]

While this research does not show that the changes in participants' opinions through the public discussions move those opinions towards some genuine consensus, it does demonstrate that ordinary people are able to assimilate information, engage in sustained discussion, and change their minds in light of that discussion. This, at least, suggests that a Citizens' Assembly, if well organized with appropriate supporting staff, might be able to generate decisions based on a reasoned evaluation of information.

The Fishkin research occurs in the artificial setting of single weekend gatherings of people who know that no real decisions will come out of their deliberations. To get some inkling of the potential of the Citizens' Assembly as a new model of democratic representation and deliberation it would thus be necessary to examine how such an assembly would function in a real world setting with meaningful stakes. One such experiment occurred in the Canadian province of British Columbia.

---

18 James S. Fishkin, "Deliberative Polling: Toward a Better-Informed Democracy," available at http://cdd.stanford.edu.

In 2003 the provincial government of British Columbia created a randomly selected Citizens' Assembly whose mandate was to formulate a referendum proposal for a new electoral system for the provincial parliament.[19] British Columbia had a typical single-member district first-past-the-post parliamentary system. Many people in the province had grown increasingly dissatisfied with the system, some on the grounds that it did not accurately reflect the preferences of voters, others on the grounds that small changes in voting preferences could generate very large changes in parliament, resulting in exaggerated political swings. The problem, then, was to choose an alternative from among the range of electoral rules. One procedure, of course, would be for parliament itself to have chosen the new rules, but since in such a situation the existing politicians would tend to support new rules that would advantage their specific political interests, this could undermine the legitimacy of the change. The solution was to create a Citizens' Assembly on Electoral Reform, consisting of 160 randomly selected delegates—one man and one woman from each of the 79 electoral districts in the province plus two delegates of "first nations" people.

The work on the Citizens' Assembly was carried out in three phases. From January to March of 2004 it met every other weekend in Vancouver for delegates to learn about alternative electoral systems through intensive lectures, seminars, and discussions. Delegates' expenses were paid along with a $150 honorarium for each weekend. In the second phase, during the summer of 2004, the delegates participated in a series of public hearings around the province to bring the issues before the broader public and get public reactions. In the third phase, in the fall of 2004, the Citizens' Assembly met again every other weekend for intensive discussions at the end of which the delegates drafted a referendum proposal for the new electoral law. To the surprise of many they did not choose a straightforward system of proportional representation, but rather what is known as the Single Transferable Vote (STV) system. Amy Lang describes the mechanism as follows:

---

19 This account is based on research by Amy Lang, "But is it For Real? The British Columbia Citizens' Assembly as a model of state-sponsored citizen empowerment," *Politics and Society* 35: 1 (2007), pp. 35–70, and *A New Tool for Democracy? The Contours and Consequences of Citizen Deliberation in the British Columbia Citizens' Assembly on Electoral Reform* (PhD dissertation, Department of Sociology, University of Wisconsin, 2007).

Single Transferable Vote is organized around multimember districts, which increases the proportional distribution of seats, if the districts have enough members. STV also uses a preferential ballot to rank-order candidates in each district. In practice, candidates from the same party compete against one another for voter's preferences, as in a primary system, giving voters more choice about who will be their representative, and undermining a party's ability to control the candidate from that district.[20]

This proposal was then submitted for a popular vote in May of 2005. As things turned out, the referendum received 57.3 percent of the vote, just short of the 60 percent needed for immediate passage.[21]

The British Columbia experiment was very successful as a process, even though the referendum did not pass on its first attempt. As an experiment it was focused on a narrow policy question—the formulation of a new electoral law—but one can imagine extending this idea to a wide range of other settings, including national legislatures.

Many legislative systems have two chambers. What, precisely, is the purpose of having a second chamber in the legislative institutions of a democracy? Roughly, there are two broad kinds of answers to this question: either you want a second chamber because you do not really trust democracy and want to impose constraints on democratic power, or because you do have faith in democracy, but believe that a second chamber is needed to make the political system more deeply democratic. A good example of the first rationale is the British House of Lords, which was based on the belief that electoral democracy is prone to excesses, so some kind of sober institutional check is needed. The device should block or, at least, slow down the process by which representative institutions generate new laws and regulations. The old House of Lords, dominated by hereditary, and then later appointed, peers was just such a brake on electoral democracy. This was only modestly altered when the House of

---

20 Lang, *A New Tool for Democracy?*, pp. 18–19.
21 The major reason the vote failed, according to analysts, was that voters at large were not sufficiently informed about the process and the proposed system. The provincial government had refrained from undertaking a heavy information campaign about the election, fearing that this would undermine the autonomy of the process by suggesting that the government was behind the specific proposal. From the analysis of exit polls, those voters who were well informed about the Citizens' Assembly and the proposal voted strongly for the referendum whereas the level of support among people uninformed about the process was much lower.

Lords was converted to a House of Appointed Notables by the Tony Blair government in 1999.[22]

The second answer to the question "why a second chamber?" imagines that democracy can be invigorated and deepened by the addition of a second chamber. The argument here is not that democracy needs to be checked, but rather that a single mechanism of representation cannot fully realize the democratic ideal. The two chambers of a legislative system, therefore, are designed to embody different mechanisms. For example, one chamber could be elected through a system of standard *territorial-district* representation and a second chamber could be elected on the basis of some principle of *functional representation*, where members represent organized groups (unions, business associations, economic sectors, etc.).

A Citizens' Assembly of *randomly selected* members is another possible form of a second chamber. There are many ways of doing this, but here is a rough sketch of one possibility:

- Members would serve staggered terms, say three years in length.

- The random selection process would be organized to ensure salient demographic groups roughly proportionate representation.

- Remuneration would be set at a high enough level to create strong financial incentives for most citizens to agree to participate, and employers would be required to reinstate members at the end of their terms with no loss of seniority.

- The Citizens' Assembly would function in a manner similar to the existing British House of Lords, being able to slow

---

22 In a federal system such as that of the United States, the second chamber of the national legislature—the Senate—serves a different sort of function since it is meant to reflect the quasi-sovereign status of the states in the federal structure. While this certainly violates principles of political equality at the national level it *could* in principle help preserve this principle at the more local level. In any case, it still operates as a brake on national-level democracy by imposing a check on the chamber which in principle more directly represents citizens with equal voting power. Of course, given the peculiarities of the US system and the serious distortions of equal representation generated by the way voting districts are drawn, it is not clear which chamber is actually more democratic.

up legislation, send it back for reconsideration, but not ultimately veto such legislation.

- The Citizens' Assembly would have a vigorous professional and technical staff to facilitate information, hearings, seminars, and other mechanisms through which Assembly members would both learn to function in the Assembly and acquire the information needed to participate in deliberations.

Prime ministers could not manipulate this system, and nor could their parties. It provides what elected chambers, by their nature, cannot: true diversity of the kinds of people involved in the legislative process. The citizens are neither career politicians nor their cronies. A randomly selected Citizens' Assembly would have a legitimacy stemming from the fact that its members were "of the people," but would always be clearly a secondary chamber. The process of legislating would be improved, but its coherence would not be threatened. The crucial thing is that it affirms the central value of democracy as rule by the people and envisions a democratic order in which ordinary citizens are empowered to be directly involved in the crucial work of law making rather than simply in the task of choosing their law makers. It counters the limitations of competitive party-based electoral democracy by deepening democracy, not constraining it.

There are many other possible uses of "randomocracy," as these kinds of randomly selected, empowered assemblies are sometimes called.[23] One idea is to use "Citizen Juries" in various kinds of policy-making contexts. A jury, after all, is a random selection of citizens empowered by the state to exercise one important type of state power: the power to pass judgments in court cases. There have been proposals to use juries for other kinds of decision making. For example, in cities where there are often complex and conflictual issues over land use and zoning regulations, a citizen jury might be a more effective body for deliberation and consensus formation over these issues than an elected city council or a professional bureaucratic planning department. The problem

---

23 The term "randomocracy" was used by British Columbia Assembly member Jack MacDonald in a pamphlet about the Citizens Assembly, *Randomocracy: A Citizen's Guide to Electoral Reform in British Columbia* (Victoria, BC: FCG Publications, 2005).

with city councils and land use policy, at least in the US, is that both elected councilors and professional planners are often overly influenced by land developers and associated business interests. A deliberative body of ordinary citizens might be better able to deliberate on "the public interest" and balance the contending claims and aspirations.

One final, very interesting idea is to use such assemblies as a way of deepening the democratic character of a long-established kind of institution for direct democracy: citizen initiatives and referenda.[24] Conventional citizen initiatives and referenda work like this: a group of citizens wants to see a new law passed or an existing law repealed, so they develop a proposal, get a required number of signatures, and the proposal then appears on a ballot to be voted on by the electorate. This kind of ballot initiative has been widely used in certain states in the US, most notably California and Washington. It has all the appearance of direct democracy: ordinary citizens decide through direct participation what legislation is passed. There are, however, two critical problems with initiatives and referenda as typically organized in the US. First, just as in ordinary representative elections, private money plays an inordinately large role in disseminating information about these initiatives, especially through the purchase of TV ads. This distorts democratic equality by giving interests backed by money vastly disproportionate influence over the referendum process. This problem is intensified by the second issue: most voters are not deeply engaged with the ballot issues and thus rely mainly on cheap information to make up their minds on how to vote. This is the classic problem of "rational ignorance" in electoral politics.[25] The result is that many voters vote on the basis of very poor-quality information about the issues at stake, and make choices which, had they been well informed, they would not have made.

---

24 "Initiatives" is the term for citizen-proposals to pass new laws; "referenda" is the term for citizen-proposals to repeal existing laws.

25 "Rational ignorance" is a term used by political scientists to describe the problem of acquiring information to make a reasoned choice in political contexts. Since for most people their individual actions are unlikely to make a big difference in the outcome of most political processes, most people are unwilling to spend a lot of time and resources acquiring good-quality information about the issues in play (unless, like academics, they enjoy being well-informed for its own sake). The result is that they rely on cheap information, which mainly means information from TV. The resulting ignorance is rational in the sense of being the outcome of a decision that reflects a rational assessment of individually borne costs and benefits.

Democracy activists in the states of Washington and Oregon have proposed using a randomly selected Citizens Initiative Review (CIR) council to address this problem, and have developed model legislation to make this possible.[26] John Gastil describes the idea this way: "In a nutshell, the CIR would gather a paid random-sample of Washington residents to scrutinize each statewide ballot measure. The results of each panel would be published in the official Voters Guide, which is distributed to every Washington household that has one or more registered voters."[27] The idea here is that this council would hear testimony about the pros and cons of the proposed legislation, read documents, position papers, and other relevant materials on the subject, and then deliberate on the issues in the manner of James Fishkin's deliberative polling. At the end of the process they would vote on the proposal and the results of their vote would be reported to the electorate. The electorate would then have a new kind of signal about how to vote: this is how ordinary citizens like me decided to vote after spending a few days seriously studying and talking about the problem. The results of the CIR council's vote could be widely disseminated in public service ads on television as a counterweight to the cheap information provided by interest groups. This signal would potentially inoculate the electorate from the effects of propaganda in the service of private interests.

ASSOCIATIONAL DEMOCRACY[28]

Of the three forms of democratic institutions, associational democracy has the least prominent place in public consciousness. Indeed, when secondary associations are considered at all in

---

26 The idea for a randomly chosen Citizens Initiative Review council to deliberate over referenda was initially proposed by Ned Crosby and Pat Benn as an extension of Crosby's earlier work on citizen juries. For a careful exposition of the theoretical rationale for a CIR and of the model legislation, see J. Gastil, J. Reedy, and C. Wells, "When Good Voters Make Bad Policies: Assessing and Improving the Deliberative Quality of Initiative Elections," *University of Colorado Law Review* 78 (2007), pp. 1435–88. For a related discussion of citizen juries, see N. Crosby and D. Nethercutt, "Citizens Juries Creating a Trustworthy Voice of the People," in J. Gastil and P. Levine (eds), *The Deliberative Democracy Handbook* (San Francisco: Jossey-Bass, 2005), pp. 111–19.

27 "Citizens Initiative Review," by John Gastil, available at http://faculty.washington.edu.

28 The section draws heavily on the first book in the Real Utopias Project: Joshua Cohen and Joel Rogers, *Associations and Democracy* (London: Verso, 1995).

the discussion of politics and government they are often viewed negatively as subverting democracy by lobbying policy makers on behalf of "special interests" and in other ways fostering "mischiefs of faction" rather than promoting rule by the people and the general interest. Nevertheless, as Joshua Cohen and Joel Rogers write, for better or worse, "such associations play a central role in the politics of modern democratic societies. They help to set the political agenda, to determine choices from that agenda, to implement (or thwart the implementation of) those choices and to shape the beliefs, preferences, self-understandings and habits of thought and action that individuals bring to more encompassing political arenas."[29] It is obvious how the capacity for action and strategy of associations can undermine democracy, hijacking power in the service of elites and particularistic interests. The question is whether political institutions can be designed in such a way as to enable secondary associations to play a positive role in deepening democracy.

Cohen and Rogers argue that there are four principal ways in which associations representing the interests of particular social groups can potentially enhance democracy: they can partially *remedy inequalities in resources* between individuals by enabling otherwise disadvantaged people to pool resources for political purposes; they can contribute to *citizen education* by functioning as "schools of democracy"; they can solve a variety of *information problems* for policy makers; and they can become the central actors within new forms of *collective problem solving*.[30] The first and second of these enhance the extent to which state policies respond to the will of the people; the third and fourth enhance the extent to which state power effectively contributes to solving collective problems that affect the lives of people. A deep democracy is one in which the state is both controlled by the people and serves their interests, and this requires that states be competent. Democracy means rule by the people *over the collective conditions of their lives*, and this requires that the state be effective in shaping those conditions in response to the will of the people. This is where associational democracy is likely to play its most distinctive role in enhancing democracy: enhancing the creative and effective problem-solving capacity of democratic institutions.

Secondary associations can potentially help democratic states

---

29   Cohen and Rogers, *Associations and Democracy*, p. 7.
30   Cohen and Rogers, *Associations and Democracy*, pp. 42–4.

solve very tricky problems of social and economic regulation. The basic issue is this: Legislative bodies establish various kinds of economic and social laws to deal with a wide range of problems; but in order for these laws to be carried out, all sorts of detailed rules, standards, and procedures need to be specified which can only be gestured at in the legislation itself. Traditionally, this task has been delegated to bureaucracies with professional staffs and technical experts whose job it is to specify such rules and implement them. There are situations in which centralized bureaucracies can do this fairly well, but as economic and social conditions have become more complex, this kind of centralized command-and-control process of rule specification and implementation has become much less effective. Centralized administrations are good at imposing uniform rules over homogeneous contexts, but have great difficulty in creating effective rules to deal with highly heterogeneous contexts. When they try to do so they typically produce heavy-handed regulations that are ineffective and often damaging. This is a chronic problem, for example, in relation to environmental and health and safety regulation: ecologies and workplaces are so diverse and complex that one-size-fits-all regulations are rarely satisfactory.

One reaction to these difficulties is to argue for deregulation. If the state cannot competently create standards and effective regulations it should abandon the effort. Let the market solve the problem by having businesses regulate themselves. This is the typical response of conservatives to regulatory failures. However, as Cohen and Rogers observe:

> In many areas of economic and social concern—from the environment and occupational safety and health to vocational training and consumer protection—egalitarian aims are badly served by the state–market dichotomy. . . . Often the right answer to the question, 'Should the state take care of the problem or should it be left to the market?' is a double negative. . . . Where these sorts of problems are encountered, associative governance can provide a welcome alternative or complement to public regulatory efforts because of the distinctive capacity of associations to gather local information, monitor behavior and promote cooperation among private actors. In such cases, the associative strategy recommends attending to the possibility of enlisting them explicitly in the performance of public tasks.[31]

The basic idea, then, is to formally include secondary associations systematically in the central tasks of governance: policy

31 Cohen and Rogers, *Associations and Democracy*, p. 45.

formation, coordination of economic activities, and the monitoring, administering, and enforcing of regulations. Associations would not simply provide external pressure by lobbying politicians and agencies for specific rules; they would be integrated as active participants into these core state functions.

The most familiar way this has occurred (in places other than the United States) is in national-level policy-formation processes involving organized labor, business associations, and the state, through what are usually called neo-corporatist institutions. In the past, especially in northern Europe, such bargaining processes have often played a pivotal role in relation to incomes policy, labor market policy, and other public policies affecting the interests of capital and labor. Many analysts have argued that such corporatist institutions have outlived their usefulness in an era of increasing globalization. Cohen and Rogers argue, to the contrary, that such national-level corporatist bargaining institutions could be even more important in formulating policies in response to the challenges of global economic forces. Consider the key domain of "active labor market policies" concerned with the supply, demand, and quality of labor. For such policies, they write:

> Cooperation among worker and employer representatives [in neo-corporatist policy-making institutions], again in the context of the availability of state assistance, can help in (1) targeting new skill needs in the population and identifying the necessary public and private components of skill delivery; (2) establishing feasible incentive structures across firms and regions—for workers, unions, employers and the unemployed—for developing or upgrading skills within such a structure; (3) providing early warning on the distributive consequences of policy choices; (4) devising programs of subsidy across different regions, or even firms, to respond to leads and lags in labor market adjustments; and (5) hammering out minimal national standards for the transferability of credentials across different local labor markets.[32]

The effectiveness of such national policy-formation processes involving the associations representing employers and workers depends upon the extent to which three conditions are met: first, the associations must be *relatively encompassing*, representing a substantial proportion of the relevant social category; second, the association leadership must be *accountable to membership* through meaningful internal democratic processes; and third, the associations must have significant *powers to sanction members*.

---

32   Cohen and Rogers, *Associations and Democracy*, p. 57.

Where associations are encompassing, the policy bargains worked out among associations are more likely to constitute genuine compromises across the conflicting interests involved. Where leadership is democratically accountable, the policy compromises are more likely to be seen as legitimate. Where associations have powers to sanction members, compliance with the results of policy bargaining is likely to be higher and free riding is less likely to occur. These are all conditions that can be facilitated by public policies, both by creating general legal rules which make the formation of such associations relatively easy and by creating high standards that must be met before an association claiming to represent a relevant group can participate in a state-organized policy-formation process.

While these kinds of neo-corporatist policy-formation processes are most strongly associated with issues of economic policy involving capital and labor, it is possible to extend this model to other policy domains. In 1996, the province of Quebec held a "Summit on Employment and the Economy" to discuss and formulate policies around a range of social questions. Community-based social movements were represented along with the traditional "social partners" of labor and employer organizations. Out of the summit, the *Chantier de l'économie sociale* (the social economy taskforce)[33] was formed to coordinate the participation of social movements in this policy-formation and implementation process. A few years later the *Chantier* became a permanent, autonomous organization, whose elected board of directors as described by its director, Nancy Neamtan, "consists of 28 individuals, elected by different electoral colleges in order to represent the diverse realities of the social economy ... The membership and board of directors includes representatives of co-operative and nonprofit enterprises, local and community development networks, and the large social movements."[34] As we will see in chapter 7, the *Chantier* has played a pivotal role both in formulating a set of public policies to deepen and expand the Quebec social economy, and in directly coordinating activities within it.

The Quebec case illustrates a very important theme for the process of deepening the associational dimension of democracy:

---

33 The literal meaning of "*chantier*" is "building site," or perhaps "workshop," but in this context it is sometimes translated as "taskforce."

34 Nancy Neamtan, "The Social Economy: Finding a Way Between the Market and the State," *Policy Options*, July–August 2005, p. 74.

the associational environment for democratic governance is not a fixed parameter; it can be changed by design. The critical encompassing association in this case, the *Chantier de l'économie sociale*, did not exist when the process was initially begun in the mid 1990s. It was created by design in order to strengthen both the effectiveness of the policy-formation process and its democratic character. The rules of its own governance were created to ensure its encompassing character with respect to the social economy through the creation of an electoral college reflecting the diversity of constituents in the social economy.[35] Its integral role in problem solving, public deliberation, and practical coordination has ensured a relatively high level of commitment of participants in the social economy to the ongoing work of the *Chantier*.

The possibilities for an expanded and deepened associative democracy are not limited to the role of encompassing associations in neo-corporatist peak-level public policy formation. Associative democracy can also function at the local and regional level to solve problems and to design and implement detailed rules and standards of various sorts. Two examples will illustrate this: skill formation within regional labor markets, and habitat conservation for endangered species.

As is well documented by economists and economic sociologists, skill formation often poses a host of serious problems for both workers and employers in capitalist economies. Many of the skills needed on the job are best acquired through training linked to work rather than in specialized vocational schools. Vocational schools certainly have a role in teaching very general skills, but except in very stable and homogeneous technological environments, they are unlikely to train for the skills needed on the job. Employers face a different sort of problem: if they devote resources to training skills that are at all portable—i.e. that workers can use in other firms—then they risk having their trained workers poached by other employers who have not bothered to make such investments. This is a classical free-rider collective action problem: all employers would be better off if they all devoted resources to upgrading the skills of workers, but each employer is tempted to refrain from doing so, thereby saving on the training costs, and

35 In the electoral college of the *Chantier*, the different networks of specific kinds of social economy organizations are each constituted as an electoral body responsible for choosing representatives of that network for the board of directors of the *Chantier*.

then luring the trained workers away from the firms that trained them. The result is that employers refrain from training workers with portable skills and opt instead for technologies that do not require such training.

One solution to this collective action problem is to form new associational institutions to govern skill formation in regional labor markets. One such institutional innovation occurred in the metalworking sector in the Milwaukee, Wisconsin, region beginning in the early 1990s. The United States does not offer an especially favorable environment for developing associational democratic solutions to economic problems—unions are weak, employers are generally skeptical of cooperative solutions to problems of economic governance, and political institutions have traditionally relied more on top-down command-and-control regulations. In spite of this, some headway in developing new associational democratic institutions has occurred in the Milwaukee area. The Wisconsin Regional Training Partnership (WRTP) has brought together labor unions, employers, the state vocational school system, community organizations, and academic researchers from the University of Wisconsin, to formulate a set of skill standards and training procedures for workers in the metalworking sector.[36]

The WRTP is outside of the state system—it is not a state agency, nor an unofficial arm of the state. Rather, it is an autonomous non-profit organization that makes contracts with various state entities, especially the technical college system, and receives significant levels of state funding from a variety of agencies. This state funding brings in its wake oversight and reporting requirements. Labor leadership, both from particular unions and from the union movement as a whole, has provided the most consistent source of initiative, information, and continuity. Employers are also critical participants, but generally their involvement is somewhat more episodic and reactive. The unions involved agreed to allow for greater flexibility in job classifications and the assignment of workers in exchange for employers accepting portable skill standards and providing

---

36 The WRTP was formed in 1992 through the initiative of the Center on Wisconsin Strategy, a research institute at the University of Wisconsin under the direction of Joel Rogers. For detailed information on the WRTP, see Annette Bernhardt, Laura Dresser, and Joel Rogers, "Taking the High Road in Milwaukee: The Wisconsin Regional Training Partnership," *WorkingUSA* 5: 3 (2004), pp. 109–30.

training; and the employers agreed to cooperate with each other and the state vocational education system in creating such standards. The WRTP thus provides an associational device, rooted in a local economy, for engaging in sustained collective problem solving over labor market and training issues and coordinating the development and execution of training programs that emerge out of these deliberations.

According to Laura Dresser, one of the academic researchers linked to the project, the WRTP has helped solve the free-riding problem over training.[37] All of the employers in the sectors involved, she believes, understood the free-riding problem and how it adversely affects the regional economy. Furthermore, there are real costs to employers for participating in the WRTP, both in terms of significant time commitments, especially of key managers, as well as the training costs once programs get established. These costs potentially add to the free-riding problem. Nevertheless, participation and cooperation from nearly all of the employers in the metalworking sectors has been reasonably high. Dresser feels that the WRTP softened the collective action problem, less by imposing sanctions on bad-faith employers (although the WRTP does have some ability to exclude firms from access to some collective resources), than by contributing to a normative environment in which at least a core of employers have come to see how working with the WRTP is of potential benefit to the region as a whole, not just themselves, and have developed a sense of obligation to contribute to this collective good.

A second example of associational democracy at a local level concerns the problem of habitat conservation for endangered species.[38] In the US, the Endangered Species Act of 1973 established relatively stringent, simple rules for protecting endangered species by regulating development in the habitats in which such species lived. In general the rule was to prohibit all economic development within the boundaries of the protected habitat. The restrictiveness of this rule meant that there were always serious battles over listing new species as endangered, since such listings threatened the interests of land owners and developers; and once

---

37 Personal interview, September 2008.
38 This example is discussed in detail in Craig Thomas's contribution to the Real Utopias Project, "Habitat Conservation Planning," in Fung and Wright, *Deepening Democracy*, chapter 5, pp. 144–72.

a species was listed, there was considerable pressure to draw the boundaries of the protected habitat as narrowly as possible. The overall result, from the point of view of species protection, was that fewer species were protected and the protection was less secure than conservationists would have liked. An alternative would have been to have a less restrictive rule in which a standard of *compatible development* (development compatible with the protection of the species), rather than no development at all, would be allowed. The problem with this standard, however, is that it is much more difficult to specify for a given habitat what precisely is "compatible," since this will vary tremendously across habitats depending on the fine-grained details of the context; and even if the rules for compatibility in a given habitat are specified, it is a more complex condition to monitor and enforce than is "no development at all." It is easy to observe a violation of the latter; it is harder to identify a violation of compatible development.

Habitat conservation is thus a good example of the problem of the weakness of bureaucratically centralized command-and-control regulations: uniform regulations are suboptimal, but regulations highly tailored to individual contexts are difficult to formulate and expensive to monitor. An associative democracy solution could look like this: Every habitat which is regulated by the endangered species act would have a habitat planning council consisting of representatives of local environmental conservation groups, landowners and developers, local government, and technical experts from the environmental protection agency. This council would have two responsibilities: first, to formulate a set of rules for compatible development, and second, to monitor compliance with those rules. Proposed rules would be reviewed by the supervising government agency, but with the presumption that the rules would be accepted. The default in the case of failure of the habitat planning council to agree on a set of habitat management rules would be the imposition of uniform no-development rules. This would give an incentive for all parties to agree to the more flexible rules. Although the interests of environmentalists and developers engaged in formulating the rules are opposed, they would both benefit from finding appropriate compatible-development rules, and this would provide the basis for the process of deliberation, pragmatic problem solving, and consensus formation. The process of sitting at the table and working through the issues could also potentially build the kind of micro-level trust needed for effective monitoring of the rules once they have been adopted.[39]

A regulatory process very much along these lines was developed by the US environmental protection agency in the 1980s and used on a selective basis in the 1990s. As analyzed by Craig Thomas, the experiment had decidedly mixed results. In some cases, where there already existed strong local environmental groups, councils were able to devise and implement effective rules of habitat management consistent with the goals of both environmentalists and developers. In other cases the councils were basically a sham, dominated by developers who manipulated the process to their own advantage.

The limitations of the habitat planning council experiments reflect the inherent difficulty of deepening associational democracy. In the absence of vigorous grass-roots secondary associations, efforts at constructing associational democratic problem-solving institutions are highly vulnerable to domination by small groups of well-resourced actors, typically representing already powerful interests. This is why the project of using associational processes to enhance democracy must be attentive to the problem of invigorating associations rooted in working-class and popular constituencies rather than simply relying on the existing array of associations.

DEEPENING DEMOCRACY AND SOCIAL EMPOWERMENT

Four of the seven pathways to social empowerment discussed in chapter 5 directly involve the state: statist socialism, social democratic statist regulation, associational democracy, and participatory socialism. In all of these the key issue is the relationship between social power in civil society and state power. Unless there are effective mechanisms for subordinating state power to social power in civil society, none of these pathways can effectively translate social power into control over the

---

39 Similar associational stakeholder councils have been used for a variety of other environmental regulations, such as watershed management and forestry management. For an example of a network of stakeholder watershed councils with some elements of associative democracy, see "2007 Watershed Councils in Oregon: An Atlas of Accomplishments," available at http://www.oregonwatersheds.org. For an example of a controversial forestry council that has had a significant impact in the management of a forest in the Sierra Mountains of California, see the discussions of the Quincy Library Group at http://www.qlg.org.

economy. If socialism as an alternative to capitalism is at its core economic democracy, it is essential, to use the words of Boaventura Santos, that democracy itself be democratized.[40]

The three forms of democracy we have looked at in this chapter—direct democracy, representative democracy, and associational democracy—constitute three solutions to the problem of how to subordinate the state to civil society. In direct democracy this occurs by delegating aspects of state power to the empowered participation and collective deliberations of ordinary citizens. In representative democracy the subordination of state to civil society is accomplished by democratically selected representatives of citizens making decisions on their behalf. And in associational democracy, subordination of the state occurs by associations rooted in civil society being empowered to perform various kinds of public functions. A thoroughly democratized democracy will involve deepening all three of these forms of democracy.

Traditional Marxist accounts of the state and democracy are generally highly skeptical of the possibility of this kind of democratic deepening, so long as the economic structure remains capitalist. The central thesis of most Marxist theories of the state is that the state in a capitalist society has a distinctively capitalist character: it is a *capitalist state*, not just a *state in capitalist society*.[41] This means that the institutions of the state are structured in such a way that they strongly tend to reproduce capitalist relations and to block anti-capitalist possibilities. Deviations from this functionally integrated configuration are possible, but when they occur they set in motion disruptions of the functioning of capitalism. These disruptions in turn tend to trigger counter-measures to restore reproductive functionality. The limits of stable deviation of the capitalist state from a form that is functionally compatible with capitalism, therefore, tend to be relatively narrow.

---

40 See Boaventura de Sousa Santos (ed.), *Democratizing Democracy: Beyond the Liberal Democratic Canon* (London: Verso, 2006).

41 The rhetorical contrast between "the state in capitalist society" and "the capitalist state" comes from an influential debate between Nicos Poulantzas and Ralph Miliband in the 1970s. See Nicos Poulantzas, "The Problem of the Capitalist State," *New Left Review* 58 (November–December 1969), pp. 67–78; Ralph Miliband, "The Capitalist State: Reply to Poulantzas," *New Left Review* 59 (January–February 1970), pp. 53–60; Ralph Miliband, "Poulantzas and the Capitalist State," *New Left Review* 82 (November–December 1973), pp. 83–92. The most systematic account of the structural properties of the state that give it a distinctively capitalist form is provided by Göran Therborn, in *What Does the Ruling Class Do When It Rules?* (London: NLB, 1978).

If these arguments are correct, then a meaningful, sustainable deepening of democracy within capitalism is just not possible. Empowered participatory governance may be a reasonable design for citizen participation in direct democracy, but within capitalism this will be confined to marginal niches. A robustly egalitarian system of representative democracy in which the people control the process of representation more profoundly may enhance the democratic quality of that representation, but again, within capitalism such devices would have little effect on the extent to which the state could actually empower civil society over capital. And while associational democracy may be an important ingredient in a radical democracy, within a capitalist economy the asymmetries of power across associations means that associational democracy will always engage in problem solving on terms favorable to capitalism.

These are important criticisms of the possibilities of social empowerment and the state within capitalism. They depend centrally on the idea that societies are coherent, integrated systems in which the parts must fit together fairly well in order for the system to function tolerably. The alternative perspective is that societies are loosely coupled systems rather than tightly integrated totalities. They are more like an *ecology* than an *organism*: quite hostile elements can coexist in shifting uneven equilibria without the system exploding. We have already encountered this idea in the notion of hybrid economic structures in which capitalist, statist, and socialist economic structures coexist in complex ways. The same kind of argument concerns forms of the state. This means that although it does make sense to elaborate the theoretical concept of a capitalist-type of state, actual state institutions can combine capitalist and non-capitalist forms. The state can contain internally contradictory elements pushing it to act in contradictory ways. States, like economic structures, are structural hybrids. So, while it is indeed the case that the state in capitalist society is a capitalist state, it is not *merely* a capitalist state: it is a hybrid structure within which capitalist forms are dominant.

This leaves open the question of how contradictory these elements within the state might become without the state becoming a chaotic institution incapable of reproducing existing class relations. There are undoubtedly limits. The nature of those limits and their implications for emancipatory transformation will be a central concern in Part III of this book.

REAL UTOPIAS II:
SOCIAL EMPOWERMENT
AND THE ECONOMY

At the center of a socialist alternative to capitalism, in whatever way socialism is understood, is the problem of economic institutions, specifically the social organization of power over the allocation of resources and control of production and distribution. In statist conceptions of socialism such power and control operates primarily through the state, in the strongest version through the direct state ownership of the principal means of production and comprehensive central planning. In the social empowerment conception of socialism proposed here, the problem of controlling economic processes is less clear-cut. There are multiple, heterogeneous institutional forms along the various pathways through which social power can be exercised over the production and distribution of goods and services.

In most of the specific proposals we will consider here, the institutional designs for social empowerment leave a substantial role for markets, and thus in one sense or another they tend to envision some sort of "market socialism." This goes against the grain of traditional Marxian conceptions of socialism as the transcendence not only of capitalist class relations but also of the market itself. In traditional Marxism the harms generated by capitalism as a system of production are attributed both to the pernicious effects of the market and to power and exploitation linked to the class relation between capitalists and workers. The vision of a world beyond capitalism thus revolves around both the move towards the egalitarianism expressed in the anti-class aphorism "to each according to need, from each according to ability," and the aspiration for a rationally ordered economy in which the production and distribution of goods and services is organized through some mechanism of collective planning.

Few theorists today hold on to the belief that a complex, large-scale economy could be viable without some role for markets—understood as a system of decentralized, voluntary exchanges involving prices that are responsive to supply and demand—in economic coordination.[1] This does not imply that an economy must be coordinated by largely unregulated "free" markets, or even that the vast majority of economic needs will be met through market exchanges, but simply that decentralized exchanges involving market-generated prices will play a significant role in economic organization. To most contemporary critics of capitalism, comprehensive planning, whether organized through centralized bureaucratic institutions or through participatory decentralized institutions, no longer seems a viable alternative. This leaves open the extent to which markets should operate under tight or weak constraints in relation to democratic priorities established through the state and other pathways of social empowerment, and the precise mechanisms by which the negative effects of market forces would be neutralized.

In this chapter we will explore a range of proposals for forms of economic structures and institutions that move us in a direction beyond capitalism by enhancing the scope and penetration of social power in economic activities. This set of proposals does not constitute a complete inventory of policy initiatives for the left. Many worthy progressive policies which would enhance the quality of life of people and contribute to solving a range of concrete problems around healthcare, inequality, poverty, energy, environmental protection, and so on, are not specifically *policies of social empowerment*. Egalitarian taxation and transfer policies that reduce inequality might further egalitarian ideals of justice, but they do not themselves shift the economic structure towards a hybrid within which social power has greater weight. Increased government environmental regulation and vigorous energy policies to develop renewable energies would be desirable and should be part of a left political program, but again, they might not do much directly to strengthen the institutions of economic democracy.

Our concern in this chapter, then, is to explore a variety of

---

1 There are some anti-capitalists who believe that a decentralized, democratically planned economy in which there is no role at all for markets is feasible. One of the more influential statements of this position is offered by Michael Albert, who argues in his book *Parecon* (a contraction of "participatory economy") (London: Verso, 2003) that even a complex global economy can be organized and coordinated through participatory planning rooted in producer and consumer councils. See the discussion at the end of this chapter for a sketch of this proposal.

institutional designs and proposals that could constitute some of the key components of a socialism of social empowerment. Some of these are purely theoretical models; others have existed in at least limited forms in various places. Some of them involve a transformation of the overall structure of capitalist institutions; others have a more partial character and can exist more or less comfortably alongside capitalism. Some of them could be instituted in limited and partial ways and then grow over time; others have more of an all-or-nothing quality and would only work if instituted in fairly developed forms. All of these designs in one way or another attempt to shift the power configurations of capitalism towards an economy animated by social empowerment.

THE SOCIAL ECONOMY

The term "social economy" has been used to cover a wide range of economic forms. Sometimes it is simply identified with the "non-profit sector"; other times it includes cooperative enterprises even if they produce for markets and compete with capitalist firms. Sometimes the social economy is defined in strictly negative terms as including non-state and non-market enterprises. Some writers, like the Quebec social economy activist Nancy Neamtan, include a specific set of internal organizational properties in the definition. A social economy enterprise, she writes, is one that

> aims to serve its members or the community, rather than simply striving for profit; is independent of the State; establishes a democratic decision-making process in its statutes and code of conduct, requiring that users and workers participate; prioritizes people and work over capital in the distribution of revenue and surplus; bases its activities on principles of participation, empowerment, and individual and collective responsibility.[2]

I will define the social economy quite broadly as economic activity that is directly organized and controlled through the exercise of some form of social power. Social power is power rooted in the voluntary association of people in civil society and is based on the capacity to organize people for collective action of various sorts. The social economy involves the production and

---

2 Nancy Neamtan, "The Social Economy: Finding a Way Between the Market and the State," *Policy Options*, July–August 2005, pp. 71–6.

distribution of goods and services—economic activity—organized directly through the use of such social power.

This definition does not imply that every organization or enterprise in the "non-profit sector" is fully part of the social economy. Some non-profit organizations are basically arms of capitalist corporations or the state, rather than voluntary associations formed in civil society. Others have large endowments of capital which provide them with the resources needed to engage in their productive activities, and are directed in the manner of a hierarchical corporation. Their control over economic activity is therefore based more on their use of economic power derived from their endowments than in their deployment of social power (i.e. power rooted in collective association in civil society). What this suggests is that many organizations will have a mixed or hybrid character: they are examples of social economy activities to the extent that they are rooted in the associational life of civil society; they are statist or capitalist organizations to the extent that their power to engage in the production and distribution of goods and services is based on state power or economic power.[3]

In this section we will examine two very different examples of social economy activity: Wikipedia, and the social economy of childcare and eldercare provision in the province of Quebec.

Wikipedia[4]

Institutional design

Wikipedia is perhaps the best-known example of the anti-capitalist potential of information technology in general and of the internet in particular.[5] Many active participants in Wikipedia might be

---

3 The argument that many organizations engaged in the production of goods and services "in" civil society have a hybrid character is analogous to the claim in chapter 4 that economic structures as a whole typically have a hybrid character, combining capitalist, statist, and socialist elements.

4 This section is jointly written with Edo Navot and based in part on an unpublished paper, "Wikipedia as a Real Utopia," presented at the 2008 Wikimania conference, Alexandria, Egypt.

5 The other well-known example would be open-source software development, most notably the Linux computer operating system begun by the Finnish computer programmer Linus Torvalds in 1991. As "open-source" software, the source code for the program was made freely available to anyone interested in working on improving the system. Over the years thousands of

surprised to see it as characterized as a fundamentally anti-capitalist organization. Indeed, the co-founder of Wikipedia, Jimmy Wales,[6] is reported to be a great fan of Ayn Rand, the iconic defender of the moral standing of pure individualistic self-interest and the virtues of capitalism.[7] What is more, at least some prominent commentators on Wikipedia see it as a paradigm of work organization for the new global capitalist economy. Don Tapscott and Anthony Williams, in their book *Wikinomics*, see the principles underlying Wikipedia, which they distill under the rubric "mass collaboration," as providing the key to new forms of business competitiveness. "For large companies," they write, "mass collaboration provide(s) myriad ways to harness external knowledge, resources and talent for greater competitiveness and growth."[8] The trick for capitalism is to harness these new, open, non-hierarchical, collaborative network processes in ways that enhance competitiveness and profitability.

Yet, Wikipedia's fundamental principles of organization are not simply *non*-capitalist; they are thoroughly *anti*-capitalist:

1. *Non-market relations: voluntary, unpaid contributions and free access.* No one is paid to write entries in Wikipedia and even much technical work on its software infrastructure is done on a volunteer basis. No one is charged to gain access to its millions of entries: it is free to anyone in the world who can get access to an internet connection. There are no advertisements on the pages of Wikipedia. No one makes a profit directly from its activities.

---

programmers around the world have worked on developing Linux, suggesting new features, adding code, identifying and correcting bugs.

6   There is some controversy among close followers of the history of Wikipedia over the precise contributions of Jimmy Wales and his early collaborator, Larry Sanger, to the idea and design of the project, but regardless of whose ideas played the bigger role in shaping the endeavor, Jimmy Wales is deeply associated with its founding and development. For a discussion of these issues see Marshall Poe, "The Hive," *The Atlantic Monthly*, September 2006.

7   See "The Free-Knowledge Fundamentalist," *The Economist*, June 5, 2008, for a discussion of Wales's attachment to Ayn Rand. While this article does not discuss in a deep way the underlying basis for Wales's views of Ayn Rand, I suspect that they have more to do with a libertarian/anarchist hostility to centralized state regulation than they do to beliefs about capitalism as such.

8   Don Tapscott and Anthony D. Williams, *Wikinomics: How Mass Collaboration Changes Everything* (New York: Penguin, 2006), p. 33. It is possible, of course, for the design of Wikipedia to be fundamentally anti-capitalist and yet for certain principles of non-hierarchical collaboration within that design to be useful for capitalist firms as well.

The financial resources needed to underwrite the hardware of the system and pay the limited staff required for some technical functions is provided by the Wikimedia Foundation, which is largely funded by contributions from the wiki community.[9]

2. *Full, open, egalitarian participation.* Wikipedia gives full editing rights to anyone who wishes to join in the production and modification of content. Anyone can be an editor and no editors have special privileges over others in the production of content. A PhD and a well-read high school student are on formally equal footing. The editorial process thus functions in a dramatically different way to conventional editorial processes that rely heavily on experts with professional credentials. While it is impossible from the available Wikipedia statistics to know how many different people have contributed to the editing process, in December 2008 there were 157,360 "active accounts," meaning accounts which had done at least one edit in the previous month.

3. *Direct and deliberative interactions among contributors.* Wikipedia contributions and decisions are generally made directly by editors in a deliberative process with other editors without mediation by any body that has editorial or managerial control. Wikipedia articles tend to display a certain life cycle, beginning as a "stub" (the wiki-term for a minimalist entry that has not yet "matured" into the normal structure of a Wikipedia article), then expanding into a proper article with an increasing rate of edits which eventually converge on some equilibrium. The "final" result is an article that either remains largely static and "complete" or undergoes only minor editing. This process is often accompanied by considerable back and forth discussion among editors, which is recorded in a discussion page linked to a given entry. It is thus possible to review the entire history of the editing process for each Wikipedia entry. The mass collaborative effort of article authorship is a slow process of *consensus formation.* On average, entries in the English Wikipedia have nearly 90 saved revisions per article.[10]

---

9 The foundation was initially established with resources from Jimmy Wales who was a successful investment banker before starting Wikipedia. Subsequently the foundation has relied mainly on contributions from individuals who use Wikipedia.

10 http://en.wikipedia.org/wiki/History_of_Wikipedia (for all references to Wikipedia web pages, content accurate as of mid 2008).

4. *Democratic governance and adjudication.* At its inception, all Wikipedians were essentially editorial administrators (called "sysops") but as vandalism and other mischief intensified with the growing notoriety of the encyclopedia, a kind of quasi-administrative structure was instituted which enabled users to acquire different levels of organizational responsibility and roles in adjudicating conflicts. This is one of the most interesting aspects of the development of Wikipedia as a real utopian institutional design: the emergence and evolution of mechanisms of social control and adjudication suitable for such a freewheeling network structure.

There are currently four basic administrative levels of users: editors, administrators, bureaucrats, and stewards. As of mid 2008 there were about 1,600 administrators, 31 bureaucrats and 36 stewards. The administrative privileges associated with these designations, however, remain focused on facilitating "cleaning" the encyclopedia; they do not confer privileges in the production of Wikipedia content. Here is how Wikipedia describes *administrators*, the basic level of this administrative structure above ordinary editors: "*Administrators*, commonly known as *admins* and also called *sysops* (*system operators*), are Wikipedia editors who have access to technical features that help with maintenance." As described in the Wikipedia website that discusses administrative procedures:

> English Wikipedia practice is to grant administrator status to anyone who has been an active and regular Wikipedia contributor for at least a few months, is familiar with and respects Wikipedia policy, and who has gained the trust of the community, as demonstrated through the Requests for adminship process. Among other technical abilities, administrators can protect and delete pages, block other editors, and undo these actions as well. These privileges are granted indefinitely, and are only removed upon request or under circumstances involving high-level intervention (see administrator abuse below). Administrators undertake additional responsibilities on a voluntary basis, and are not employees of the Wikimedia Foundation.[11]

Access to these administrative roles is gained through democratic means. The process, as described on the page in Wikipedia discussing "Requests for Adminship," stresses the open, consensus-seeking character of the process:

> Any user may nominate another user with an account. Self-nominations are permitted. If you are unsure about nominating yourself for adminship, you may wish to consult *admin coaching*

---

11   http://en.wikipedia.org/wiki/Wikipedia:Administrators.

first, so as to get an idea of what the community might think of your request. Also, you might explore adoption by a more experienced user to gain experience. Nominations remain posted for seven days from the time the nomination is posted on this page, during which time users give their opinions, ask questions, and make comments. This discussion process is not a vote (it is sometimes referred to as a *!vote* using the computer science negation symbol). At the end of that period, a *bureaucrat* will review the discussion to see whether there is a consensus for promotion. This is sometimes difficult to ascertain, and is not a numerical measurement, but as a general descriptive rule of thumb most of those above ~80% approval pass, most of those below ~70% fail, and the area between is subject to bureaucratic discretion. . . . Any Wikipedian with an account is welcome to comment in the Support, Oppose, and Neutral sections. The candidate may respond to the comments of others. Certain comments may be discounted if there are suspicions of fraud; these may be the contributions of very new editors, sockpuppets, and meatpuppets.[12] Please explain your opinion by including a short explanation of your reasoning. Your input will carry more weight if it is accompanied by supporting evidence.[13]

Selection procedures to other levels of the hierarchy have somewhat different rules, but they all involve open democratic processes.[14]

One of the key roles for these different levels of administrators is resolving conflicts. There are, of course, topics in which there is considerable disagreement among editors over content. Sometimes this makes it difficult for an entry to converge on a consensus text. There are also instances of malicious vandalism of Wikipedia entries. Wikipedia urges the resolution of disagreement between editors on the basis of open communication and users have written numerous guides and essays offering instruction and advice to this end.[15] Most evidence indicates that warring between

---

12   As explained on Wikipedia, *sockpuppet* is a wiki expression referring to "an online identity used for purposes of deception within an Internet community," while *meatpuppet* is "commonly used to deprecate contributions from a new community member if the new member was (allegedly) recruited by an existing member only to back up the recruiting member's position."

13   http://en.wikipedia.org/wiki/Wikipedia:RFA.

14   One cautionary note about this description: Edo Novat presented the analysis presented here as a paper, "Wikipedia as a Real Utopia," at the 2008 Wikimania conference. Afterwards in discussions with long-time participants in Wikipedia, some people expressed skepticism that the actual processes by which people gained access to levels of the hierarchy were as straightforward as the procedures described in Wikipedia.

15   The "See Also" links at the bottom of the "dispute resolution process" page in Wikipedia gives several sources, though there are many more.

editors is rare, relative to the total number of editors and the vast amount of content over which disagreement may arise. Yet, disputes do arise and when the editors fail to resolve the issues themselves, a neutral administrator may be called in to manage the conflict through negotiation, mediation, and arbitration—all processes that emphasize the empowerment of aggrieved parties, consensus, and mutually beneficial outcomes. If disputes remain unresolved, then a series of escalating interventions become available. A dispute may be referred to formal mediation and finally to arbitration. The Arbitration Committee, which was formed in early 2004, is the mechanism of last resort for dispute resolution and is the only body that can impose a decision, including sanctions, against users.[16] The members of the Arbitration Committee are appointed by Jimmy Wales on the basis of advisory elections by the broader Wikipedia community. At this ultimate level of control, the Wikipedia process contains a residual, if nevertheless important, element of undemocratic power.[17]

Taken together these four characteristics of Wikipedia— non-market relations, egalitarian participation, deliberative interactions among contributors, democratic governance and adjudication—conform closely to the normative ideals of radical democratic egalitarianism. What is remarkable is that these principles have underwritten the collaboration of tens of thousands of people across the world in the *production* of a massive global resource. The statistics are stunning. According to the numbers provided by Wikipedia, by mid 2009 there were over 2.9 million English-language entries, and a total of almost 7 million in over 200 other language versions of Wikipedia. By 2007, the daily number of English articles accessed in Wikipedia surpassed 2 million. Whatever else may be the case, Wikipedia shows that productive non-market egalitarian collaboration on a very wide scale is possible.

---

16   See http://en.wikipedia.org/wiki/Wikipedia:Arbitration Committee.

17   Jimmy Wales continues to hold "ultimate authority" within the Wikipedia organization. He appoints the members of the Arbitration Committee from a list of candidates voted on by the broader wiki community, and has reserved the right to impose new rules and policies in special circumstances, although he has thus far refrained from using this power. Wales has argued that retaining this power is a necessary protection against takeover of the project by the concerted efforts of mischievous or ill-intentioned users. As it stands, Wikipedia remains a largely democratic institution with unexercised autocratic authority.

Criticisms of Wikipedia

The most serious criticisms of Wikipedia center on the reliability of its entries. Three issues are in play here. First there is the simple problem of inaccuracy in entries written by amateurs, and the problem that the loudest voice—not necessarily the most reasoned and well-informed—may win out in debates. Even though a number of studies have shown that the error rate of Wikipedia entries compares favorably to more established sources, nevertheless many people remain skeptical. Second, there are instances marked by genuine, deep disagreements over particular topics. The general editorial policy of Wikipedia is for articles to be written with a "neutral point of view" (NPOV), but for some topics— like Israel and Palestine—this is virtually impossible. This creates significant problems for the Wikipedia model. One solution could be creating multiple entries reflecting different stances, but there is as yet no consensus among Wikipedians that this is the best way to resolve such problems. Third, there is the problem of deliberate distortion. Sometimes this is simply mischief, as when the entry for Aardvark was deleted and replaced with "A very ugly animal." But sometimes deliberate distortions are introduced in an effort to shape a person's or institution's reputation by adding false information to an entry or deleting unflattering material. The Wikipedia page on controversies in the history of Wikipedia contains many examples. One of the best known instances, which occurred in 2006, is the congressional aides scandal, "in which several political aides are caught trying to influence the Wikipedia biographies of several politicians to remove undesirable information (including pejorative statements quoted, or broken campaign promises), add favorable information or 'glowing' tributes, or replace the article in part or whole by staff authored biographies."[18] Corporations have engaged in similar strategies, hiring people to write favorable entries and in other ways attempting to use Wikipedia entries as part of a marketing strategy to leverage legitimacy for their products. While many deliberate falsifications have been discovered, it is impossible to know how many go unnoticed, and this adds to the skepticism about the reliability of entries.

In response to these problems, a number of other internet encyclopedia projects have been launched. Two of these are particularly interesting: Larry Sanger's Citizendium project and

18   http://en.wikipedia.org/wiki/History_of_Wikipedia.

Google's rival to Wikipedia, Knol. The first of these retains many of the social economy aspects of Wikipedia, but tries to correct the problem of reliability by giving a more authoritative role to certified experts. The second rejects the social economy model altogether, and tries to enlist the profit motive into the development of the information compendium.

Citizendium was founded by the co-founder of Wikipedia, Larry Sanger, who left Wikipedia in 2002 after recurring conflicts with the editor community.[19] He was disappointed by the often less-than-civilized contentiousness of the project and was convinced that Wikipedia's rejection of privileged expertise and lack of discipline were weaknesses that undermined the credibility and accuracy of the encyclopedia. When Sanger left Wikipedia he started his own online encyclopedia, which he called Citizendium.

Citizendium remains a "beta" project and so may evolve, but it bills itself as "a 'citizens' compendium of everything' . . . an open wiki project aimed at creating an enormous, free, and *reliable* encyclopedia."[20] Citizendium hopes to achieve credibility by using "gentle expert oversight," requiring contributors to use their real names, and creating a parallel hierarchy within its contributors and its articles. Anyone can create a Citizendium account and begin *authoring* articles but in order to become an *editor*, a person must first open an account then apply for editorship by submitting a CV as well as proof of expertise that verifies the claims of the CV, like links to online conference proceedings or an academic department home page. All applications for authorships as well as editorships must include verifiable personal information, especially your real name, a biography, and specification of areas of expertise. "Constables" review all applications:

---

19   There is some controversy over whether Sanger was actually a co-founder of Wikipedia, or simply a collaborative employee of Jimmy Wales. When they worked together they both referred to Sanger as a co-founder, but after 2004 Wales insisted that he alone founded Wikipedia. For a journalistic account of the history of Wikipedia, their collaboration and eventual falling out, see Poe, "The Hive." There are many accounts of Sanger's role in Nupedia (the forerunner to Wikipedia), and his subsequent departure from the project. For Sanger's own narrative and critique see his article "The Early History of Nupedia and Wikipedia: A Memoir" posted on *Slashdot* on April 18, 2005, available at http://features.slashdot.org.

20   The "About" page of Citizendium (italics in original), http://en.citizendium.org/wiki/CZ:About.

Citizendium's "community managers" or "moderators," [who] oversee adherence to basic policies, resolve behavioral—not editorial—disputes, and rein in troublemakers. ... They operate within a "separation of powers" and are held to a strict conflict of interest policy. All Citizendium constables hold at least a bachelor's degree and are at least 25 years old.[21]

Since the project is a wiki, anyone can create an article, edit it, etc. The privileges of editorship include all the responsibilities of authors and include the ability to officially "approve" articles, guide content creation by authors, and participate in governance.[22] Citizendium distinguishes between articles that are works in progress, or "live," and those that have been "approved" by the community of editors within a certain specialty working group in what is essentially a peer-review process.[23] As of May 1, 2008, there were 61 approved articles and slightly fewer than 7,000 total articles as of January 1, 2008.[24]

Sanger's hope for Citizendium is that it will synthesize the work of the general public, and exploit the fervor for participation in projects like Wikipedia, with the informed approval of accredited experts. In this institutional framework, experts supply discipline and inform the public's contributions. Thus Citizendium has a collegial institutional structure that is a sort of hybrid of the openness of Wikipedia with a paternal role for academic experts. It remains an exemplar of social economy production—production based on the mobilization of voluntary cooperation for the provision of needs—even though it adopts a less strictly egalitarian model in the process of production itself.

Knol is Google's attempt to compete directly with Wikipedia. In the summer of 2008, Knol was officially launched as an active site. Knol is Google's short-hand for knowledge, as well as the word they use to signify a "unit of knowledge," or a single web page on a given topic. Google intends to provide free, easy-to-use software that will let authors produce articles, or knols, on a topic in which they have some expertise. Anybody will be

---

21 Citizendium's explanation page of its "Constabulary": http://en.citizendium.org/wiki/CZ:Constabulary.

22 For more details about the roles of editors, see http://en.citizendium.org/wiki/CZ:The_Editor_Role.

23 For more on the approval process, see http://en.citizendium.org/wiki/CZ:Approval_Process.

24 http://en.citizendium.org/wiki/CZ:Statistics.

able to produce an article and Google will host it for free (much like Google's blogging software). Udi Manber, a Google VP of Engineering who first announced the intention to launch Knol, writes that "Knols will include strong community tools. People will be able to submit comments, questions, edits, additional content, and so on. Anyone will be able to rate a knol or write a review of it. Knols will also include references and links to additional information." However, editing is the sole responsibility of the author. Finally, at an author's discretion, Google will place advertisements relevant to each knol and "Google will provide the author with substantial revenue share from the proceeds of those ads." The purpose of these articles is "to be the first thing someone who searches for this topic for the first time will want to read. The goal is for knols to cover all topics, from scientific concepts, to medical information, from geographical and historical, to entertainment, from product information, to how-to-fix-it instructions."[25]

Google expects people to write competing knols on the same subject and welcomes that competition. The purpose is to create a competitive marketplace of knowledge in the general mold of Google's brand of velvet-glove capitalism. Google hopes to siphon off the enthusiasm with which people contribute to Wikipedia by offering them remuneration, while undermining Wikipedia's ranking prominence in Google searches. Google's strategy for signaling the legitimacy of knols is to prominently showcase authors and their credentials. Thus the system will favor knols created by accredited experts.

It is unclear whether or not either of these alternatives to Wikipedia will constitute serious rivals. It is also unclear, of course, how Wikipedia will develop into the future, both in response to projects like Citizendium and Knol, and in response to its own internal dynamics. Will the level of energetic participation that has occurred in the first years of Wikipedia be sustained into the future? What will the process look like after twenty years? Will the kind of broad-based editorial diligence, commitment, and enthusiasm that has been crucial both to the rapid expansion of the number of entries and to the relatively effective monitoring of quality be indefinitely sustainable on a voluntary basis?

---

25 Udi Manber, "Encouraging people to contribute knowledge," *The Official Google Blog*, posted 12/31/2007, http://googleblog.blogspot.com/2007/12/encouraging-people-to-contribute.html.

The Quebec social economy

One of the most vibrant examples of an emerging social economy is to be found in the Canadian province of Quebec.[26] While Quebec has a long history of cooperatives in various sectors, and other economic activities which could be broadly considered part of a social economy, the term only became part of public discourse over economic alternatives in the mid 1990s. The pivotal event, noted in chapter 6, was a "Summit on Employment and the Economy" convened by the provincial government in 1996 to deal with long-term problems of unemployment and economic development in Quebec. A wide variety of organizations from civil society and the economy were invited to participate. Such corporatist policy forums are a familiar thing in many countries with strong social democratic or Catholic-corporatist traditions. What was rather special about the 1996 summit in Quebec, however, was the inclusion of social movement organizations, community organizations, and other grass-roots civil society associations in the dialogue.

Out of this meeting came a set of concrete policy proposals for the state and action plans for civil society to enhance the vitality of the social economy in Quebec. Some of these proposals have subsequently been adopted. They involve, among other things, making it much easier for non-profit associations engaged in social economy activities to acquire the necessary financial resources, through government grants, indirect subsidies, or access to credit; the creation of a social economy office within

---

26 This discussion draws from personal discussions with Marguerite Mendell, a Montreal economist who studies the social economy, and Nancy Neamtan, director of the *Chantier de l'économie sociale*, and from the following works: Marguerite Mendell, Benoit Levesque, and Ralph Rouzier, "The Role of the Non-profit Sector in Local Development: New Trends," Paper presented at OECD/LEED Forum on Social Innovation, August 31, 2000; Marguerite Mendell "The Social Economy in Québec: Discourses and Strategies," in Abigail Bakan and Eleanor MacDonald (eds), *Critical Political Studies: Debates From the Left* (Kingston: Queen's University Press, 2002), pp. 319–43; Neamtan, "The Social Economy"; Nancy Neamtan and Rupert Downing, "Social Economy and Community Economic Development in Canada: Next Steps for Public Policy," *Chantier de l'économie sociale* issues paper, September 19, 2005; Marguerite Mendell, "L'empowerment au Canada et au Québec: enjeux et opportunités," in *Economie, géographie et société* 8: 1 (janvier–mars 2006), pp. 63–86; Marguerite Mendell, J-L. Laville, and B. Levesque, "The Social Economy: Diverse Approaches and Practices in Europe and Canada," in A. Noya and E. Clarence (eds), *The Social Economy: Building Inclusive Economies* (France: OECD Publications, 2007), pp. 155–87.

the provincial government; and the consolidation of an umbrella organization in civil society, the *Chantier de l'économie sociale*, to coordinate strategies for enlarging and deepening the role of the social economy.[27] While the social economy in Quebec is still only a small part of the total Quebec economy, it is firmly rooted institutionally, growing in importance, and broadly accepted as desirable.

Two examples illustrate different ways in which the social economy in Quebec functions. The first example is childcare services. Such services can be organized in four basic ways. First, they can be organized within personal networks of family, kinship, and friends. This is certainly the most common way that childcare is traditionally provided, motivated by private concerns and regulated primarily by moral norms of care and concern for the well-being of others. Second, childcare can be organized through markets, either by for-profit capitalist daycare centers, or by self-employed individual childcare service providers. The central motivation for the provision of childcare through markets is private profit, and the norms regulating the provision are anchored in property rights: people have the right to set up businesses to provide services, and parents have the right to sign contracts for these services. This is the primary way in which non-family childcare services are provided in the United States. Third, the state can directly provide childcare services, as in France. The motivations for provision involve some conception of the common good, and the norms regulating the provision generally include some notion of citizenship rights. Finally, the services can be provided by civil society associations of one form or another. As in the state provision, the motivations here are rooted in collective interests, but the norms are more directly grounded in moral concerns for caregiving. This is the Quebec solution. These four possibilities are mapped in Figure 7.1.

In Quebec, the provincial government guarantees universal

---

27 An earlier organization, the *Conseil de la coopération du Québec* (recently renamed the *Conseil québécois de la Coopération et de la Mutualité*), played an important role in one aspect of the social economy, the cooperative movement, since the 1940s. The *Chantier* differs from the *Conseil* in trying to represent the full gambit of social economy organizations and activities—collective enterprises, non-profit organizations, and cooperatives—and in its governance structure which includes old and new social movements. The *Conseil* continues to exist alongside the *Chantier*, and at times there have been tensions between these two organizations.

FIGURE 7.1 *Four Ways of Providing Childcare*

Central Norms Regulating
Provisions of Childcare

		Rights	Caring
Primary Interests Motivating Provision of Childcare	Collective	State-provided childcare	Social economy childcare
	Private	Capitalist market childcare	Family childcare

childcare at a charge (in 2008) of seven Canadian dollars per day, but it does not directly run daycare centers. Rather, it provides subsidies to non-profit daycare centers run jointly by daycare workers and parent volunteers so that the combination of the parent charges and the state subsidies provides a solid living wage for the childcare providers. By 2008 there were over 40,000 childcare workers in this subsidized social economy sector.[28] As originally designed, the rules governing the subsidies made them available only to childcare service providers organized as non-profit associations or worker cooperatives, thus blocking the entry of capitalist firms into this market. Capitalist childcare services were not prohibited from operating in Quebec, but they did not receive the social economy subsidy that underwrites the financial viability of the co-ops. Needless to say, for-profit daycare providers strenuously objected to this policy, saying that it created "unfair competition." More recently, under the initiative of a more conservative government with a more neoliberal ideology, private firms have been allowed to receive the subsidy as well, although the sector is still overwhelmingly dominated by non-profit associations.

The second example is that of non-medical homecare services for the elderly. This innovation was launched in 1997 based on a proposal by the *Chantier de l'économie sociale* in its action

---

28   Personal communication from Nancy Neamtan.

plan at the summit in October 1996. Quebec, like most economically developed places, faces a series of difficult issues around
the care of the elderly which are seen as increasingly pressing
with the aging of the population and increased life expectancy.
As elderly persons become less able to take care of themselves
one option is for them to move into retirement communities and
nursing homes. Depending upon the location of such facilities,
such moves can be extremely disruptive of social networks and,
in any case, are generally very expensive (even when they are
of low quality). An alternative is for various kinds of services
to be created to provide the kind of ongoing practical support
that makes it possible for the elderly to stay in their own homes.
This would include things like house-cleaning, meal preparation,
shopping assistance, and odd jobs. Such services are beginning
to be provided on a fairly wide scale in Quebec through the
social economy. As described by Nancy Neamtan, the director
of the *Chantier*, ten years after this initiative was launched, the
network of non-profit and cooperative homecare businesses
across Quebec

> employs almost 8,000 people, half of whom were previously unskilled
> welfare recipients. By offering over 5.6 million hours of home care
> services to over 76,000 clients, the majority of whom are over 75 years
> old, these organizations have created jobs, taken pressure off public
> sector services, delayed institutionalization for many elderly people,
> reduced the welfare rolls and assured access to home care services in
> record time to all communities across the province.[29]

The clients pay a sliding scale of $4–18 (Canadian dollars)
per hour depending on household income for the service. The
provincial government provides subsidies to bring the wages
of service providers to a level slightly above the legal minimum
wage.[30]

These eldercare home services providers are organized as
various types of cooperatives and non-profit organizations. Nancy
Neamtan reports that the ideal model for this sector is what has
come to be known as a "solidarity cooperative."[31] This is a kind
of hybrid model between a pure producer-owned cooperative,

---

29 Neamtan, "The Social Economy," p. 74.
30 The homecare services sector of the social economy has received much lower
subsidies than the childcare sector, and thus wages (as of 2009) are much lower for
service providers.
31 Personal interview.

in which the ownership and control of the firm is entirely in the hands of the service providers, and a non-profit organization, in which the ownership and control of the firm is in the hands of a community non-profit association. In a solidarity cooperative the board of directors includes representatives of all of the key stakeholders in the activities of the cooperative: the workers, the users of the service, and the broader community. The community involvement helps root the cooperative territorially; the user involvement enhances its responsiveness to the needs of the elderly; and the worker involvement ensures that the direct providers of the service have significant control over their conditions of work. The solidarity cooperative model more fully embodies the principle of social empowerment than the simpler cooperative model or community non-profit model of social economy provision.

The development and vitality of both of these examples of social economy care-giving services—childcare services and homecare services for the elderly—depend significantly on the existence of the *Chantier de l'économie social*, the association responsible for coordinating and promoting the social economy in Quebec.[32] The *Chantier* characterizes itself as a "network of networks," a forum in which all of the elements of the social economy can meet, discuss problems, formulate new initiatives, and generate synergies. It includes a wide range of categories of members: networks of social economy enterprises including such things as daycare and housing cooperatives; regional associations in the social economy; community development centers; technical resource centers that support social economy activities; social movements including labor unions, the environmental movement, the women's movement, and various kinds of community movements. Recently a network of First Nations has been added to the *Chantier*. Each of these categories of membership elects people to sit on the board of directors of the *Chantier*. Various categories of non-voting members also have seats on the board. The board is responsible for strategic decisions and new initiatives, especially those involving financial instruments created by and under the control of the *Chantier*. The *Chantier* constitutes the pivotal associational mechanism through which the diverse activities in the Quebec social economy contribute to a collective process of social empowerment.

---

32 The following description of the *Chantier* comes from personal discussions with Nancy Neamtan.

Elements of institutional design for a vibrant social economy

The range of economic activities that can potentially be organized through the social economy in an effective manner is quite broad. In Quebec, aside from childcare and homecare services, the social economy already plays a significant role in recycling activities, sheltered workshops for people with intellectual and physical disabilities, and housing. In many places in the world, much of the performing arts is organized in ways that have a significant social economy component. Healthcare services are another arena where social economy organizations play an important, if usually secondary, role in the form of healthcare cooperatives and community clinics of various sorts. In the United States, charter schools and some forms of school voucher programs can also be viewed as instances of a social economy: the state pays for these educational services, but they are actually produced by associations in civil society.[33]

The Quebec experience suggests four elements of institutional design to facilitate the expansion and deepening of these kinds of initiatives in ways that would contribute to the broader agenda of social empowerment:

1. *State subsidies targeted to the social economy.* There are a number of difficult issues bound up with alternative mechanisms for providing financial resources for social economy activities and enterprises. One source of funding is private donations from individuals and private foundations. Many NGOs receive their funding from these sources, and sometimes this works well. Wikipedia was initially bankrolled by a combination of funds from private foundations and the personal wealth of Jimmy Wales, and has subsequently been substantially funded by contributions from participants. But for many social economy initiatives, such private funding will be inadequate for two reasons. First, for many projects, private donations and foundations are unlikely to provide adequate levels of funding. It is hard to imagine the Quebec social economy of

---

33 These examples from the US indicate, of course, that social economy initiatives may not always be progressive. School vouchers in particular are often a strategy for de-funding public education rather than advancing a general process of radical democratic egalitarian social empowerment, and charter schools are often a strategy for getting around teacher unions.

childcare and eldercare services reaching the scale it has on the basis of private donations. Secondly, private foundations typically have their own agendas derived from the priorities of their founders and boards of directors. Sometimes these can be quite progressive, rooted in democratic egalitarian ideals, but more often wealthy foundations have close ties to elites and corporations and their priorities are firmly rooted in existing structures of power and inequality. For social economy initiatives to be dependent on such foundations for financial resources, therefore, almost inevitably constrains their radical potential.

Of course, it is also true that the dependence of the social economy on the state for financial resources imposes constraints. Capitalist states are also deeply connected to elites and corporations and their priorities are also firmly rooted in existing structures of power and inequality. But at least the state is a terrain for democratic struggle and contestation, and this can increase the prospects of acquiring stable funding which allow for relatively high levels of autonomy.

In any case, for better or worse, private funding is unlikely to be sufficient for a vibrant, dynamic social economy and thus it is important for the state to underwrite social economy enterprises and activities through subsidies of various sorts. Furthermore, the rules of the game for such subsidies should block access to them by capitalist firms. A reasonable objection by capitalist firms is that this gives social economy cooperatives an "unfair" competitive advantage in certain markets. As noted above, this objection was raised in Quebec against the targeted subsidies to non-profit organizations and cooperatives which facilitated the rapid growth of social economy eldercare home services and childcare services. The appropriate response to this is to point out that state subsidy is a way of recognizing the positive social externalities that come from the cooperative, non-profit organization of production in the social economy. This is especially crucial in care-giving services in which the profit motive is in inherent tension with the values of nurturance and care.[34] The capitalist logic of meeting needs is that it is only worth doing when you can make a profit from it: I help you because it's good for me. The social economy logic of meeting

---

34 For a discussion of the tension between care-giving and the market, see Nancy Folbre, *The Invisible Heart: Economics and Family Values* (New York: The New Press, 2001).

needs is other-directed: I help you because it is good for you.[35] The widespread existence of cooperative needs-oriented production of such services contributes positively to supporting a sociocultural context that affirms these values. If this is indeed a positive social and cultural externality of needs-oriented production, then in the absence of a subsidy less of this public good will be produced. This provides a justification *even within the economic logic of a capitalist market economy* for a tax-based state subsidy to the social economy form of cooperative needs-oriented production.

2. Development of social economy investment funds. While state subsidies are crucial for the social economy, in the long term it is also important for the social economy itself to develop internal mechanisms for raising funds and directing them to innovative social economy projects. To the extent that the social economy manages to gain such funds, its capacity for autonomous growth would increase. In Quebec in a limited way, the *Chantier* has helped develop and coordinate venture capitalist funds for social economy enterprises. If the social economy is to expand to become a major source of employment and economic activity, then new financial instruments for social economy savings and investment need to be devised.

3. Governance through associational democracy. At the dynamic center of the development of the Quebec social economy is the *Chantier de l'économie sociale*—the kind of encompassing association that enables the heterogeneous set of projects and organizations in the social economy to coalesce into an enhanced form of social empowerment. This is a difficult task because of the conflicting interests and identities that mark civil society. Quebec, in many ways, was a highly favorable social environment for the development of this kind of associational solution, for prior to the creation of the *Chantier* there were already in place various networks of social movements, cooperatives, and civic associations. The status of Quebec as a French-speaking province

---

35 This formulation of the contrast comes from G. A. Cohen's essay, "Back to Socialist Basics," *New Left Review* 207, September–October 1994. See also the discussion in chapter 3 above on the way commodification threatens certain important broadly held values.

in an English-speaking country also contributed to a strong sense of solidarity that facilitated the elaboration of thick associational solutions to coordination problems. These factors help to explain why the social economy has developed the way it has in Quebec.

In places where civil society is less associationally rich and the social bases of solidarity are weaker, building such encompassing associations poses a greater challenge. The key task of institutional design is to foster associations that are deeply connected to social economy activities within civil society and create a coordinating body that democratically represents key networks of these associations.

4. *Participatory democratic forms of organization.* The goal of enlarging the social economy is not simply that in and of itself this is a good thing because it contributes to improving the lives of people. The social economy is also one of the important pathways in the broader project of social empowerment in which the ultimate goal is broad social control over the economy. For this to occur, the social economy needs to be a setting within which solidarity and social cohesion are enhanced and a broad notion of the collective good is practiced. This is one of the main reasons why cooperatives play such a central role in social economy activities: cooperatives affirm the emancipatory values of egalitarianism. More generally, a social economy organized along participatory democratic forms of governance at both the micro- and macro-levels of organization is likely to contribute more consistently to the wider agenda of social empowerment.

Potential problems

The social economy has clearly demonstrated that it can occupy a niche within capitalist economies, especially when specific sectors of social economy activity are subsidized by the state, as in Quebec. But can it expand in ways that would significantly encroach upon capitalism itself? Two central problems face such an expansion as a pathway to increasing social empowerment: the problem of involvement in the social economy of inegalitarian, exclusionary associations in civil society, and the problem of the potential distortion of the social economy by capitalist market relations.

Exclusionary associations

Inherent in the construction of a social economy is the problem of potentially exclusionary and inegalitarian associations in civil society. Engaging in needs-oriented social production within the associational context of civil society is no guarantee of embodying the central emancipatory values of democratic egalitarianism.

In the United States there is a range of associationally organized economic activities that satisfy the general criteria for the social economy and yet have at best an ambiguous relation to the emancipatory project of social empowerment. Many of the proposals that go under the rubric "faith-based initiatives" consist of social economy activities for the provision of needs: the state provides religious groups with funding for various kinds of social services which were previously run directly by the state. Churches are civil society associations that in addition to providing religious services often also provide a wide range of needs-oriented services: educational services, summer and after-school programs for children, food pantries for the indigent, counseling services, and much more. In faith-based initiatives these services are funded through tax money, but organized by churches. Sometimes the subsidies do contribute to a broad process of social empowerment, organized in an egalitarian, participatory way, giving communities greater control over the provision of certain kinds of services, but they can also become a vehicle for advancing the sectarian religious agenda of the church.

School vouchers are another good example of the problem of potentially inegalitarian, exclusionary processes within the social economy.[36] In a fully developed school voucher system, all parents are given a voucher worth a certain amount of money which they then give to whatever school, public or private, their child attends. School choices function like a market where the money follows the students. Schools compete with each other for students. Good schools—the argument goes—will attract many

---

36 The existing publicly funded voucher programs in the US are quite limited, being heavily targeted to poor minority children who otherwise would go to extremely bad public schools, and are therefore supported by some progressives within minority communities. The strongest political support for vouchers, however, comes from right-wing social forces who see it as a way of ultimately shifting public funding from state-run schools to religious schools and private schools. The special voucher programs for the poor are a kind of Trojan horse strategy to establish and normalize the principle in the hope of drastically expanding it in the future.

students and thrive; poor schools will either improve under pressure or disappear. The competition of the market will work its magic and schooling will improve. Insofar as the private schools are organized by voluntary associations in civil society—which is often the case—a voucher system for funding education can be viewed as a way of channeling resources into the social economy.

In the political and social context in the US of the early twenty-first century, while the small existing voucher programs may help a few poor children exit disastrous public schools, the broader proposal to universalize vouchers is supported primarily by anti-state conservatives who see vouchers as a way of undermining state-run education by transferring tax funds from public schools to privately run schools through the choices of parents. Since these proposals generally allow private schools to charge tuition fees on top of the voucher payments, this could ultimately become a state subsidy to high-priced private education. Also, since a majority of private schools are organized by religious associations, a voucher-based system organized through the social economy in the US would be supporting associations which often have extremely conservative social values. A fully developed voucher system to replace direct government-run schools with social economy schools organized by associations could easily end up supporting highly inegalitarian schools run on the basis of exclusionary, sectarian principles.

There is no automatic way that a growth of state transfers, incentives, and subsidies to underwrite the social economy can avoid these kinds of pernicious effects. It is crucial, then, that specific rules are instituted in the state support of social economy projects that ensure its universalistic, egalitarian, and democratic character. This is one of the critical functions played by the *Chantier* in Quebec: it is explicitly committed to democratic, universalistic, and egalitarian values, and this systematically affects the way it coordinates the elaboration of the Quebec social economy. In terms of schools, Sam Bowles and Herb Gintis—in their book in the Real Utopias Project, *Recasting Egalitarianism*—propose rules for a radical egalitarian design for school vouchers that would mitigate their inegalitarian and exclusionary potential.[37] Their proposal would institute a generous voucher system, but prohibit schools from "topping up" the voucher funds with any other source of funding—from tuitions, gifts, endowments, etc. This means that the vouchers cannot become

---

37 Samuel Bowles and Herb Gintis, *Recasting Egalitarianism* (London: Verso, 1999).

a subsidy for expensive private schools for the rich. They also propose a system in which vouchers would be worth differing amounts to schools depending upon the existing demographic characteristics of the students already in the school and the characteristics of the child with the voucher. A poor child's voucher, for example, will be worth more to a school with lots of middle-class students than to a school with mainly poor children. This creates incentives for schools to have a diverse student body. Finally, Bowles and Gintis propose a fairly strong licensing and monitoring procedure to ensure that schools receiving vouchers adopt certain broad curricular standards. The schools in such a system would retain a genuinely public character in the sense of maintaining publicly regulated standards and educational content, but would nevertheless be run in diverse and flexible ways by associations rooted in civil society. These rules would not eliminate all of the potential problems in a voucher system, but they would avoid its inegalitarian and exclusionary potentials.

Capitalism and the social economy

The second general problem faced by attempts to significantly expand and deepen the social economy concerns its articulation to capitalist markets. Two issues are especially important: the problem of competition with the capitalist economy, and the dependency of the social economy on capitalism for financial resources.

According to prevailing views, competition keeps individuals and firms on their toes, putting pressure on them to innovate and improve the quality and efficiency of what they do. Why should the social economy worry about competition from capitalist firms if in fact the social economy is a better way of providing certain kinds of services? Especially salient here are three issues that make it difficult for the social economy to enter sectors which are potentially profitable to capitalist firms. First, capitalist corporations are in a position to poach talented leadership from the social economy. Leaders in social economy enterprises often face challenging organizational tasks and develop highly valuable people skills. Where capitalist corporations can identify this talent, they are able to offer vastly higher salaries and drain off at least some of the most talented labor from the social economy. This may not pose a serious threat to some aspects of the social economy, such as childcare services, which are generally not especially profitable for capitalist firms, but it could constrain the advance of the social economy into new arenas. Second, capitalist firms can engage in forms of competition which undermine the social economy. Capitalist firms have greater access to credit than non-profit social economy enterprises and are therefore generally more capitalized. They can offer more lavish, if also expensive, services and thus siphon off the more affluent potential consumers of social economy services, leaving the social economy to provide services for those least able to pay. Third, capitalist firms do not have to worry about generating positive social externalities of their market activities and thus they do not need to devote any resources to this objective, whereas such positive externalities are part of the core motivation for much social economy activity. This gives capitalist firms a competitive advantage over social economy enterprises within ordinary markets. Unless there are strong rules protecting the markets for social economy enterprises by providing financial subsidies to the social economy that reflect these positive externalities, capitalist competition will tend to erode their commitment to social economy principles.

Beyond the issue of direct competition with capitalist markets, the social economy is potentially distorted by its need to acquire financial input from capitalist sources. If social economy enterprises take out loans from banks, they then have to generate sufficient income to pay the interest and eventually pay back the principal. If they seek capital investment from individuals and associations, they then need to offer a reasonable "rate of return." Both loans and investments mean that social economy enterprises have to behave more like capitalist firms, making decisions on the basis of expected rates of profit. The alternative, of course, is to seek subsidies, rather than investments, in the form of donations from private individuals and foundations and grants from the state. Such grants potentially do offer greater autonomy for social economy firms, but they also depend upon the willingness of political authorities and (usually) wealthy individuals to make these grants and donations and this leaves the social economy vulnerable to shifts in the political balance of power and the spending priorities of elites.

What the social economy really needs, then, is some way for a significant part of its core funding to become unconditional and non-contingent. One institutional device for this would be an *unconditional basic income*.

UNCONDITIONAL BASIC INCOME

The basic mechanism

Though the idea of an unconditional basic income (UBI) has a long pedigree, it has only recently been revived, particularly in European discussions.[38] The proposal has appeared under a variety of names: universal basic income; demogrant; citizen dividend; negative income tax.[39] While the details may vary, the basic idea, as already described in chapter 1, is quite simple: Every legal resident of a country receives a monthly living stipend sufficient to live at a culturally defined respectable standard of living, say 125 percent of the "poverty line." The grant is *unconditional* on the performance of any labor or other form of contribution, and it is *universal*—everyone receives the grant as a matter of citizenship right, rich and poor alike. Grants go to individuals, not families. Parents are the custodians of minority children's grants. Usually basic income is treated as a national policy in which taxes within a country are used to provide a basic income to all citizens or legal residents, but some discussions explore the desirability and feasibility of a global basic income, using some kind of global tax mechanism to provide all people on earth at least a minimal basic income.[40]

---

38 Basic income was the central concern of volume V in the Real Utopia Project: Bruce Ackerman, Anne Alstott, and Philippe Van Parijs, *Redesigning Distribution: Basic Income and Stakeholder Grants as Cornerstones of an Egalitarian Capitalism* (London: Verso, 2006). For earlier discussions, see Robert Van der Veen and Philippe Van Parijs, "A Capitalist Road to Communism," *Theory and Society* 15: 5 (1986), pp. 635–55; David Purdy, "Citizenship, Basic Income and the State," *New Left Review* 208, November–December 1994, pp. 30–48; Philippe Van Parijs, "The Second Marriage of Justice and Efficiency," in Philippe Van Parijs (ed.), *Arguing for Basic Income* (London: Verso, 1992), pp. 215–34.

39 There are technical details which differentiate some of the proposals under these various rubrics, but basically they all envision a mechanism for giving everyone an income without conditions attached.

40 One proposal for a global basic income argues that the natural resources of the world should be treated as "owned" by all of humanity, and thus the economic rents that are derived from the private ownership of those resources should be taxed and treated as income for all people in the world. Because of the uneven spatial distribution of those resources, a global tax and redistribution of the rents would involve substantial global redistribution as well. For a discussion of this stance towards a globally redistributive basic income, see Hillel Steiner, "Three Just Taxes," in Van Parijs (ed.), *Arguing for Basic Income*.

The rationale

Universal basic income has several very attractive features from the point of view of radical egalitarianism.[41] First, it significantly reduces one of the central coercive aspects of capitalism. When Marx analyzed the "proletarianization of labor," he emphasized the "double separation" of "free wage labor": workers were separated from the means of production, and thus were also separated from the means of subsistence. The conjoining of these two separations is what forced workers to sell their labor power to obtain subsistence. In this sense, proletarianized labor is fundamentally unfree. Unconditional, universal basic income breaks this identity of separations: workers remain separated from the means of production (they are not themselves owners), but they are no longer separated from the means of subsistence (this is provided through the basic income grant). The decision to work for a wage, therefore, becomes much more voluntary. Capitalism between freely consenting adults is much less objectionable than capitalism between employers and workers who have little choice but to work for wages. By increasing workers' capacity to refuse employment, basic income generates a much more egalitarian distribution of real freedom than ordinary capitalism, and this directly contributes to reducing inequalities in access to the means to live a flourishing life.[42]

Second, universal basic income is likely to generate greater egalitarianism within labor markets. If workers are more able to refuse employment, wages for unpleasant work are likely to increase relative to wages for highly enjoyable work. The wage structure in labor markets, therefore, will begin to reflect more systematically the relative disutility of different kinds of labor rather than simply the relative scarcity of different kinds of labor power. This, in turn, will generate an incentive structure for employers to seek technical and organizational innovations that eliminate unpleasant work. Technical change would therefore have not just a labor-saving bias, but a labor-humanizing bias.

---

41 Some egalitarians have objected to universal basic income on the grounds that it constitutes a form of exploitation of those who produce by those who live entirely off the grant. Defenders of universal basic income argue that this is a misdescription of the process by which a surplus is produced and distributed in a complex society. For a discussion of this issue, see Jon Elster, "Comment on Van der Veen and Van Parijs," *Theory and Society* 15: 5 (1986), pp. 709–21.

42 The call for "real freedom for all" is the central justification for basic income proposed by Philippe Van Parijs, *Real Freedom for All* (Oxford: Oxford University Press, 1997).

Third, universal basic income directly and massively eliminates poverty without creating the pathologies of means-tested anti-poverty transfers. There is no stigmatization, since everyone gets the grant. There is no well-defined boundary between net beneficiaries and net contributors, since many people and families will move back and forth across this boundary over time. Thus, it is less likely that stable majority coalitions against redistribution will form once basic income has been in place for some length of time. There are also no "poverty traps" caused by threshold effects for eligibility for transfers.[43] Everyone gets the transfers unconditionally. If you work and earn wages, the additional income is taxed, of course; but the tax rate is progressive, so there is no disincentive for a person to enter the labor market to acquire discretionary income.

Fourth, universal basic income is one way of socially recognizing the value of a range of decommodified care-giving activities that are badly provided by markets, particularly care-giving labor within families, but also within broader communities. While universal income would not, by itself, transform the gendered character of such labor, it would counteract some of the inegalitarian consequences of the fact that such unpaid labor is characteristically performed by women. In effect, universal basic income could be considered an indirect mechanism for achieving the "wages for housework" proposals by some feminists: recognizing that care-giving work is socially valuable and productive and deserving of financial support.[44]

Fifth, a secure, unconditional basic income would potentially increase the collective power of organized labor, not just the freedom of exit of individual workers, and thus contribute to the broader agenda of social empowerment of popular social forces. This increased power of labor, of course, also poses a problem for

43 In standard income transfer programs designed to reduce poverty, recipients receive a cash benefit if their income falls below some threshold. This means that they lose their benefit when their income rises above this level. They are thus likely to end up economically worse off if their earnings rise to just above the threshold. This disincentive to increase earnings is called a "poverty trap."

44 The net effects of universal basic income on gender inequality are ambiguous. On one hand, the grants go to individuals, not households, and this reduces inequality between men and women. The grants also provide income for unpaid care-givers, and this too will disproportionately benefit women. On the other hand, universal basic income could reinforce the gendered division of labor within care-giving, making it harder for women to resist pressures to assume full responsibility for such activities.

the sustainability of basic income, for the fear of such increased collective power is one of the reasons why basic income is likely to be strongly opposed by capitalists. If workers treated the basic income as an unconditional strike fund and used it to relentlessly raise wages, this would undermine the economic viability of the basic income itself by triggering disinvestment. However the increased working-class power underwritten by a basic income need not be used merely for short-term economic gain; as we will discuss in detail in chapter 11, it can also be used to forge what can be termed *positive class compromise*, which creates the conditions for a sustainable shift in the balance of class power.

Finally, and of particular importance in the present context, universal basic income can be viewed as a massive subsidy to the social economy and the cooperative market economy. One of the main problems that collective actors face in the social economy is generating a decent standard of living for the providers of social economy services. This is, of course, a chronic problem in the arts, but it also affects efforts by communities to organize effective social economy services for various kinds of caring activities—childcare, eldercare, home healthcare, respite care. The problem of providing an adequate standard of living to members is also a chronic problem for worker-owned cooperatives, especially in the early stages in which a cooperative is being established and members are learning how to function, work out organizational details, and develop productive capacity. A basic income would make it much easier for a cooperative to survive this learning phase and reproduce itself as an ongoing economic organization. Basic income can thus be viewed as mechanism to transfer part of the social surplus from the capitalist market sector to the social economy, from capital accumulation to what might be termed social accumulation and cooperative accumulation—the accumulation of the capacity of society for self-organization of needs-oriented economic activity and cooperatively based market activity.

Problems

Two issues typically are raised by skeptics of unconditional basic income: the problem of *labor supply*, and the problem of *capital flight*.

A universal basic income is feasible only if a sufficient number of people continue to work for wages with sufficient effort to generate the production and taxes needed to fund the universal grant. If too many people are happy to live just on the grant (either because they long to be couch potatoes or simply because they have a strong preference for non-income-generating activities over discretionary income) or if the necessary marginal tax rates were so high as to seriously dampen incentives to work, then the whole system would collapse. Let us define a "sustainable basic income grant" as a level of the grant that, if it were instituted, would generate a sufficient labor supply to provide the necessary taxes for the grant. The highest level of such grants, therefore, could be called the "maximally sustainable basic income grant." The empirical question, then, is whether this maximally sustainable level is high enough to provide for the virtuous effects listed above. If the maximally sustainable grant was 25 percent of the poverty line, for example, then it would hardly render paid labor a non-coercive, voluntary act, and probably not reduce poverty dramatically.[45] If, on the other hand, the maximally sustainable grant was 150 percent of the poverty level, then a universal basic income would advance the egalitarian normative agenda significantly. Whether or not this would in fact happen is, of course, a difficult empirical question to study, and would depend upon the distribution of work preferences and productivity in an economy.[46] A generous basic income is likely to be more sustainable in countries that already have very generous redistributive welfare states, since the additional taxes would in such cases be relatively small, and in societies with strong work ethics and cultural norms of work participation, since in such cases a smaller proportion of the labor force is likely to opt out of labor market work entirely. Ironically perhaps, a basic income is also likely to be more sustainable in a society with a strong consumerist culture, since people in such a society are likely to have strong preferences for discretionary income.

Apart from the labor supply problem, universal basic income is also vulnerable to the problem of capital flight and disinvestment. If a high universal basic income grant significantly increases the

---

45 Even a miserly grant might have positive anti-poverty effects by constituting a kind of wage subsidy to the low end of the labor market. Such a grant would function something like the earned income tax credit currently in place in the United States, or like a modest negative income tax, as proposed in the early 1970s.

46 It is very difficult to make credible estimates of these effects because they are likely to involve significant nonlinearities and dynamic interactions. It is thus very difficult to extrapolate from the effects of existing earnings subsidy programs to generous basic income grants, or even from low-level grants to high level grants.

bargaining power of labor, if capital bears a significant part of
the tax burden for funding the grant, and if tight labor markets
dramatically drive up wages and thus the costs of production
without commensurate rises in productivity, then a universal
basic income could well precipitate significant disinvestment
and capital flight. It is for this reason that socialists have traditionally argued that a real deproletarianization of labor power
is impossible within capitalism—that the necessary condition for
sustainable high-level universal basic income is significant political
constraints over capital, especially over the flow of investments.[47]

As in the labor supply problem, it is very difficult to make meaningful projections in order to determine how serious a problem
capital flight would be under different levels of a universal basic
income. What we do know is that a well-functioning, sustainable
capitalist economy is possible in a country like Sweden in which
taxation amounts to over half of the gross domestic product and
over 75 percent of the labor force is unionized. If, in the early
twentieth century before the rise of Swedish social democracy,
someone had asked whether a capitalist economy would be
sustainable with such high levels of taxation and working-class
organization, the answer would undoubtedly have been no.

SOCIAL CAPITALISM

The expression "social capitalism" refers to a wide range of institutional mechanisms and social processes through which social
power rooted in civil society directly impinges on the exercise of
capitalist economic power, especially in capitalist corporations.
The most widespread example of this is, of course, labor unions.
Unions are secondary associations and while they organize workers
in the economy—in firms and labor markets—their main source
of power comes from their capacity as an association to mobilize
people for collective action, and in this sense they are also part
of civil society.[48] When unions are heavily regulated by the state

---

47 I argued in an earlier analysis of basic income that socialism was a
necessary condition for a sustainable universal basic income. I no longer think
that my arguments in that essay are entirely compelling. See Erik Olin Wright,
"Why Something like Socialism is Necessary for the Transition to Something like
Communism," *Theory and Society* 15: 5 (1986).
48 For a discussion of the capacity to mobilize voluntary collective action
as the pivotal source of power within unions, see Claus Offe and Helmut

and their roles in governance of economic power are restricted to collective bargaining over wages and limited aspects of working conditions, then the social empowerment enacted through unions is quite limited. But in some times and places unions have a much more expansive role and modify the functioning of capitalism in significant ways. They may have the rights to elect representatives on boards of directors of large corporations, as in the German system of co-determination, or they may participate in various kinds of workplace governance and works councils within firms. Unions may also become deeply involved in community activism and coordinate their efforts with social movements in civil society. Such "social movement unionism" potentially contributes to building solidarities across the diverse interests in civil society thus enhancing the coherence of social empowerment.[49]

In what follows I will not discuss the conventional role of unions even though this is an important aspect of social capitalism. Instead I will focus on less familiar institutional proposals which attempt to create more democratic ways of directly controlling economic power through associational forms of various sorts. There already exist in capitalist societies large pools of capital controlled by public and quasi-public bodies. Endowments of public universities and the pension funds of unions and governmental units are typical examples. Modest efforts occur, from time to time, to make use of these kinds of capital pools to impose social constraints on investment. Perhaps the best-known example was the concerted effort to divest university endowments of investments in South Africa during the apartheid period. Certain kinds of pension funds have also vetted investments on the basis of some criterion of social responsibility. More radically, as we shall see, in the 1970s in Sweden, unions and the left of the Social Democratic Party proposed that union-run wage-earner funds be used to gradually gain significant control over Swedish corporations. The proposal came under concentrated attack and was modified to such an extent that the final version lost these radical features.

The question, then, is whether a broad institutional redesign

Wiesenthal, "Two Logics of Collective Action: Theoretical Notes on Social Class and Organizational Form," in Maurice Zeitlin (ed.), *Political Power and Social Theory*, Vol. 1 (Greenwhich, CT: JAI Press, 1980), pp. 67–116.

49   For a discussion of the distinctive character of social movement unionism, see Gay Seidman, *Manufacturing Militance: Workers' Movements in Brazil and South Africa, 1970–1985* (Berkeley: University of California Press, 1994).

of the rules and practices governing the creation and control of such public capital pools would enable them to play a much more significant role in constraining capital, imposing democratic direction and social priorities on accumulation. In particular, pension funds already constitute a vast pool of capital that could be used for these purposes, and the general trend of converting *defined benefit* pensions into *defined contribution* pensions is likely to increase the importance of such capital pools in the future.[50] Is there a way of organizing and funding such large pension funds, especially when they are run by associations like unions, in such a way that they can be used proactively to discipline corporations and reduce the capacity of capital to escape public regulation?

A variety of strategies have been either adopted or proposed with the goal of enabling people and associations to use capital funds to influence corporate behavior. Some of these have already been well integrated into the capitalist economy. Socially screened mutual funds, for example, establish various kinds of ethical criteria for the purchase of stocks in corporations. Some of these are highly targeted to a particular kind of ethical concern such as excluding military firms, oil companies, or tobacco companies from a portfolio. Others adopt a broader, ethically denser positive social screen by requiring that firms be certified as having high labor or environmental standards. These kinds of socially screened funds certainly make it easier for socially concerned people and associations to invest with a clear conscience, but it is a matter of some debate how much real effect this has on corporate behavior. Skeptics argue that social screening might have virtually no impact on stock values of non-screened firms. On the one hand, screening could have negative effect on the stock price of non-screened corporations since the demand for their stock would be slightly less, but on the other hand, this would mean that those stocks would become better bargains

---

50 A "defined benefit" pension is one in which people know in advance how much income they will receive from their pension when they retire. Traditional social security in the US is like this as were many pension plans in large corporations. A "defined contribution" pension is one in which the amount of pension you receive depends upon the returns on investments derived from the specific contributions you make. Typically in such schemes there is a choice over different kinds of mutual funds and other investment instruments, and the amount of income generated in the pensions depends both on the amount of contribution and upon how well these funds do in the market. The proposal for the "privatization" of social security consists of converting it from a defined benefit pension to a defined contribution pension.

for investors who don't care about social screening, and this would increase the demand for such stocks. The net effect, the skeptics insist, is likely to be minimal, and thus social screening would not put much real pressure on "bad" firms. Defenders of social screening argue that even if the direct effect of ethical investing on stock prices is small, it does contribute to a changed set of cultural expectations about corporate behavior, and over time this could have a larger effect. Corporate practices are never simply driven by the ruthless, single-minded pursuit of maximum profits; they are also governed to some degree by social norms, and the existence of visible socially screened investment funds contributes to strengthening the moral climate of capitalist behavior.

Here we will explore two strategies for democratic control over pools of capital that go considerably beyond social screening of stock portfolios. One of these—labor-controlled venture capital funds—exists in limited form in a few places, and the other— share-levy wage-earner funds—has been proposed but not adopted. Both strategies, if adopted on a wide scale, would offer significant prospects for a direct impact of social power on the exercise of economic power.

Labor-controlled solidarity funds

The Quebec Federation of Labour (QFL) Solidarity Fund was begun in 1983 as a capital investment pension fund designed to provide direct investments in small and medium-sized firms in Quebec.[51] It has subsequently grown to be one of the most important sources of equity capital in the province. The Fund has a number of distinctive characteristics:

1. *The role of the labor movement.* The Quebec Federation of Labour directly manages and controls this Fund and organizes the recruitment of individuals to contribute to it. Through the Solidarity Fund, the labor movement begins to play a role in the allocation of capital to different purposes. This is a critical aspect of the design of the Solidarity Fund as an instrument for social empowerment. While other kinds of associations in civil society could also, potentially, organize equity capital funds to serve the

---

51 The fund is primarily used not to buy stock on the stock market, but to directly invest in firms in the form of venture capital investments for new firms and what are called "private equity investments" in established "privately held" firms.

interests of their members, unions are in a unique position to place working conditions and capital–labor relations at the center of the social agenda of such investments.

2. *Social criteria for investment.* Before any investments are made, a "social assessment" of the workplace is conducted which involves "a meticulous examination of the operation of the enterprise with regard to: its employees, its style of management, the employees' profile, the working conditions, the working relationships, the production, competition and respect for the principal policies of the Federation of Labour, in particular as regards health and safety at work, and environmental laws."[52] Investments are made only in firms that satisfy this social audit.

3. *Working-class investors.* The majority of individuals investing in the Fund—58 percent—are union members. Part of the official Mission Statement of the Fund is to "Make workers aware of the need to save for retirement and encourage them to do so, as well as encourage them to participate in the development of the economy by purchasing Fund shares."

4. *Volunteer worker representatives.* The process of enrolling people into the Fund is undertaken largely by voluntary workers, referred to as *Responsables Locaux* (local representatives) who enroll fellow employees in their own workplaces. The Fund provides extensive education and training for these volunteer local representatives of the Fund: "It is these [*Responsables Locaux*] who form the spine of the Solidarity Fund. Under the Fund over 2,000 volunteers [as of 2004] have received training, attended courses, taken part in the public actions of the Fund (i.e. meetings) and have become, in their work environment, the experts, the people who have a good knowledge of the operation of the Fund."[53]

5. *Long-term perspective on profitability.* Profit-making continues to be a priority in decisions about the use of solidarity funds. The funds are treated as a source of investment savings for retirement of workers, and the Fund thus takes seriously the need to generate a reasonable rate of return. But the Fund is also committed to the

---

52 ILO Department of Communication, "Solidarity Fund: Labour-sponsored Solidarity Funds in Quebec are Generating Jobs," *World of Work* 50 (2004), p. 22.
53 ILO, "Solidarity Fund," p. 22.

idea that a secure retirement for its contributors depends on the health of the Quebec economy, and this depends upon a long-term perspective on economic development, job retention and creation, and support for strategic sectors. The focus of investment on small and medium enterprises is especially important. These are firms that are much more locally rooted and geographically immobile than large corporations. In the aggregate, they also provide more jobs than large firms. In the context of globalized capitalism, then, the vitality of small and medium enterprises is pivotal to a robust economic environment.

6. *Patient capital.* The Fund places great emphasis on what it terms "patient capital" designed to give small and medium enterprises long time-horizons in which to develop their market capacities. The 2007 Annual Report of the Fund states:

> Our success is based on expertise and patient capital. To help our partner companies meet the numerous challenges they face, we provide patient capital—capital that will truly allow them to carry out modernization or expansion projects and to boost their competitiveness . . . [B]ecause of our mission and size, we can stand by our partners through tough times when they need the most support to carve out a competitive position or to grow.[54]

Henri Masé, the chairman of the board of directors of the Fund, explains this priority:

> For us, investing is part of an approach to create collective wealth by focusing on quality jobs: those we can create and those we must preserve. . . . It certainly is no secret that I am against purely speculative investments, particularly those made by U.S. private funds. There is no medium- and long-term vision behind these strategies; the investors are not at all concerned with the survival of the companies in which they invest. Their sole interest is to turn a quick profit. To be sure, we have nothing against seeking out attractive returns to increase wealth, but not to the detriment of our social values or mission to create and protect jobs and help grow the economy.[55]

7. *Government support.* The Fund is indirectly (and was in its early years directly) subsidized by the government. Contributions to the Fund receive very favorable tax treatment in the form of tax credits from both the provincial government and the federal

---

54 QFL, *Annual Report of the Solidarity Fund 2007*, p. 13.
55 QFL, *Annual Report of the Solidarity Fund 2007*, p. 3.

government. When it was first set up it received direct seed grants from the government to augment the amount of investment the Funds were able to undertake.

8. *Active involvement with "company partners."* The Fund is actively involved with the companies in which it invests, which it refers to as its company partners, providing various kinds of training and education for employees, and technical and marketing consultation for management. It functions in part as a development agency and not simply a source of capital. This close involvement in the partner companies reduces the risks that might otherwise accompany the priority of the Fund in providing firms with "patient" capital.

9. *Education functions.* One of the purposes of the employee education programs is to educate employees in its company partners in the basics of financial and economic processes so that they better understand the nature of the problems their employer faces. As stated in the 2007 Annual Report:

> The economic training provided by the Fund is geared toward all the employees of its partner companies, and springs from the Fund's desire to contribute to their growth. By counting on transparency and good communication practices between management and employees of the companies receiving training, the economic training program seeks, among other things, to establish a common understanding, from a financial perspective, of the issues and challenges the companies face. In this way, everyone 'speaks the same language' and is better equipped and mobilized to make suggestions that may help secure the company's future while maintaining and creating quality jobs.[56]

When combined with the emphasis on the social assessment of firms, this is designed to increase the level of collaboration within firms between employers and employees in solving problems.

In 1985, two years after it was founded, the Fund had assets of 14.3 million Canadian dollars, just over 5,000 member shareholders, and investments in four partner companies. In 2007 this had grown to assets of 7.2 billion Canadian dollars, 574,794 members, and investments in 1,696 companies, making it a significant player in providing capital for small and medium enterprises, accounting for nearly one third of all venture capital in Quebec.[57] Because of this success,

---

56 QFL, *Annual Report of the Solidarity Fund 2007*, p. 11.
57 QFL, *Annual Report of the Solidarity Fund 2008*, p. 3.

beginning in the early 1990s, solidarity funds along the lines of the QFL fund were started in other Canadian provinces.[58]

These funds are prime examples of social capitalism as a pathway of social empowerment. They do not challenge capitalism as such. Mostly they invest in ordinary capitalist firms, although they also provide equity investments for worker-owned cooperatives. Their investment strategy is to strengthen the competitiveness of firms within the Quebec economy, not to weaken Quebec capitalism, and to foster more collaborative relations between employers and workers through financial education and other devices, not to increase class antagonism. Social capitalism is thus a hybrid form within which capitalism remains an essential element. But it is a hybrid within which social power has greater weight than within ordinary capitalist structures because of the pivotal role of the labor movement in running the funds and setting the priorities.

So far, even in Canada where solidarity funds are a significant institution, they constitute a relatively small part of total investment. There is no fundamental reason, however, why such funds could not be dramatically expanded. One strategy for doing this would be for the state to provide direct subsidies to such funds rather than simply the current indirect subsidies in the form of tax expenditures.[59] This is what the Canadian government did when the QFL Solidarity Fund was initially established, but such direct subsidies could be an ongoing feature of state economic intervention. The rationale for the state providing seed money to the QFL Solidarity Fund was that in order to make it an attractive place for individual workers to place their savings it needed to be large enough to have credibility, and seed capital allowed the Fund to cross this threshold. The rationale for ongoing direct subsidies is that this increases the capacity of the people of Quebec to control the long-term development of the local economy by underwriting

---

58   Other labor-sponsored funds include the Working Opportunity Fund in British Columbia, Crocus Investment Fund in Manitoba, and the First Ontario Fund in Ontario.

59   The tax deductions people receive for contributing to solidarity funds constitute what is called a "tax expenditure" on the part of the government. If the marginal income tax rate on a person contributing to the fund is 20 percent and the person contributes $1,000 to the fund, the person only pays $800, so, in effect, the additional $200 is an expenditure by the state. Tax expenditures have the special feature of not being visible forms of state subsidy, since they appear in the form of lowered tax revenues rather than explicit state allocations, and thus tend to be less vulnerable to political attack. They also have the property of allowing citizens to decide individually where some of their tax money goes rather than having this organized entirely by the state itself.

more systematically geographically rooted small and medium enterprises as well as worker-owned cooperatives while at the same time enhancing the role of social power in the regulation of capital accumulation. This is an objective which could be supported by a coalition of small-business owners and organized labor.

Share-levy wage-earner funds

Solidarity funds, as just described, are primarily a device for social power to influence the direction of development of small and medium enterprises and worker-owned cooperatives. Share-levy wage-earner funds are a device for labor unions (and potentially other civil society associations) to gain substantial control over the operation of large corporations. The institution was originally proposed in the 1970s by Rudolf Meidner, the prominent Swedish social democratic economist who was one of the key architects of the Swedish welfare state.[60]

A share-levy system is based on a particular way of taxing corporations. In an ordinary corporate tax, corporations pay to the state some percentage of their profits in taxes, say 20 percent (the proposed rate in the Meidner plan for a share-levy). The remainder of the profits can be used for reinvestment or distributed to shareholders as dividends. Such taxes are relatively standard in capitalist economies. A share-levy works quite differently:

1. *Payment of corporate taxes as new shares.* In a share-levy system, rather than pay corporate taxes in cash, corporations pay profit taxes in the form of *new issues of shares in the corporation* equal in value to the profit tax. This means that the tax has no effect on the immediate stream of income available to a corporation: the corporation retains control over its entire monetary profits. Instead, the profit tax takes the form of a tax on the wealth of the shareowners of the corporation calibrated on the basis of the corporation's profitability.

2. *Wage-earner fund.* These shares are paid into a "wage-earner fund" representing all employees in the economy and controlled through some democratic process. In Sweden the proposal was for the fund to be organized through a network of local and

---

60 For a comprehensive discussion of the Meidner plan for wage-earner funds, see Jonas Pontusson, *The Limits of Social Democracy* (Ithaca, NY: Cornell University Press, 1992).

workplace funds largely controlled by the unions, but the fundamental principle is that the wage-earner fund is controlled by democratically accountable popular associations, and other associational arrangements besides unions would be possible.

3. *Status of shares in the fund*. The shares in the wage-earner fund confer all of the usual share rights—rights to dividends, rights to vote for the board of directors, and in some circumstances the right to vote on company policies. These shares cannot, however, be sold; they become, in effect, inalienable ownership rights of the collective of wage-earners as represented by the wage-earner fund organization. The effect of the annual issue of new shares by corporations in order to pay the share-levy is to dilute the value of individual shares (i.e. because the number of shares increases, each share represents a smaller fraction of the total ownership rights in the firm). In effect, therefore, the share-levy constitutes a modest wealth tax on private shareowners.[61]

4. *Dynamic trajectory of ownership*. Over time the accumulation of shares in the wage-earner funds would gradually shift control rights over firms from private shareowners to these collective entities. Initially this would enable the wage-earner funds to elect some of the members of the board of directors, but over a period of several decades this would result in majority ownership of the shares by the wage-earner funds, thus conferring on these funds effective control over the corporations. Since the funds represent the broad population and are under democratic control, this trajectory constitutes an increasing socialization of the ownership rights in corporations. This need not mean that corporations would ever become entirely socially owned, for corporations could continue to sell shares on the open stock market which private investors could purchase. The fact that private investors would face a wealth tax on their share holdings does not necessarily mean that their share purchase would be a bad investment, any more than the fact that there is a property tax on real estate means that real estate becomes a bad investment. What the share-levy does mean is that over time the power relations over

---

61 The share-levy is a wealth tax in the sense that the dilution of share value that results from issuing the new shares is the equivalent of forcing wealth holders to give some of the shares they own to the wage-earner fund. It is, however, a special kind of wealth tax: a wealth tax that requires an asset transfer, not a wealth tax like a property tax on home owners that can be paid for with money.

corporations will shift heavily towards social power. This is accomplished without reducing the financial profits of corporations and their capacity to invest those profits; what changes gradually over time is the balance of ownership rights over the use of those profits and over the policies of the management of the corporation.

5. *Variations*. There are many possible variations on this basic institutional design that could be adopted. For example, rules could be put in place specifying that the wage-earner funds can own no more than 51 percent of the shares in a company, giving the wage-earner funds control over corporations but still allowing individual private investors to own a substantial part of the total shares. This would imply a hybrid ownership structure in which social ownership predominated, but capitalist ownership was still allowed. The organizational structure of the funds could also vary from the proposed Swedish model. In Sweden the wage-earner funds were to be organized as a network of regional funds and workplace funds. As described by Robin Blackburn: "A portion of these funds would go to an enterprise-level body run by the employees, who would thereby acquire a growing stake in their employer. But the bulk of the funds would be channeled to the regional network, representing local communities and trade unions."[62] There are many other possibilities. There could be national-level funds, regional funds, local funds, perhaps sectoral funds. The funds could be controlled by unions and labor federations, as in the Meidner plan, or by civic associations or specially elected public boards. The key principle is that socially empowered associations rooted in civil society have democratic control over corporations via their control over these funds.

A general plan along these lines was endorsed by the Swedish labor federation in 1976. It triggered a massive, hostile reaction by the Swedish capitalist class which launched a successful campaign to discredit it.[63] There were dire warnings about how the plan would lead to capital flight, disinvestment, and the collapse of the Swedish economy. While the union leadership supported the plan, the Swedish Social Democratic Party, lead by Olaf Palme, was at best

---

62 Robin Blackburn, "Economic Democracy: Meaningful, Desirable, Feasible?," *Daedalus* 136: 3 (2007), p. 42.

63 For a good discussion of the political battle over the Swedish share-levy proposal, see Jonas Pontusson, "Sweden: After the Golden Age," in Perry Anderson and Patrick Camiller (eds), *Mapping the West European Left* (London: Verso, 1994), pp. 23–54.

ambivalent. The result was that the Social Democratic Party lost an election for the first time in over forty years. Eventually in the 1980s a modified version of the wage-earner fund plan was introduced, but it specifically blocked the possibility of effective control of corporations shifting to these funds. In 1992, when the Swedish Conservative Party came to power, even this modified version of the system was dismantled.

The idea of a share-levy has recently been revived in discussions of pension reform, particularly in the work of Robin Blackburn.[64] Blackburn argues that all developed capitalist economies face a future crisis in the delivery of adequate pensions for an aging population. As the dependency ratio increases—the ratio of people outside of the labor force supported by active workers—it will be harder and harder to fund adequate pensions on a pay-as-you-go basis through payroll taxes and income taxes on current workers. It would be better, Blackburn argues, to effectively pre-fund pensions through some kind of share-levy scheme. The central obstacle to this is the steadfast reluctance of governments to tax shareholding wealth: "It is a striking fact that while most governments are happy to tax the homes people live in, they all refuse to have any direct levy on share-holding wealth or to allow—as Meidner boldly imagined—social funds to exercise control over the large corporations."[65]

---

64   Robin Blackburn's proposal to use a share-levy system to fund pensions was the centerpiece of a conference in the Real Utopias Project held in 2003. Two of the conference papers were subsequently published in the journal *Politics and Society*: Robin Blackburn, "The Global Pension Crisis: From Gray Capitalism to Responsible Accumulation," *Politics and Society* 34: 2 (2006), pp. 135–86, and Ewald Engelen, "Resocializing Capital: Putting Pension Savings in the Service of 'Financial Pluralism'?," *Politics and Society* 34: 2 (2006), pp. 187–218. See also Robin Blackburn, *Banking on Death, or, Investing in Life: The History and Future of Pensions* (London: Verso, 2002), and "Capital and Social Europe," *New Left Review* 34, July–August 2005, pp. 87–114.

65   Robin Blackburn, "Rudolf Meidner, 1914–2005: A Visionary Pragmatist," *Counterpunch*, December 22, 2005. Blackburn likens the reluctance of capitalist states to tax share-wealth to the unwillingness of the *ancien régime* in France to tax the nobility prior to the French Revolution: "Increasingly, it seems, we live in a society like the French Ancièn Regime before 1789. Then the wealth of the feudal aristocracy was largely exempt from tax; now it is the holdings of the corporate millionaires and billionaires that escape taxation. Other signs reminiscent of the age of Louis XVI include the spirit of 'après nous le deluge', the reliance on lotteries, and the emergence of modern variants of 'tax farming'—for example, laws which oblige citizens to pay their taxes (pension contributions) to commercial fund managers rather than to an accountable public body. But the taboo on effective taxation of corporate wealth is the most crucial sign of the reign of privilege."

Solidarity funds and share-levy funds constitute forms of social capitalism that attempt to modify core features of property relations within capitalism in ways that push it towards a structural hybrid within which social power has greater weight. Of these two proposals, the solidarity funds are more easily integrated into capitalism, since they can be instituted in piecemeal fashion on a small scale, and at least on such a scale they do not immediately threaten the power of corporate capitalism. The share-levy mechanism is inherently more threatening. If a share-levy mechanism were established and stably backed by the state, this would create a new institutional equilibrium within which capitalist power would be diminished in the overall configuration of a capitalist economy. Depending upon the details of the design and its trajectory over time, this could even signal an equilibrium in which social power—democratic control over economic power—became dominant. This, of course, is why it was so stridently opposed by the Swedish capitalist class, which recognized that the share-levy proposal was a long-term threat to its class interests and class power. In the end, therefore, it was not politically achievable in the historical conditions in which it was proposed, and wherever it might be proposed in the future it will certainly encounter sharp opposition. But the inevitability of sharp opposition does not necessarily mean that the proposal is inherently unachievable. There may be unexpected circumstances in the future when this institutional strategy could become possible.

COOPERATIVE MARKET ECONOMY

The oldest vision for an emancipatory alternative to capitalism is the worker-owned firm. Capitalism began by dispossessing workers of their means of production and then employing them as wage-laborers in capitalist firms. The most straightforward undoing of that dispossession is its reversal through worker-owned firms. In the nineteenth century the cooperative movement was animated by a strongly anti-capitalist ideology and constituted a central idea of the currents that Marx derided as "utopian socialism" and which subsequently became loosely identified with some versions of anarchism. Proudhon, one of the principal targets of Marx's attack, saw workers' cooperatives both as the cellular units of a socialist alternative and as the centerpiece of the struggle against capitalism. In 1853 he described the cooperative principle thus:

Mutuality, reciprocity exists when all the workers in an industry, instead of working for an *entrepreneur* who pays them and keeps their products, work for one another and thus collaborate in the making of a common product whose profits they share amongst themselves. Extend the principle of reciprocity as uniting the work of every group, to the Workers' Societies as units, and you have created a form of civilization which from all points of view—political, economic and aesthetic—is radically different from all earlier civilizations.[66]

Such mutualist worker co-ops would cooperate with each other through a kind of voluntary federal structure which would facilitate coordination and joint action. Mutualism within production and voluntary federalism among productive units would form the basis of a new society, initially within capitalism itself but eventually replacing capitalism altogether.

Marx had a quite ambivalent attitude towards this strategic vision.[67] In the *Communist Manifesto* he derisively dismissed the likes of producer-owned cooperatives as "little experiments, inevitably abortive." In the *Eighteenth Brumaire of Louis Bonaparte* he sharply criticized the French working class for engaging in "doctrinaire experiments, exchange banks, and workers' associations," which in his eyes constituted a "movement which, having given up the struggle to overthrow the old world despite all the means at its disposal, prefers to seek its own salvation behind society's back, privately, inside the narrow framework of its existence, and which will thus necessarily come to grief."[68] On the other hand, in 1864 in his Inaugural Address to the International Working Men's Association, Marx heralded the cooperative movement as a major achievement of the working class, of even greater significance than the passage of the ten-hour law:

> But there was in store a still greater victory of the political economy of labor over the political economy of property. We speak of the co-operative movement, especially the co-operative factories raised by the unassisted efforts of a few bold "hands." The value of these great social experiments cannot be overrated. By deed instead of by argument, they have shown that production on a large scale, and in accord with the behests of modern science, may be carried on without the existence of a class of masters employing a class of hands; that to

---

66 Pierre-Joseph Proudhon, *The Stockjobber's Handbook*, quoted in Martin Buber, *Paths in Utopia* (Boston: Beacon Press, 1958 [1949]), pp. 29–30.

67 This account of Marx's views of worker co-ops comes from Buber, *Paths in Utopia*, chapter VIII.

68 Quoted by Buber, *Paths in Utopia*, p. 84.

bear fruit, the means of labor need not be monopolized as a means of dominion over, and of extortion against, the laboring man himself; and that, like slave labor, like serf labor, hired labor is but a transitory and inferior form, destined to disappear before associated labor plying its toil with a willing hand, a ready mind, and a joyous heart.[69]

Building workers' cooperatives, therefore, became for Marx a legitimate element of socialist strategy, although he continued to believe that they would be contained within relatively narrow limits so long as capitalist power remained intact:

To save the industrious masses, co-operative labor ought to be developed to national dimensions, and, consequently, to be fostered by national means. Yet the lords of the land and the lords of capital will always use their political privileges for the defense and perpetuation of their economic monopolies. So far from promoting, they will continue to lay every possible impediment in the way of the emancipation of labor . . . To conquer political power has, therefore, become the great duty of the working classes.[70]

Workers co-ops have continued throughout the subsequent history of capitalist development, although today, with a few notable exceptions, they are mostly relatively small, local operations. When they are successful, they often tend to evolve in the direction of more conventional capitalist firms, hiring non-member employees as a way of expanding production rather than enlarging the full membership of the producer co-op itself.[71] While many, perhaps most, people who work as members in cooperatives continue to see them as an alternative way of life to working in a conventional capitalist firm, for most participants they are no longer part of a broad strategy for building an alternative to capitalism and are certainly not part of an organized anti-system strategy as was the case with the nineteenth-century cooperative movement. Nevertheless, worker-owned cooperatives remain one of the central expressions of a democratic egalitarian vision of an alternative way of organizing economic activity.

---

69 Karl Marx, "The Inaugural Address to the International Working Men's Associations" (1864) in Karl Marx and Frederick Engels, *Selected Works in Two Volumes* (Moscow: Foreign Languages Publishing House, 1962), volume I, p. 383.
70 Marx, "Inaugural Address," pp. 383–4.
71 Buber notes that Marx saw that the tendency for cooperatives to become ordinary firms was a significant problem: "[Marx] clearly recognizes the danger of the Co-operatives degenerating into ordinary bourgeois joint-stock companies, and even recommends the right remedy: that all the workers employed should receive the same share" (Buber, *Paths in Utopia*, p. 85).

The basic properties of worker-owned cooperatives

There are many different institutional designs that in one way or another embody the idea that producers should "own" their means of production. These vary in the extent to which they depart from ordinary capitalist principles. At one end of the spectrum are *employee stock ownership plans* (ESOPs) in which workers share in the profits of a firm by owning varying amounts of stock which confer on them the rights of any other stock-owner. As described on the website of the National Center for Employee Ownership:

> An ESOP is a kind of employee benefit plan, similar in some ways to a profit-sharing plan. In an ESOP, a company sets up a trust fund, into which it contributes new shares of its own stock or cash to buy existing shares ... Shares in the trust are allocated to individual employee accounts. Although there are some exceptions, generally all full-time employees over 21 participate in the plan. Allocations are made either on the basis of relative pay or some more equal formula. As employees accumulate seniority with the company, they acquire an increasing right to the shares in their account, a process known as vesting ... When employees leave the company, they receive their stock, which the company must buy back from them at its fair market value (unless there is a public market for the shares). Private companies must have an annual outside valuation to determine the price of their shares. In private companies, employees must be able to vote their allocated shares on major issues, such as closing or relocating, but the company can choose whether to pass through voting rights (such as for the board of directors) on other issues. In public companies, employees must be able to vote all issues.[72]

ESOPs depart from strictly capitalist relations since workers share in the profits and have some voting rights in the governance of the firm. However, since the power of workers within an ESOP firm is proportional to the amount of stock they own and since in most ESOPs this is a very small proportion of the total stock of the company, the real power relations within firms with ESOPs are not dramatically different from ordinary capitalist firms.[73]

---

72 http://www.nceo.org.
73 Still, it is worth noting that the economic performance of capitalist firms with ESOPs appears to be somewhat better than firms without ESOPs. The National Center on Employee Ownership reports that "In the largest and most significant study to date [2005] of the performance of employee stock ownership plans (ESOPs) in closely held companies, Douglas Kruse and Joseph Blasi of Rutgers have found that ESOPs appear to increase sales, employment, and sales

At the other end of the spectrum are firms characterized by two principles: they are *fully owned by their employees* and they are *democratically governed by their members* on a one-person-one-vote basis. Such firms are called worker cooperatives.[74] The precise details of how these principles are realized vary considerably. In terms of ownership, in some cooperatives all workers in the firm are full members, while in others some of the workers are non-member employees without voting rights in the governance of the firm. In some cooperatives all worker-owners have an equal capital-stake in the firm; in others, while all members must have a minimum capital-stake, these stakes can vary considerably. The governance structures of cooperatives also vary. Some cooperatives are governed through direct democracy in which important decisions are made by assemblies of all workers; in others there is an elected board of directors. While in principle in all worker-owned cooperatives managers are accountable to workers through democratic processes, in some co-ops the work of management is rotated among members, while in others there is a distinct managerial structure with professionally and technically trained managers.

These variations in institutional forms reflect adaptations to the practical complexities of realizing the principles of worker ownership and democratic governance under different conditions. The optimal organization for a small bakery cooperative will be different from that of a large industrial cooperative. No one organizational form could function equally well under such different conditions of technology, skill and training requirements, scale of production, and other factors.

There is no question that worker-owned cooperatives, *in some settings*, constitute a viable alternative to capitalist firms. It is much less clear how important an element they could be in an alternative to capitalism itself. According to the US Federation of Worker Cooperatives, in the United States today there are probably only about 300 democratic workplaces with a total employment of

---

per employee by about 2.3% to 2.4% per year over what would have been expected absent an ESOP. ESOP companies are also somewhat more likely to still be in business several years later." See http://www.nceo.org.

74 There are many other kinds of cooperatives: consumer cooperatives, such as grocery stores; marketing cooperatives; housing cooperatives; purchasing cooperatives (as when small farmers join together in a cooperative to purchase inputs together). Each of these may embody some principles of social empowerment, but they do not pose as sharp a contrast—and perhaps challenge—to capitalism as worker-owned cooperatives.

only about 3,500 people generating around $400 million in annual revenues.[75] This obviously represents a miniscule section of the US economy. Skeptics of cooperatives argue that this reflects the fact that in a competitive market economy, worker-owned cooperatives can only effectively survive in small niches in which there is a relatively homogeneous workforce in stable markets with low capital requirements. Once a cooperative increases in size, complexity and, above all, worker-heterogeneity, democratic decision-making simply becomes too cumbersome and conflictual to allow for effective business practices. In short, the reason cooperatives are a marginal part of a capitalist economy is because they are less efficient than capitalist firms.[76]

Defenders of cooperatives counter that this marginalization of cooperatives reflects the lack of a supportive social and economic infrastructure for cooperative activity in contemporary capitalist economies, and particularly the deep imperfections in credit markets which make it difficult for cooperatives to acquire adequate capitalization. Cooperatives characteristically face significant credit constraints because worker-owners lack the collateral of established capitalist firms and are thus seen as higher risk by banks. It may be true that in certain respects the governance structures of democratically run firms are more cumbersome than those of hierarchical, bureaucratically organized capitalist firms, but it is also the case that there are other ways in which cooperatives are potentially more efficient and productive than capitalist firms: the collaborative processes within a cooperative can enhance its problem-solving capacities; the commitment of its worker-owners to the success of the enterprise can increase their willingness to work diligently and productively; the closer alignment of interests of workers and managers can reduce the "transaction costs" of monitoring work effort.[77] How these opposing forces play out,

---

75 See http://www.usworker.coop. These figures are reported as conservative estimates since, according to the US Federation of Worker Cooperatives, "we lack comprehensive data on the nature and scope of worker cooperatives in the U.S." Still, even if this estimate was doubled, democratic firms would remain a tiny proportion of the American economy.

76 For an excellent treatment of the problems faced by worker-owned cooperatives within the framework of "transaction cost" analysis and neoclassical economics, see Henry Hansmann, *The Ownership of Enterprise* (Cambridge, MA: Harvard University Press, 1996).

77 For the view that worker-owned firms reduce transaction costs by more closely aligning the interests of workers and managers and are thus in this respect more efficient than capitalist firms, see Bowles and Gintis (eds), *Recasting Egalitarianism*.

defenders of cooperatives would argue, will be highly dependent upon both the details of how cooperative firms are organized and on the socioeconomic contexts in which they operate. In any case, the empirical reality of the limited presence of cooperative firms in capitalist economies is not evidence of their inherent inefficiency relative to capitalist firms, but only of their lower profitability under these unfavorable socioeconomic conditions.

It is, of course, very difficult to adjudicate between these contending diagnoses, and it is beyond the scope of the present analysis to provide a thorough review of the empirical research on cooperatives and their dilemmas. What we can do is look at what is generally regarded as the world's most successful group of worker-owned cooperatives: Mondragón in the Basque region of Spain. Examining the factors that have contributed to its success and some of the dilemmas it faces may help clarify the real utopian potentials of cooperatives as a pathway to social empowerment.

Mondragón

What has come to be known as the Mondragón cooperatives began as a single cooperative firm, Ulgor, in the Basque city of Mondragón in 1956, producing paraffin heaters and gas stoves with 24 workers.[78] In the years that followed, under the direction and inspiration of a Spanish priest, José María Arizmendiarrieta, a series of new cooperatives were created. Crucially, in 1959, Arizmendiarrieta helped found a cooperative bank, the *Caja Laboral Popular*, which functioned both as a savings bank and a credit union for its members, but also as a coordinating institution for the producer cooperatives in the area. The *Caja Laboral Popular* was formally linked to all of the other cooperatives and supported them by providing critical investment funds and other services. As this complex of cooperatives grew they created additional cooperative organizations to provide a range of services and support on such things as

78 This account of the development of Mondragón comes from personal interviews with Mondragón officials and from a number of published sources: George Cheney, *Values at Work: Employee Participation Meets Market Pressures at Mondragón* (Ithaca: ILR Press, 1999); the official website of Mondragon: http://www.mcc.es; and Baleren Bakaikoa, Anjel Errasti, and Agurtzane Begiristain, "Governance of the Mondragón Corporacion Cooperativa," *Annals of Public and Cooperative Economics* 75: 1 (2004), pp. 61–87.

legal matters and accounting, research and development, insurance and social security, and training and educational services. Various governance structures were elaborated in tandem with the expansion of this network of cooperative institutions. Some of the governance structures were rooted in the geographical proximity of specific cooperatives within particular valleys in the Basque region, and others concerned cooperative institutions such as the *Caja Laboral*.

In 1991 the overall institutional matrix was reconfigured into what is now known as the Mondragón Cooperative Corporation (MCC). This reorganization was an attempt at creating a more efficient system of governance and coordination that would enable the complex of cooperatives to compete more effectively in markets outside of the Basque region itself. Now, instead of the governance structure being mainly based on geographical proximity, it is based on functional specialization organized into three primary sectoral groups—industrial, distribution, and financial. Individual cooperative enterprises, the units that are directly owned by the worker-members, constitute the most fundamental level of this organizational structure. They retain what the members of the MCC refer to as "sovereign power." These individual cooperatives are then represented at more comprehensive levels of organization of the MCC as a whole.

The individual cooperatives within the MCC contribute a portion of their profits to various collective functions of the corporation as a whole. In particular they contribute to a kind of solidarity investment fund which enables the MCC to provide some redistribution from those firms with the highest rates of profit to firms that are having difficulties. The network of cooperatives also provides mechanisms through which workers from one cooperative can be temporarily transferred to another to smooth out variations in production needs especially during economic downturns. While individual cooperatives can in principle go bankrupt, this has never happened because of these solidaristic processes within the Mondragón network of cooperatives. This is the sense in which the Mondragón Cooperative Corporation constitutes an emergent form of a *cooperative market economy* rather than simply a cooperative firm within a capitalist market economy. The MCC constitutes a social infrastructure for the reproduction and expansion of cooperative ownership which partially insulates each cooperative firm from the full force of the competitive, profit-maximizing pressures of capitalist markets.[79]

The details of the governance structure of the MCC as a whole are quite complex. The critical points are these:

1. *Dual Structure of Governance* The individual cooperatives are internally governed by democratic procedures, although mostly this takes the form of democratic elections to various kinds of councils and boards rather than a direct democracy of worker assemblies.

Within the individual cooperatives there are two governance structures, one referred to as the sociopolitical structure and the other as the techno-structure. The former involves direct democratic election by worker-owners. The techno-structure, which is basically responsible for the managerial and technical functions of the cooperative, is formally under the control of the sociopolitical structure. In practice the techno-structure has quite a bit of autonomy. Some critics of Mondragón argue that in many cooperatives the techno-structure effectively dominates the governance procedures and operates only under very thin constraints of democratic accountability.

2. *General Assemblies* There are also periodic General Assemblies of worker-members within individual cooperatives. The General Assembly is formally the sovereign body of the cooperative. It is responsible for appointing the managing director and, in principle, has the power to determine the broad strategies of the cooperative. The General Assemblies are required to meet on an annual basis, but they can also be convened on an ad hoc basis to deal with specific policy issues that concern basic strategies of the cooperative. Attendance varies a lot across cooperatives, but is generally relatively modest.

3. *Representative Councils* The individual cooperatives choose representatives to sit on various councils and standing committees at higher organizational levels of the MCC. These governing bodies of the MCC both coordinate activities across individual cooperatives, encouraging synergies of various sorts, and formulate long-term strategic plans for Mondragón as a whole.

---

79 As described in chapter 5, a cooperative market economy combines the pathways to social empowerment of the social economy with social capitalism. It is a form of social capitalism insofar as social power controls economic power in the production of goods and services; it is a form of social economy insofar as the voluntary association of cooperatives involves the direct production of collective goods needed for the flourishing of cooperation.

4. *Withdrawal Rights* The individual cooperatives are voluntary members of the MCC conglomerate structure and retain the right to withdraw if they want to. In 2008 two quite profitable cooperatives left the MCC, much to the dismay of the corporation as a whole.[80] The ostensible reason was disagreement on the direction of the MCC, but many people at Mondragón believe that the exit was mainly based on the economic self-interest of the breakaway cooperatives not wanting to participate in the redistributive practices of the MCC.

Taken together, this governance structure constitutes a mixture of representative democracy and direct democracy within a confederation of sovereign organizational units. It is predictably fraught with contradictions and tensions: between democratic accountability from below and managerial autonomy; between decentralized decision making and more centralized coordination; between solidaristic principles across cooperatives and the economic interests of individual cooperatives; between a commitment to wider social solidarity with the welfare of surrounding communities and the corporate welfare of inside members of cooperatives. Left critics of Mondragón argue that within each of these antinomies, the MCC looks more and more like an ordinary capitalist corporation. Defenders of the MCC argue that in spite of these tensions, the worker-owners of the cooperatives retain meaningful democratic control over the broad strategies of the individual firms and the larger corporation, and in this respect function very differently from capitalist corporations.

Concerns about the long-term trajectory of development of the cooperatives within the MCC have intensified in recent years. Since the mid 1990s, the MCC has adopted an aggressive strategy of expansion beyond its historical home in the Basque country. This has, above all, taken the form of buying up capitalist firms and turning them into subsidiaries of the cooperatives within the

---

80   The two cooperatives which quit Mondragón were Irizar and Ampo. In the early 1990s both had encountered severe economic difficulties and were close to bankruptcy but were rescued through the economic solidarity of the MCC. This was underwritten especially by the strong economic performance of Fagor at the time. Now Fagor is in economic trouble, perhaps even in a crisis, and had expected to receive support from enterprises that are going well, like Irizar and Ampo. The leadership of the cooperatives that left MCC argue that they left because of disagreements over the management model, particularly over the issue of the need for a new generation of directors, but people in Mondragón with whom I discussed the issues believe that they left because it was economically advantageous to do so, thus violating the core principles of economic solidarity in the MCC.

corporation. The most striking example is the massive expansion of the Mondragón grocery chain, Eroski, through the purchase of other large grocery chains in Spain. By 2008 Eroski had become the largest chain of grocery stores in the country. Other MCC cooperatives have purchased capitalist firms in other countries. For example, the Fagor cooperative that manufactures high-quality dishwashers and refrigerators purchased a kitchen furniture firm in France, hoping that synergies between these two lines of production would improve its market position. Fagor Elian, a cooperative that manufactures various kinds of auto-parts, created a new wholly owned parts subsidiary in Brazil, to manufacture parts for the Brazilian arm of Volkswagen. The director of the MCC explained to me that although the Fagor Brazilian plant loses money, the Volkswagen Corporation insisted that Fagor Elian provide parts to its Brazilian operation if it wanted to continue to supply parts to Volkswagen in the EU. Setting up a Brazilian operation was therefore a defensive move to protect the standing of the Fagor Elian cooperative in the Basque country as a parts supplier.

The leadership of MCC believes that, given market pressures linked to globalization, this strategy of national and global expansion is necessary for the survival of the Mondragón cooperatives in the twenty-first century. Whether or not this diagnosis is correct is a matter of considerable controversy, but in any case the result of this expansion has been to intensify the capitalist dimension of the Mondragón economic hybrid. In 2007, of the roughly 100,000 workers in the various cooperative firms of the MCC, somewhat less than 40 percent were owner-members of the cooperatives. The rest were ordinary employees. Some of these were temporary employees working directly within the cooperatives in the Basque region who had some prospect of eventually becoming owner-members of the cooperative.[81] But the vast majority were employees of the subsidiaries of the MCC cooperatives. In effect, therefore, the owner-members of the cooperatives within the MCC have become, collectively, capitalist employers of the workers within the

---

81 Traditionally between 10 percent and 20 percent of the workers in a Mondragón cooperative were non-member employees. In the past the expectation was that most of these employees would have the opportunity to eventually become members of the cooperative after a probationary period of one or two temporary employment contracts. In more recent years, however, the rate at which temporary employees become permanent members of cooperatives has declined. The employment structure within the cooperatives, therefore, has more of a dualistic character than in the past.

subsidiary firms. This global configuration of economic and class relations within the conglomerate structure of the Mondragón cooperatives is in deep tension with its cooperativist principles.

The future of Mondragón as an embryonic model of a cooperative market economy will depend, in significant ways, on how the cooperatives handle this global melding of capitalist and cooperativist principles. There are a number of possible solutions. The first would be to create a mechanism through which substantial numbers of these new employees could themselves become full owner-members within the parent Mondragón cooperative. In my discussions in Mondragón, no one felt this would be a broadly feasible strategy, given that the effective functioning of a cooperative depends heavily on trust and solidarity. Even in the case of subsidiaries within Spain such expansion of cooperative members is a challenge. After considerable debate, the Eroski cooperative that now has grocery stores throughout Spain has decided to allow its employees in stores outside of the Basque region to become worker-owners. This was a difficult and contentious decision because of serious concerns that the character and democratic potential of the vastly enlarged cooperative would dramatically change with the dilution of solidarity resulting from the inclusion of so many worker-members from outside the region. The problem of incorporating the workers in the Brazilian Fagor subsidiaries in the governance structure of a Basque cooperative like Fagor Elian would be even greater.

Another solution would be to create mechanisms to turn foreign subsidiary firms into separate self-managed cooperatives owned and governed by the local workers. These newly cooperativized firms would then form some kind of long-term strategic alliance with the parent cooperative. This has been done successfully, on occasion, within the Basque region itself. Mondragón cooperatives have sometimes purchased failing capitalist firms within the region, restructured them, and then helped the workers within the firm gradually turn the subsidiary into a separate cooperative. This has always been a difficult and protracted process, however, and at least in the conditions faced by the MCC cooperatives in 2008, no one I spoke with felt that such a process of "cooperativization" was likely to be feasible for foreign subsidiaries of MCC.[82]

---

82 An additional problem, revealed in my interviews with Mondragón members, was a high level of distrust and prejudice about the Brazilian workers in these subsidiaries. Several people remarked that they were pretty unreliable and lazy, and lacked the motivation needed to run a successful cooperative.

A final solution would be to actively encourage the formation of strong unions and other forms of worker empowerment within the subsidiary firms, including such things as works councils and worker co-determination. This solution recognizes the deeply hybrid quality of a global cooperative firm under capitalist market conditions and the difficulty of pushing this hybrid in the direction of greater social empowerment through a simple, unitary organizational form. The globalization of cooperative firms could still contribute to expanding the potential for social power if the parent cooperatives facilitate empowering workers within their capitalist subsidiaries through various mechanisms of social capitalism. At least so far, Mondragón has not pursued this strategy either, adopting a rather hostile attitude to unions within its subsidiaries. For the time being, therefore, the foreign subsidiaries of the MCC are run pretty much like conventional capitalist firms.

TWO MODELS OF COMPREHENSIVE SYSTEM ALTERNATIVES

All of the examples of social empowerment over the economy discussed so far focus on partial aspects of the overall relationship between social power and the economy. Taken together they might amount to a system-level transformation, but each example on its own only constitutes movements along a particular pathway of social empowerment. This is in keeping with the general framework for envisioning real utopias proposed earlier: rather than attempting to specify the design for the final destination, the strategy is to examine specific mechanisms which move in the right direction.

This is not the only way to approach the problem of moving beyond capitalism. Much of the twentieth century was dominated by a model of a comprehensive system alternative to capitalism: statist socialism with central planning. Few people give much credibility to that model any longer. Here we will look at two alternative system designs that are responses to the inadequacy of centrally planned statist socialism. The first sees the absence of markets as the pivotal problem with centrally planned socialism, and thus proposes a model of market socialism as the alternative. The second identifies the bureaucratic centralism of planning as the core problem, and thus proposes a decentralized form of democratic participatory planning as the alternative. I think both of these models contain suggestive elements relevant to building a socialism of social empowerment, but neither constitutes a satisfactory stand-alone model of an alternative to capitalism.

Market socialism

John Roemer has proposed a theoretical model of market socialism that attempts to eliminate capitalist class relations while retaining market mechanisms of economic coordination almost intact.[83] By *socialism* Roemer means a society within which capitalist exploitation has been eliminated and ownership of the means of production is held *equally by all citizens*. His central idea for socialism is thus different from the one I have proposed: whereas I define socialism in terms of broad democratic control over the economy, Roemer defines it in terms of equal ownership of means of production. Nevertheless, his arguments are of relevance to the present discussion for two reasons. First, the equal ownership principle, if it were achieved, would be a significant advance in social justice as defined in chapter 2. Second, while equal ownership is not itself a democratic principle since it does not mandate any process of democratic control over the economy, nevertheless by eliminating concentrations of private economic power it considerably enlarges the space of such democratic control in the political sphere. Roemer's proposal, therefore, represents a quite different approach to the problem of democratizing the economy: rather than directly designing institutional mechanisms for enhanced social empowerment he proposes a mechanism for undermining the exercise of concentrated economic power, and thereby removing a critical impediment to the functioning of democracy.

In contrast to the traditional statist model of socialism, Roemer proposes a mechanism for distributing ownership equally which relies on a stock market and decentralized decision making rather than centralized bureaucratic administration. While his investigation is purely theoretical in the sense that no economy has ever been organized even partially in the way he proposes, it nevertheless attempts to specify the institutional design in a way that is attentive to our understanding of how various mechanisms work in actual market economies.

---

83 John Roemer, *A Future for Socialism* (Cambridge, MA: Harvard University Press, 1994) and *Equal Shares: Making Market Socialism Work* (London: Verso, 1996).

The institutional design

Imagine an economy with two kinds of money that we will call "dollars" and "coupons." Dollars are used to purchase commodities, whether for purposes of consumption or production. Coupons are used in only one kind of market: the market for ownership shares of corporations. Shares are therefore denominated in coupons rather than dollars. Dollars cannot be used to buy shares, and dollars and coupons cannot be legally traded. Coupons also cannot be given as gifts (this is, in effect, selling them at zero price in dollars) or inherited. Everyone, upon becoming an adult, is given an amount of coupons equal to his or her per capita portion of the total coupon-value of the shares in the economy. With these coupons, people purchase shares in corporations, either by investing directly in the stock market or by delegating some intermediary—call it a coupon mutual fund—to manage their coupon investments on their behalf. The ownership of shares, then, gives people the usual rights of shareowning in a capitalist economy—a right to a flow of dividends (which are in dollars and thus can be used to purchase consumption goods) and a right to vote for the board of directors and perhaps other corporate policies. At death, all of one's coupons revert to the common pool, to be redistributed to the next generation. There is, again, no inheritance of coupons.

In only one circumstance can coupons be exchanged for dollars: Corporations, when they issue new shares and sell them on the stock market for coupons, take the coupons they acquire to the government-run Central Bank and exchange these coupons for dollars, thus acquiring the ordinary commodity-buying money they need for new capital investments. The Central Bank determines the exchange rate between coupons and dollars. This becomes a pivotal policy tool for economic planning: if for public policy reasons there was a desire to encourage investments in some sectors over others, the rates of conversion of coupons for investment dollars could be higher in the preferred sectors.

Most people, being risk-averse, will invest in mutual funds with relatively balanced portfolios, but some will invest directly in the stock market. Over the course of a lifetime, therefore, some people will become relatively coupon-rich and others coupon-poor. Nevertheless, inequalities in coupon wealth will be fairly muted because no intergenerational transfers are allowed, and because the dollar-poor cannot act on the temptation to liquidate their coupon holdings for cash. The proposal thus differs significantly from the share distribution schemes adopted in the 1990s to privatize former state socialist economies, in which there were no constraints on the right of people to sell their shares for cash, and as a result very quickly most people ended up with no shares and some with high concentrations.

The state plays a central role in this model, even though the state does not itself own the means of production. The state is necessary to enforce the "missing market" (i.e. to prevent the exchange of coupons for dollars), to organize the continual redistribution of coupons to each new generation, and to govern the conversion rate of corporate-owned coupons for dollars through the Central Bank. These interventions are essential to reproducing the egalitarian quality of the model and allocating capital efficiently, but they all involve articulating state activity to market mechanisms rather than supplanting markets by the state.

A full elaboration of a model of coupon-based market socialism would require a range of additional institutional details. For example, there needs to be some mechanism for dealing with small shops and firms that would remain privately owned, and some mechanism for converting private venture capital start-up firms into coupon-share public corporations. There would also need to be an elaboration of how the banking system would work, since people with high labor market earnings would presumably save part of their income in banks and banks would make loans to firms. The banking system thus could become a backdoor mechanism for unequal claims on corporate profits via interest rates on loans linked to savings assets. Roemer's model also contains no specification for how the mutual funds that are at the heart of the process—since most people would invest their coupons in such funds rather than directly in firms—would be run and controlled. The fund managers could become a kind of crypto-capitalist class, controlling vast amounts of capital and effectively reconstituting the influence of concentrated economic power. Obviously if a coupon-based form of market socialism were ever to be instituted in practice, such details would be important, and conceivably the viability of the institutional design for advancing democratic egalitarian ideals might hinge on how well these practical considerations were dealt with. For our present purposes, however, we will bracket these complexities and examine the rationale of the central institutional device.

Rationale

Market socialism as modeled by Roemer has two fundamental rationales. First, coupon-based market socialism directly eliminates one of the central sources of inequality in capitalism because inequalities in incomes derived from inequalities in investments would be greatly attenuated.[84] Even if this left inequalities in labor market earnings unaltered, there would no longer be a strong tendency for those inequalities to be accentuated by inequalities in unearned income derived from investments out of high earnings. However, a radically egalitarian distribution of capital wealth probably would also have an indirect impact on the inequalities linked to labor markets as well. While there is much debate on the determinants of inequality in labor market earnings, there is considerable evidence that this is significantly shaped by power relations, not simply by the spontaneous forces of competition over skills in the market. One of the reasons labor market inequality rose so dramatically in the US in the last quarter of the twentieth century was that the decline of unions and the weakening of other mechanisms of labor market regulation (especially the minimum wage) undermined constraints on corporations pushing down wages and increasing the salaries of executives. If capital ownership were to be equally distributed in the entire population, the social forces arrayed against unions and other mechanisms of egalitarian labor market regulation would most likely be weakened. The equalization of capital ownership would not in and of itself change the distribution of labor market earnings, but dynamically it seems probable that inequalities in labor markets would be significantly reduced as well.

The second principal rationale for coupon-based market socialism centers on democracy. By eliminating high concentrations of wealth, market socialism enhances democratic equality in three ways. First, and most obviously, high concentrations of capitalist wealth constitute a resource that can be deployed politically. The potential for social empowerment over the state and the economy is enhanced when concentrations of economic power are eliminated. Second, and perhaps less obviously, dispersing share ownership so widely in the general population

---

84 In a Marxian framework this also implies the elimination of most forms of capitalist exploitation, since capitalist exploitation rests on the exclusion of direct producers from ownership of the means of production.

should make it much easier to balance priorities that people have as equal citizens in a polity with priorities they have as relatively equal owners of means of production. In a conventional capitalist economy, democratic decision making is highly constrained by the problems of capital flight and disinvestment when public policy measures have adverse effects on specific private capitalist interests. If ownership is fully and sustainably dispersed among workers and citizens, and if the mutual funds in which most people place their coupons are themselves democratically controlled by their members, then the threat of disinvestment and capital flight would be greatly reduced. Market socialism would not completely eliminate economic constraints on democracy, at least not if competition on a global scale remains a feature of market economies. But it would reduce the pressures, because there would be such a close correspondence between the distribution of political votes over public decisions and "ownership" votes over investment decisions. Third, in existing capitalist economies, for an important range of policies designed to reduce "public *bads*" (the opposite of "public goods"), concentrations of ownership create actors with both a concentrated interest in producing the public bad and a concentrated capacity to act on that interest. For example, a coalition of wealthy owners in a polluting industry will have an interest in and capacity for using their wealth as a political investment to block anti-pollution policies, both through lobbying and through contributions to political parties with weak commitments to environmental protection. Coupon-based market socialism, therefore, should increase democratic capacity to reduce these kinds of public bads.

Roemer's institutional design can be considered a variety of "market *socialism*"—rather than simply a peculiar variety of capitalism—for two principal reasons. First, the state has a relatively high capacity for planning, albeit planning that works through market mechanisms. Democratically determined priorities for directions of economic development would thus have much greater play in coupon-based market socialism than in capitalism. Second, the exclusion of direct producers from ownership of the means of production—a central feature of capitalist class structures—has been largely overcome.

Potential problems

Coupon-based market socialism faces many potential problems. As already noted, the institutional design in Roemer's account is underspecified, particularly with respect to the precise structure of power relations over banks and the mutual fund investment process. Much rides on how these institutions would actually work and they could certainly develop in ways that would subvert the socialist quality of the system. But even if these problems are adequately solved, there are important potential issues concerning unanticipated incentive effects. How will risk-taking around innovations be managed? How will principal/agent problems between equal-owner stockholders and corporate managers be solved, given the extremely high levels of diffusion of ownership? To contend with such problems, coupon-based market socialism would need to develop an elaborate array of institutional devices for the system to function well, with the potential for many unintended consequences, incentive failures, principal/agent problems, and so on. To give just one example, as people age they will want to shift their coupon-based investments from shares in firms with strong growth potential to firms that pay out high dividends. This creates the potential for some firms to become "cash cows," where people invest their coupons in the firm in exchange for such high-dividend payouts that the firms drain their assets until the coupon value of the shares drops to zero. In effect, this would amount to an indirect device by which people would be able to exchange their coupons for dollars, in violation of the basic logic of the model. Preventing this would require complex regulations and apparatuses for monitoring the behaviour of firms. The administrative structure of coupon-based market socialism may carry many fewer burdens than was required of classical centralized state socialism, but nevertheless involves considerable complexity. Because of such complexity it is hard to anticipate what the broader ramifications and unintended consequences of these arrangements might be.

Parecon: a non-market participatory democratic economy

Market socialism, as envisioned by John Roemer, retains most of the features of a market economy but attempts to remove its distinctively capitalist character by blocking the private accumulation of capital and thus the private exercise of economic power. The idea, then, is that a market system without capitalist class relations would advance the egalitarian side of democratic egalitarianism by distributing wealth in a sustainably egalitarian manner and would also advance the democratic side by largely neutralizing the possibility of economic power undermining the democratic control of state power.

Michael Albert proposes a much more radical break with capitalism by completely eliminating both private ownership and market relations. The problem, of course, is how to do this without shifting power over economic activities to the state. Albert's proposal—"participatory economics," or "parecon" for short—is to reorganize economic institutions through a complex array of participatory councils with the power to make all decisions concerning the allocation and use of society's productive resources.

Institutional design

The institutional design of parecon as elaborated by Albert is constructed around five core principles: social ownership understood as equal ownership by all citizens; egalitarian democratic empowerment based on a principle of participation proportional to effects; jobs constructed as "balanced complexes"; remuneration for work according to effort/sacrifice and needs; and economic coordination based on comprehensive participatory planning. Briefly, the central features of each of these principles are as follows:

1. *Social ownership*. Albert endorses a much stronger concept of equal ownership of the means of production than does Roemer. In Roemer's model citizens are given an equal quantity of *coupons* with which to purchase shares in the total corporate assets of the economy, but they retain individualized rights to those shares and to the dividends connected to them, and over a lifetime some inequality in the value of such shares will emerge. In Albert's model "each workplace [is] owned in equal part by all citizens so that ownership conveys no special rights or income advantages . . . We would own it equally, so that ownership would have no bearing on the distribution of income, wealth, or power."[85]

85 Michael Albert, *Parecon* (London: Verso, 2003), p. 9. Albert later clarifies this idea of social ownership: "We simply remove ownership of the means of production from the economic picture. We can think of this as deciding that no one owns the means of production. Or we can think of it as deciding everyone owns a fractional share of every single item of the means of production equivalent to what every other person owns of that item. Or we can think of it as deciding

This means that people do not acquire any income directly via their connection to specific economic assets, but via some public mechanism of distribution.

2. *Egalitarian democratic empowerment*. Most visions of democratic equality are rooted in a principle of one-person-one-vote. On the surface this seems like a fine embodiment of egalitarian principles. Albert argues that this is the case only in special circumstances. The more general principle is that people should have decision-making influence proportional to the effects of those decisions on their lives. This is a much more complex idea: "the norm for decisions being that methods of dispersing information and for arriving at and tallying preferences into decisions should convey to each party involved, to the extent possible, *influence over decisions in proportion to the degree he or she will be affected by them*."[86] This principle means that for some kinds of decisions each individual would have complete control over the decision since the decision only affects him or herself, whereas in other types of decisions the influence of a given person would be variable. In workplaces this means that some decisions are made by work teams, others by departments, and still others by assemblies of the entire workforce. Of course it would be impossible to precisely calibrate all decision-making venues this way, but the principle would stamp the basic contours of the rights to participate in different democratic arenas.

3. *Job complexes.* In any economy, the great variety of tasks that need to be done gets packaged into "jobs." Mostly, in capitalism, the bundle of tasks that constitute a job is decided by capitalists and managers. The result is a very strong tendency for the division of labor to take the form of some jobs being interesting, challenging, and empowering, while others are boring, routinized, and disempowered. Albert proposes a radical redesign of jobs in which each worker would work in a "balanced job complex, meaning the combination of tasks and responsibilities each worker has would accord them the same empowerment and quality of life benefits as the combination every other worker has."[87] In the iconic example, a brain surgeon would thus spend part of each day changing bed pans or doing other

---

that society owns all of the means of production but that it has no say over any of the means of production nor any claim on their output on that account" (p. 90).

86 Albert, *Parecon*, p. 9 (emphasis added).
87 Albert, *Parecon*, p. 10.

menial, tedious work in a hospital. In cases where workplaces as a whole had, relative to the economy-wide average, high or low levels of desirable tasks, then the balance in a job complex would be created through appropriate productive activities outside of the workplace. The net result is that there would be little difference across people in the quality of life experienced within work.

4. *Remuneration according to effort/sacrifice and to need.* Albert formulates two distinct principles through which people acquire their income, one that is linked to work and one that is not. The former states that remuneration for work should reflect

> how hard we have worked, how long we have worked, and how great a sacrifice we have made in our work. We shouldn't get more because we use more productive tools, have more skills, or have greater talent, much less should we get more because we have more power or own more property. We should get more only by virtue of how much effort we have expended or how much sacrifice we have endured in our useful work.[88]

This principle of remuneration is in keeping with the strong intuition of many egalitarians that a just system of payment for work rewards "only what we can affect and not what is beyond our control."[89] The second remuneration principle provides income to people on the basis of special needs that cannot be met through remuneration for effort.[90] This implies a recognition that the moral issues involved in distributing the income generated in an economy cannot be satisfied entirely through

---

88   Albert, *Parecon*, p. 10.
89   Albert, *Parecon*, p. 10.
90   This second basis for remuneration Albert describes not as a principle of justice, but as a principle of compassion. Payment according to need "is not really a candidate for a definition of economic justice . . . It is one thing for an economy to be equitable, fair, and just. It is another thing for an economy to be compassionate. A just economy is not the last word in morally desirable economics" (*Parecon*, p. 37). The definition of social justice I offer in chapter 2 combines Albert's norm of compassion into the concept of social justice. In effect I argue that it would be unjust to deprive people of the resources needed to live a flourishing life if they were unable to obtain these through their own efforts. I do not think, however, that a lot rides on whether or not justified compassion is viewed as an aspect of social justice or a stand-alone principle. I agree with Albert that "justice" is not the only relevant value for evaluating social institutions, and functionally the term "equal access" in my "equal access to the necessary means to live a flourishing life" includes both equal access to income-generating work in which effort is the central determinant of income, and equal access to a compassionate distribution of income reflecting special needs.

fair payment for the contributions people make to generating that income.

5. *Economic coordination through participatory planning.* This is, in many ways, the most controversial element in Albert's proposed institutional design for parecon. It provides the mechanisms through which Albert believes markets could be completely eliminated in ways which would actually increase aggregate social efficiency. The core of the proposal is the creation of a nested structure of worker councils and consumer councils which would be responsible for formulating and revising comprehensive plans for production and consumption. Here is how Albert initially describes the overall character of this system:

> participatory planning [is] a system in which worker and consumer councils propose their worker activities and consumer preferences in light of true valuations of the full social benefits and costs of their choices. The system utilizes cooperative communication of mutually informed preferences via a variety of simple communicative and organizing principles and means including . . . indicative prices, facilitation boards, and rounds of accommodation to new information.[91]

Worker councils are organized at every level of productive activity: work teams, units, divisions, whole workplaces, and industrial sectors. Consumer councils are similarly organized at every scale: families would belong to neighborhood councils, neighborhood councils would belong to federations of councils for larger parts of cities, federations would belong to city consumption councils, city councils would belong to state or regional councils, and these in turn would belong to national consumption councils. "This nested federation of democratic councils would organize consumption," Albert writes, "just as the nested federation of democratic workers councils organizes production."[92]

How is this supposed to work? The basic idea is that actors within these various worker and consumer planning councils make proposals for the work activities they want to perform in the coming planning period (specified as a year in Albert's formulation) and the consumption they want to have. These plans are first formulated at the most local level of the system and then reviewed by councils at more encompassing scales and either accepted or

91   Albert, *Parecon*, p. 12.
92   Albert, *Parecon*, p. 93.

rejected in light of information from facilitation boards (which provide various kinds of technical information, especially "indicative prices" meant to reflect the true social costs of different choices given the full array of choices being made throughout the economy). In the case of consumption councils, participatory planning would work like this:

> In participatory planning every actor (individual or council) at every level will propose its own activities, and, after receiving information regarding other actors' proposals, and the response of other actors to its proposal, each actor makes a new proposal.
>
> Thus, each consumption "actor," from individuals up to large consumer federations, proposes a consumption plan. Individuals make proposals for private goods such as clothing, food, toys, etc. Neighborhood councils make proposals that include approved requests for private goods as well as the neighborhood's collective consumption requests that might include a new pool or local park. Higher-level councils and federations of councils make proposals that include approval requests from member councils as well as the federation's larger collective consumption request.[93]

This is an iterated process of plans being proposed, passed onward to the more encompassing level, evaluated, and then returned to the proposing council with new information, reevaluated and reconfigured, and passed back for new consideration:

> In a first iteration, where consumers propose in part a "wish list" and workers propose substantial improvements in their work lives, while some goods may be in excess supply, for most goods initial proposals taken together will not equal a feasible plan. As the next step, every council receives new information indicating which goods are in excess supply or demand and by how much, and how the council's proposal compares to those of other comparable units. Facilitation boards provide new estimates of indicative prices projected to equilibrate supply and demand.
>
> At this point consumers reassess their requests in light of the new prices and most often "shift" their requests for goods in excess demand toward goods whose indicative prices have fallen because they were in excess supply or at least less in demand than others. Consumers' councils and individuals whose overall requests were higher than average would feel obliged to whittle down their requests in hopes of winning approval for their proposals. Equity and efficiency emerge simultaneously from this negotiation stage.[94]

---

93 Albert, *Parecon*, p. 28.
94 Albert, *Parecon*, p. 131.

This entire process is aided by a parallel structure of nested "facilitation boards" that provide an array of technical services—computer services, simulations, accounting, etc.—to each level of the councils:

> parecon will have various "facilitation boards" or agencies that facilitate information exchange and processing for collective consumption proposals and for large-scale investment projects, workers requests for changing places of employment, and individuals and families seeking to find membership in living units and neighborhoods, among other functions.[95]

Albert acknowledges that this is a complex process and that the quality of the final plan coming out of the process will depend on the quality of the information flowing through the system. This is partially accomplished through the use of quantitative "indicative prices," but it also requires the assimilation of meaningful *qualitative* data:

> to both assure accuracy and to foster solidarity we need not only set quantitative prices but also continually socially reset them in light of changing qualitative information about work lives and consumption activity . . . Not only must a participatory economy generate and revise accurate quantitative measures of social costs and benefits in light of changing conditions, it must also communicate substantial qualitative information about the conditions of other people.[96]

Given sufficient iterations and appropriate technical support using powerful computer software, Albert believes that this process will converge on a coherent annual plan for both production and consumption. If it works as forecast, this plan will take into account the full social costs of alternative uses of an economy's available resources and align these with the comprehensive consumption preferences of equal citizens.

The problem of viability

In terms of the general framework of pathways to social empowerment we have been exploring, Michael Albert's model of parecon can be viewed as a vision for moving beyond capitalism that relies on a single pathway, *the social economy*: all production

---

95   Albert, *Parecon*, p. 127.
96   Albert, *Parecon*, p. 126.

in Albert's parecon is organized around the direct provision for needs on principles of reciprocity and voluntary association. Economic power, as I have defined it, is eliminated completely, and with it, the market. And state power exercises no direct role in organizing the economy; economic activity is entirely governed by the locally grounded process of democratic planning through voluntary participation in worker and consumer councils. This, then, is a model for going beyond capitalism that rejects six of the seven pathways we have been exploring.

As a statement of the *moral vision* for an alternative to capitalism, Albert's five principles of institutional design have much in common with the arguments of this book. While he uses a somewhat different language for discussing these issues, the deeply egalitarian and democratic values that animate the design principles of parecon are close to the normative principles underlying the analysis of this book:

- *Social ownership* is similar to the way I framed the problem of social ownership as a contrast to both state and private ownership in the concept of socialism.

- *Democratic self-management* is closely connected to the concept of political justice as equal access to the necessary means to control the conditions of one's life.[97]

- *Job complexes* are a useful way of deepening the radical egalitarian principle of social justice as equal access to the necessary means to live a flourishing life, since interesting and meaningful work is an important condition for flourishing.

- *Remuneration to effort*, when combined with the additional norm of *remuneration for needs*, is very close to the principle of equal access to the material means to live a flourishing life.

---

97 The principle that an individual's influence on decisions should be proportional to the effects of those decisions on their lives was not an explicit part of my specification of what political justice entails, but I think it is an appropriate elaboration of the idea that people should have equal access to those decisions which affect their lives.

- *Democratic participatory planning* as an ideal is a further expression of democracy as equal access to participation in decisions that influence one's life.

So, at the level of ideals, parecon and socialism-as-social-empowerment are operating in very much the same moral universe. Nevertheless, they differ substantially in terms of the framework for translating these ideals into a practical institutional structure within which people can live and work. In spite of his efforts to give many concrete details on how participatory planning would work, Albert's model is more like a utopian vision that does not take sufficiently seriously pragmatic problems of complexity, difficult trade-offs, and unintended consequences, than it is a viable design for a real utopian alternative to capitalism.

One way of posing the problem is to ask: How confident can we realistically be, in the world in which we live now, that we understand the likely dynamics of an entirely new kind of social structure? How certain is our scientific understanding of the key problems that would be set in motion in an economic system organized along the lines of parecon? This would include, for example: our theory of how people make decisions under different social conditions and facing different problems of complexity; how solidarity is formed and fractured under different rules of allocation; how information complexity can generate chaotic processes; how preferences are formed under different micro- and macro-processes of cooperation and competition; how variations in selfish and altruistic dispositions and preferences are both generated and reproduced; how accurate information can be generated in complex interactive contexts where there may be advantages to distorting information; and many other things. I think we have sufficient insight into such problems to justify believing that it is possible to move along the pathways of social empowerment from the existing world; but I do not think we have enough of a grasp of the issues to know how a complex economic system organized through decentralized planning councils without any markets would actually function, or even whether such a structure would be even minimally viable. What we have observed and can study are specific workplaces in which democratic-participatory principles are rigorously in place, as well as a variety of more macro-settings where meaningful forms of participatory councils have operated (as in the participatory budget in Porto Alegre). But these

limited settings hardly constitute an empirical basis for making
confident claims about how an entire economic system built on
these principles would or could function. This, of course, does
not imply the converse—that we know enough now to be sure
that parecon as envisioned by Michael Albert is impossible—but
admitting that parecon *might* be possible (because of our ignorance on a range of problems) is insufficient grounds upon which
to propose a transformative project that confidently rejects any
role for markets in a democratic egalitarian society.

For his part, Albert never flinches in his absolute certainty that
parecon will work well enough to constitute an improvement
over both capitalism and any possible market socialism. This is
not to say that he fails to acknowledge that in practice the institutions of a future parecon economy will only approximate the
ideals. He emphasizes that there will be mistakes and failures: job
complexes will only approximate perfect balance; democratic self-
management will never be able to perfectly calibrate voting and
participation rules to the proportionality of effects on the lives
of participants; and participatory planning will never be able to
perfectly reflect all of the social costs and benefits of alternative
allocations of economic resources. And he embraces, appropriately, a pragmatic experimentalist view of how parecon institutions
would be instituted and developed: if they don't work, then they
will be modified in ways that cannot be anticipated in advance.
Nevertheless he insists unequivocally that whatever pragmatic
limitations parecon might have it will be superior to even the best-
designed form of market socialism, and, however unexpected the
direction of its evolution, it will not include markets.

Albert's uncompromisingly extreme position against markets
is anchored in two propositions. The first is the claim that the ills
associated with capitalism come as much from the fact that capitalism is a type of market economy as from the distinctive class
relations of capitalism. It is for this reason that Albert believes
that any form of market socialism, even if it completely eliminated
capitalist ownership, would be at most a very modest improvement over capitalism:

> whatever gains over capitalism have been achieved in attaining market
> socialism, market socialism is still not an economy that by its intrinsic
> operations promotes solidarity, equity, diversity, and participa-
> tory self-management while also accomplishing economic functions
> efficiently. Instead *all of the intrinsic ills of markets*—particularly
> hierarchical workplace divisions, remuneration according to output

and bargaining power, distortion of personality and motives, and mispricing of goods and services, etc.—persist, while *only* the aggravating presence of private capital is transcended.[98]

He therefore sees markets as inherently entailing not simply voluntary, decentralized exchange, but also things like hierarchy and remuneration according to output and bargaining power, whereas I see those as consequences of unregulated markets, not of markets as such.

Albert's second basic proposition is the claim that the presence of even limited markets is destructively corrosive of democratic egalitarian values: "Having a little markets in a parecon is a bit like having a little slavery in a democracy, though even less tenable. The logic of markets invalidates the logic of participatory planning and of the whole parecon, and it is also imperial, once it exists trying to spread as far as wide as it can."[99] Albert thus fundamentally rejects the concept of reproducible hybrid forms of economic structures that combine opposing logics: the presence of markets within what I have termed a socialist hybrid would, for him, inevitably destroy the socialist elements.

If one accepts these two propositions, then it might make sense to argue for the complete abolition of markets and their replacement by decentralized participatory planning, even if one lacked convincing evidence that a complex economy without any role for markets would in fact work very well. I do not, however, think there are good grounds for this absolutist rejection of markets. Even if they are corrosive of egalitarian and democratic values it does not follow that it is impossible to impose upon markets forms of social and political regulation that would largely neutralize these corrosive effects. Albert insists that we have unequivocal empirical evidence that markets as such generate all of these negative effects, but in fact all that we have unequivocal empirical evidence for

---

98   Albert, *Parecon*, p. 79 (emphasis added).
99   Albert, *Parecon*, p. 277. I do not find this analogy between slavery and the market compelling. Slavery is inherently morally abhorrent. Markets become abhorrent, if they do, because of their aggregate emergent properties and effects, not their molecular character. A bilateral voluntary exchange between equals is not morally objectionable. If there were a mechanism that sustained that equality, then the regularization of such exchanges would also not be inherently objectionable in the same sense that slavery is. It could be the case that the emergent properties and negative externalities of markets in the aggregate are so powerful that no form of democratic regulation can neutralize them, but this is a much more complex argument than is the case with regard to slavery.

is that markets *combined with capitalist class relations* generate these effects; we don't know what the effects of markets combined with other forms of economic organization would be. Markets can generate inequalities in wages, but after-market income taxes can substantially redistribute income. Firms operating within markets may ignore negative externalities, but democratic regulatory processes can assess those externalities and impose constraints on market decisions, particularly if those regulatory processes are themselves organized through associational democracy rather than as centralized command-and-control regulation. What is more, in a hypothetical context where concentrations of *capitalist* power have been reduced through progress along the multiple pathways of social empowerment, such regulatory processes are likely to be much more effective than in capitalism for reasons we have already discussed. Of course such attempts at regulating markets will themselves always be imperfect. But so will the attempts at system-wide planning within parecon. We cannot know in advance whether the problems generated by such "imperfections" would be greater in a pure participatory economy of the sort Albert proposes or in a hybrid form within which markets continued to play a meaningful role.

Once we drop the assumption that markets are like cancer—so that if you have a little in the mix it will inevitably corrode and destroy social empowerment—then the issue of the optimal balance between participatory planning and unplanned market allocations is not one that can be decided in advance of the pragmatic learning process of social transformation. There is certainly no *a priori* reason to suppose that the balance that would be arrived at through a process of deliberative democracy would be 100 percent planning + 0 percent markets.

There are at least four reasons why the participants in a vigorously democratic participatory process rooted in the democratic egalitarian values of parecon might nevertheless opt for a significant presence of markets.[100] First, participants in a democratic process know that their preferences are formed within social interactions and that people today cannot have a fully rational grasp of possible preferences tomorrow. They might therefore recognize the virtues of having a chaotic unplanned element in the process of creating an economic environment for preference formation: a

---

100   I am framing the issue here in terms of the balance between markets and participatory planning, but a similar argument could be made concerning the balance between centralized state regulation and participatory planning.

democratically planned participatory economy might be better if it
had a significant, if still circumscribed, unplanned component—a
little "anarchy of production" *might* function more effectively than
a more thoroughly planned economic process, even if this meant
that there would be some negative market-effects that would need
to be counteracted through regulations.

Second, participants in an economy that is experimenting with
various combinations of participatory democratic economic forms
and market forms might discover that markets provide some
advantages for certain desirable forms of risk taking. It might be
good to have a space for risk taking without having to get permission from councils and committees before taking the risks, and this
less planned form of risk taking might be most easily facilitated by,
again, allowing space for market activities and market incentives.
This does not mean that innovation requires markets. But it could
still be the case that the optimal level of risk taking with respect
to innovations may require having a mix of innovation-inducing
social processes, and this could include allowing individuals and
collectivities to take risks through markets without prior permission for the specific risk-project.

Third, the information complexity of the iterated planning
process described in *Parecon* might in the end simply overwhelm
the planning process. Albert is confident that with appropriate
computers and software this would not be a problem—and he
dismisses people who disagree with him on this. Perhaps he is right.
But he may also be utterly wrong. As described in *Parecon* the
information process seems hugely burdensome, particularly since
it includes workers and consumers writing qualitative accounts
of their needs and activities, and councils absorbing such qualitative information and deploying it in evaluating plans. The sketch
of the information process provided by Albert is useful in giving
a sense of how things could take place, but it does not provide a
convincing case that this would actually generate coherent plans
that would converge on a set of quantities and prices for all products in a large economy.

Finally, there is the question of how people want to live their lives
and whether the amount of time spent on paperwork, in meetings,
and at computer terminals in a pure parecon system is the amount
that participants would democratically choose. Of course, if
parecon really is an all-or-nothing proposition—either you have a
full-blown participatory economy with no markets, or the system
will degenerate back to a full-blown market economy—then

democratic egalitarians might opt for parecon even if they were generally unhappy about the time required for such participation. Life involves trade-offs, and this could be worth it if the choice was such a stark one. But if economic social empowerment is not an all-or-nothing proposition, if hybrids are possible, then choices can be made over the trade-offs between a participatory economy without markets involving more time devoted to the tasks of participatory decision making and a hybrid which would require less time to be taken up on such tasks. It is impossible to decide what the optimal balance is before the people who will live within these institutions have had a chance to experience different possibilities and figure things out through a process of pragmatic, democratic experimentalism.

CONCLUSION: AN EXPANSIVE AGENDA OF SOCIAL EMPOWERMENT

This chapter has touched on only a selected number of proposals of institutional designs that would increase social empowerment over the economy. There are many other empirical examples and theoretical ideas which could have been discussed. To just give a sense of the wider range of possibilities, here are some of the other forms of social empowerment over the economy:

Community land trusts. These are forms of collective ownership of land—by community groups, social movement organizations, NGOs, or sometimes government organizations—which take land out of the real estate market, place it into a distinctive legal form of property rights called a "land trust" which significantly restricts the subsequent transfer of ownership, and then uses the land for various kinds of social purposes such as low-income housing, nature conservancy, and various projects of community development. The idea is that land should be controlled by socially rooted collective associations rather than by private individuals or capitalist developers.

International labor standards campaigns. It is widely recognized that one of the reasons capital moves production facilities from the developed world to developing countries is because of cheap labor and lower labor standards. One reaction to this by the labor movements in the North is to try to erect trade barriers to imports of industrial products produced in low-wage countries or in other ways to impede the "export" of jobs through outsourcing. But another response is to attempt to create international labor standards which would be effectively enforced in the developing world. There are a number of difficulties involved in such endeavors: establishing a set of labor standards that are not simply a disguised form of protectionism; creating an effective monitoring apparatus that will provide reliable information about compliance, especially given the complex subcontracting relations that occur in many sectors; and being able to impose meaningful sanctions for noncompliance. As Gay Seidman has forcefully argued, transborder labor standards campaigns are most effective when they involve collaboration between social movements in the North and South along with the participation of the state in the monitoring and enforcement process.[101]

United Students Against Sweatshops. Universities in the United States control the use of the name of their university and university logos in commercial products like t-shirts and sweatshirts. The United Students Against Sweatshops (USAS) was formed to pressure universities to license their logos only to manufacturers who agree to a strict labor standards code.[102] To this end, in 2000 the USAS formed a monitoring organization, the Workers' Rights Consortium (WRC), to investigate working conditions in factories that produce apparel with university logos on them. There existed at the time a clothing-industry-backed monitoring organization—which was renamed the Fair Labor Association—which offered universities a much weaker set of standards. As the result of a protracted struggle on university campuses, including sit-ins in administration offices and rallies and demonstrations, many universities ended up adopting the stronger standards. More recently, the USAS has tried to increase the effectiveness of its anti-sweatshop drive by creating a designated supplier program which lists factories that have been positively certified as compliant by the WRC. As of the end of 2008 over forty universities have agreed to restrict contracts for university apparel to factories in the designated supplier program.

---

101 Gay Seidman, *Beyond the Boycott: Labor Rights, Human Rights and Transnational Activism* (New York: Russell Sage Foundation, 2007). See also Cesar Rodriguez-Garavito, "Global Governance and Labor Rights: Codes of Conduct and Anti-Sweatshop Struggles in Global Apparel Factories in Mexico and Guatemala," *Politics and Society* 33: 2 (2005).

102 http://www.studentsagainstsweatshops.org.

Forestry conservation certification. Social movements have also been involved in struggles over environmental issues in which they use information campaigns, boycotts, and other strategies to try to get multinational corporations to comply with various kinds of good environmental standards. In the early 1990s, one such campaign resulted in the creation of the Forestry Stewardship Council (FSC) in an effort at specifying high ecological standards for forestry management and establishing a mechanism for certifying that specific forests meet these standards. The structure of the FSC embodies many elements of associational democracy. As described by Christine Overdevest:

> the FSC scheme is characterized by a deliberative and democratic governance structure. Representatives of traditionally oppositional, formal interest groups make up the FSC's "balanced," participatory and deliberative membership-based governance structure. The membership currently is composed of 561 members worldwide, with 79 from the U.S., but voting weight is equally distributed among three chambers—economic, social, and environmental. The economic chamber is constituted by forestry firms, secondary processors and retailers, auditing organizations, and consultants. The social chamber includes civil society groups and individuals who represent community development, poverty, and human and worker rights organizations, and the environmental chamber includes a variety of environmental interests groups ranging from activist-oriented organizations like Greenpeace and Friends of the Earth to mainstream organizations such as the World Wildlife Fund and the Nature Conservancy. Each chamber has one-third of the vote. Because of the variability in the meaning of conservation, within each FSC chamber one-half of the voting power has been further assigned to "northern hemisphere members" and one-half to the "southern hemisphere members," to "balance" the interests of developed and developing countries.[103]

This governance body sets certification standards and oversees the monitoring process of forests. The certification of forests, in turn, provides a basis for certifying that wood products from those forests were produced in a way consistent with environmental sustainability.

The complexities of this certification and monitoring process are considerable. Not only is it necessary to closely monitor forestry practices over a very wide area, it is also necessary to keep track of the products derived from these forests to be sure that uncertified products do not mix with them on their way through the

---

103 Christine Overdevest, "Codes of Conduct and Standard Setting in the Forest Sector: Constructing Markets for Democracy?," *Relations Industrielles/ Industrial Relations* 59: 1 (2004), pp. 179–80.

supply chain. Furthermore, the forestry industry itself has created certification programs, typically with lower standards, which often confuses consumers. Nevertheless, such campaigns have had modest success in getting some large retailers to carry lumber that has been certified by the Forestry Stewardship Council, and pressure from the FSC also appears to have forced the forest industry's own standard-setting and certification organization, the Sustainable Forestry Initiative, to gradually raise its standards.[104] These campaigns, when they become institutionalized as monitoring organizations rooted in social movement associations, constitute a form of social capitalism: social power constrains the exercise of economic power over particular aspects of production and distribution.

The Equal Exchange trade cooperative and the Fair Trade movement. There is a small but growing effort of worker-owned cooperatives in the global North to become involved in the trade of commodities produced by cooperatives in the global South. The best-known example of this is the worker-owned coffee cooperative Equal Exchange, founded in Massachusetts in 1986. Its central objective is to import coffee (and subsequently tea and chocolate) produced within agricultural cooperatives from the global South. In the 1990s Equal Exchange joined with other organizations in what had come to be known as the Fair Trade movement. The idea here is to create global standards for "fair trade" and a reliable organization for certifying that goods have been produced according to those standards. In recent years the integrity of the official fair trade certification process has come into question as the Fair Trade movement has attempted to get large retailers like Starbucks and Whole Foods to include fair trade products. This has led, some people argue, to a dilution of the certification standards as fair trade certification has been extended to commodities grown on large farms and plantations so long as they met certain minimal conditions. For this reason some coffee cooperatives, such as Just Coffee in Madison, Wisconsin, have pulled out of the fair trade certification organization and are attempting to create more direct connections between coffee cooperatives in the global South and roasters and retailers in the global North.[105]

*   *   *

---

104 See Overdevest, "Codes of Conduct and Standard Setting."
105 Information about Just Coffee can be found on its website: http://justcoffee.coop. For a through study of fair trade coffee, see Daniel Jaffee, *Brewing Justice: Fair Trade Coffee, Sustainability, and Survival* (Berkeley: University of California Press, 2007).

This array of institutional proposals for moving along the pathways of social empowerment constitutes a rich, diverse menu of possibilities. Some of the institutional designs we have explored can be constructed by a few people single-mindedly working together. This is the case for many worker-owned cooperatives, including those which have a transformative mission. Others require the concentrated effort of social movements and collective associations, as in some of the social capitalism proposals we have examined. And still others can only happen with the strong involvement of the state, as is the case for basic income. While individually each proposal can be seen as contributing to expanding and deepening social empowerment, the real progress in shifting the power configuration of the economic hybrid will come from the interactions and synergies among them: basic income can facilitate the formation of cooperatives and social economy enterprises; various forms of social capitalism can contribute to expanding the cooperative market economy; and all of these can increase the political will for new forms of participatory socialism.

The prospects for such synergies, however, depend upon the possibilities for transformative struggles. And to understand those possibilities, we need a theory of transformation. This is the subject of the next four chapters.

III: TRANSFORMATION

ELEMENTS OF A THEORY OF
TRANSFORMATION

Even if one accepts the vision of social empowerment we have been exploring as both *desirable* and *viable*, the question remains: how could this possibly be *achievable*? A skeptic might argue thus: If indeed these institutional arrangements constitute central components of a viable movement in the direction of radical democratic egalitarian emancipatory ideals, then the creation of these institutions would be massively opposed by elites whose interests would be threatened by such changes. And so long as capitalism remains the dominant component in the economic structure, those elites will have sufficient power to block or subvert any serious movement along the pathways of social empowerment.

This, then, is the fundamental problem for a theory of transformation: in order to advance democratic egalitarian ideals it is necessary to radically extend and deepen the weight of social empowerment within economic structures in capitalist societies, but any significant movement in this direction will be a threat to the interests of powerful actors who benefit most from capitalist structures and who can use their power to oppose such movement. How, then, can significant movement on the pathways of social empowerment be accomplished? To answer this question we need a theory of emancipatory social transformation.

A fully developed theory of social transformation involves four interlinked components: A theory of *social reproduction*, a theory of the *gaps and contradictions of reproduction*, a theory of *trajectories of unintended social change*, and a theory of *transformative strategies*. The first of these provides an account of the obstacles to emancipatory transformation. The second shows how, in spite of these obstacles, there are real possibilities of transformation. The third attempts to specify the future prospects of both obstacles and possibilities. And finally, the fourth component attempts to answer the question "what is to be done?" in light of the prior account of the obstacles, possibilities, and future trajectories. While for the purposes of exposition we will distinguish these four theoretical agendas, they are deeply interconnected. The processes of reproduction, contradiction, and dynamic trajectories of change are not sharply distinct: the process of social reproduction is intrinsically contradictory, and the very practices involved in such contradictory reproduction endogenously generate the trajectories of unintended social change.

In this chapter I will briefly sketch each of these agendas. I will not attempt to explore any of them thoroughly, since this would require a book in its own right. Rather, the purpose is to set the stage for a discussion of alternative modes of emancipatory transformation in the following three chapters.

SOCIAL REPRODUCTION

The term "social reproduction" is used in a variety of distinct ways in social theory. Sometimes it refers to the problem of intergenerational reproduction of social status: social reproduction is primarily about the ways in which parents transmit status to their children, through socialization, education, wealth transfers, and so on. Sometimes social reproduction is used as a contrast to "production": reproduction refers to those activities that reproduce people over time, particularly the caring and nurturing activities performed especially by women, in contrast to activities that produce goods and services. Here I am using the term to refer to the processes that reproduce the underlying structure of social relations and institutions of a society. While this certainly involves mechanisms for the intergenerational transmission of status and includes the problem of reproducing people on a day-to-day basis, in the present context I will use the term to refer to the reproduction of social structures.

All forms of emancipatory social theory contain at least a rudimentary account of social reproduction. Sometimes this can be quite simple, emphasizing the ways in which powerful and privileged actors use coercion to maintain their advantages. But more characteristically theories of social reproduction involve complex accounts of how people's subjectivities and mundane practices are formed in such a way as to help stabilize social systems.

Social reproduction in capitalist society takes place through two sorts of interconnected processes which I will call *passive reproduction* and *active reproduction*. Passive reproduction refers to those aspects of social reproduction that are anchored in the mundane routines and activities of everyday life. This is social reproduction of "the dull compulsion of everyday life." People go about their daily life with ingrained habits and dispositions, a sense of the naturalness and taken-for-grantedness of the social world that comes simply from living in it. Workers go to work and follow orders on the job, and in so doing they not only produce commodities for the market but also reproduce their own status as workers.[1] This passive aspect of social reproduction is not the result of specialized effort and consciously constructed institutions designed for the purpose of social reproduction. Passive social reproduction is simply a by-product of the ways in which the daily activities of people mesh in a kind of self-sustaining equilibrium in which the dispositions and choices of actors generate a set of interactions that reinforces those dispositions and choices.[2]

Active social reproduction, in contrast, is the result of specific institutions and structures which at least in part are designed to serve the purpose of social reproduction. These include a wide variety of institutions: the police, the courts, the state administration, education, the media, churches, and so on. This is not to say that the only purpose of such institutions is social reproduction. Most complex social institutions serve a variety of "functions." Nor does the claim that these are institutions of active social reproduction imply that

---

1 Some treatments of the idea of social reproduction, especially within the Marxist tradition, also emphasize the ways in which passive social reproduction is simultaneously a process of dynamic development. The process of capitalist production and accumulation consists of workers going to work, entering the labor process and producing commodities which then get sold by capitalists to realize a profit which capitalists invest in capitalist production, etc. This process does not reproduce itself as a static, fixed structure, but as a dynamically developing structure of relations and processes. Through their interconnected mundane practices, therefore, workers and capitalists both reproduce these relations and transform them. This endogenous developmental aspect of reproduction is foregrounded in the discussion of the third element in the theory of transformation: the problem of trajectories of unintended social change.

2 Much of Pierre Bourdieu's analysis of social reproduction concerns various aspects of what I am here calling passive reproduction. Bourdieu's concept of *habitus* identifies the ways in which individuals acquire unconscious dispositions which enable them to function smoothly within a structure of relations. This constitutes the basis for a process of social reproduction to the extent that these dispositions lead to practices that reinforce the dispositions. Göran Therborn's brilliant discussion, in *The Power of Ideology and the Ideology of Power* (London: Verso, 1980), of "subjection" and "qualification" in his analysis of how ideological practices shape social subjects is also largely an analysis of passive reproduction. Passive reproduction is also very close to the notion of equilibrium in certain strands of institutional economics informed by game theory: the preferences, norms, and expectations of each actor in an institutional equilibrium are continually reinforced by the spontaneous strategies of other actors. See, for example, Masahiko Aoki, *Comparative Institutional Analysis* (Cambridge, MA: MIT Press, 2001).

they are always effective. Indeed, the limits and contradictions of such institutions are of pivotal importance for a theory of social emancipation. What is at issue here is that social reproduction is the result of the deliberate actions of individuals and the deliberate design of institutions and not simply the unconscious by-product of mundane activities.

Active and passive reproduction interact in important ways. Passive reproduction is aided by various institutions which help stabilize the mundane routines of everyday life. The regulation of contracts by the state, for example, facilitates predictable routines in labor markets and work, which in turn underwrite the passive reproduction generated by daily activities in workplaces. Accordingly passive reproduction can be disrupted when the institutions that shape the contexts of daily life are themselves disrupted for one reason or another. But equally, the burden on institutions of active social reproduction is much greater if the processes of passive reproduction are weak and contradictory. Active and passive social reproduction thus constitute a system of variable coherence and effectiveness.

The basic (implicit) proposition of theories of social reproduction within most currents of emancipatory social theory is this: *Social structures and institutions that systematically impose harms on people require vigorous mechanisms of active social reproduction in order to be sustained over time.* Oppression and exploitation are not sustained simply through some process of social inertia rooted only in the mechanisms of passive reproduction; they require active mechanisms of social reproduction in order to be sustained.[3] This proposition is itself derived from three underlying claims:

---

3 This way of framing the issues gives the theory of social reproduction a certain "functionalist" cast: The argument begins with a claim that oppressive social structures "require" an array of processes in order to survive; we observe that these structures do survive; and therefore we conclude that there must exist the requisite kinds of mechanisms. Traditional Marxist analyses of the state, for example, often treat it as "fulfilling the function" of reproducing the economic structure. G. A. Cohen has forcefully argued that the classical base/superstructure analysis of capitalism in historical materialism relied on functional explanations: the superstructure exists and takes the form it does because it reproduces the economic base; see G. A. Cohen, *Karl Marx's Theory of History: A Defense* (Princeton: Princeton University Press, 1978). Such functional reasoning, however, need not imply that mechanisms of reproduction are generated by some automatic, non-intentional process operating "behind the backs" of people. Social reproduction is a contested, partial, and contradictory reality. If there are strong tendencies for particular institutions to contribute functionally to social reproduction, this is the result of the history of struggles over social reproduction and the resulting process of institution building, not some automatic, functional logic of the system.

1. *The reality of harms.* The harms specified in the diagnosis and critique of capitalism do not simply reflect the peculiar values and ideas of theorists; they are to a greater or lesser extent experienced by people as real harms.[4] This does not mean, of course, that people necessarily understand the *source* of these harms. This is why emancipatory social science begins with a diagnosis and critique of existing social structures and institutions. But while the nature and causes of harms may not be transparent, nevertheless the harms are real, not simply a matter of perspective: they are embodied in lived experience by actual people and would in general be recognized as socially generated harms if people had all of the relevant information.

2. *Human capacities and motivations.* People universally have certain basic capacities (intelligence, imagination, problem-solving abilities, etc.) and motivations (for material well-being and security, social connection, autonomy, etc.) which would lead one to predict that when they experience things which are harmful to their lives, they will try to do something about it. When the source of harms is social, this means that *in the absence of counteracting forces*, people will try to change the social conditions which generate these harms. This does not mean that people never resign themselves to a life of suffering, but that such resignation requires explanation, given human intelligence and problem-solving capacity. Something must be interfering with a response that would improve their situation.

3. *Obstacles.* In the absence of mechanisms which block social transformation, there will thus be a tendency for people to challenge those social structures and institutions which generate harms, and while this does not necessarily mean they will fully succeed, it does mean that those structures and institutions are likely to change. *The absence of challenges to oppression, therefore,*

---

4   There are some currents of contemporary social theory which reject the idea that it is possible to make objective claims about harms and suffering, or about their antithesis, human flourishing. Suffering and flourishing, the argument goes, are entirely derived from arbitrary and variable cultural standards. It is possible to talk about "real harms" only in culturally defined terms. While culture plays a pivotal role in the interpretation of harms and suffering, and affects the ways in which people cope with them, I do not think that the problem of harms can be reduced to a problem of culturally determined perceptions. For a penetrating discussion of a realist view of suffering and flourishing, see Andrew Sayer, *The Moral Significance of Class* (Cambridge: Cambridge University Press, 2005).

requires an explanation. This is what a theory of social reproduction attempts to provide for an emancipatory social science:
understanding the specific mechanisms that generate obstacles
to such processes of oppression-reducing social transformation.
This is not to suggest that oppressive social structures are always
precarious, vulnerable to challenge, and in need of finely tuned
active mechanisms to hold them together. Capitalism is not like
a biological organism which can survive only under very specific
and restrictive conditions. What an oppressive social system like
capitalism needs are reasonably effective mechanisms that will
contain social conflicts within tolerable limits, sufficiently muting
their disruptive effects so that capitalist investment and capital
accumulation can take place.

Understood in this way, the problem of social reproduction
within an emancipatory social science is *not* the same as the classical "problem of social order" within sociology. Theories of
social order and of social reproduction both attempt to explain
social integration and stability, but they do so against different
counterfactuals. The counterfactual to social order is Hobbesian
chaos; the counterfactual to social reproduction is social transformation. The problem of social order is grounded in the latent
potential for individuals to act in normatively unconstrained
predatory ways—the war of all against all. The theory of social
order attempts to explain the mechanisms that generate stable
forms of cooperation and social integration by counteracting such
individualistic anti-social tendencies of predation. The problem of
social reproduction is grounded in the latent potential for people
collectively to challenge structures of domination, oppression,
and exploitation. The theory attempts to explain the mechanisms
that generate sufficiently stable forms of cooperation and system
integration to mute such collective tendencies for transformation. Both the problem of social order and the problem of social
reproduction are important themes in social theory, and certain
institutions may contribute to both—the police, for example, can
both prevent chaos and obstruct emancipatory transformation.
Our concern here, however, is not with the issue of social order
as such, but with the processes that contribute systematically to
the reproduction of the fundamental social structures of power,
oppression, and privilege in capitalist society.

What, then, are the central ingredients for a theory of social
reproduction? Four clusters of mechanisms through which

institutions of various sorts affect the actions of people, individually and collectively, are especially important: *coercion*, *institutional rules*, *ideology*, and *material interests*. These constitute mechanisms of capitalist social reproduction to the extent that they, first, obstruct individual and collective actions which would be threatening to capitalist structures of power and privilege, and, second, channel actions in such a way that they positively contribute to the stability of those social structures, particularly through the ways in which the actions contribute to passive reproduction.[5] The core problem for a theory of the reproduction of capitalism is to understand the ways in which the institutions of capitalist society accomplish this.

Coercion, rules, ideology, and material interests interact in a variety of ways, some more effective than others in creating a system of coherent social reproduction. Two configurations are especially important, which I will refer to as *despotism* and *hegemony*.[6] In the former, coercion and rules are the central mechanisms of social control; ideology and material interests mainly function to reinforce coercion and rules. In the latter, ideology and material interests play a much more central role in social reproduction. In what follows we will first look briefly at each of the clusters of mechanisms and then examine the contrast between the configurations of despotism and hegemony.

1. *Coercion: mechanisms which raise the costs of collective challenge*

At the center of active social reproduction are various processes which raise the cost of collective challenges to existing structures of power and privilege by imposing various kinds of punishments on people for making such challenges. These include both costs

---

5   Obstructing threatening actions and promoting stability are not the same thing, since among non-threatening actions some actively contribute to sustaining power and privilege while other actions may have no systematic effects on the issue of stability.

6   This particular terminology for the contrast comes from Michael Burawoy's reworking of Gramsci's understanding of hegemony. In his discussions of the problem of workers' cooperation with capitalists within the labor process Burawoy distinguishes between what he calls hegemonic factory regimes and despotic factory regimes. This is a specific instance of the more general idea of despotic and hegemonic forms of social reproduction. See Michael Burawoy, *Manufacturing Consent: Changes in the Labor Process Under Monopoly Capitalism* (Chicago: University of Chicago Press, 1979) and *The Politics of Production: Factory Regimes Under Capitalism and Socialism* (London: Verso, 1985).

to individuals for participating in collective actions and costs to collectivities for organizing such actions.

Of particular importance here are the ways in which the state regulates the situation by making certain forms of collective action illegal. This is not simply a question of the state proscribing insurrectionary violence by revolutionary movements that directly challenge existing power structures; it also includes the state's attempts to regulate a wide range of associational practices that bear on the problem of forming collective organization for transformative social struggle. For example, part of the explanation for the weakness of the American labor movement is the particularly restrictive legal rules imposed on unions for organizing workers and engaging in collective action. Regulations that raise the costs of collective action for individuals and unions include such things as the legal right of employers to hire permanent replacement workers during strikes, laws that bar secondary boycotts by unions, rules governing union certification and decertification elections that are advantageous to employers, and so on. A union which violated these rules would face directly repressive actions by the state, ranging from heavy fines to imprisonment of union members and leaders. This adverse legal environment for labor organizing is further aggravated by the administrative practices of the state regulatory apparatuses which only weakly enforce rules favorable to labor. The overall result, therefore, is a relatively repressive and hostile regulatory environment for union organizing.

Beyond direct state regulation, non-state actors in various ways also use coercion and the threat of coercion to raise the costs of collective challenge to structures of power and privilege. Sometimes these non-state forms of repression are themselves authorized by the state, as in rules which allow employers to fire employees who are seen as troublemakers, or rules which prevent people from handing out leaflets in shopping malls. Other times private repressiveness may not be formally authorized, but is nevertheless tolerated by the state, as in the long history of privately organized coercion to maintain structures of racial domination and exclusion.

Repression, as we know, does not always work. It can breed anger, undermine legitimacy, and contribute to solidarities of shared victimization. In some situations, therefore, coercion can trigger intensified resistance and thus fail as a mechanism of social reproduction. A key problem for a theory of social reproduction then is to understand the conditions which reinforce or undermine the effectiveness of coercive means of social reproduction. We will examine this issue in the discussion of hegemony below.

2. *Institutional rules: creating gradients of collective action opportunities*

While the importance of direct repression of illegal activity should not be underestimated, it would be a mistake to see the state's role in social reproduction as operating exclusively through such explicit coercion. Of equal importance are the procedural "rules of the game" which make some courses of action difficult to pursue and others much easier. Such gradients of collective action opportunities contribute to social reproduction when the easier, less risky strategies are much less likely to be threatening to the stability of capitalism than the more difficult strategies.

Consider, for example, the core institution of representative democracy in capitalist societies. Prior to the advent of the universal franchise, the general fear among ruling elites in capitalism was that democracy would threaten the stability of capitalism. This seems straightforward enough: if you give people who are harmed by capitalism the vote, this would surely only make it easier for them to challenge capitalism. Marx himself expressed this expectation when he wrote about representative democracy:

> The comprehensive contradiction of this constitution, however, consists in the following: the classes whose social slavery the constitution is to perpetuate, proletariat, peasantry, petty bourgeoisie, it puts into the possession of political power through universal suffrage. And from the class whose old social power it sanctions, the bourgeoisie, it withdraws the political guarantees of this power. It forces the political rule of the bourgeoisie into democratic conditions, which at every moment help the hostile classes to victory and jeopardize the very foundations of bourgeois society.[7]

As it turned out, representative democracy has been one of the critical sources of social stability in developed capitalism. Adam Przeworski, in his brilliant analysis of the dynamic reproductive effects of capitalist democracy, explains this outcome in terms of the mechanisms by which capitalist democracy channels social conflicts in ways that tend to reproduce capitalist social

---

7 Karl Marx, "Class Struggles in France," in Karl Marx and Frederick Engels, *Selected Works in Two Volumes*, Vol. I (Moscow: Foreign Languages Publishing House, 1962), p. 172.

relations.[8] The dilemma faced by socialist parties historically was basically this: if they participated seriously in electoral competition, then they would be subjected to a whole series of systematic pressures to act responsibly and play by the rules which over time would erode militancy; if, on the other hand, they abstained from electoral competition in order to avoid these pressures, then they risked political marginalization since other parties would be better positioned to champion the immediate economic interests of workers and other potential supporters of socialist parties. To avoid such marginalization, socialist parties historically chose to participate energetically in elections, but in order to win elections they had to support policies which would attract middle-class voters whose interests were less sharply at odds with capitalism, and when they won elections from time to time, if they wanted to remain in power they had to pursue policies which would foster robust capital accumulation. This does not mean, Przeworski stresses, that socialist and social democratic parties have not in fact served important material interests of workers, but they have done so in ways which broadly strengthen rather than undermine capitalism. Representative democracy has greatly facilitated this integrative process.

The design of electoral institutions in capitalist states is a specific instance of a more general phenomenon that Claus Offe has termed "negative selection"—the organization of state institutions in such a way as to filter out ("negatively select") those practices and policies which would have especially disruptive effects on the reproduction of capitalism.[9] Negative selection mechanisms built into the state would include things like the formal rules of bureaucratic administration (which insulate the state bureaucracy from popular pressures), the procedures of courts (which make it difficult for anti-system forces to effectively use the courts), and the rules though which the state acquires revenues for its activities (which make the state dependent on income generated within the capitalist economy for its tax base). Offe argues that the critical reproductive property

---

8 Adam Przeworski, *Capitalism and Social Democracy* (Cambridge: Cambridge University Press, 1985) and Adam Przeworski and John Sprague, *Paper Stones: A History of Electoral Socialism* (Chicago: University of Chicago Press, 1988). See also the superb analysis of the system-maintaining features of capitalist democracy in Joshua Cohen and Joel Rogers, *On Democracy* (New York: Penguin Books, 1983).

9 See Claus Offe, "Structural Problems of the Capitalist State: Class Rule and the Political System. On the Selectiveness of Political Institutions," in Klaus Von Beyme (ed.), *German Political Studies*, Vol. I (London: Sage, 1974), pp. 31–54.

of these mechanisms lies in what they systematically *exclude*: these filter mechanisms all have the effect of systematically impeding the possibility of systematic challenges to the basic structures of capitalism being translated into actions by the state.[10] When critics of capitalism argue that the capitalist state is systematically biased in favor of the capitalist class, much of what they are describing is the class character of these negative selection mechanisms built into the institutional rules of the state apparatuses.[11]

3. *Ideology and culture: mechanisms which shape the subjectivities of actors*

There are many different idioms one can use to discuss the social processes through which the subjectivities of actors are formed and the ways this contributes to (or perhaps undermines) social reproduction in the sense we are using this term here. One way of doing this is by drawing a contrast between *ideology* and *culture*. As I will use the terms here, ideology refers to the *conscious* aspects of subjectivity: beliefs, ideas, values, doctrines, theories, and so on. Culture refers to the *nonconscious* aspects of subjectivity: dispositions, habits, tastes, skills. Thus, for example, the *belief* that intense competitive individualism is a good thing would be an aspect of capitalist ideology; the personal habits, skills, and dispositions to act in intensely individualistic and competitive ways is an aspect of capitalist culture.[12]

---

10   The argument that the structure of the state imposes negative selectivity on state actions is a form of weak functionalism. The structure of the state excludes highly *dysfunctional* actions, actions which would seriously undermine capitalism, but among the non-excluded possibilities there is no claim that functionally optimal actions are selected.

11   The most extended, systematic analysis of the class biases built into the machinery of the capitalist state and of the complex ways in which these contribute to the reproduction of capitalism is Göran Therborn's *What Does the Ruling Class Do When it Rules?* (London: Verso, 1978).

12   This is not the standard way of explicitly defining the contrast of culture and ideology even if it corresponds in practice to the main ways these two terms are used in explanations. In many discussions, culture is an all-embracing term within which ideology would be a specific type of cultural product. In other discussions, ideology is used more restrictively to refer to coherent, codified doctrines rather than the full set of conscious elements of subjectivity. The definition of culture being adopted here, centering on the noncognitive aspects of subjectivity, corresponds closely to Pierre Bourdieu's concept of *habitus* as the internalized individual dispositions that connect people to their locations within social structures.

A central issue in the theory of social reproduction is the extent to which ideology and culture defined in this way contribute to the sustainability of structures of power, inequality, and privilege. Why should it be the case that the ideas people hold as well as their inner dispositions should contribute to the stability of a social structure? A variety of mechanisms have been proposed to answer this question. The simplest centers on the way the production and dissemination of ideas are in significant ways controlled by individuals and institutions that benefit substantially from existing structures of power and privilege.[13] The domination of the mass media by capitalist corporations, for example, would be a particularly salient aspect of this process. While this does not guarantee that the only messages people receive are those consistent with the interests of people in power, it does mean that system-affirming ideas will be more prevalent, disseminated more widely, cheaper to be exposed to, and backed by higher-status media and institutions than are ideas which challenge structures of power and privilege. To the extent that the beliefs and ideas people hold are shaped by the explicit messages they receive, this will tend to generate a rough correspondence between prevalent beliefs and the requirements of social reproduction.

Whatever tendency exists for there to be a correspondence of ideology and culture to the requirements of the social reproduction of capitalism, it is not, however, simply the result of the deliberate inculcation of ideas by powerful actors. Such correspondence is also generated by the micro-processes of the formation of beliefs and dispositions. Institutions of socialization, such as the family and schools, are generally concerned with instilling habits and dispositions that will enable children to function well in the world when they are adults, to live the best lives possible given

---

13 This mechanism for establishing a correspondence between the ideas people hold and the interests of ruling classes is one of the themes in Marx and Engels's well-known account of ideology in *The German Ideology* (New York: International Publishers, 1970): "The ideas of the ruling class are in every epoch the ruling ideas, i.e. the class which is the ruling material force of society, is at the same time its ruling intellectual force. The class which has the means of material production at its disposal, has control at the same time over the means of mental production, so that thereby, generally speaking, the ideas of those who lack the means of mental production are subject to it." (p.64) The mechanism which underlies this claim is the control over the process of production and dissemination of ideas by capitalists and their proxies.

the constraints they are expected to face. This means that parents and teachers try as best they can to encourage dispositions that are at least compatible with effective functioning within existing structures of power, inequality, and privilege. This does not always work well, but it generates at least a rough correspondence between the kinds of social subjects needed for the social structure to be reproduced and the kinds of social subjects produced within the society.[14]

Beliefs, of course, are not simply inculcated in the process of childhood socialization, but are continually formed and reformed throughout life, and this also bears on the processes of social reproduction. Here the issue is the various ways in which psychological processes of belief formation interact with the lived experience of people in the social settings in which they act. This is where the processes of active and passive social reproduction meet. Jon Elster, for example, argues that *adaptive preference formation* is one psychological process by which people come to align their beliefs about what is desirable with their perceptions of what is possible. This provides psychological foundations for certain key elements of inequality-supporting ideologies.[15] Göran Therborn has elaborated a simple learning model in his analysis of ideology and the formation of the human subject: As individuals go about their lives they act on the basis of certain kinds of beliefs about the nature of the social world in which they live. If they believe that the individual acquisition of education is a way to improve their material condition, then they are more likely to attempt to get education than if they believe education doesn't matter, and if they get more education then their economic prospects are likely to be better than those of people who did not. Every day when people go to work they act on the basis of their expectations about how other people will behave and what will be the consequences of their actions. In a well-functioning set

---

14   Göran Therborn, in *The Power of Ideology and the Ideology of Power*, aptly describes this as the process by which children are *subjected* to a form of subjectivity which *qualifies* them to function effectively in the society. The broad functional correspondence between the process of formation of social subjects in schools and the requirements of capitalist organizations is a longstanding theme in Marxist and critical studies of education. For an influential account of this correspondence see Samuel Bowles and Herbert Gintis, *Schooling in Capitalist America* (New York: Basic Books, 1976).

15   See Jon Elster, *Making Sense of Marx* (Cambridge: Cambridge University Press, 1985), especially chapter 8, "Ideologies," pp. 458–510.

of institutions with interlocking expectations and patterns of
behavior, these expectations and predictions will be fairly consistently affirmed, and the underlying beliefs thus reinforced; when
the predictions fail, the beliefs will tend to be weakened. To the
extent that the social system generates a pattern of "affirmations
and sanctions" (to use Therborn's expression) consistent with
the beliefs in a given ideology, that ideology will be strength-
ened. Ideology contributes to social reproduction, then, when
beliefs that contribute to social stability are affirmed in the daily
practices of individuals.

Of the various aspects of ideology and belief formation that
bear on the problem of social reproduction and potential challenges to structures of power and privilege, perhaps the most
important are beliefs about *what is possible*.[16] People can have
many complaints about the social world and know that it generates significant harms to themselves and others, and yet still
believe that such harms are inevitable, that there are no other real
possibilities that would make things significantly better, and that
thus there is little point in struggling to change things, particularly since such struggles involve significant costs. Such beliefs are
formed in part through education, the media, and other processes
by which people are told what is possible. But they are also forged
through daily, mundane activities in the world which make
existing institutions, social relations, and structures seem natural
and inevitable.

4. Material interests: mechanisms which tie the welfare of individuals to the effective functioning of capitalist structures

Joan Robinson, the Cambridge University economist from the
1930s through the 1950s, is reputed to have said: "The one
thing worse than being exploited in capitalism is not being
exploited." By this she meant, of course, that unemployment
was a worse condition than being exploited within work, not
that exploitation as such was desirable. This quip reflects a
central point about the process of the social reproduction of

---

16 Therborn, in *The Power of Ideology and the Ideology of Power*, identifies
three core questions for which ideology gives people answers: What is good?
What exists? What is possible? The first of these defines the normative dimension
of beliefs. The second centers on descriptions and explanations about how the
social world works. And the third concerns what alternatives are imaginable.

capitalist society: capitalism organizes the material conditions of life of people in such a way that nearly everyone fares better when the capitalist economy is doing well than when it is doing badly. The famous slogan, "What is good for General Motors is good for America" thus contains a crucial truth: within a well-functioning capitalism the material interests of almost everyone depend to a significant degree upon successful capitalist economic activity.

This near-universal dependence of everyone's material interests on the pursuit of profits by capitalist firms is perhaps the most fundamental mechanism of the social reproduction of capitalist society. It lends credibility to the claim that capitalism is in fact in everyone's interest, not just the interests of the capitalist class, and it places a considerably greater burden on the argument that an alternative to capitalism would be preferable. It underwrites broad public support for a wide range of state policies designed to sustain robust capital accumulation and acts as a systematic constraint on the pursuit of policies that might in other ways benefit a large majority of people but which might threaten capitalist profits. So long as capitalism can effectively tie the material interests of the large majority of the population to the interests of capital, other mechanisms of social reproduction have less work to do.

It is because of the centrality of this mechanism that economic crises in capitalism loom so large in discussions of social reproduction, for in crisis conditions the close link between individual material interests and capitalism is weakened. In a prolonged crisis large numbers of people may become relatively marginalized from the labor market and the core mechanisms of capitalist integration, and may thus begin to find ideologies and movements that challenge capitalism more credible. Marx and Engels's famous last lines from the Communist Manifesto—"The proletarians have nothing to lose but their chains. They have a world to win. Working Men of All Countries, Unite!"—have particular cogency when capitalism fails to provide for basic material welfare and security rather than simply when workers perceive it as obstructing their freedom. The stability of capitalism and its robustness against transformative challenges thus depend in significant ways on the extent to which it remains able to generate this kind of economic integration for large numbers of people.

Despotic and hegemonic reproduction

Coercion, rules, ideology/culture, and material interests should not be understood as four independent, autonomous clusters of mechanisms each of which additively contributes its bit to the process of social reproduction. Rather, social reproduction is the result of the complex forms of interaction among these processes. Institutional rules function best when people believe that they are legitimate (an aspect of ideology), when following them is in their material interests, and when there is a predictable sanction for violating them.[17] Coercion is more effective when rarely used because most people comply with laws out of duty or self-interest. Ideologies are more robust when they mesh with important aspects of material interests. To understand the problem of social reproduction, therefore, we must study configurations of mechanisms and not just the mechanisms taken separately.

Two configurations of these mechanisms of reproduction are particularly important: despotic reproduction and hegemonic reproduction.

In the despotic form, coercion is the primary mechanism of social reproduction, coupled with the specific institutional rules through which coercion is exercised. Social order is maintained primarily through fear, and potential transformative challenges are blocked primarily by various forms of repression. There is still a role for ideology and culture, and for material interests, if only to provide cohesion within elites and a necessary degree of loyalty within the repressive forces themselves. But most of the burden of social reproduction is carried by coercive processes.

In the hegemonic form of reproduction, coercion recedes to the background, and the active consent of subordinate classes and groups becomes much more important.[18] Active consent means

---

17   The point here is not that most people follow institutional rules simply out of fear of punishment. Compliance for most people most of the time follows from a belief in the obligation to follow rules. Nevertheless, the reality and predictability of sanctions still matters, for it shows those people who have a sense of obligation that *other people* who may lack that sense and who violate the rules are likely to be punished for doing so. This prevents the erosion of this sense of obligation that is likely to occur if people are able to violate the rules with impunity. For a systematic discussion of this interplay of obligation and coercion, see Margaret Levi, *Of Rule and Revenue* (Berkeley: University of California Press, 1989).

18   In Antonio Gramsci's well-known expression, hegemony is "protected by the armour of coercion." See Antonio Gramsci, *Selections From the Prison Notebooks*, edited and translated by Quintin Hoare and Geoffrey Nowell Smith (London: Lawrence and Wishart, 1971), p. 263.

that people willingly participate and cooperate in reproducing existing structures of power and inequality not mainly out of fear, but because they believe that doing so is both in their interests and is the right thing to do. Active consent requires more than the simple recognition that one's livelihood depends upon capitalist profits. That much is true even in a despotic system of capitalist social reproduction. It requires a much stronger sense that at least some of the gains from capital accumulation and capitalist development are shared with ordinary people, either through productivity-linked wage increases or through state redistribution in the form of a "social wage." This kind of *quid pro quo* of workers' active cooperation in exchange for gains from growth is called a "class compromise."

Active consent also depends on the ways in which the dominant class, to use Gramsci's expression, is seen as providing "moral and intellectual leadership" to the society as a whole. *Leaders* are different from *bosses*: bosses are obeyed because of their power; leaders are followed because of the belief that they are on your side, that they have your interests at heart and that you share with them a vision of the good society. When this is the case, the ideology which supports the status quo is not experienced as an alien body of ideas imposed on the society, but as a "common sense" that links elites and masses together in a common project.[19]

Institutional rules of the state are much more complex in hegemonic systems than in despotic systems of social reproduction. In a despotic system, the institutional rules of the state affect social reproduction primarily through their role in the exercise of threats and sanctions. The main problem they face is containing arbitrary, self-destructive forms of repression. In the hegemonic form of social reproduction there is a much greater burden on institutional rules, since they are called upon to facilitate class compromise and forge at least a rough ideological consensus. The rules of the game, therefore, need to channel the behavior of the elite and ruling classes in positive ways, not just the behavior of subordinate classes.

Despotic and hegemonic configurations of social reproduction are ideal types. Most actual capitalist systems contain both

---

19   For an excellent exposition of Gramsci's notions of ideological hegemony that emphasizes the ways in which it involves forging real ideological links between elites and masses, see Chantal Mouffe, "Hegemony and Ideology in Gramsci," in Chantal Mouffe (ed.), *Gramsci and Marxist Theory* (London: Routledge and Kegan Paul, 1979), pp. 168–206.

despotic and hegemonic processes. In the United States today, despotic reproduction plays a key role with respect to certain segments of the population, especially inner city minorities. The extraordinarily high level of imprisonment of African-American young men reflects the failure of any hegemonic project. A substantial segment of the "middle class," on the other hand, participates enthusiastically in the tasks of social reproduction through fully hegemonic processes. For much of the working class, social reproduction takes a mixed form.

LIMITS, GAPS, AND CONTRADICTIONS

If processes of social reproduction were comprehensive, effective, and fully coherent, then there would be little possibility for effective strategies of radical social transformation. The only kinds of deliberate social change that would be possible would be those entirely compatible with reproducing existing structures of power and privilege.

There are currents in social theory which come close to this view. Certain interpretations of the work of Foucault, for example, see domination as penetrating so deeply into the fabric of everyday life that there is virtually no room for transformative resistance. Some accounts of ideology and culture make the hold of dominant ideologies and cultural forms seem so powerful that it is hard to see how meaningful challenges can occur. And some accounts of the repressive capacity of the state make it seem that even if people were somehow to break out of the straightjacket of the hegemonic ideology, they would never be able to organize collective actions capable of seriously threatening dominant classes and elites without triggering levels of repression that would render such challenges futile.

There are reasons to be skeptical of this radical pessimism. One of the central tasks of emancipatory social science is to try to understand the contradictions, limits, and gaps in systems of reproduction which open up spaces for transformative strategies. There is, of course, no *a priori* guarantee in any time and place that those spaces are large enough to allow for significant movement in the direction of fundamental transformations of structures of domination, oppression, and exploitation. But even when the spaces are limited, they can allow for transformations that matter. In any case, emancipatory theory should not simply map the mechanisms of social reproduction, but should also identify the processes that generate cracks and openings in the system of reproduction.

What, then, are the sources of limits and contradictions to social reproduction in capitalist societies? Four themes are especially important:

1. Complexity and inconsistent requirements for social reproduction

The first and perhaps most fundamental source of limits and gaps to social reproduction is complexity. Social systems, particularly when they are built around deep cleavages and forms of oppression, have multiple requirements for their stable reproduction and in general there is no reason to believe that these requirements are entirely consistent. What this means is that the process of social reproduction is continually faced with dilemmas and trade-offs in which solutions to one set of problems create conditions which potentially intensify other problems.

Let me illustrate this with what might be called the "Frankenstein problem" of the state. For a whole host of familiar reasons, capitalism would destroy itself in the absence of an effective state capable of regulating various aspects of the market and production. There is thus what can be termed a functional necessity for "flanking systems" through which the state intervenes to prevent such self-destructive processes. The financial system must be regulated, infrastructures must be built, training and education must be provided, predatory business practices must be controlled, contracts must be enforced, negative externalities countered, monopolies regulated, and so on. In order for these interventions to work well the state needs to have both a degree of autonomy and an effective capacity to act—autonomy from the particular interests of specific capitalists and corporations and a real capacity to intervene to discipline capitalists and sectors. In the absence of this autonomy, parts of the state can be captured by particular groups of capitalists and state power used to protect their specific interests rather than manage the functioning of the capitalist system as a whole; in the absence of an effective capacity to act, the state's regulatory interventions will be ineffective. This autonomy and capacity, however, also mean that the state will have the ability to damage capital accumulation as well as facilitate it. This creates the specter of the state undermining social reproduction either by making serious mistakes or because the political leadership of the state begins to pursue anti-capitalist objectives for one reason or another. Thus the Frankenstein problem: in order to be able to autonomously intervene functionally the state must have the capacity to do so destructively; it has the potential to become a monster out of control.[20]

This potential problem becomes particularly intense as the conditions for a stable capitalist economy become more complex and require a broader array of state regulations and interventions. The extension and deepening of the interventionist capacity of the state creates a perpetual problem of lines of demarcation between the state and the economy as domains of action. These are no longer seen as "naturally" separated spheres and thus the scope and purposes of state action with respect to the economy are perpetually contested. In response to such contestation, capitalist elites and the political representatives they support might for a time argue for a radical retreat of the state towards deregulation and privatization, but a serious withdrawal of the state from the economic regulation of capitalism is an illusion. If the anti-statist mantra of neoliberalism were ever really implemented, capitalist crises would intensify and social reproduction would become even more problematic. Thus the dilemma: significantly reduce the regulatory role of the state and the likelihood of serious economic disruptions of the sort that began in 2008 increases; give the state the capacity and autonomy needed for effective intervention, and risk the continual politicization of the capitalist economy.[21] This dilemma means that there is unlikely to ever be a stable, sustainable equilibrium in the articulation of capitalist state power and the capitalist economy; the trajectory over time is more likely to involve episodic cycles of regulation/deregulation/reregulation.

---

20 The description of the state as a potential Frankenstein comes from Claus Offe. See in particular, Claus Offe, "The Capitalist State and the Problem of Policy Formation," in Leon Lindberg (ed.), *Stress and Contradiction in Contemporary Capitalism* (Lexington: D.C. Heath, 1975), pp. 125–44, and "The Crisis of Crisis Management: Elements of a Political Crisis Theory," in Claus Offe, *Contradictions of the Welfare State* (London: Hutchinson, 1984), pp. 35–61.

21 Claus Offe describes this tension in the role of the state in reproducing the capitalist economy as "the problem of whether the political administrative [system] can politically regulate the economic system without politicizing its substance and thus negating its identity as a capitalist economic system. . ."; see Offe, "The Crisis of Crisis Management," p. 52.

There are many other contradictions and dilemmas generated by the multiple requirements for the stable social reproduction of capitalism: tensions between the conditions for the reproduction of global corporations and local capitalist firms; between the requirements of different sectors of the economy (e.g., oil versus transportation; healthcare versus manufacturing); between reproducing the long-term environmental conditions for capitalism and the short-term rates of capital accumulation; and so on. There is no stable equilibrium possible in which all the conditions are simultaneously met in a satisfactory way such that all of these tensions are resolved, and this creates openings for strategies of social change.

2. Strategic intentionality and its ramifications

The active social reproduction of capitalism occurs through institutions that solve problems of various sorts which, were they to be left unsolved, would render capitalism more vulnerable to challenge and transformation. Functionally adequate solutions to problems of social reproduction, however, are not somehow generated automatically by the spontaneous workings of a society; they are produced through the intentional, strategic actions of people grappling with problems and struggling over the power to define the shape and practices of institutions. This means that institutions of social reproduction necessarily face three important problems: first, the problem of institutional design being the result of struggles over design rather than simple imposition; second, the problem of inadequate knowledge about the effects of alternative institutional designs and practices (and sometimes the problem of sheer stupidity on the part of powerful actors); and third, the problem of the accumulation of unintended and unanticipated consequences of intentional action.

The institutions that play a pivotal role in social reproduction are not the result of careful intentional design by powerful actors with a free hand to build such institutions as they wish; they are the result of struggles, especially among different factions of various sorts among elites, but also between elites and popular social forces. Marx's quip that people "make history, but not just as they choose" applies to elites just as much as to the masses. Institutional designs therefore reflect the balances of power and compromises of the social forces involved in their creation and development. The resulting institutions may certainly be "good enough" for adequate social reproduction most of the time, but they are very unlikely to constitute finely tuned, optimal machinery capable of blocking all efforts at transformative social change.

Second, even apart from the relatively messy conditions affecting the design and development of institutions important for social reproduction, inadequate knowledge is a chronic problem. Powerful actors may have access to more sophisticated economics and social science than ordinary citizens, but they are still prone to simple-minded theories about how society works and ideological blinders about optimal policies for social reproduction. Even if the leaders of the state and of other institutions of social reproduction are motivated to enact policies which secure the interests of capital and the social reproduction of capitalism, in many circumstances they act on the basis of a quite faulty grasp of what is needed to accomplish these goals, at times with astounding stupidity. It is a serious error to overestimate the intelligence and foresight, let alone the wisdom, of the rich and powerful. Mistakes, including quite serious mistakes, are therefore to be expected.

Finally, even when policies are based on sound theories, most have unintended side effects and over time the accumulation of unintended consequences can undermine the value of initially effective institutions. Gaps in the process of social reproduction, therefore, are both present from the start because of the strategic conditions under which those institutions are built, and develop over time through the ramifications of unintended consequences.

3. *Institutional rigidities and path dependency*

The problem of unintended consequences is particularly important because of the third source of limits on social reproduction—institutional rigidity. The issue is a familiar one: the institutions which play an important role in macro-social reproduction are created under specific historical conditions, facing particular problems and design possibilities. Their subsequent development bears the stamp of these initial conditions. Furthermore, they are themselves social systems in their own right, with internal cleavages, hierarchies, power structures, conflicts of interest, and so on. In order to be sustained over time they too need mechanisms for their own social reproduction.[22] These mechanisms of internal social reproduction render institutions relatively rigid—that is, they help sustain the basic structures of power and inequality within these institutions. This rigidity, however, makes it harder for institutions to respond flexibly when the requirements for broader social reproduction change.[23] States have particular kinds of electoral rules, political jurisdictions, administrative structures; capitalist firms have particular corporate structures, managerial hierarchies, divisions of labor; educational systems are designed to deal with particular kinds of students, labor markets, and cultural conditions. Thus, even those institutions that have contributed effectively to social reproduction in one period under one set of conditions may easily become much less effective as conditions change. But because of the vested interests in those institutions and the strength of their own mechanisms of reproduction, they may be very difficult to change or replace.[24]

Three examples will illustrate these issues. In the United States most people get their health insurance from their employers. In the 1950s and 1960s large corporations embraced this arrangement as a way of tying their employees to the firm. It was a relatively inexpensive fringe benefit and was seen as part of a package that contributed to ensuring a stable, loyal workforce. Gradually the benefit expanded, particularly to include retired workers who had worked for the firm for an extended period of time. By the end of the twentieth century, with an aging population and rapidly rising health costs, these health insurance obligations have become a significant liability to many firms. It is one of the reasons large US auto manufacturers are in serious economic difficulty at the beginning of the twenty-first century. Yet this particular institution of social reproduction is locked in to a large and powerful

22 In a sense, to use traditional Marxist language, superstructures contain superstructures: some of the structural properties of states have the "function" of reproducing the state itself.

23 This problem, it should be noted, applies to organizations committed to challenging existing institutions as well as to those institutions themselves: political parties and labor unions are institutions with internal hierarchies and power relations and internal mechanisms of social reproduction which generate path-dependent rigidities and may make it difficult for these organizations to adapt to changing strategic imperatives in their social environment.

24 This is one of the robust findings of the school of organizational sociology called "organizational ecology." In studies of capitalist firms, the basic organizational design of corporations changes mainly as one kind of firm replaces another rather than through processes of internal transformation.

private health insurance system which has, at least until now, effectively blocked any serious movement towards an alternative universal public insurance system. From the point of view of the overall stability and social reproduction of capital accumulation in the United States, by the 1990s some form of universal publicly funded insurance would almost certainly have been better than employer-funded private insurance, yet the institutional rigidity of the existing system and the interests bound up with it have prevented this change from occurring.

A second example is the pattern of urban transportation and housing in most American cities. In the 1950s and beyond a massive project of highway construction and suburbanization helped fuel a vibrant automobile-based process of capitalist economic growth in the US. These policies transformed the built environment of American cities and changed normative expectations about the balance between public and private modes of transportation. The twin processes of suburbanization and automobilization were central components of the hegemonic integration of the material interests of workers with capitalist development in the decades following World War II. These processes also destroyed much of the physical infrastructure of public transportation, most noto-riously in Los Angeles, and imposed serious constraints on the future development of transportation systems. Today, under conditions of rapidly rising energy costs and concerns about global warming, this lack of infrastructure and the prevalence of low-density residential development and urban sprawl in most large US cities make it very difficult to move towards a renewed system of mass urban transit that would be desirable, not just for individuals, but for capitalism as well.

The third example concerns the specific institutional devices designed to make it difficult to raise taxes in the state of California, particularly the requirement for a super-majority at the state level and the severe restriction on property taxes at the local level. These mechanisms were set in place by conservative anti-taxation forces who opposed the expansion of state services in the 1970s. The rules of the game created then are difficult to change, requiring constitutional amendments. The result was that in the fiscal crisis of the state government of California in 2009 it proved almost impossible to raise the revenues needed for even basic state services. The resulting paralysis of state government is highly dysfunctional for the interests of capital, not just for the population in general.

4. Contingency and unpredictability

Institutional rigidity would not necessarily generate significant gaps in the process of social reproduction if the tasks and problems of such reproduction remained fairly constant or if the changes in those tasks were sufficiently predictable that they could be anticipated well in advance. But this is not the case: perhaps the one thing we can predict with certainty is that the future is uncertain. One might imagine that the key institutions of social reproduction could be designed in such a way that they could quickly and flexibly respond to whatever new demands were placed on them. After all, learning capacity and adaptive capacity are the hallmarks of well-designed institutions. To some extent this is what liberal democracy has accomplished within capitalism, for democratic institutions do in fact make learning and change possible more effectively than do more closed authoritarian institutional structures. Nevertheless, even well-functioning liberal democratic institutions are plagued by institutional inertia, and the contingency and unpredictability of socioeconomic and political changes continually disrupt smooth adjustments.

These four arguments for the gaps and contradictions in the process of social reproduction do not imply that the social reproduction of capitalism is perpetually precarious. The mechanisms of coercion, institutional rules, ideology, and material interests generally enable capitalist societies to muddle through pretty well and to weather the storms of disruptive change when they occur. But the inevitable limits and contradictions in social reproduction do mean that even during periods when the prospects for transformative challenge seem quite limited, spaces for such a challenge are likely to open up in the future as a result of unexpected, contingent changes.

THE UNDERLYING DYNAMICS AND TRAJECTORY OF UNINTENDED SOCIAL CHANGE

The first two components of a theory of emancipatory transformation tell us that any project of radical social transformation will face systematic obstacles generated by the mechanisms of social reproduction, but that these obstacles will have cracks and spaces for action because of the limits and contradictions of reproduction which, at least periodically, make transformative strategies possible. However, these components by themselves do not suggest any specific prognosis about the long-term prospects for emancipatory change. They do not tell us whether such spaces of action are likely to expand or contract in the future, or whether the mechanisms of reproduction will tend to become more coherent or more crisis-prone. For this we need a theory of the trajectory of social change.

The actual trajectory of large-scale social change that we observe in history is the result of the interaction of two kinds of change-generating processes: first, the cumulative *unintended by-products of the actions* of people operating under existing social relations, and second, the cumulative intended effects of *conscious projects of social change* by people acting strategically to transform those social relations. The first includes such things as capitalists introducing new technologies or adopting new strategies of investment and competition, families changing their fertility behavior, and women deciding not to interrupt their labor market participation after the birth of a child. In each of these cases people engage in actions not in an effort to change the world, but to solve specific problems which they face. The cumulative aggregate effects of such individual actions, however, are social changes with very broad ramifications. They are "unintended effects" not because they are necessarily unwanted—women, for example, may welcome the collective erosion of traditional gender norms that is the cumulative effect of their individual adaptive strategies—but because the broad macro-effects were not part of the intentions and strategies that explain the actions in the first place.

The second change-generating process includes actions by collective actors of various sorts—political parties, unions, social movements, non-profit foundations, corporations, states—to deliberately transform social structures and institutions in various ways: through state policies, social protests, pressures on powerful organizations, practical institution-building efforts, sometimes through violent confrontations. These actions, of course, also have cumulative unintended effects, and thus also constitute instances of the first kind of process, but they differ in also being directly motivated by the goal of generating social change.

Both deliberate and unintended processes of social change are crucial for emancipatory transformation. Significant movement

towards radical egalitarian democratic social empowerment is
not something that will happen just by accident as a by-product
of social action for other purposes; it requires deliberate
strategic action, and since such popular empowerment threatens
the interests of powerful actors, this strategic action typically
involves struggle. But strategy and struggle are not enough. For
radical transformation to occur conditions must be "ripe"; the
contradictions and gaps in the processes of social reproduction
must create real opportunities for strategy to have meaningful
transformative effects. It may, of course, also be possible in
some historical periods for the deliberate strategies of collective actors to "ripen the conditions," but more generally the
central problem for collective actors engaged in struggles for
social emancipation is to "seize the time" when opportunities
for transformation occur for reasons not mainly of their own
making.

This confluence of trajectories of unintended social change
with deliberate strategies of transformation has marked every
major contemporary episode of emancipatory transformation.
Consider the dramatic transformation of changes in gender relations since the middle of the twentieth century. Men and women
went about their lives looking for jobs, fighting within their intimate lives over housework, trying to make ends meet, raising
their children. Employers adopted new technologies, faced new
kinds of labor requirements, and looked for workers. Mostly
people were not deliberately trying to change the world; they
were trying to deal with the concrete problems they encountered
as they made their lives as best they could. However, because
of the nature of the opportunities they faced, the resources they
controlled, the beliefs they held, and the choices they ultimately
made, they did things which cumulatively contributed to the
transformation of gender relations. This is not, of course, the
end of the story. Deliberate efforts at social change were also
crucial. Women joined together to fight for equal rights. They
formed consciousness-raising groups with the explicit purpose
of changing their understanding of the world. They engaged in
local projects of institution-building for gender equality, and
larger-scale political mobilization for system-level change. Men
often (but not always) resisted these changes, mocking feminists, but overall the forces for transformation were stronger.
An important reason they were stronger is that the cumulative
effect of the unintended processes had weakened the interests of

powerful actors in the maintenance of male dominance.[25] By the beginning of the twenty-first century, as a result of the interplay of the unintended consequences of individual actions and the deliberate strategies of transformation, the gender order of the mid twentieth century had been pervasively transformed. This is not to say that deep gender equality has been realized, but the transformations have still been profound in an emancipatory direction.

A similar argument has been made by David James for the successful transformation of the segregationist institutions of racial domination in the US South by the Civil Rights Movement of the 1950s and 1960s compared to the failure of such movements in earlier decades.[26] James argues that in the late nineteenth century the segregationist racial state emerged and consolidated in the South to a significant extent because of its importance for the social reproduction of oppressive forms of control over agrarian labor, especially sharecropping. The destruction of sharecropping in the 1930s and the mechanization of Southern agriculture played a key role in eroding the material basis for this form of the state and made it much more vulnerable to transformation under changed political conditions in the post-World War II period. When the Civil Rights Movement intensified its struggles against segregationist institutions in the 1950s, therefore, the capacity for mobilization was greater, and the forms of resistance to change were more uneven than they had been half a century earlier. Those struggles were still crucial for the destruction of the segregationist state, but the likelihood of their success was greatly enhanced by the cumulative effects of unintended social changes over the previous quarter century.

This duality to the processes which generate trajectories of social change poses a serious problem for people committed to emancipatory projects of transformation. The problem is this: any

---

25 The specific emphasis on the gradual erosion of interests of *powerful* men in actively opposing gender equality comes from Robert Max Jackson, *Destined for Equality: The Inevitable Rise of Women's Status* (Cambridge, MA: Harvard University Press, 1998). For a more extended discussion of my views on the contradictory transformation of gender relations in the US, see Erik Olin Wright and Joel Rogers, *American Society: How it Really Works* (New York: W. W. Norton, 2010), chapter 15, "Gender Inequality."

26 David James, "The Transformation of the Southern Racial State: Class and Race Determinants of Local-State Structures," *American Sociological Review*, 53 (1988), pp. 191–208.

plausible strategy for the fundamental emancipatory transformation of existing institutions of power, inequality, and privilege,
especially in developed capitalist societies, has to have a fairly long
time-horizon. There is simply no short-term strategy that could
plausibly work. If we believed that the basic social structural
parameters within which we formed our strategies would remain
constant, then perhaps we could avoid worrying too much about
how conditions change over time. But since this is not the case,
in order to have a coherent long-term strategy we need at least
a rough understanding of the general trajectory of unintended,
unplanned social changes into the future. This turns out to be a
daunting theoretical task.

Classical Marxism proposed precisely such a theory. As argued
in chapter 4, historical materialism is basically a theory of the
history of the future of capitalism. Marx attempted to identify
how the unintended consequences of capitalist competition and
exploitation in the process of capital accumulation generate "laws
of motion" of capitalism which push it along a specific trajectory
of development. This trajectory was marked by several salient
features: an ever-expanding breadth and depth of market relations culminating in global capitalism and the commodification
of social life; an increasing concentration and centralization of
capital; a general tendency for capital intensity and productivity
to increase over time; a cyclical intensification of economic crisis; a
tendency towards both the expansion of the working class and its
homogenization, and as a result, its increasing collective capacity
for struggle; and a weakening of the mechanisms of active social
reproduction as a result of the long-term tendency of the rate of
profit to fall. In this classical theory there is a deep connection
between the processes of social reproduction, dynamic trajectories, and contradictions: the very processes through which the
capital/labor relation is passively reproduced—exploitation and
capital accumulation—dynamically transform those relations in
ways that produce a trajectory of increasing contradictions in the
active reproduction of the system as a whole.

Many of the predictions of historical materialism have in fact
been borne out by the actual history of capitalism. In particular,
capitalism has become a global system of capital accumulation;
corporations have grown in both absolute and relative size; and
capitalist commodification penetrates ever more pervasively into
social life. But other predictions do not seem adequate. Capitalism
does not seem to be faced with a systematic tendency towards

intensification of crisis; the class structure has not become simplified into a more polarized structure and the working class has not
become ever more homogeneous; and the economic mechanisms
of social reproduction that tie the immediate material interests of
most people to capitalism do not seem to have been dramatically
weakened. Historical materialism (understood as the theory of capitalism's future), therefore, does not seem to be an adequate theory
of the trajectory of unintended social change on which to ground the
problem of developing strategies for emancipatory transformation.

At present we do not have such a theory. At best our theories of
the immanent tendencies of social change beyond the near future
are simply extrapolations of observable tendencies from the recent
past to the present or speculations about longer-term possibilities.
There is thus a disjuncture between the desirable time-horizons
of strategic action and planning for radical social change and the
effective time-horizons of our theories. This may simply reflect
the lack of development of good theory. But it may also reflect the
inherent complexity of the problem. It is possible, after all, to
have very powerful theories explaining the historical trajectory of
development in the past without being able to develop a theory
of future tendencies. This is the case for evolutionary biology,
which has sound explanations for the trajectory of living things
from single-celled creatures to the present, but virtually no theory
of what future evolution will look like.[27] This may also be the
case for the theory of social change: we may be able to provide
rigorous and convincing explanations for the trajectory of change
up to the present, but still have almost no ability to explain very
much about what the future holds in store.

In any event, for whatever reasons, at present we lack a compelling theory of the long-term immanent trajectory of unintended
social change. This places a greater burden on the fourth element
of a theory of transformation, the theory of transformative strategies, for it is forced to grapple with the problem of transformative
struggles without a satisfactory understanding of the trajectory of
conditions such struggles are likely to encounter.

---

27 The reason for this impossibility of theorizing the future of biological
evolution is because of the enormous role of contingent events—asteroids hitting
the earth, for example—in explaining the actual course of evolution. For a
discussion of the distinctive quality of the historical explanations of evolutionary
theory, see Erik Olin Wright, Andrew Levine, and Elliott Sober, *Reconstructing
Marxism: Essays on Explanation and the Theory of History* (London: Verso,
1992), chapter 3.

STRATEGIES OF TRANSFORMATION

The final element of a theory of transformation focuses directly on collective action and transformative strategy. The central question is this: given the obstacles and opportunities for emancipatory transformation generated by the process of social reproduction, the gaps in that process, and the uncertain trajectory of unintended social change into the future, what sort of collective strategies will help us move in the direction of social emancipation?

In the next three chapters we will focus on three basic logics of transformation through which new institutions of social empowerment might potentially be built: *ruptural*, *interstitial*, and *symbiotic*. These logics of transformation differ both in terms of their visions of the trajectory of systemic transformation and in their understanding of the nature of the strategies needed to move along that trajectory. These differences are summarized in an idealized way in Figure 8.1.

Vision of the trajectory of systemic transformation.

The central distinction among visions of the trajectory of system transformation is between the view that any trajectory beyond capitalism will necessarily involve a decisive *rupture* and those views which foresee a trajectory of sustained *metamorphosis* without any system-wide moment of discontinuity. Ruptural transformations envision creating new institutions of social empowerment through a sharp break within existing institutions and social structures. The central idea is that through direct confrontation and political struggles it is possible to create a radical disjuncture in institutional structures in which existing institutions are destroyed and new ones built in a fairly rapid way. Smash first, build second. A revolutionary scenario for the transition to socialism is the iconic version of this: a revolution constitutes a decisive, encompassing victory of popular forces for social empowerment resulting in the rapid transformation of the structures of the state and the foundations of economic structures.

Within the alternative visions of change through metamorphosis, there are two conceptions: *interstitial* metamorphosis and *symbiotic* metamorphosis. Interstitial transformations seek to build new forms of social empowerment in the niches and margins of capitalist society, often where they do not seem to

FIGURE 8.1 *Three Models of Transformation: Ruptural, Interstitial, Symbiotic*

Vision of Trajectory of Systemic Transformations Beyond Capitalism	Political Tradition Most Closely Associated with Logic of Transformation	Pivotal Collective Actors for Transformation	Strategic Logic with Respect to the State	Strategic Logic with Respect to the Capitalist Class	Metaphors of Success
Ruptural	Revolutionary socialist/communist	Classes organized in political parties	Attack the state	Confront the bourgeoisie	War (victories and defeats)
Interstitial Metamorphosis	Anarchist	Social movements	Build alternatives outside of the state	Ignore the bourgeoisie	Ecological competition
Symbiotic Metamorphosis	Social democratic	Coalitions of social forces and labor	Use the state: struggle on the terrain of the state	Collaborate with the bourgeoisie	Evolutionary adaptations

pose any immediate threat to dominant classes and elites. This is the strategy of building institutions of social empowerment that is most deeply embedded in civil society and which often falls below the radar screen of radical critics of capitalism. While interstitial strategies are at the center of some anarchist approaches to social change, and play a big practical role in the endeavors of many community activists, socialists in the Marxist tradition have often disparaged such efforts, seeing them as palliative or merely symbolic, offering little prospect of serious challenge to the status quo. Yet, cumulatively, such developments can not only make a real difference in the lives of people, but potentially constitute a key component of enlarging the transformative scope for social empowerment in the society as a whole.

Symbiotic transformations involve strategies in which extending and deepening the institutional forms of popular social empowerment simultaneously helps solve certain practical problems faced by dominant classes and elites. The democratization of the capitalist state had this character: democracy was the result of concentrated pressures and struggles from below which were initially seen as a serious threat to the stability of capitalist dominance, but in the end liberal democracy helped solve a wide range of problems, and in doing so contributed to that stability. The increase in social empowerment was real, not illusory, but it also helped to solve problems in ways that served the interests of capitalists and other elites. Symbiotic transformations thus have a contradictory character to them, both expanding social power and strengthening aspects of the existing system.

These three visions correspond broadly to the revolutionary socialist, anarchist, and social democratic traditions of anti-capitalism.

Pivotal collective actors for transformation.

Different strategies are linked to different conceptions of the core collective actors engaged in transformation. In ruptural strategies, *classes organized through political parties* are the central collective actors. The aphorism "class struggle is the motor of history" captures this in the Marxist tradition. Interstitial strategies revolve around *social movements* rooted in a heterogeneous set of constituencies, interests, and identities. No one social category is privileged as the leader of the project of transformation. Different collective actors will be best positioned to engage in different kinds of interstitial strategies, and whether or not there is a collective actor that could be considered the "most important" will be historically and contextually variable. Finally, symbiotic strategies are built around *popular coalitions* within which, typically, the labor movement plays a particularly central role because of its importance in forging positive class compromises.

Strategic logic with respect to the state.

Ruptural strategies envision a political process that culminates in a *frontal attack on the state*. This is the characteristic idea of revolutionary political strategies. State power is essential for transcending capitalism, and state power can only be stably secured by anti-system forces through the destruction of the core institutions of the capitalist state. Interstitial strategies in contrast operate *outside the state* and try as much as possible to avoid confrontations with state power. The core idea is to build counter-hegemonic institutions in society. There might be contexts in which struggles against the state could be required to create or defend these spaces, but the core of the strategy is to work outside the state. Finally symbiotic strategies see the state itself as a terrain of struggle in which there exists a possibility of *using the state* to build social power both within the state itself and in other sites of power.

Strategic logic with respect to the capitalist class.

Ruptural strategies envision class struggles with the capitalist class taking the form of *sharp confrontations*: capitalists must be forced to make concessions, and the only way such concessions can be sustained is through the continual capacity to threaten the use of force. Only through a confrontational class struggle is it possible to move along the trajectory of transformation to the point where ruptural break become historically possible. Interstitial strategies try to avoid confrontation. *Ignore the bourgeoisie* is the strategic goal: challenge capitalism by building the alternative, not by directly confronting it. Symbiotic strategies seek to create the conditions for *positive collaboration*—what I call positive class compromise. This may also require confrontations, but in the service of creating conditions for positive cooperation by closing off certain alternatives for capitalists.

Metaphors of success in the process of transformation.

The central metaphor of ruptural strategies is war. Movement occurs through the uneven process of victories and defeats in the confrontations with capital and the attacks on the state. This is not a linear process—there are reversals and stalemates. Still, successful movement along the trajectory depends upon victories in these struggles and building the capacity for a more comprehensive victory in the future. Interstitial success is more like a complex ecological system in which one kind of organism initially gains a foothold in a niche but eventually out-competes rivals for food sources and so comes to dominate the wider environment. Symbiotic success is more like a process of evolution, in which structural properties are modified through adaptations which progressively enhance social power and eventually result in a new species.

None of these strategies is simple and unproblematic. All contain dilemmas, risks, and limits, and none of them guarantee success. In different times and places, one or another of these modes of transformation may be the most effective, but often all of them are relevant. It often happens that activists become deeply committed to one or another of these strategic visions, seeing them as being universally valid. As a result, considerable energy is expended fighting against the rejected strategic models. A long-term political project of emancipatory transformation with any prospect for success must grapple with the messy problem of combining different elements of these strategies, even though on the ground it is often the case that they work at cross-purposes. Examining these three modes of transformation in more detail is the task of the next three chapters.

RUPTURAL TRANSFORMATION

It may seem odd at the beginning of the twenty-first century to have an extended discussion of ruptural transformations of capitalism. While revolutionary rhetoric has not completely disappeared, few critics of capitalism today imagine that a revolutionary overthrow of the state in the developed capitalist countries is a plausible strategy of emancipatory social transformation. Quite apart from any moral considerations about the immediate consequences of adopting such a strategy, or the desirability of the ultimate outcomes that would be generated by such an overthrow, the idea that the strategy itself could possibly succeed seems very far-fetched.

In spite of this, I believe that there are four reasons why it is worthwhile discussing ruptural strategies. First, political activists, especially when they are young, are often attracted to the idea of a radical rupture with existing institutions. The existing structures of power, privilege, and inequality seem so malevolent and so damaging to aspirations for human flourishing that the idea of simply smashing them and creating something new and better can be appealing. This may be because of wishful thinking or romantic illusions, but nevertheless the idea of revolutionary rupture continues to excite the imagination of at least some activists. Second, a clear understanding of the logic and limits of a ruptural strategy of social transformation can help clarify alternative strategies. Theoretical and political debates on the left have been waged since the nineteenth century in terms of the "reform" versus "revolution" opposition, and in important ways the specificity of the former comes from this contrast. Third, while I am quite skeptical of the possibility of system-wide ruptural strategies, more limited forms of rupture in particular institutional settings may be possible, and there are aspects of the ruptural strategy—such as its emphasis on sharp confrontation with dominant classes and the state—which can certainly be important under specific circumstances. The logic of ruptural transformation need not be restricted to totalizing ruptures in entire social systems. Finally, even if systemic ruptural strategies for social empowerment in developed capitalist countries are not plausible at the beginning of the twenty-first century, no one has a crystal ball which tells what the future holds. In the world as it currently stands, the robustness of the institutions of the state in developed capitalist democracies make ruptural strategies implausible, but it is possible that in some unanticipated future the contradictions of these societies could dramatically undermine those institutions. Equilibria unravel. Systemic crises destroy the foundations of hegemony. Ruptures may happen rather than be made, and in such conditions a ruptural strategy may become what Marxists used to call an historical "necessity."[1] The idea of ruptural strategy still needs to be part of our strategic thinking about social transformation since such strategies may become more relevant in some places at some point in the future.

THE KEY QUESTION AND UNDERLYING ASSUMPTIONS

The question I want to address in this chapter is this: under what conditions is it plausible to imagine that there could be broad popular support for a ruptural strategy against capitalism in advanced capitalist countries? The analysis is based on three assumptions:

First, I assume that in developed capitalist countries with functioning liberal democratic institutions, a ruptural strategy for socialism would have to work in significant ways through the ordinary democratic processes of the capitalist state. This does not

---

1 Theda Skocpol argued in her influential book *States and Social Revolutions* (Cambridge: Cambridge University Press, 1979) that revolutions are not made; they happen. By this she meant that the crisis conditions which make possible the revolutionary seizure of state power are not themselves the result of the strategies of revolutionaries, but of the intersection of large dynamic processes operating behind the backs of actors and contingent historical conjunctures of events which create a "revolutionary situation." Revolutionary parties "seize the time," and for this they undoubtedly have to be in some sense prepared, but actual ruptural strategies only really become operative in the context of such moments. (These issues were raised in a discussion of ruptural logics of transformation by two graduate students at Johns Hopkins University, Sefika Kumral and Erdem Yoruk).

mean that the ruptural strategy would not include fundamental transformations of the form of the state itself—democratic deepening of the state is certainly a central part of the agenda of social empowerment. And it does not mean that a ruptural strategy would not also include political actions outside of the state in civil society and in the economy. My assumption is simply that if a ruptural strategy of transformation is at all feasible, it will not take the form of a violent insurrectionary assault and overthrow of the state by extra-parliamentary means in the model of classical revolutions. The reason for making this assumption is not a rejection of revolution on the basis of some absolute moral objection to insurrectionary violence, but rather a belief that under foreseeable historical conditions such means would be incapable of actually creating a deeply egalitarian democratic form of social empowerment in developed capitalist societies.[2] However difficult it might be, therefore, if a ruptural strategy is to be pursued *for the goal of democratic egalitarian socialism*, then the strategy will have to work through the existing, imperfect state machinery.[3]

Second, I assume that given the necessity of working through the institutions of representative democracy, broad popular support is a necessary if not sufficient condition for a plausible ruptural strategy. While there have certainly been historical instances in which a rupture in political institutions occurred because a well-organized political force that did not have the support of a large majority of the population was able to "seize the time" and take advantage of a severely weakened state, this has not resulted in a subsequent trajectory of broad democratic social empowerment of the sort we have been exploring in this book. Throughout this

---

2 It is often said that "ends cannot justify the means," but unless the means are completely innocuous, *only* the ends can justify them. It may be that certain means cannot be justified by any ends, but in most real-world situations the means of struggle do have undesirable side effects on bystanders and unintended negative consequences of various sorts, and in deciding whether or not those means are nevertheless justified, the justification of the ends must play some role. In any case, if the means in fact cannot plausibly lead to the ends for which they are intended, then they are unjustified.

3 This does not imply, of course, that coercion would not be part of a ruptural strategy, since once state power is being used for a ruptural transformation, the defense of the state against counter-revolution may require coercion, particularly if the counter-revolution is itself violent. My assumption here is simply that the control of state power was achieved through ordinary democratic means rather than through a violent insurrection and overthrow of the regime in power, and the democratic structure of the state is maintained during the ruptural transformation.

chapter, therefore, I assume that if a ruptural strategy is to be a central part of the construction of a robust socialism of social empowerment, then it would have to be supported by a substantial majority of the population.

Third, I assume, following the influential work of Adam Przeworski,[4] that a necessary condition for broad, *sustainable* popular support is that socialism (however this is defined) will be in the all-things-considered material interests of most people.[5] This is not to imply that in struggles against capitalism moral commitments that are not directly connected to material interests are not important. They matter tremendously and help forge the solidarities and willingness to make sacrifices that are essential for collective action to be robust. Nevertheless, I will assume that while ideology and moral commitment may strengthen support for a radical rupture with capitalism, they build on a base of material interests; in the absence of such interests, ideological commitments would not by themselves be able to generate durable popular support.[6] Socialism of whatever form will not be sustainable in the long run if the material conditions of life for most people are worse than under capitalism.

The analysis which follows is based on these three assumptions. At the end of the chapter we will examine the implications of relaxing the assumptions.

RUPTURAL TRANSFORMATION AND TRANSITION TROUGHS

The key problem to sort out, then, is this: Under what conditions is a ruptural strategy for socialism sufficiently in the material interests of the majority of people to render it a plausible strategy of transformation? The material interests of people with respect to any large project of social change involving a sharp rupture with existing institutions depend upon three key parameters:

---

4   See Adam Przeworski, *Capitalism and Social Democracy* (Cambridge: Cambridge University Press, 1985), and Adam Przeworski and John Sprague, *Paper Stones* (Chicago, Chicago University Press, 1986).

5   In this context, "material interests" should be understood in an expansive way to include leisure as well as consumption, quality of work as well as earnings.

6   The issue here is not the standard collective action problem of whether or not individuals will actively join a political struggle for such a rupture, but rather under what conditions people will see such a rupture as being in their *interests*. The pragmatic "collective action problem" of overcoming free riding only becomes relevant if in fact people believe they would benefit from the success of the collective action.

- The trajectory of their material well-being *in the absence of the rupture*. This is what life would look like if the existing structures of power and privilege continued.

- The trajectory of their material well-being *after the period of rupture is over* and the new institutions are fully in place and functioning effectively.

- The trajectory of their interests *during the period between* the initiation of the rupture and the new institutional equilibrium. Given that under any plausible scenario, a rupture with the existing economic structure is likely to be highly disruptive, this period of transition will almost certainly involve a significant decline in average material conditions of life. Adam Przeworski thus dubs this part of the long-term trajectory of material conditions the "transition trough."

A simple representation of these trajectories in developed capitalism, derived from the work of Przeworski, looks something like the pictures in Figures 9.1 and 9.2. Figure 9.1 presents a hypothetical trajectory of the level of material well-being of the median person

FIGURE 9.1 *Hypothetical Trajectory of Material Interests in Developed Capitalism*

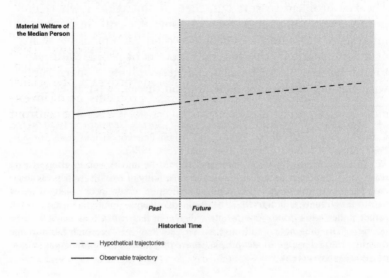

in developed capitalist economies from the past to the present and into the future within capitalist society. From the standpoint of the present moment, of course, the future is uncertain. But let us assume that the most likely trajectory of standards of living for the median person in developed countries is flat or slowly rising.[7] This prediction could certainly be wrong. It is possible that at some point in the future for a variety of reasons—economic crises, ecological deterioration, technologically induced mass unemployment, etc.—standards of living for most people could significantly fall over their lifetimes, and if this were to occur, the analysis which follows would need to be modified (as we will discuss towards the end of this chapter). But let us assume here that the standard of living for the average person will either be fairly constant or will slowly rise.

The question then is this: what would be the likely trajectory of material conditions of life for the median person *if there was a successful ruptural strategy for a socialist transformation?*[8] Let us examine this problem under a relatively optimistic scenario. Suppose that through a democratic process an emancipatory socialist party were to gain control of the state with a large majority of the vote and had sufficient power to launch a serious program of socialist transformation, either in the sense of implementing the full agenda of social empowerment institutions we have discussed or in the narrower sense of pursuing a democratic version of a statist socialist program of state ownership and control of the most important economic organizations. Also let us suppose, perhaps unrealistically, that this does not meet with violent resistance from social forces opposed to socialism. There is no armed counter-revolution. We are therefore making quite optimistic assumptions: a radical democratic egalitarian socialist party is elected through democratic means, it has sufficient power to enact and implement a serious program of socialist transformation, and while it may face problems of disinvestment and incentive failures of various sorts, it does not confront violent opposition in the form of a counter-revolution. Everyone

---

7 It is important to note here that even in a period of prolonged stagnation of average wages, the standard of living of most individuals still tends to rise over time because of the positive age profile of earnings. While in the last quarter of the twentieth century in the United States median earnings stagnated, the median person's earnings still increased over the course of their work life.

8 I am pegging this question here to the "median person" because the socialist transformation needs to be supported by the majority of the population if a socialist party is to receive continued electoral support under democratic rules.

FIGURE 9.2 *Socialist Rupture and Trajectories of Material Interests*

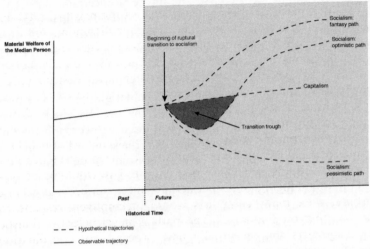

agrees to respect the existing political rules of the game. We are thus examining the problems with a ruptural strategy under quite favorable conditions. What would happen to the material welfare of the average person? Figure 9.2 indicates three general possibilities.

The "socialist fantasy path" imagines that a rupture with capitalism immediately brings with it an improvement in the material conditions of life of the median person in the society. Either there is no significant economic disruption, or the immediate gains from redistribution are so large as to swamp whatever short-term economic decline occurs due to the disruptions of rapid institutional change. This path is unrealistic, at least in a complex, developed capitalist economy. Even if it is the case that the material conditions of life of ordinary people would be much better in a socialist economy, it is not plausible that a ruptural transition from capitalism would instantly improve things.

The "pessimistic path" is predicted by anti-socialists. The disruption of capitalist mechanisms causes an economic collapse, but the system never recovers and the new equilibrium is permanently below what it would have been had capitalism continued. If one believes in this path, then socialism is simply undesirable. The issue is not the costs of a transition from capitalism to socialism, but the relative steady-state economic performance of the two systems.

The "optimistic path" recognizes that any rupture with capitalism would necessarily entail significant economic disruption and thus sacrifice. Even if we assume that the rupture occurs under democratic conditions and that there is no violent resistance, any serious move towards socialism would trigger significant destruction of the incentive and information structures that animated economic coordination under capitalism. Supply chains, systems of distribution, credit markets, pricing systems, and many other pivotal elements of economic integration would be deeply disrupted. This would certainly precipitate a significant decline in production and standards of living for some period of time. This would be intensified by capital flight and disinvestments in the run-up to a socialist rupture, since many capitalists would preemptively respond to the "writing on the wall." The path is nevertheless optimistic for it predicts that eventually new processes of coordination are effectively installed, appropriate incentives are restored, and production and distribution under the new rules of the game are institutionalized. As this happens conditions improve, eventually crossing the predicted trajectory of capitalism itself and moving towards a higher general level. The shaded area in Figure 9.2, then, constitutes the "transition trough" between the ruptural break with capitalism and the point where material conditions of life under socialism exceed those under the previous social order for the median person.

Let us assume that the most likely trajectory is some variant of the optimistic path. The key issue then becomes the size of the transition trough. Depending upon how deep and prolonged the transition trough is, it may not be in the material interests of most people to support a ruptural path to socialism *even if they firmly believe that life would be better once the transition was weathered*. Interests must always be understood within specific time-horizons, and if the transition trough continues for a sufficiently extended period it is unlikely to be seen by most people as in their material interests.

Furthermore, it is important to remember that from the perspective of the actors encountering a transition, the shape of these curves is not an empirical observation, but a hypothesis about the future. The future is uncertain, and in any case such predictions are always based on highly contestable theoretical arguments. Even if

FIGURE 9.3 *Projections into the Future from Part-Way Through a Transition*

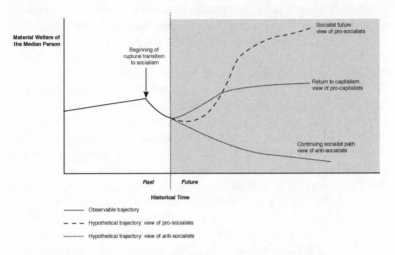

Past | Future

Historical Time

——— Observable trajectory

— — — Hypothetical trajectory: view of pro-socialists

.... Hypothetical trajectory: view of anti-socialists

these arguments are well-founded, most people are unlikely to have unshakable confidence in them. In the period of the downward slope of the transition trough, as indicated in Figure 9.3, the empirical trajectories of the optimistic and pessimistic paths look very similar. As the economy declines political forces opposed to socialism will argue strenuously that the trajectory will continue downwards to catastrophe and that the transition should be reversed. Of course socialists will counter with arguments that eventually the economy will improve and people should stay the course, but this may look like wishful thinking to many people if the transition is prolonged. In the midst of the transition trough, the observable trajectory of material conditions in the recent past looks rather like the predicted path of the anti-socialist pessimists. The political coalition of supporters for a democratic ruptural transition to socialism, therefore, is likely to become increasingly strained and fragile over time if the transition trough is relatively deep and prolonged.

The situation is actually likely to be even more precarious than this, for so far we have looked only at the trajectory of material interests of the median person. Let us suppose that there are two classes of people whose material interests would ultimately be broadly served by a successful transition to socialism. Let us call

FIGURE 9.4 *Class Variations in Trajectories of Material Interests*

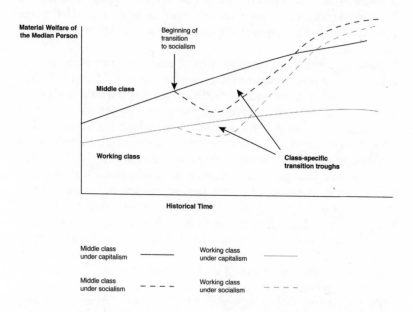

them the "working class" and the "middle class."[9] In capitalism the middle class has in general a higher material standard of living than the working class and let us suppose that this inequality has been growing over time. Figure 9.4 indicates the nature of the transition troughs for these two classes of people in a ruptural transition to socialism. A ruptural transition to socialism under democratic conditions requires a broad coalition between the middle class and the working class, but the experience of transition is likely to be different for individuals in different parts of the coalition. Specifically, if the socialist government takes the egalitarian principles seriously, then the transition trough is likely to be deeper

---

9 I am using the term "middle class" here in a deliberately loose way. The issue is to distinguish, within the coalition of people whose lives would be improved by socialism (and thus would potentially support its goals on the basis of their material interests), those people who are relatively advantaged within capitalism from those who are not. The precise definition of the middle class and working class does not matter for this specific purpose. If one prefers an expansive concept of the working class, then the issue would be one of a coalition between the relatively advantaged and disadvantaged segments of the working class.

and longer for the middle class, even if they remain materially better off than workers throughout the process. This means that in addition to the general problem of a decline in political support in a prolonged transition trough, there is likely to be a particularly acute problem of middle-class defections from the socialist coalition.

If these arguments are roughly correct, and if the transition trough resembles the general pattern suggested in Figures 9.2 and 9.4, then it is unlikely that a ruptural transition to socialism would be sustainable *under democratic conditions*. Political support simply would not remain sufficiently strong or intact for a long enough period of time. This means that a democratically elected socialist government attempting to build socialist institutions through a ruptural strategy would either face political defeat in a subsequent election or, in order to stay in power and traverse the transition, would have to resort to undemocratic means. A turn to authoritarian party rule, however, would undermine the radical democratic egalitarianism of the institution-building project itself. The result is therefore more likely to be a transition to some form of authoritarian statism than a radically democratic form of social empowerment.

Some revolutionary socialists have believed that a turn to authoritarian one-party rule during a transition from capitalism need not destroy the possibility of the subsequent evolution of meaningful egalitarian democracy. Historical experience suggests that this is very unlikely: the concentration of power and unaccountability that accompanies the abrogation of multi-party representative democracy and the "rule of law" generates new rules of the game and institutional forms in which ruthlessness is rewarded, democratic values are marginalized, dissent is dealt with repressively, and the kinds of autonomous capacities for collective action in civil society needed for democracy are destroyed. The legacies of such practices during the difficult times of a transition make a democratic socialist destination implausible.

REJOINDERS

There are a number of possible responses to this generally pessimistic view of the possibility of a ruptural strategy. First, and most simply, it may be that the transition trough would not be deep and prolonged. While the "fantasy path" may be unrealistic, perhaps the optimistic path is itself too pessimistic. If the duration of the trough were reasonably short, and especially if the upturn occurred relatively quickly, then a democratic coalition for transformation might remain intact.

Second, it might be argued, the projection of material conditions of life for people *under capitalism* is wrong. If developed capitalism were to enter a prolonged period of endemic crisis with long-term prospects of deterioration, then the likely transition trough out of capitalism might not look so bad. This, of course, is what Marx in part believed: In the long term capitalism undermines its own conditions for profitable accumulation with

FIGURE 9.5 *Socialist Rupture and Trajectories of Material Interests Under Alternative of Long-Term Intensification of Capitalist Crisis*

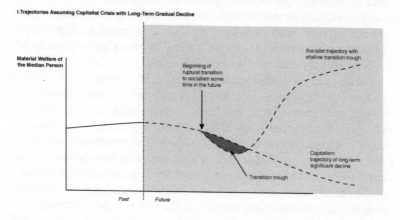

I. Trajectories Assuming Capitalist Crisis with Long-Term Gradual Decline

Material Welfare of the Median Person

Socialist trajectory with shallow transition trough

Beginning of ruptural transition to socialism some time in the future

Capitalism: trajectory of long-term significant decline

Transition trough

Past   Future

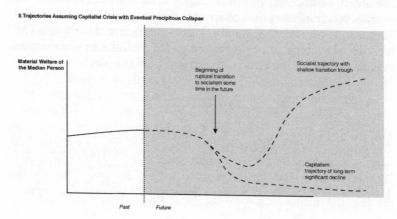

II. Trajectories Assuming Capitalist Crisis with Eventual Precipitous Collapse

Material Welfare of the Median Person

Socialist trajectory with shallow transition trough

Beginning of ruptural transition to socialism some time in the future

Capitalism: trajectory of long-term significant decline

Past   Future

a resulting intensification of crisis tendencies. As illustrated in Figure 9.5, as crises deepen, transition troughs become shallower because the counterfactual trajectory within capitalism becomes increasingly downward sloping. It may even become plausible, if crises take the form of a sharp and enduring collapse, that the socialist trajectory would be more like the "fantasy path" in Figure 9.2: material conditions immediately improve for most people relative to what they would have been in the absence of the rupture.

Third, actors may be motivated for a transition to socialism by values other than material interests, and it is not necessarily the case that with respect to these other values a sharp transition trough would exist. For example, it is certainly possible that with respect to the values of democratic participation and community solidarity the very process of rupture and transition enhances their realization. Thus, if these values constituted a robust and powerful source of motivation for people, then it is possible that support for the socialist project over the course of even a prolonged trough in material conditions could be sustained.

None of these responses are, I believe, convincing. It is possible that the disruption accompanying a rapid transformation of capitalist relations might be less than anticipated here, but historical experience of patterns of disinvestment in the face of even mild state-initiated threats to capital suggests that the disruption would more likely be quite severe. It is also possible that capitalism will enter into a long-term process of intensifying crisis and permanent decline that lowers the standard of living of most people, but in the absence of a compelling theory of the mechanisms that generate such intensification, this is a purely speculative argument. And while motivations other than material interests are profoundly important for the struggle for human emancipation, there is little historical evidence that over an extended period these motivations could neutralize the effects of a sharp economic decline accompanying a project of radical transformation of capitalism.

Large-scale ruptural strategies for constructing a democratic egalitarian socialism, therefore, seem implausible in the world in which we currently live, at least in the developed capitalist economies. If we wish to work for such a transformation, therefore, we need to think about some broadly different approaches to the problem. The question becomes: is it possible to expand the space for new forms of social empowerment within capitalism? What are the limits on this process?

10

INTERSTITIAL TRANSFORMATION

If one believes that systemic ruptural strategies of emancipatory transformation are not plausible, at least under existing historical conditions, then the only real alternative is some sort of strategy that envisions transformation largely as a process of metamorphosis in which relatively small transformations cumulatively generate a qualitative shift in the dynamics and logic of a social system. This does not imply that transformation is a smooth, non-conflictual process that somehow transcends antagonistic interests. A democratic egalitarian project of social emancipation is a challenge to exploitation and domination, inequality and privilege, and thus emancipatory metamorphosis will entail power struggles and confrontations with dominant classes and elites. In practice, therefore, an emancipatory metamorphosis will require some of the strategic elements of the ruptural model: the history of the future—if it is to be a history of emancipatory social empowerment—will be a trajectory of victories and defeats, winners and losers, not simply of compromise and cooperation between differing interests and classes. The episodes of that trajectory will be marked by institutional innovations that will have to overcome opposition from those whose interests are threatened by democratic egalitarianism, and some of that opposition will be nasty, recalcitrant, and destructive. So, to invoke metamorphosis is not to abjure struggle, but to see the strategic goals and effects of struggle in a particular way: as the incremental modifications of the underlying structures of a social system and its mechanisms of social reproduction that cumulatively transform the system, rather than as a sharp discontinuity in the centers of power of the system as a whole.[1]

---

1 This understanding of metamorphosis suggests that the stark contrast between "rupture" and "metamorphosis" is in some ways misleading since

Understood in this way, there are two broad approaches to the problem of transformation as metamorphosis: *interstitial transformation* and *symbiotic transformation*. These differ primarily in terms of their relationship to the state. Both envision a trajectory of change that progressively enlarges the social spaces of social empowerment, but interstitial strategies largely by-pass the state in pursuing this objective while symbiotic strategies try to systematically use the state to advance the process of emancipatory social empowerment. These need not constitute antagonistic strategies—in many circumstances they complement each other, and indeed may even require each other. Nevertheless, historically many supporters of interstitial strategies of transformation have been very wary of the state, and many advocates of more statist symbiotic strategies have been dismissive of interstitial approaches.

In the next chapter we will explore symbiotic transformations. Here we will examine the logic of interstitial strategies. We will begin by distinguishing between interstitial *strategies* and what might be called interstitial *processes*. This will be followed by a discussion of different types of interstitial strategies and a discussion of the underlying logic of the ways such strategies might contribute to broader emancipatory transformation. The chapter will conclude with a discussion of the limits of interstitial strategies.

WHAT IS AN INTERSTITIAL *STRATEGY*?

The adjective "interstitial" is used in social theory to describe various kinds of processes that occur in the spaces and cracks within some dominant social structure of power.[2] One can speak of the interstices of an organization, of a society, or even of global capitalism. The underlying assumption is that the social unit in question can be understood as a system within which there is some kind of dominant power structure or dominant logic which

---

emancipatory metamorphosis can itself be thought of as a trajectory of partial and limited social ruptures—institutional innovations—that cumulatively constitute a qualitative transformation. What is really at issue here is therefore the extent to which a large-scale comprehensive rupture with the fundamental structures of power in capitalism is possible.

2   As a way of capturing the strategic logic being discussed here, the term "interstitial" was suggested to me by Marcia Kahn Wright.

organizes the system, but that the system is not so coherent and integrated that those dominant power relations govern all of the activities occurring within it. Even in so-called "totalitarian" systems in which centralized power penetrates quite deeply into all spheres of social life there are still spaces within which individuals act in relatively autonomous ways, rather than following the dictates of the logic of the system. This need not imply that such interstitial practices are subversive or that they necessarily corrode the logic of the system, but simply that they are not directly governed or controlled by the dominant power relations and principles of social organization.[3]

Interstitial processes often play a central role in large-scale patterns of social change. For example, capitalism is often described as having developed in the interstices of feudal society. Feudal societies were characterized by a dominant structure of class and power relations consisting of nobles of various ranks who controlled much of the land and the principal means of military violence. Peasants with different kinds of rights engaged in agricultural production and produced a surplus which was appropriated by the dominant feudal class through a variety of largely coercive mechanisms. Market relations developed in the cities, which were less fully integrated into feudal relations, and over time this created the context within which proto-capitalist relations and practices could emerge and eventually flourish. Whether one believes that the pivotal source of ultimate transformation of feudalism came from the dynamics of war-making and state-building, from contradictions in the process of feudal surplus extraction, from the corrosive effects of markets, from the eventual challenge of emerging capitalists, or some combination of these processes, the interstitial development of capitalism within feudal societies is an important part of the story.

While interstitial *processes* and *activities* clearly play a significant

---

3 One of the fundamental issues in social theory is the extent to which society can be viewed as a "system" and, if so, what kind of system. At one extreme is the view of society as a system in much the same way as an organism is a system with well articulated parts that fulfill interconnected functions. But societies can also be viewed as a system more like an ecology in nature: there are systematically interconnected causal relations among the component parts, and some of these may have the character of functional connections and feedback processes, but they are not governed by a coherent logic and there are no necessary functional relations that smoothly integrate the whole. Here I will be treating the systemness of social phenomena in this way, as a loosely coupled system.

role in social change, it is less obvious that there are compelling interstitial *strategies* for social transformation. The urban artisans and merchants in feudal society whose interstitial activities fostered new kinds of relations did not have a project of destroying feudal class relations and forging a new kind of society. They were simply engaged in profit-seeking activities, adapting to the opportunities and possibilities of the society in which they lived. The broader ramifications for long-term social change were basically unintended by-products of their activities, not a strategy as such. An interstitial strategy, in contrast, involves the deliberate development of interstitial activities for the purpose of fundamental transformation of the system as a whole.

There are certainly many interstitial activities in contemporary capitalist societies which are candidates for elements of an interstitial strategy of social emancipation: worker and consumer co-ops, battered women's shelters, workers factory councils, intentional communities and communes, community-based social economy services, civic environmental councils, community-controlled land trusts, cross-border equal-exchange trade organizations, and many others. All of these are consciously constructed forms of social organization that differ from the dominant structures of power and inequality. Some are part of grand visions for the reconstruction of society as a whole; others have more modest objectives of transforming specific domains of social life. Some are linked to systematic theories of social transformation; others are pragmatic responses to the exigencies of social problem-solving. What they have in common is the idea of building alternative institutions and deliberately fostering new forms of social relations that embody emancipatory ideals and that are created primarily through direct action of one sort or another rather than through the state.

This vision of interstitial transformation has a long and venerable place in anti-capitalist thinking, going back to the anarchist tradition in the nineteenth century and continuing in various anarchist and "autonomist" currents to the present.[4] While there is no

---

4 I will use the term "anarchism" to describe the theoretical foundations of interstitial strategies because anarchist writers have placed the greatest emphasis on such strategies. As is the case for many political labels, terms like "anarchism" become infused with different meaning depending upon the historical context in which the label becomes linked to concrete political movements. The classical anarchist vision of social emancipation revolves around the idea of a stateless society in which social cooperation is organized through voluntary activity within relatively small communities linked through some kind of voluntary federation.

inherent reason why strategies of interstitial transformation should be restricted to the specific anarchist vision of emancipatory alternatives, there is an obvious affinity between the anarchist vision of an ultimate destination without a coercive state and the idea of interstitial strategies that largely ignore the state. The preamble of the Constitution of the Industrial Workers of the World, the influential US anarcho-syndicalist movement of the early twentieth century, proclaimed: "By organizing industrially we are forming the structure of the new society within the shell of the old."[5] Half a century later, Colin Ward, the prominent British anarchist writer, described the central idea of an anarchist strategy thus:

> Far from being a speculative vision of a future society . . . [anarchy] is a description of a mode of human organization, rooted in the experience of everyday life, which operates side by side with, and in spite of, the dominant authoritarian trends of our society . . . [T]he anarchist alternatives are already there, in the interstices of the dominant power structure. If you want to build a free society, the parts are all at hand.[6]

At times, however, anarchism became identified with particularly violent attacks on centers of authority and with visions of chaos rather than non-coercive community. The term "autonomist" became popular in some European political contexts in the second half of the twentieth century to identify movements that were part of the anarchist tradition, but which emphasized the voluntary, autonomous formation of egalitarian cooperation.

5 The literature of the IWW continually refers to new forms of worker organization as "embryonic" forms of the future society, suggesting again the idea that the future is built within the interstices of the present. For example, in a 1913 pamphlet titled "The Trial of a New Society" by Justuys Ebert (IWW: Chicago, 1913) the metaphor of embryonic development is used to characterize the process of transformation. The solidaristic organization of workers in the Lawrence, Massachusetts, textile strike of 1912, the pamphlet proclaims, was "The crude embryo—the rough outline of the future state, where industry and government shall be by, for, and of the workers direct." In the conclusion to the pamphlet the author asks: "The fact that a new economic power has arisen and is achieving new political and social triumphs within the old social order cannot be denied. But the question arises, can it endure? Will the embryo thus conceived develop until it overgrows and dominates all institutions in the interests of a new era?" In answering in the affirmative, the author draws on the history of the rise of the bourgeoisie which "developed their own institutions, their crafts, their trade, their guilds, their communes and confederations outside of and in opposition to the institutions peculiar to the original feudal constitution. They built the new society within the shell of the old; they evolved out of the old by means of new institutions in keeping with their new aspirations."

6 Colin Ward, *Anarchy in Action* (London: Allen and Unwin, 1973), p. 18, quoted in Stuart White, "Making Anarchism Respectable? The Social Philosophy of Colin Ward," *Journal of Political Ideologies* 12: 1 (2007), p. 15.

At the beginning of the twenty-first century when activists at the World Social Forum proclaim "another world is possible," much of what they have in mind are anarchist-inflected grass-roots initiatives to create worker and consumer cooperatives, fair trade networks, cross-border labor standards campaigns, and other institutions that directly embody the alternative world they desire in the here and now.

As already noted, many socialists, especially those enmeshed in the Marxist tradition, are quite skeptical of such projects. The argument goes something like this: While many of these efforts at building alternative institutions may embody desirable values and perhaps even prefigure emancipatory forms of social relations, they pose no serious challenge to existing relations of power and domination. Precisely because they are "interstitial" they can only occupy the spaces that are "allowed" by capitalism. They may even strengthen capitalism by siphoning off discontent and creating the illusion that if people are unhappy with the dominant institutions they can and should just go off and live their lives in alternative settings. Ultimately, therefore, interstitial projects amount to a retreat from the political struggle for radical social transformation, not a viable strategy for achieving it. At best they may make life a little better for some people in the world as it is; at worst they deflect energies from the real political challenge of changing the world for the better.

There are certainly instances in which this negative diagnosis seems plausible. The hippy communes of the 1960s may have been inspired by utopian longings and a belief that they were part of the "dawning of the Age of Aquarius," but in practice they functioned more as a flight from the realities of capitalist society than as nodes of radical transformation. Other examples, like organic grocery cooperatives, while not flights from capitalist society, nevertheless seem constrained to occupy small niches, often catering to relatively affluent people who can afford to "indulge" their preferences for a particular kind of "lifestyle." Organic grocery cooperatives may embody some progressive ideals, but they do not pose a threat to the system.

As a general indictment of interstitial strategies of transformation, these negative judgments are too harsh. They assume both that there is an alternative strategy which does pose a serious "threat to the system" and also that this alternative strategy is undermined by the existence of interstitial efforts at social transformation. The fact is that in present historical conditions no strategy credibly poses a direct threat to the system in the sense that there are good grounds for believing that adopting it will generate effects in the near future that would really threaten capitalism. This is what it means to live in a hegemonic capitalist system: capitalism is sufficiently secure and flexible in its basic structures that there is no strategy possible that immediately threatens it. The strategic problem is to imagine things we can do now which have a reasonable chance of opening up possibilities under contingent conditions in the future. Interstitial strategies, of course, may ultimately be dead ends and be permanently contained within narrow limits, but it is also possible that under certain circumstances they may play a positive role in a long-term trajectory of emancipatory social transformation.

The question, then, is this: what is the underlying model of social transformation in which interstitial activities can be viewed as part of an overall strategy for emancipatory social empowerment? What is the implicit theory of the ways in which such activities can cumulatively transform the society as a whole? Writers in the anarchist tradition devote remarkably little attention to this problem. While anarchist writing criticizes existing structures of capitalist and statist power and defends a vision of a federated cooperative alternative without the coercive domination of the state, there is very little systematic elaboration of how to actually "build the new society within the shell of the old" and how this might lead to a systemic transformation.

HOW INTERSTITIAL STRATEGIES CAN CONTRIBUTE TO EMANCIPATORY SOCIAL TRANSFORMATION

Many of the specific examples used in chapter 7 to illustrate social empowerment and the economy were substantially the result of interstitial strategies. Wikipedia is the result of people building an alternative non-capitalist form of knowledge dissemination within the extraordinary space of interstitial activity called the internet. Many projects within the social economy are the result of interstitial strategies, even if, as in Quebec, some of them receive important subsidies from the state. Worker-owned cooperatives are the quintessential form of interstitial organization at the center of classical anarchist strategies of interstitial transformation. To this list many other empirical examples could be added: a wide variety of internet-based strategies that subvert capitalist intellectual property rights (e.g., Napster, the music-sharing site); open-source software and technology projects; fair trade networks designed to link producer cooperatives in poor countries to consumers in rich countries; efforts to create global labor and environmental standards through various kinds of monitoring and certification projects. Within each of these interstitial activities, many of the actors involved see what they are doing as part of a strategy for broad social change, not simply as self-limiting activities motivated by lifestyle preferences or the desire to "do good works." The question then is how these kinds of interstitial activities could have broad transformative, emancipatory effects for the society as a whole. What is the underlying logic through which they might cumulatively contribute to making another world possible?

There are two principal ways that interstitial strategies within capitalism potentially point the way beyond capitalism: first, by altering the conditions for eventual rupture, and second, by gradually expanding the effective scope and depth of their operations so that capitalist constraints cease to impose binding limits. I will refer to these as the *revolutionary anarchist* and *evolutionary anarchist* strategic visions, not because only anarchists hold these views, but because the broad idea of not using the state as an instrument of social emancipation is so closely linked to the anarchist tradition.

PAVING THE ROUTE TO RUPTURE

Many nineteenth-century anarchists shared with Marxist-inspired revolutionary socialists the belief that ultimately a revolutionary rupture with capitalism would be necessary. Where they differed sharply was in the belief of what sorts of transformations were needed within capitalism in order for a revolutionary rupture to plausibly usher in a genuinely emancipatory alternative. For Marx, and later for Lenin, the central task of struggles within capitalism was to forge the collective capacity of a politically unified working class needed to successfully seize state power as the necessary condition for overthrowing capitalism. The task of deep social reconstruction to create the environment for a new way of life with new principles, new forms of social interaction and reciprocity, would largely have to wait until "after the revolution."[7]

For revolutionary anarchists, on the other hand, significant progress in such reconstruction is not only possible within capitalism, but is a necessary condition for a sustainable emancipatory rupture with capitalism. In discussing Proudhon's views on revolution, Martin Buber writes:

> [Proudhon] divined the tragedy of revolutions and came to feel it more and more deeply in the course of disappointing experiences. Their tragedy is that as regards their *positive* goal they will always result in the exact opposite of what the most honest and passionate revolutionaries strive for, unless and until this [deep social reform] has so far taken shape *before* the revolution that the revolutionary act has only to wrest the space for it in which it can develop unimpeded.[8]

If we want a revolution to result in a deeply egalitarian, democratic, and participatory way of life, Buber writes,

> the all-important fact is that, in the social as opposed to the political sphere, revolution is not so much a creative as a delivering force whose function is to set free and authenticate—i.e. that it can only perfect, set free, and lend the stamp of authority to something that has already been foreshadowed in the womb of the pre-revolutionary society; that, as regards social evolution, the hour of revolution is not an hour of begetting but an hour of birth—provided there was a begetting beforehand.[9]

A rupture with capitalism is thus necessary in this strategic vision, but it requires a deep process of interstitial transformation beforehand if it is to succeed.

---

7   Martin Buber, in his excellent study of anarchist thinking, *Paths in Utopia* (Boston: Beacon Press, 1958), argues that while Marx eventually came to acknowledge some virtues in the creation of cooperatives, he remained critical of views that saw this as a centerpiece of struggles within capitalism, feeling that it was an illusion that cooperatives could contribute much to remaking society so long as the bourgeoisie remained in power.

8   Martin Buber, *Paths in Utopia* (Boston: Beacon Press, 1958), p. 44.

9   Buber, *Paths in Utopia*, pp. 44–5. The metaphor of birth combines the idea of incremental metamorphosis with rupture: the moment of birth is a rupture with the past. There is a "before" and "after," a discontinuity in the life course. But birth can only happen after a successful, incremental gestation in which future potentials are brought to the brink of full actualization, and after birth this incremental process continues through maturation.

There are, I think, four different arguments implicitly in play in this vision of pre-revolutionary (i.e. pre-ruptural) interstitial social transformation within capitalism. These arguments are represented in Figure 10.1, a modified version of the transition trough diagrams from the previous chapter.

First, supporters of the necessity of interstitial transformations within capitalism claim that such transformations can bring into capitalism some of the virtues of a society beyond capitalism. Thus the quality of life of ordinary people in capitalism is improved by such transformation. In phase I of Figure 10.1 interstitial transformations in capitalism are initiated and these generate an improvement of the quality of life for the average person relative to a capitalism without such transformations.[10]

Second, the revolutionary anarchist strategy affirms that at some point such interstitial social transformations within capitalism hit limits which impose binding constraints (phase II in the figure). Capitalism ultimately blocks the full realization of the potential of socially empowering interstitial transformations. A rupture with capitalism (phase III) becomes necessary to break through those limits if that potential is to advance further.

Third, if capitalism has already been significantly internally transformed through socially empowering interstitial transformations, the transition trough will be tolerably shallow and of relatively short duration (phase IV). Successful interstitial transformations within capitalism mean that economic life becomes less dependent upon capitalist firms and capitalist markets as capitalism continues. Workers' cooperatives and consumer cooperatives have developed widely and play a significant role in the economy; the social economy provides significant basic needs; collective associations engage in a wide variety of socially empowered forms of regulation; and perhaps power relations within capitalist firms have been significantly transformed as well. Taken together, these changes mean that the economic disruption of the break with capitalism will be less damaging than in the absence of such interstitial transformations. Furthermore, the pre-ruptural transformations are palpable demonstrations to workers and other potential beneficiaries of socialism that alternatives to capitalism

---

10 I am using the general expression "quality of life" here to indicate the all-things-considered well-being of people, without giving any particular weights to things like income, working conditions, quality of leisure, the nature of community, etc.

FIGURE 10.1 *Interstitial Transformations Paving the Way to Rupture*

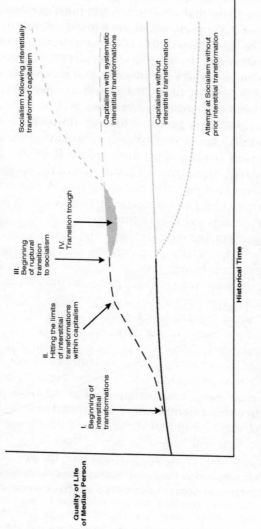

Quality of Life
of Median Person

Beginning of
interstitial
transformations

I.

II.
Hitting the limits
of interstitial
transformations
within capitalism

III.
Beginning
of ruptural
transition
to socialism

IV.
Transition trough

Socialism following interstitially
transformed capitalism

Capitalism with systematic
interstitial transformations

Capitalism without
interstitial transformation

Attempt at Socialism without
prior interstitial transformation

Historical Time

Before Rupture   After Rupture

Capitalism without interstitial transformation

Capitalism with systematic interstitial transformations

Socialism following interstitially transformed capitalism

Attempt at Socialism without prior interstitial transformation

in which the quality of life is better are viable. This contributes to forming the political will for a rupture once the untransgressable limits within capitalism are encountered.[11] The transition trough in figure 10.1 is thus much shallower than it would otherwise be.

And finally, egalitarian, democratic social empowerment will be sustainable after a rupture only if significant socially empowering interstitial transformations had occurred before the rupture. In the absence of such prior social empowerment, the rupture with capitalism will unleash strong centralizing and authoritarian tendencies that are likely to lead to a consolidation of an oppressive form of statism. Even well-intentioned socialists will be forced by the contradictions they confront to build a different kind of society than the one they wanted. The result will be a decline in the quality of life for most people below the trajectory it would have had even under capitalism itself.

ERODING THE BINDING LIMITS OF CAPITALISM

The strategic scenario in Figure 10.1 assumes that capitalism ultimately imposes untransgressable limits on the possibilities of democratic egalitarian emancipatory transformations. The evolutionary anarchist scenario for social emancipation through interstitial transformation drops this assumption. The basic idea, as illustrated in a stylized way in Figure 10.2, is this: Capitalist structures and relations do impose limits on emancipatory social transformation through interstitial strategies, but those limits can themselves be eroded over time by appropriate interstitial strategies. The trajectory of change through interstitial strategy,

---

11 An alternative way of expressing these arguments is to use the language of Antonio Gramsci. Gramsci argued that in the West, with its strong civil society, socialist revolution required a prolonged "war of position" before a successful "war of maneuver" was possible. This means that the period before a rupture is a period of building an effective *counter*-hegemony. Gramsci's emphasis was on building political and ideological counter-hegemony. While he did not directly discuss the issue of interstitial transformations in the economy and civil society, they could be viewed as transforming key aspects of the "material bases of consent" necessary for such a counter-hegemonic movement to be credible and sustainable. For a discussion of Gramsci's ambiguous views on the possibilities of transforming civil society within capitalism in ways that would enhance social empowerment, see Jean L. Cohen and Andrew Arato, *Civil Society and Political Theory* (Cambridge, MA: MIT Press, 1994), section on "Gramsci and the Idea of Socialist Civil Society," pp. 142–59.

FIGURE 10.2 *Interstitial Transformations Eroding Capitalism's Limits*

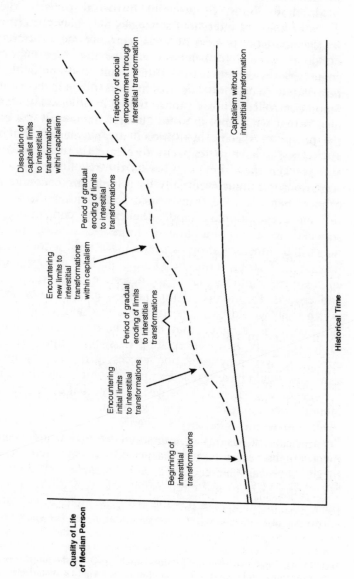

therefore, will be marked by periods in which limits of possibility are encountered and transformation is severely impeded. In such periods new interstitial strategies must be devised which erode those limits. In different historical periods, therefore, different kinds of interstitial strategies may play the critical role in advancing the process of social empowerment. Strategies for building workers' cooperatives may be the most important in some periods, the extension of the social economy or the invention of new associational devices for controlling investments (e.g., union-controlled venture capital funds) in others. The important idea is that what appear to be "limits" are simply the effect of the power of specific institutional arrangements, and interstitial strategies have the capacity to create alternative institutions that weaken those limits. Whereas the revolutionary anarchist scenario argues that eventually hard limits are encountered that cannot themselves be transformed from within the system, in this more evolutionary model the existing constraints can be softened to the point that a more accelerated process of interstitial transformation can take place until it too encounters new limits. There will thus be a kind of cycle of extension of social empowerment and stagnation as successive limits are encountered and eroded. Eventually, if this process can be sustained, capitalism itself would be sufficiently modified and capitalist power sufficiently undermined that it no longer imposed distinctively capitalist limits on the deepening of social empowerment.[12] In effect, the system-hybridization process generated by interstitial strategies would have reached a tipping point in which the logic of the system as a whole had changed in ways that open up the possibilities for continued social empowerment.

Of course the trajectory in Figure 10.2 is highly simplified. Even optimistic visions of interstitial strategies understand that there can be reversals and the periods of thwarted advance of social empowerment could be quite extended. And there may be contingent historical circumstances in which interstitial strategies may no longer be possible—for example, in conditions of authoritarian statism where the political space for such strategies

---

12 Other kinds of structural limits might still exist—limits imposed by gender or global political divisions or some other kind of social relations—and this means that the cycle of encountering limits and devising new limit-eroding strategies would continue. But the specific limits to social empowerment imposed by capitalism would no longer impose binding constraints.

has been closed off. In such circumstances, ruptural strategies may be necessary, not so much to directly transform capitalism as to unbottle the interstitial processes blocked by authoritarian statism. The key idea, however, is that there is nothing inherent in the structures of capitalism as such which prevents interstitial strategies from having these transformative effects, and thus an interstitial trajectory towards social emancipation is possible within a world dominated by capitalism.[13]

INTERSTITIAL STRATEGIES AND THE STATE

It is possible to acknowledge that interstitial strategies of transformation can expand the scope of social empowerment and improve the quality of life of people without embracing these broad strategic visions. Interstitial strategies may create enlarged spaces for non-commodified, non-capitalist economic relations, but it seems unlikely that this could sufficiently insulate most people from dependency on the capitalist economy and sufficiently weaken the power of the capitalist class and the dependency of economic activity on capital accumulation to render the transition trough in the revolutionary scenario short and shallow. And while interstitial strategies may expand the scope of social empowerment, it is difficult to see how they could ever by themselves erode the basic structural power of capital sufficiently to dissolve the capitalist limits on emancipatory social change.

The basic problem of both scenarios concerns their stance towards the state. Those in the anarchist tradition of social emancipation understand that both civil society and the economy are only loosely integrated systems which allow considerable scope for direct action to forge new kinds of relations and practices. In contrast, they tend to view the state as a monolithic, integrated institution, without significant cracks and with only marginal potentials for emancipatory transformation. For revolutionary

---

13 This claim—that capitalism as such does not generate untransgressable limits of possibility—is sometimes couched in a language of "anti-essentialism." See, for example, J. K. Gibson-Graham (Julie Gibson and Katherine Graham), *The End of Capitalism (As We Knew It): A Feminist Critique of Political Economy* (Oxford: Blackwell, 1996). They argue that not only are economic systems always hybrids, but also that the capitalist dimension or component of the hybrid has no deep, unalterable "essence" which imposes rigid limits of possibility on the character of the hybrid as a whole.

anarchists, in fact, the state is precisely the institution which makes an ultimate rupture necessary: the coercive power of the state enforces the untransgressable limits on social empowerment. Without the state, the erosion of capitalist power through interstitial transformation could proceed in the manner described by evolutionary anarchists.

This is not a satisfactory understanding of the state in general or of the state in capitalist societies in particular. The state is no more a unitary, fully integrated structure of power than is the economy or civil society. And while the state may indeed be a "capitalist state" which plays a substantial role in reproducing capitalist relations, it is not *merely* a capitalist state embodying a pure functional logic for sustaining capitalism. The state contains a heterogeneous set of apparatuses, unevenly integrated into a loosely coupled ensemble, in which a variety of interests and ideologies interact. It is an arena of struggle in which contending forces in civil society meet. It is a site for class compromise as well as class domination. In short, the state must be understood not simply in terms of its relationship to social reproduction, but also in terms of the gaps and contradictions of social reproduction.

What this means is that struggles for emancipatory transformation should not simply ignore the state as envisioned by evolutionary interstitial strategies, nor can they realistically smash the state, as envisioned by ruptural strategies. Social emancipation must involve, in one way or another, engaging the state, using it to further the process of emancipatory social empowerment. This is the central idea of symbiotic transformation.

11

SYMBIOTIC TRANSFORMATION

The basic idea of symbiotic transformation is that advances in bottom-up social empowerment within a capitalist society will be most stable and defendable when such social empowerment also helps solve certain real problems faced by capitalists and other elites. While there are historical moments in which it may be possible, through effective popular mobilization and solidarity, to deepen and extend forms of social empowerment even when this sharply threatens the interests of capitalists and other dominant elites, such gains will always be precarious and vulnerable to counterattack. Gains won in a period of heightened mobilization will therefore tend to be undone in periods where such mobilization declines. Forms of social empowerment are likely to be much more durable and to become more deeply institutionalized, and thus harder to reverse, when, in one way or another, they also serve some important interests of dominant groups, and solve real problems faced by the system as a whole. Joel Rogers and Wolfgang Streeck formulate this idea in terms of the general conditions for the robust success of the democratic left: "The democratic left makes progress under capitalism when it improves the material well-being of workers, solves a problem for capitalists that capitalists cannot solve for themselves, and in doing both wins sufficient political cachet to contest capitalist monopoly on articulating the 'general interest.'"[1]

Historically the most important examples of this mode of transformation were the relatively stable forms of "class compromise" between capital and labor mediated by the state in many

---

[1] Joel Rogers and Wolfgang Streeck, "Productive Solidarities: Economic Strategy and Left Politics," in David Miliband (ed.), *Reinventing the Left* (Cambridge: Polity Press, 1994), p. 130.

developed capitalist countries in the second half of the twentieth century. Forging the conditions which make such class
compromise possible has been at the center of the more progressive currents in social democratic politics. In this chapter we will
explore the implicit logic of this kind of strategy and its emancipatory potential.

CLASS COMPROMISE[2]

The concept of "class compromise" invokes three quite distinct
images. In the first, class compromise is an illusion. Leaders of
working-class organizations—especially unions and parties—strike
opportunistic deals with the capitalist class which promise general
benefits for workers but which, in the end, are largely empty. Class
compromises are, at their core, one-sided capitulations rather than
reciprocal bargains embodying mutual concessions.

In the second image, class compromises are like stalemates on
a battlefield. Two armies of roughly similar strength are locked
in battle. Each is sufficiently strong to impose severe costs on
the other; neither is strong enough to definitively vanquish the
opponent. In such a situation of stalemate the contending forces
may agree to a "compromise": to refrain from mutual damage in
exchange for concessions on both sides. The concessions are real,
not phony, even if they are asymmetrical. Still, they don't constitute a process of real cooperation between opposing class forces.
This outcome can be referred to as a "negative class compromise."

The third image sees class compromise as a form of mutual
cooperation between opposing classes. This is not simply a situation of a balance of power in which the outcome of conflict falls
somewhere between a complete victory and a complete defeat
for either party. Rather, here there is a possibility of a non-zero-
sum game between workers and capitalists, a game in which both
parties can improve their position through various forms of active,
mutual cooperation. This outcome can be called a "positive class
compromise."

The central idea of symbiotic transformation is that the possibilities for stable, positive class compromise generally hinge on
the relationship between the *associational power* of the working

2 Much of this section is drawn from a previously published article, Erik
Olin Wright, "Working-Class Power, Capitalist-Class Interests, and Class
Compromise," *American Journal of Sociology* 105: 4 (2000), pp. 957–1002.

class and the *material interests* of capitalists.[3] The conventional wisdom among both neoclassical economists and traditional Marxists is that in general there is an inverse relationship between these two variables: increases in the power of workers adversely affect the interests of capitalists (see Figure 11.1). The rationale for this view is straightforward for Marxist scholars: since the profits of capitalists are closely tied to the exploitation of workers, the material interests of workers and capitalists are inherently antagonistic. Anything which strengthens the capacity of workers to struggle for and realize their interests, therefore, negatively affects the interests of capitalists. The conventional argument by neoclassical economists is somewhat less straightforward, for they deny that in a competitive equilibrium workers are exploited by capitalists. Nevertheless, working-class associational power is seen as interfering with the efficient operation of labor markets by making wages harder to adjust downward when needed and by making it harder for employers to fire workers. Unions and other forms of working-class power are seen as forms of monopolistic power within markets, and like all such practices generate monopoly rents and inefficient allocations. As a result, unionized workers are able to extort a monopoly rent in the form of higher wages at the expense of both capitalists and non-unionized workers.

An alternative understanding of the relationship between workers' power and capitalists' interests sees this as a curvilinear *reverse-J* relationship rather than an inverse relationship (see Figure 11.2).[4] As in the conventional wisdom, capitalist class interests are

---

3 Throughout this discussion of class compromise I will rely on a simple, polarized concept of the class structure of capitalism in which workers and capitalists are the only classes. For some purposes it is important to deploy a highly differentiated class concept which elaborates a complex set of concrete locations within class structures. My work on the problem of the "middle class" and "contradictory locations within class relations" would be an example of such an analysis. See Erik Olin Wright, *Classes* (London: Verso, 1985), and *Class Counts* (Cambridge: Cambridge University Press, 1997). For some problems, the causal processes cannot be properly studied without specifying a range of fine-grained differentiations and divisions within classes on the basis of such things as sector, status, gender, and race. For other purposes, however, it is appropriate to use a much more abstract, simplified class concept, revolving around the central polarized class relation of capitalism: capitalists and workers. This is the class concept I will mainly use in this chapter.

4 The reverse-J shaped relationship between working-class power and capitalist interests was first suggested to me in a paper by Joel Rogers, "Divide and Conquer: Further 'Reflections on the Distinctive Character of American Labor Law'," *Wisconsin Law Review* 13: 1 (1990), pp. 1–147.

FIGURE 11.1 *Conventional View of the Relationship Between Working-Class Power and Capitalist-Class Interests*

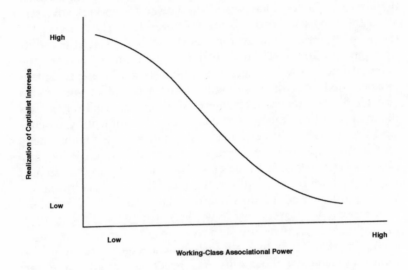

best satisfied when the working class is highly disorganized, when workers compete with each other in an atomized way and lack significant forms of associational power. As working-class power increases, capitalist class interests are initially adversely affected. However, once working-class power crosses some threshold, working-class associational power can begin to have positive effects on capitalist interests. The classic example of this was the role of organized labor in helping to solve certain problems posed by Keynesian macroeconomic policy. Full employment, insofar as it implies high levels of capacity-utilization and higher aggregate demand for the products of capitalist firms, potentially serves the interests of capitalists. But it also risks a profit squeeze from rapidly rising wages and spiraling levels of inflation. Keynes himself recognized this as a serious problem: "I do not doubt that a serious problem will arise as to how wages are to be restrained when we have a combination of collective bargaining and full employment."[5] The emergence and consolidation in a number of countries of strong, centralized unions capable of imposing wage restraint on both workers *and employers*

---

5 Andrew Glynn, "Social Democracy and Full Employment," *New Left Review* 211 (1995), p. 37.

FIGURE 11.2 *Curvilinear Relationship Between Working-Class Power and Capitalist-Class Interests*

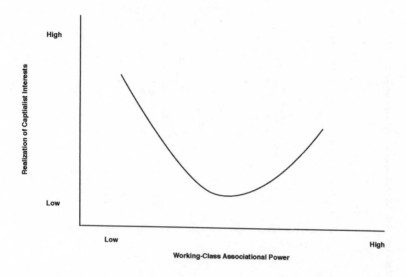

was perhaps the most successful solution to this problem. In this sense, a powerful labor movement need not simply constitute the basis for a *negative* class compromise, extracting benefits for workers through threats to capital. If a labor movement is sufficiently disciplined, particularly when it is articulated to a sympathetic state, it can positively contribute to the realization of capitalist interests by helping to solve macroeconomic problems.

In order to more deeply understand the social processes reflected in the reverse-J hypothesis of Figure 11.2, we need to elaborate and extend the model in various ways.[6] First we will examine more closely the underlying causal mechanisms which generate this curve. Second, we will extend the range of the figure by examining what happens at a very high levels of working-class associational power. Finally, we will examine various ways in which the institutional environment of class conflict determines which regions of this curve are historically accessible as strategic objectives.

---

6   A more formal elaboration of the theoretical foundations of this model can be found in Wright, "Working-Class Power, Capitalist-Class Interests and Class Compromise," pp. 969–76.

FIGURE 11.3 *Decomposition of the Relationship Between Interests of Capitalists and Associational Power of Workers*

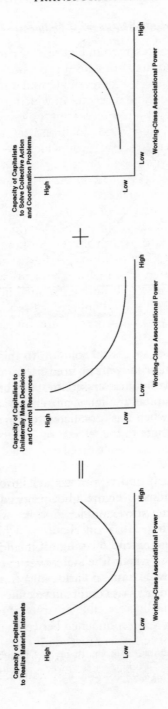

Mechanisms underlying the reverse-J relation

The reverse-J curve presented in Figure 11.2 can be understood as the outcome of two kinds of causal processes—one in which the interests of capitalists are increasingly undermined as the power of workers increases, and a second in which the interests of capitalists are enhanced by the increasing power of workers. These are illustrated in Figure 11.3. In broad terms, the downward-sloping curve reflects the ways in which the increasing power of workers *undermines the capacity of capitalists to unilaterally make decisions and control resources* of various sorts, while the upward-sloping curve reflects ways in which the associational power of workers may *help capitalists solve certain kinds of collective action and coordination problems.*

Class struggle and compromise do not occur within an amorphous "society," but within specific institutional contexts—firms, markets, states. The real mechanisms which generate the reverse-J curve in figure 11.3 are embedded in such institutional contexts. Three institutional spheres within which class struggles occur and class compromises are forged are particularly important:

- *The sphere of exchange.* This concerns above all the labor market and various other kinds of commodity markets, but in some situations financial markets may also be an arena within which class conflicts occur and class compromises are forged.

- *The sphere of production.* This concerns what goes on inside of firms once workers are hired and capital is invested. Conflicts over the labor process and technology are the characteristic examples.

- *The sphere of politics.* Class conflict and class compromise also occur within the state over the formation and implementation of state policies, and the administration of various kinds of state-enforced rules.

There is a rough correspondence between each of these institutional spheres of class conflict and class compromise and characteristic kinds of working-class collective organizations: *labor unions* are the characteristic associational form for conflict/

compromise in the sphere of exchange; *works councils* and related associations are the characteristic form within the sphere of production; and *political parties* are the characteristic form within the sphere of politics.

The central task of our analysis, then, is to examine the mechanisms which enable these different forms of working-class associational power—unions, works councils, parties—to forge *positive* class compromises within the spheres of exchange, production, and politics. These mechanisms are summarized in Figure 11.4.

The sphere of exchange

Capitalists have a range of material interests within the sphere of exchange that bear on their relationship with the working class: minimizing labor costs; having an unfettered capacity to hire and fire without interference; selling all of the commodities they produce; having a labor force with a particular mix of skills in a labor market that provides predictable and adequate supplies of labor. As has often been argued by both Marxists and non-Marxist political economists, some of these interests contradict

FIGURE 11.4 *Decomposition of Relation Between Working-Class Power and Capitalist-Class Interests in the Spheres of Politics, Exchange and Production*

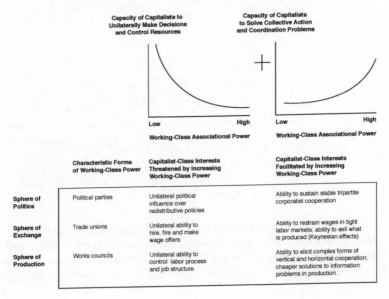

	Characteristic Forms of Working-Class Power	Capitalist-Class Interests Threatened by Increasing Working-Class Power	Capitalist-Class Interests Facilitated by Increasing Working-Class Power
Sphere of Politics	Political parties	Unilateral political influence over redistributive policies	Ability to sustain stable tripartite corporatist cooperation
Sphere of Exchange	Trade unions	Unilateral ability to hire, fire and make wage offers	Ability to restrain wages in tight labor markets; ability to sell what is produced (Keynesian effects)
Sphere of Production	Works councils	Unilateral ability to control labor process and job structure	Ability to elicit complex forms of vertical and horizontal cooperation; cheaper solutions to information problems in production.

each other. Most notably, the interests of capitalists in selling commodities means that it is desirable for workers-as-consumers to have a lot of disposable income, whereas capitalists' interests in minimizing their own wage bill implies an interest in paying workers-as-employees as little as possible.

Increases in working-class associational power generally undermine the capacity of individual capitalists to unilaterally make decisions and allocate resources within labor markets. In the absence of unions, capitalists can hire and fire at will and set wages at whatever level they feel is most profitable given existing market conditions. Working-class associational power reduces capitalists' individual capacity to make profit-maximizing decisions on labor markets and thus hurts their material interests.

If capitalists' interests within the sphere of exchange consisted entirely of interests in their individual ability to buy and sell with minimal constraint, then something close to the inverse relation portrayed in Figure 11.1 would hold. But this is not the case. The material interests of capitalists—their ability to sustain a high and stable rate of profit—depends upon the provision of various aggregate conditions within the sphere of exchange, and these require coordination and collective action. The solution to at least some of these coordination problems can be facilitated by relatively high levels of working-class associational power.[7]

The classic example of this is the problem of inadequate aggregate demand for the consumer goods produced by capitalists. This is the traditional Keynesian problem of how raising wages and social spending can underwrite higher levels of aggregate demand and thus help solve "under-consumption" problems in the economy. Inadequate consumer demand represents a collective action problem for capitalists: capitalists simultaneously want to pay their own employees as low wages as possible and want other capitalists to pay as high wages as possible in order to generate adequate consumer demand for products. High levels of unionization, in effect, prevent individual firms from "defecting" from the cooperative solution to this dilemma.

---

7 This does not mean that working-class associational power is a necessary condition for the solution to such coordination problems. There may be other devices which may constitute alternative strategies for solving these coordination problems. All that is being claimed is that working-class associational power can constitute a mechanism which makes it easier to solve such problems.

Working-class strength can also contribute to more predictable and stable labor markets. Under conditions of tight labor
markets where competition for labor among capitalists would
normally push wages up—perhaps at rates higher than the rate
of increase of productivity, thus stimulating inflation—high
levels of working-class associational power can also contribute
to wage restraint.[8] Wage restraint is an especially complex collec-
tive-action problem: individual capitalists need to be prevented
from defecting from the wage restraint agreement (i.e. they must
be prevented from bidding up wages to workers in an effort to
lure workers away from other employers given the unavailability
of workers in the labor market), and individual workers (and
unions) need to be prevented from defecting from the agreement
by trying to maximize wages under tight labor market conditions. Wage restraint in tight labor markets, which is important
for long-term stable growth and contained inflation, is generally
easier where the working class is very well organized, particularly in centralized unions, than where it is not.

A second example concerns the serious problem of skill formation in labor markets faced by capitalists. As we discussed in
chapter 7, while it is in the interests of capitalists to have a labor
force with high levels of flexible skills, it is not in the interests
of individual capitalists to provide for the needed training since
in a free labor market other capitalists, who have not provided
such training, can poach such well-trained workers. Strong unions
can play an active role in helping to solve this kind of problem
by ensuring greater job security for workers, stabilizing and
enforcing seniority rules, and in other ways reducing the possibilities of poaching.

These positive effects of working-class associational power on
capitalist interests in the sphere of exchange need not imply that
capitalists themselves are equally well organized in strong employers'
associations, although as the history of Northern European neo-
corporatism suggests, strongly organized working-class movements
tend to stimulate the development of complementary organization

---

8 For a discussion of union power and wage restraint, see L. Calmfors and J.
Driffill, "Bargaining Structure, Corporatism, and Macroeconomic Performance,"
Economic Policy 6 (1988), pp. 13–61; Glynn, "Social Democracy and Full
Employment"; Jonas Pontusson, "Between Neo-Liberalism and the German
Model: Swedish Capitalism in Transition," in Colin Crouch and Wolfgang
Streeck (eds), *Political Economy of Modern Capitalism: Mapping Convergence
and Diversity* (Thousand Oaks, CA: Sage, 1997), pp. 50–70.

on the part of employers. In any case the ability of workers' power to constructively help solve macroeconomic problems is enhanced when capitalists are also organized.

Assuming that the positive Keynesian and labor market effects of working-class power are generally weaker than the negative wage-cost and firing discretion effects, the combination of these processes yields the reverse-J relationship for the sphere of exchange in Figure 11.4.

The sphere of production

A similar contradictory quality of the interests of capitalists with respect to workers occurs within the sphere of production: on the one hand, capitalists have an interest in being able to unilaterally control the labor process (choosing and changing technology, assigning labor to different tasks, changing the pace of work, etc.), and on the other hand they have an interest in being able to reliably elicit cooperation, initiative, and responsibility from employees.

As working-class associational power within production increases, capitalists' unilateral control over the labor process declines. This does not mean that they are necessarily faced with rigid, unalterable work rules, job classifications, and the like, but it does mean that changes in the labor process need to be negotiated and bargained over with representatives of workers, rather than unilaterally imposed. Particularly in conditions of rapid technical change, this may hurt capitalist interests.

On the other hand, at least under certain social and technical conditions of production, working-class associational strength within production may enhance the possibilities for more complex and stable forms of cooperation between labor and management. To the extent that working-class strength increases job security and reduces arbitrariness in managerial treatment of workers, then workers' time-horizons for their jobs are likely to increase, and along with this their sense that their future prospects are linked to the welfare of the firm. This in turn may contribute to a sense of loyalty and greater willingness to cooperate in various ways.

The German case of strong workplace-based worker organization built around works councils and co-determination is perhaps the best example. Wolfgang Streeck describes how codetermination and works councils positively help capitalists solve certain problems:

What, then, is specific about codetermination? Unlike the other factors that have limited the variability of employment, codetermination has not merely posed a problem for enterprises, but has also offered a solution. While on the one hand codetermination has contributed to growing organizational rigidities, on the other hand, and at the same time, it has provided the organizational instruments to cope with such rigidities without major losses in efficiency. . .

. . .the works council not only shares in what used to be managerial prerogatives, but also accepts responsibility for the implementation and enforcement of decisions made under its participation. This constellation has frequently been described as "integration" or "cooptation" of labor or organized labor, in management; with the same justification, however, it can be seen as "colonization" of management, and in particularly manpower management, by the representatives of the workforce. The most adequate metaphor would probably be that of a *mutual incorporation of capital and labor* by which labor internalizes the interests of capital just as capital internalizes those of labor, with the result that works council and management become subsystems of an integrated, internally differentiated system of industrial government which increasingly supersedes the traditional pluralist-adversarial system of industrial relations.[9]

This tighter coupling of the interests of labor and capital with the resulting heightened forms of interclass cooperation helps employers solve a range of concrete coordination problems in workplaces: more efficient information flows within production (since workers have more access to managerial information and less incentive to withhold information as part of a job-protection strategy); more efficient adjustments of the labor process in periods of rapid technological change (since workers are involved in the decision making, and are thus less worried that technological change will cost them their jobs, they are more likely to actively cooperate with the introduction of new technologies); more effective strategies of skill formation (since workers, with the most intimate knowledge of skill bottlenecks and requirements, are involved in designing training programs). Most broadly, strong workplace associational power creates the possibility of more effective involvement of workers in various forms of creative problem-solving.[10]

---

9 Wolfgang Streeck, *Social Institutions and Economic Performance: Studies of Industrial Relations in Advanced Capitalist Economies* (Newbury Park, CA: Sage, 1992), pp. 160 and 164.

10 It is possible, under certain social and cultural conditions, for some of these forms of cooperation to emerge and be sustained without strong workplace

With so many positive advantages of such cooperative institutions, it might seem surprising that strong workplace associational power is so rare in developed capitalist countries. The reason is that such cooperative advantages come at a cost to capital. Streeck recognizes this even in the German case:

> Above all, codetermination carries with it considerable costs in managerial discretion and managerial prerogatives . . . Integration cuts both ways, and if it is to be effective with regards to labor it must bind capital as well. This is why codetermination, for all its advantages, is seen by capital as a thoroughly mixed blessing . . . Both the short-term economic costs and the long-term costs in authority and status make the advantages of codetermination expensive for the capitalist class, and thus explains the otherwise incomprehensible resistance of business to any extension of codetermination rights.[11]

Because of these costs, capitalists in general will prefer a system of production in which they do not have to contend with strong associational power of workers in production. Thus, again, the reverse-J shape of the functional relation between workers' power and capitalists' interests within production.

The sphere of politics

The two components of the reverse-J relationship between working-class associational power and capitalist interests are perhaps most obvious in the sphere of politics. As a great deal of comparative historical research has indicated, as working-class political power increases, the capitalist state tends to become more redistributive: the social wage increases and thus the reservation wage of workers is higher; taxation and transfer policies reduce income inequality; and in various ways labor power is partially de-commodified. All of these policies have negative effects on the material interests of high-income people in general and capitalists in particular. Working-class political power also tends to underwrite institutional arrangements which increase working-class power within the sphere of exchange

---

associational power of workers. This is often the way the relatively cooperative system of employment relations in Japan is described (see, e.g., Chie Nakane, *Japanese Society* [London: Weidenfeld and Nicholson, 1970]), although others have criticized such culturalist views (e.g., Masahiko Aoki, *Comparative Institutional Analysis* [Cambridge, MA: MIT Press, 2001], pp. 304 ff.). In any event, under many conditions high levels of worker cooperation within production are likely to be difficult to sustain if they are not backed by some form of significant associational power.

11 Streeck, *Social Institutions*, p. 165.

and often within the sphere of production as well. Working-class associational power in the political sphere, therefore, may also indirectly contribute to the downward-sloping curves in the spheres of exchange and production.

The upward-sloping class compromise curve in the sphere of politics is the central preoccupation of social democracy. The large literature on tripartite state-centered corporatism is, in effect, a literature on how the interests of capitalists can flourish in the context of a highly organized working class.[12] Sweden (up until the mid 1980s) is usually taken as the paradigm case: the Social Democratic Party's control of the Swedish state facilitated a set of corporatist arrangements between centralized trade unions and centralized employers' associations that made possible a long, stable period of cooperation and growth. The organizational links between the labor movement and the Social Democratic Party were critical for this stability, since it added legitimacy to the deals that were struck and increased the confidence of workers that the terms of the agreement would be upheld in the future. This made it possible over a long period of time for Swedish capitalism to sustain high capacity utilization, very low levels of unemployment, and relatively high productivity growth. State-mediated corporatism anchored in working-class associational strength in the political sphere played a significant role in these outcomes.

The inventory of mechanisms in Figure 11.4 provides a preliminary set of variables for characterizing the conditions of class compromise within different units of analysis across time and space. Class compromises within the sphere of exchange can occur in local, regional, and national labor markets, or within labor markets linked to particular sectors. Production level compromises typically occur within firms, but they may also be organized within sectors.[13] Class compromises in the sphere of politics are espe-

---

12 See, for example, Gøsta Esping-Andersen, *Three Worlds of Welfare Capitalism* (Princeton, NJ: Princeton University Press, 1990); Philippe Schmitter, "Corporatism is Dead! Long Live Corporatism! Reflections on Andrew Schonfield's *Modern Capitalism*," *Government and Opposition* 24 (1988), pp. 54–73; Philippe Schmitter and G. Lembruch (eds), *Trends Towards Corporatist Intermediation* (London: Sage, 1979).

13 In the spheres of production and exchange, there may be considerable heterogeneity in the shape of the class compromise curves and the degree of working-class associational power across firms and sectors. The result is that within a given country the conditions for class compromise may be much more

cially important within the nation state, but local and regional political class compromises are also possible. The emergence of various forms of corporatism involving local and regional levels of government may indicate the development of political class compromises within sub-national units. The reverse-J curves that map the terrain of class compromise, therefore, can be relevant to the analysis of class compromises in any unit of analysis, not simply entire countries.

Different countries, then, will be characterized by different combinations of values on these three pairs of class compromise curves.[14] In Germany, for example, working-class associational power has traditionally been especially strong within the sphere of production, somewhat less strong in the sphere of exchange, and rather weaker in the sphere of politics. In Sweden—at least in the heyday of social democracy—it was very strong in the spheres of exchange and politics, and perhaps a bit weaker in the sphere of production. In the United States, working-class associational power has dwindled within all three spheres, but is strongest in the sphere of exchange within certain limited sectors. The overall reverse-J curve for class compromise within a society, therefore, is the result of a complex amalgamation of the component curves within each of these spheres.

Making the model more complex: extending the theoretical domain of variation

The range of variation in Figures 11.3 and 11.4 can be considered the typical spectrum of possibilities in contemporary, developed capitalist societies. It will be helpful for our subsequent analysis to consider what happens when working-class power increases

---

favorable in some firms and sectors than in others. The aggregate reverse-J curve characterizing a given sphere, therefore, is itself an amalgamation of the distribution of such curves across firms, sectors, and other less aggregated units of analysis.

14 The actual variation across time and place is, of course, much more complicated than is being portrayed here. Countries will vary not simply in where they are located on each of these curves, but also on: 1) the relative weights of the various curves in defining the overall configuration for the society; 2) the units of analysis within countries within which class compromises are most rooted; 3) the specific shapes of the component curves themselves. In some times and places, for example, the upward-sloping segments of some of the curves might be relatively flat, in other cases, quite steep. My theoretical understanding of these relations is insufficient to say anything very systematic about either of these two sources of variation.

FIGURE 11.5 *Interests of Capital and Power of Workers with Respect to Control Over Investments*

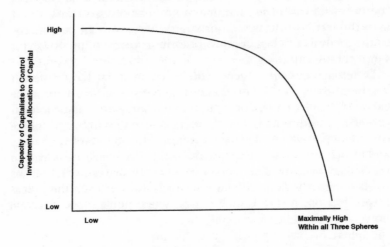

Working-Class Associational Power

towards the limiting case of society-wide working-class organization and solidarity simultaneously in all three spheres of class compromise. This corresponds to what might be termed "democratic socialism," understood as working-class collective democratic control over capital.

What happens to capitalist class interests as working-class associational power approaches this theoretical maximum? Figure 11.5 presents the relationship between one crucial aspect of capitalists' interests—their control over investments and accumulation (allocation of capital)—and working-class power. The control over investments is perhaps the most fundamental dimension of "private" ownership of the means of production within capitalism. In most capitalist societies, even as working-class power increases, this particular power of capital is not seriously eroded. Even with strong unions and social democratic parties, capitalists still have the broad power to disinvest, to choose their individual rate of savings, to turn their profits into consumption or allocate them to new investments, etc. Of course, all capitalist states have capacities to create incentives and disincentives for particular allocations of capital (through taxes, subsidies, tariffs, etc.). And in special circumstances "disincentives" can have a significant coercive character, effectively constraining capitalists' capacity to allocate capital. Still, this fundamental aspect of capitalist property rights is not generally threatened within the normal range of variation of working-class power. When working-class associational power approaches its theoretical maximum, however, the right of capitalists to control the allocation of capital is called into question. Indeed, this is the heart of the definition of democratic socialism—popular, democratic control over the allocation of capital. This is what so scared the Swedish capitalist class when the Meidner plan of share-levy wage-earner funds was proposed in 1976. This suggests the shape of the curve in Figure 11.5: a relatively weak negative effect of working-class power on capitalist interests with respect to the control over the basic allocation of capital until working-class power reaches a very high level, at which point those interests become seriously threatened.[15]

When Figure 11.5 is added to Figure 11.2, we get the roller-coaster curve in Figure 11.6. There are two *maxima* in this theoretical model: the *capitalist utopia*, in which the working class is sufficiently atomized and disorganized to give capitalists a free hand in organizing production and appropriating the gains from increased productivity without fear of much collective resistance; and the *social democratic utopia*, in which working-class associational power is sufficiently strong to generate high levels of corporatist cooperation between labor and capital without being so strong as to threaten basic capitalist property rights. These two maxima, however, constitute quite different strategic environments for workers and

---

15 The x-axis in figure 11.5 is working-class associational power undifferentiated into the spheres of production, exchange, and politics. It thus represents an under-theorized amalgam of the associational power within the three spheres (which are themselves amalgams of associational power across the various units of analysis that make up a sphere). The underlying intuition is that viable democratic socialism requires high levels of workers' associational power within all three spheres, and that a *sustainable* threat to fundamental capitalist property rights under democratic conditions can only occur when such unified associational power occurs. This does not imply, however, that the three spheres are of equal weight in this theoretical gestalt. Traditionally Marxists have argued that working-class power at the level of the state is most decisive for challenging capitalist property rights, whereas anarcho-syndicalists have argued that the pivot is workers' power within production.

FIGURE 11.6 *Expanded Model of Working-Class Associational Power and Capitalist-Class Interests*

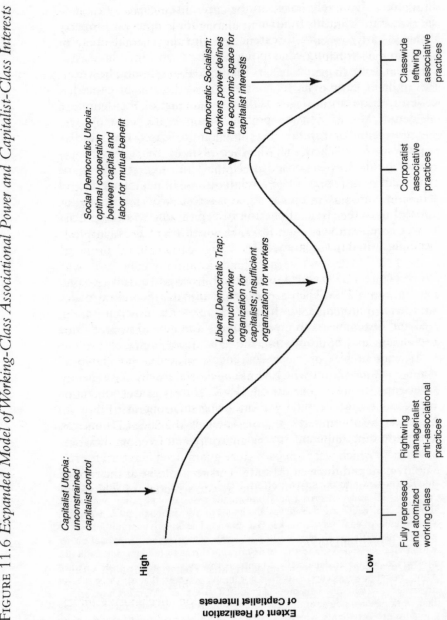

Working-Class Associational Power in Economic Organization and Politics

capitalists. Statically, capitalists should only care about where they sit on the vertical axis of this figure: if you draw a horizontal line through the figure that intersects the curve at three places, capitalists should be statically indifferent among these three possibilities. Understood dynamically, however, capitalists in general will prefer points in the left hand region of the curve.

It is at least in part because of this threat of a society-wide shift in the balance of class power that capitalists might prefer for working-class associational power to remain to the left of the social democratic "peak" of this curve, even though this peak might be theoretically advantageous to capitalist interests. Arriving at the peak looks too much like a Trojan horse: small additional changes in associational power could precipitate a decisive challenge to capitalist interests and power. The local maximum of the "social democratic utopia" in Figure 11.6 may thus be a kind of tipping point which is seen by capitalists as too risky a zone to inhabit. This is one interpretation of the strident opposition by Swedish capitalists to the initial formulation of the "wage-earners fund" proposal in the 1970s. The wage-earners fund, as initially conceived, was a proposal through which Swedish unions would gain increasing control over the Swedish economy via the use of union pension funds to acquire controlling interests in Swedish firms. From the point of view of economic performance and even the middle-run profit interests of Swedish firms, it was arguable that this might be beneficial for Swedish capital, but it raised the possibility of a long-term slide towards democratic socialism by significantly enhancing the power of Swedish labor. The result was a militant attack by Swedish capital against the Social Democratic Party. As Andrew Glynn writes: "The policies which the Social Democrats were proposing impinged on the authority and freedom of action of business which was supposed to be guaranteed in return for full employment and the welfare state. This seems to lie at the root of the employers' repudiation of the Swedish model, of which full employment was a central part."[16]

Zones of unattainability

In the practical world of real capitalist societies, not all values within this theoretically defined range are historically accessible. There are two different kinds of exclusion mechanisms which

---

16 Glynn, "Social Democracy and Full Employment," pp. 53–4.

have the effect of narrowing the range of real possibilities. These can be termed *systemic* exclusions and *institutional* exclusions.

Systemic exclusions define parts of the curve that are outside the limits of possibility because of the fundamental structural features of a social system. Specifically, the presence of a *constitutionally secure democracy* removes the fully repressed and atomized working class part of the curve from the historical stage, and the presence of *legally secure capitalist property rights* removes the democratic socialism part of the curve. This does not mean that there are no historical circumstances in which these zones of the curve might become strategically accessible, but to get there would require a fundamental transformation of the underlying social structural principles of the society.

Institutional exclusions refer to various kinds of historically variable institutional arrangements, formed within the limits determined by the systemic exclusions, which make it difficult or impossible to move to specific regions of the curve. For example, restrictive labor laws can make it difficult to extend working-class associational power towards the corporatist associative practices part of the curve.[17] On the other hand, generous welfare state provisions which render workers less dependent on capital, and strong associational rights which facilitate unionization, may make it difficult to move towards the right-wing managerialist region. Such institutional exclusions, of course, are themselves the outcomes of historical conflicts and should not be viewed as eternally fixed. But once in place, they help to define the range of feasible strategies immediately open to actors, at least until the time when actors can effectively challenge these institutional exclusions themselves.

These two forms of exclusion are illustrated in Figure 11.7. The central region of the curve defines the space that is immediately accessible strategically. To use a game theory metaphor adopted by Robert Alford and Roger Friedland,[18] this is the domain of ordinary politics, of *liberal* versus *conservative* struggles over "plays" within a well-defined set of institutional "rules of the game."[19] The other regions of the curve become the objects of

17 This is the core argument of Rogers, "Divide and Conquer."
18 Robert Alford and Roger Friedland, *Powers of Theory* (Cambridge: Cambridge University Press, 1985).
19 The use of the term "liberal" and "conservative" in this context refers to the standard usage in US politics. The term "conservative" here corresponds to what in many European countries would be called "liberal."

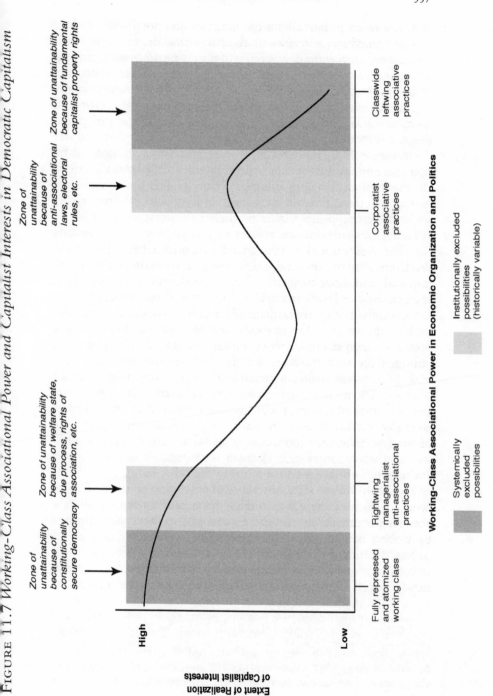

FIGURE 11.7 *Working-Class Associational Power and Capitalist Interests in Democratic Capitalism*

politics only episodically. *Reformist* versus *reactionary* politics are struggles over the rules of the game that define institutional exclusions; *revolutionary* versus *counter-revolutionary* politics are struggles over the systemic constraints that define what game is being played. The creation and destruction of these systemic barriers of exclusion are the central stakes in processes of ruptural transformation, where the key issues are mobilization of power resources for system-defining victories and defeats.

In Figure 11.7, the "zones of unattainability" defined by the systemic and institutional exclusions symmetrically span the tails of the theoretical curve of possibilities. There is no reason, of course, to believe that the real world is this neat. Indeed, one of the reasons for introducing this complexity is precisely to provide tools for understanding forms of variation across time and place in these exclusions. This historical variability is illustrated in Figure 11.8 which compares the United States and Sweden in the periods of most stable Swedish social democracy and American liberal democracy.

Systemic exclusions in the United States and Sweden are roughly comparable: both have structurally secure democratic states with stable representative institutions and the rule of law, and both securely guarantee capitalist property rights. Where they differ substantially is in the nature of the historically variable institutional exclusions which confront their respective working classes.

In the US, a variety of institutional rules create a fairly broad band of institutional exclusions to the right of the central trough of the curve. Electoral rules which solidify a two-party system of centrist politics and anti-union rules which create deep impediments to labor organizing all push the boundary of this zone of institutional exclusion to the left. On the other hand, such factors as the weak welfare state, the very limited job protections afforded workers, and laws which guarantee managerial autonomy all have the effect of narrowing the institutional exclusions centered around right-wing managerialist anti-associational practices. The band of accessible strategy in the US, therefore, affords labor very little room to maneuver and keeps working-class associational practices permanently lodged on the downward-sloping segment of the curve to the left of the trough.

Swedish institutional exclusions, particularly during the most stable period of social democracy, work towards facilitating working-class associational power. Labor law is permissive, making it quite easy to form and expand union membership, and the generous welfare state and job protections significantly reduce

FIGURE 11.8 *Working-Class Associational Power and Capitalist Interests in Liberal Democratic Capitalism (United States) and Social Democratic Capitalism (Sweden)*

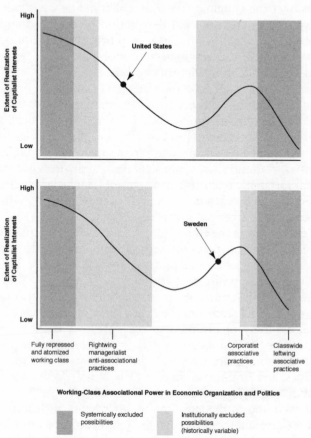

Working-Class Associational Power in Economic Organization and Politics

the scope of right-wing managerialist strategies. The result has been that the Swedish labor movement has for a long time been located on the upward-sloping section of the curve to the right of the trough.

Actors living within these systems, of course, do not directly see this entire picture. To the extent that the institutional exclusion mechanisms have been securely in place and remained unchallenged for an extended period of time, they may become entirely invisible

FIGURE 11.9 *Strategic Environment for Feasible Associational Politics as Seen by the Actors in Social Democratic Capitalism and Liberal Capitalism*

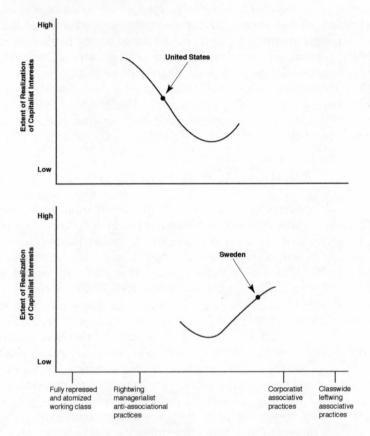

Working-Class Associational Power in Economic Organization and Politics

and the parts of the curve which they subsume may become virtually unimaginable. From the vantage point of actors within the system, therefore, the range of "realistic" possibilities may look like those portrayed in Figure 11.9 rather than Figure 11.7. The American labor movement faces a terrain of possibilities which places it chronically on the defensive. Every marginal increase of workers' strength is experienced by capitalists as against their interests, so whenever the opportunity arises, capitalists attempt to undermine labor's strength. Anti-union campaigns are common and decertification elections a regular occurrence. In Sweden, even in the somewhat less favorable economic environment at the beginning of the twenty-first century, the institutionally delimited strategic environment is much more benign for workers. The central pressure on capitalists has been to forge ways of effectively cooperating with organized labor, of creating institutional spaces in which the entrenched forms of associational power of workers can be harnessed for enhanced productivity. This need not imply that employers actively encourage enhanced working-class associational power, but it does suggest less sustained effort to undermine it.

THE LOGIC OF SYMBIOTIC STRATEGIES

Symbiotic strategies of emancipatory transformation imply that movements in the direction of a long-term metamorphosis of social structures and institutions in a democratic egalitarian direction is facilitated when increasing social empowerment can be linked to effective social problem-solving in ways that also serve the interests of elites and dominant classes. Positive class compromise is one example of such a linkage, but this logic is not restricted to class-based collective action; there is a wide range of projects of social change not directly rooted in class relations that have at least some elements of this logic. In particular, there are many kinds of local processes of collaborative problem-solving, sometimes grouped together under the rubric "the civic renewal movement," in which civic groups of various sorts are empowered to participate in problem-solving collaboration with powerful local actors such as city governments, regional authorities, and business elites.[20] These efforts at locally rooted symbiotic transformations have involved such things as watershed councils, community development projects, community health projects, labor market training partnerships, and many other things. In each of these instances there are practical problems which in one way or another challenge the interests of elites as well as ordinary citizens and in which, under some conditions, a collaborative strategy of seeking

---

20 For an extensive review of such projects and their potential contribution to a revitalized American democracy, see Carmen Siriani and Lewis A. Friedland, *The Civic Renewal Movement: Community Building and Democracy in the United States* (Dayton, OH: Kittering Foundation Press, 2005).

solutions to the problem becomes attractive to contending social forces. Watershed and ecosystem management, for example, poses problems for the interests of developers, manufacturers, agribusiness, and other elite groups, as well as environmentalists, sportsmen, and other constituencies in civil society. Under at least some conditions, collaborative problem-solving involving empowered stakeholders in civil society can create "win-win" solutions in everyone's advantage. Creating the conditions for this to occur is the core of symbiotic strategies of transformation.

Because symbiotic transformations involve systematic forms of collaboration and mutually beneficial cooperation between opposing social forces, it might be thought that the *strategies* in pursuit of such collaboration would also be collaborative and nonconfrontational. There is a current in contemporary social analysis that sees failures to achieve such collaborative solutions as mainly failures of trust and enlightenment between opposing groups, not failures of struggles over power. In this view, most conflict situations should be viewed as failures of the participants to discover the positive-sum possibilities of their situation. Typically this is because the positive-sum, collaborative potential is obscured to the participants by ideologies and preconceived notions of interest. Social actors, the argument goes, do not have real fixed interests; rather, interests are always something constructed in the specific contexts of problem-solving interactions. "Win-win solutions" to problems should therefore be generally possible as long as the actors engage in good-faith experimental, collaborative interactions.

An influential statement of this view, already noted in chapter 7, has been elaborated by Charles Sabel, particularly in his important coauthored essay with Michael Dorf, "A Constitution of Democratic Experimentalism."[21] Building on the pragmatist tradition of democratic theory of John Dewey, Sabel and Dorf develop what they refer to as a democratic experimentalist approach to social and economic regulation which attempts "to rethink American constitutionalism and the design of our representative democracy in the light of those urgent doubts about the possibilities of democratic government in an age of complexity."[22] Complexity poses two crucial problems for the functioning of

---

21 Michael Dorf and Charles Sabel, "A Constitution of Democratic Experimentalism," *Columbia Law Review* 98: 2 (1998).
22 Dorf and Sabel, "A Constitution," p. 274.

democratic institutions: First, it becomes increasingly difficult for legislators to effectively pass legislation which adequately specifies the necessary forms of government regulation to deal with a very wide range of problems, from environmental protection to skill formation. The result is that legislation effectively delegates the rule-making responsibility to centralized bureaucracies and leaves the actual task to experts within such agencies. But, second, the centralized bureaucracies equally find it impossible to specify detailed regulations that are responsive to the real variability of local conditions generated by complexity and are incapable of effectively responding to the unintended consequences of particular rules by their continual refinement and development. The solution proposed by Sabel and Dorf is the reconstruction of state institutions along pragmatist lines. The core institutional design consists of rule formulation and reformulation through decentralized experiments governed by deliberative bodies consisting of empowered stakeholders. More centralized authority takes responsibility for monitoring these experiments and disseminating information so that these deliberative bodies can effectively compare the relative success of different experiments. Once this process is set in motion, Sabel and Dorf believe, the actors will begin to reconstruct their interests (and perhaps their identities as well) in ways that reinforce the positive-sum collaboration of pragmatic problem-solving and gradually marginalize obstructionist forces that insist on pursuing antagonistic, exclusionary interests. Through such a "bootstrapping" process, a broad society-wide diffusion of collaboration will be generated through the very process of collaboration.

The argument throughout this book challenges this benign view of the stakes in class-based conflict, although it does not reject the potential for positive-sum compromises and problem-solving collaboration within those conflicts under certain conditions. The antagonistic interests of workers and capitalists are real, built into the underlying structure of relations that define capitalism. In general, privileged elites and dominant classes prefer disorganized, disempowered popular forces; only when that possibility is historically closed off does the second-best equilibrium of a positive class compromise become attractive to them. And closing off the disempowered alternative is a question of struggles over power, not just enlightenment.

Symbiotic strategies of transformation, therefore, always involve a counterpoint between two kinds of processes. First, there are struggles over the institutional zones of exclusion which attempt to open up the upward-sloping part of the curve to collective action and close off as much of the downward-sloping curve as possible; and second, there is the process within these institutional limits of reaching the most favorable equilibrium. Most of the time in stable capitalist democracies these institutional parameters seem fairly fixed and unassailable, and perhaps even invisible. But episodically opportunities arise for serious challenges to those institutionally imposed limits of possibilities, and when this occurs the changes will depend in significant ways on the outcomes of confrontations and mobilizations. When these institutional limits of possibility block the exit options for powerful elites and open up empowered forms of popular participation, then collaborative problem-solving experimentalism can become a real possibility for movements in the direction of democratic egalitarianism.

SYMBIOTIC TRANSFORMATIONS BEYOND CAPITALISM?

It is one thing to say that symbiotic strategies can potentially enlarge the space for social empowerment and create relatively stable forms of positive collaboration. But why should we believe that this also has the potential of cumulatively transforming the system as a whole? Why is a symbiotic strategy any more plausible than ruptural strategies or interstitial strategies as a strategy not simply for improvement of life within capitalism but for the transcendence of capitalism? After all, the historically most impressive examples of symbiotic strategies—the first resulting in extending the franchise to the working class and the second in empowering the labor movement as a central player in the expansive welfare state—both contributed to consolidating very robust forms of capitalism. As was the case for ruptural strategies and for interstitial strategies, therefore, it is difficult to make an abstract case that symbiotic strategies provide a basis for social transformation beyond capitalism.

What we are left with, then, is a menu of strategic logics and an indeterminate prognosis for the future. The pessimistic view is that this condition is our fate, living in a world in which capitalism remains hegemonic: systemic ruptures for a democratic egalitarian alternative to capitalism are extremely unlikely to ever muster mass popular support within developed capitalist democracies; interstitial transformations are limited to restricted spaces; and symbiotic strategies, when they are successful, strengthen the hegemonic capacity of capitalism. The optimistic view is that we don't know what system challenges and transformative possibilities there will be in the future: interstitial strategies today can strengthen popular understandings that another world is possible and contribute to moving along some of the pathways of social empowerment; symbiotic strategies can potentially open up greater spaces for interstitial strategies to work; and the cumulative effect of such institution-building around expanded forms of social empowerment could be to render ruptural transformations possible under unexpected future historical conditions.

CONCLUSION:
MAKING UTOPIAS REAL

At the end of the first decade of the twenty-first century, capitalism is once again in a period of serious crisis. The self-satisfied triumphalism of the last two decades of the twentieth century has largely disappeared; a new period of uncertainty about the future of capitalism has begun. Institutions designed to steer capitalism forward and preserve the conditions for stable capital accumulation seem at a loss about what to do. In the press there are facile discussions about whether or not capitalism can survive the current turmoil.

Capitalism will survive, for the foreseeable future anyway. The disruptions following the economic crisis which began in 2008 may cause great suffering to many people, and the disastrous effects of the mania for deregulating markets may reveal the irrationalities of capitalism, but suffering and irrationality are never enough to generate fundamental social transformations. As in previous periods of financial collapse in the aftermath of speculative frenzies, so long as a viable alternative to capitalism is not actively on the historical agenda—and with broad popular support linked to a political movement able to translate that support into political power—capitalism will remain the dominant structure of economic organization.

This book has tried to contribute to the task of placing alternatives on the historical agenda. This has involved clarifying the diagnosis and critique of capitalism as an economic structure, elaborating a conceptual framework for thinking about emancipatory alternatives, and specifying the central elements of a theory of social transformation. Here are the key lessons:

1. *Capitalism obstructs the realization of both social justice and political justice*   This is the fundamental starting point in the search for alternatives: the critique of capitalism as a structure of power and inequality. The argument here is that the central mechanisms and processes that make capitalism a distinctive way of organizing economic activity inherently create obstacles to

universalizing the conditions for human flourishing and deepening democracy. This does not imply all social injustices are attributable to capitalism, nor does it imply that the complete elimination of capitalism is a necessary condition for significant advances in social and political justice. But it does imply that the struggle for human emancipation requires a struggle against capitalism, not simply a struggle within capitalism.

2. Economic structures are always hybrids While it is useful for analytical purposes to define "capitalism," "statism," and "socialism" as three qualitatively distinct types of economic structure, differentiated by the form of power that organizes economic activity, no concrete economic system is ever purely one or another of these forms. All actually existing contemporary economic systems are complex configurations of capitalist, statist, and socialist forms. This idea applies not just to national economies, but to all units of analysis within economic systems including firms: a capitalist firm with a strong works council combines capitalist and socialist elements, as does a worker-owned cooperative that hires some employees.

Within such hybrid configurations, to call an economic structure "capitalist" is to identify the dominant form of power within this configuration. A firm is capitalist if it is the case that the allocation and use of economic resources within the firm is primarily the result of the exercise of economic power. An economy is capitalist when capitalist power is the dominant form of power over economic activities within that economy. This has critical implications for our understanding of the problem of transformation: emancipatory transformation should not be viewed mainly as a binary shift from one system to another, but rather as a shift in the configuration of the power relations that constitute a hybrid.

3. The socialist hybrid The pivotal thesis of this book is that transcending capitalism in a way that robustly expands the possibilities for realizing radical democratic egalitarian conceptions of social and political justice requires social empowerment over the economy. This means taking democracy very seriously. A broad and deep social empowerment means, first, subordinating state power to social power rooted in civil society. This is the ordinary meaning of the idea of "democracy." Rule by the people means that power derived from voluntary association in civil society controls power rooted in the state. Social empowerment, however, is not restricted to meaningful democratic control of the state; it also means the subordination of economic power to social power. Fundamentally this means that private ownership of the means of production ceases to govern the allocation and use of productive resources. Finally, and perhaps most elusively, social empowerment means democratizing civil society itself: creating an associationally thick civil society populated by both narrow and encompassing associations organized on democratic egalitarian principles. Taken together, these processes of democratization would constitute a fundamental transformation of the class structure, for the core of the class relations of capitalism involves economic power linked to private ownership of the means of production. The full subordination of that power to social power means the end of the subordination of the working class to the capitalist class.

4. *Institutional pluralism and heterogeneity: multiple pathways of social empowerment* The long-term project of social empowerment over the economy involves enhancing social power through a variety of distinct kinds of institutional and structural transformations. Socialism should not be thought of as a unitary institutional model of how an economy should be organized, but rather as a pluralistic model with many different kinds of institutional pathways for realizing a common underlying principle. In chapter 5 I identified seven such pathways: statist socialism, social democratic economic regulation, associational democracy, social capitalism, social economy, cooperative market economy, and participatory socialism. These pathways are embodied in different ways in the specific real utopian innovations and proposals we explored in chapters 6 and 7: urban participatory budgeting, Wikipedia, the Quebec social economy for childcare and eldercare, unconditional basic income, solidarity funds, share-levy wage-earner funds, Mondragón, market socialism, and "parecon." No one of these pathways and specific proposals by itself is likely to constitute a viable framework for a socialist economy, but taken in combination they have the potential to shift the underlying configuration of power that controls economic activity.

5. *There are no guarantees: Socialism is a terrain for working for social and political justice, not a guarantee for realizing those ideals* Social justice, as I defined it in chapter 2, requires that all people have equal access to the necessary social and material means to live flourishing lives; political justice entails that all people

have equal access to the political means to participate in decisions that affect their lives. The dominance of social power over the economy does not guarantee the realization of these radical democratic egalitarian ideals. Civil society is an arena not only for the formation of democratic egalitarian associations, but also for exclusionary associations rooted in particularistic identities opposed to universalizing the conditions for human flourishing. Enhancing the role and power of associations within an economic structure could have the effect of reproducing oppressions within civil society rather than eroding them.

The argument for socialism defined as democratic power over the allocation and use of productive resources is thus not that socialism guarantees social and political justice, but rather that it creates the most favorable socioeconomic terrain on which to struggle for justice. This, basically, rests on what might be termed "faith in democracy": the belief that the more democratic the distribution of power is in a system the more likely it is that humane and egalitarian values will prevail. This presupposes not a belief in the innate goodness of people, but rather the belief that under conditions of a wide and deep democracy people will interact in ways in which the more humane impulses of our nature are more likely to prevail. But democracy can be hijacked. Exclusionary solidarities can be fostered as well as universalistic ones. There are no guarantees.

Philosophers and political activists share a common fantasy: If only we can design institutions in the perfect manner we can relax. If we had the best possible institutional form of democracy it would generate self-reinforcing dynamics which would continually strengthen democracy. Economists have fantasized the self-reproducing market: if only we designed the institutions of property rights just right, then markets would be self-reproducing, perpetually generating precisely the kinds of incentives and motivations needed for markets to function well. And at least some socialists have hoped that if capitalist power were destroyed and the new economic institutions run by workers were designed in just the right way then socialism would be self-reinforcing: the kinds of people needed to make socialism work smoothly would be engendered by those institutions, and the conflicts in society which might undermine those institutions would gradually disappear. This kind of aspiration underlay Marx's famous prediction of the "withering away of the state" as socialism evolved into communism.

All of these visions imagine that institutions can be designed in such a way as to produce precisely the kinds of people needed for those institutions to run smoothly and to marginalize any social processes which might undermine or disrupt the institutions. In short, they imagine a social system without contradictions, without destructive unintended consequences of individual and collective action, a system in a self-sustaining emancipatory equilibrium.

I do not believe that any complex social system, including certainly any socialist system, could ever conform to this ideal. Of course the design of institutions matters. The whole point of envisioning real utopias and thinking about the relationship between institutional designs and emancipatory ideals is to improve the chances of realizing certain values. But in the end the realization of those ideals will depend on human agency, on the creative willingness of people to participate in making a better world, learning from the inevitable mistakes, and vigorously defending the advances that are made. A fully realized socialism in which the arenas of power in society—the state, the economy, civil society—have been radically democratized may foster such willingness and increase the learning capacity of people to cope with unanticipated problems, but no institutional design can ever be perfectly self-correcting. We can never relax.

6. *Strategic indeterminacy: there is no one way* Movement towards radical democratic egalitarian ideals of social and political justice will not happen simply as an accidental by-product of unintended social change; if this is to be our future, it will be brought about by the conscious actions of people acting collectively to bring it about. This implies that a theory of transformation needs to include a theory of conscious agency and strategy.

Just as there are multiple institutional forms through which social power can be increased, there are multiple strategic logics through which these institutions can be constructed and advanced. We have examined three strategic logics of transformation: ruptural, interstitial, and symbiotic. No one of these strategic logics of transformation is likely to be adequate for the task of enhancing social power. Any plausible long-term trajectory of transformation needs to draw elements from all three. I argued in chapter 8 that at least within developed liberal democratic capitalist societies, systemic ruptures are implausible strategies for democratic egalitarianism. This does not imply, however, a rejection of all aspects of the ruptural logic of transformation. Partial ruptures, institutional breaks, and decisive innovations in specific spheres may be possible, particularly in periods of severe economic crisis. Above all, the conception of struggle within ruptural visions—struggle as challenge and confrontation, involving victories and defeats, rather than just collaborative problem-solving—remains essential for a realistic project of social empowerment.

These aspects of the ruptural logic must be combined with interstitial and symbiotic strategies. Interstitial strategies make possible the creation and deepening of socially empowered institutions from the bottom up. These new relations both function as practical demonstrations that another world is possible, and can potentially expand in ways which erode economic power. When this happens they are likely eventually to hit limits and confront organized opposition from capitalist forces, in which case the kind of political mobilizations and confrontations characteristic of ruptural strategies may be required in order to enlarge the spaces within which interstitial transformations can occur. Symbiotic strategies and transformations link ruling class interests to enlarged social power, thus stabilizing the institutional basis for social empowerment. This creates contexts for "positive class compromises" involving positive-sum games and active forms of problem-solving collaboration between opposing interests. Such contexts, however, are themselves embedded within rules of the game that make defections by powerful groups costly, and these rules are often the result of victories and defeats within more confrontational struggles.

How these strategic elements are best combined within a political project of social empowerment is highly dependent on specific historical settings and the real possibilities for (and limits on) "making history" that those settings create. What is more, given both the complexity of even the most favorable historical settings and the Pandora's box of unintended consequences, it is unlikely that even the most astute people in any setting will really know precisely how best to configure these strategic visions. Flexible strategic pluralism is the best we can do.

7. *Opacity of the future limits of possibility: We cannot know in advance how far we can go in this trajectory of social empowerment* The seven pathways of social empowerment provide a rough map of the direction of transformation needed to enhance the socialist component of the economic system. The logics of transformation tell us something about the strategies that

might move us along those pathways. But we cannot specify in advance the full array of institutional forms which will enable us to consolidate particular ways of deepening and enlarging social power on these pathways. Nor can we really know how far it is possible to move along them.

Earlier generations of socialists had greater confidence that a radically democratic economy in which capitalism had been overcome was actually possible. In the terms we have been using in this book, they were confident that social power, especially when it worked through the state, could become the dominant form of power over economic activity. Marx put forward the most forceful argument for such a view. He believed that he had discovered the laws of motion of capitalism with sufficient rigor to be able to predict that, in the long run, capitalism itself would destroy its own conditions of existence. As a result, capitalist economic power would eventually become a fragile and ineffective basis for organizing economic activity. The predicted long-term erosion of capitalist power, then, provided a fairly strong basis for the complementary prediction of the rise of social power organized by the working class to the dominant position within a radically transformed economic order. This thesis was based less on a systematic theory about how a deeply democratic and egalitarian structure of economic relations would function, and why it would be sustainable, and more on the claim that capitalism in the long term itself becomes impossible.

Once this strong theory of the demise of capitalism is dropped, as I argued in chapter 4, it becomes much more pressing to demonstrate that socialism itself is viable. It could be the case, however, that, contrary to aspirations for social emancipation, it is impossible in a complex economic system to construct a sustainable institutional and structural configuration within which social power would be the dominant form of power. A radical, democratic egalitarian economic system simply might not be viable under the conditions of scale and complexity of the contemporary world. Attempts to create such a socialist configuration might always prove unstable and degenerate into some form of either a statist or a capitalist economy. The best we can do might be to try to neutralize some of the most harmful effects of capitalism. In spite of the will there might be no way. That could be true.

But it could also be the case that the apparent limits to the expansion of social power are much weaker than we might suppose. And it could certainly be the case that, under future conditions which we cannot anticipate, those limits will be radically different from what they are today and that dramatic advances in social power would become possible. The world might then look something like this: Unconditional basic income frees up time for social economy participation. Share-levy wage-earner funds and solidarity funds enhance the capacity of unions and other associations to control firms and investments. Worker-owned cooperatives are revitalized by new information technologies which make cooperation among cooperatives easier, and new cooperative market infrastructures are developed which buffer producer cooperatives from destructive market pressures. Direct state involvement in the economy is combined with new forms of associational participation which improve the efficiency and accountability of state enterprises. Participatory budgeting diffuses across a wide range of cities and extends to new domains of government spending. And entirely new institutions as yet unforeseen are invented to push forward social empowerment in new ways. This too could be true.

I do not believe that my lack of confidence about the limits of possibility simply reflects a failure of theoretical imagination (although, of course, I could be wrong about this as well). Rather, I think it reflects the inherent problems involved in understanding the ramifications of unintended consequences within complex systems. But it is crucial, really crucial, not to slide from this frank admission of ignorance about the future limits of possibility to a belief that socialism is impossible. We simply do not know what the ultimate limits to the expansion of democratic egalitarian social empowerment might be. The best we can do, then, is treat the struggle to move forward on the pathways of social empowerment as an experimental process in which we continually test and retest the limits of possibility and try, as best we can, to create new institutions which will expand those limits themselves. In doing so we not only envision real utopias, but contribute to making utopias real.

BIBLIOGRAPHY

Abers, Rebecca, "From Clientelism to Cooperation: Participatory Policy and Civic Organizing in Porto Alegre, Brazil," *Politics and Society* 26: 4 (1998), pp. 511–37.

Ackerman, Bruce, *Voting With Dollars: A New Paradigm for Campaign Finance* (New Haven: Yale University Press, 2004).

Ackerman, Bruce, and Ann Alstott, *The Stakeholder Society* (New Haven: Yale University Press, 2000).

Ackerman, Bruce, and James S. Fishkin, *Deliberation Day* (New Haven: Yale University Press, 2005).

Ackerman, Bruce, Anne Alstott, and Philippe Van Parijs, *Redesigning Distribution: Basic Income and Stakeholder Grants as Cornerstones of a More Egalitarian Capitalism* (London: Verso, 2007).

Albert, Michael, *Parecon* (London: Verso, 2003).

Alexander, Jeffrey, *The Civil Sphere* (New York: Oxford University Press, 2006).

Alford, Robert, and Roger Friedland, *Powers of Theory: Capitalism, the State and Democracy* (Cambridge: Cambridge University Press, 1985).

Aoki, Masahiko, *Comparative Institutional Analysis* (Cambridge, MA: MIT Press, 2001).

Arrighi, Giovanni, *The Long Twentieth Century: Money, Power and the Origins of Our Times* (London: Verso, 1994).

Avritzer, Leonardo, "New Public Spheres in Brazil: Local Democracy and Deliberative Politics," *International Journal of Urban and Regional Research* 30: 3 (2006), pp. 623–37.

Baiocchi, Gianpaolo, *Militants and Citizens: The Politics of Participatory Democracy in Porto Alegre* (Stanford: Stanford University Press, 2005).

—— "Participation, Activism and Politics: The Porto Alegre Experiment," in Fung and Wright, *Deepening Democracy*, pp. 45–76.

Bakaikoa, Baleren, Anjel Errasti, and Agurtzane Begiristain, "Governance of the Mondragón Corporacion Cooperativa," *Annals of Public and Cooperative Economics* 75: 1 (2004), pp. 61–87.

Bernhardt, Annette, Laura Dresser, and Joel Rogers, "Taking the High Road in Milwaukee: The Wisconsin Regional Training Partnership," *WorkingUSA* 5: 3 (2004), pp. 109–30.

Blackburn, Robin, *Banking on Death, or, Investing in Life: The History and Future of Pensions* (London: Verso, 2002).

—— "Capital and Social Europe," *New Left Review* 34, July–August 2005, pp. 87–114.

—— "Rudolf Meidner, 1914–2005: A Visionary Pragmatist," *Counterpunch*, December 22, 2005, available at counterpunch.org.

—— "The Global Pension Crisis: From Gray Capitalism to Responsible Accumulation," *Politics and Society* 34: 2 (2006), pp. 135–86.

—— "Economic Democracy: Meaningful, Desirable, Feasible?," *Daedalus* 136: 3 (2007), pp. 36–45.

Boldrin, Michele, and David Levine, *Against Intellectual Monopoly* (Cambridge: Cambridge University Press, 2007).

Bowles, Samuel, "Policies Designed for Self-Interested Citizens May Undermine 'The Moral Sentiments': Evidence from Economic Experiments," *Science* 320: 5883 (June 20, 2008), pp. 1605–9.

Bowles, Samuel, and Herbert Gintis, *Schooling in Capitalist America* (New York: Basic Books, 1976).

Bowles, Samuel, and Herbert Gintis, *Recasting Egalitarianism: New Rules for Equity and Accountability in Markets, Communities and States* (London: Verso, 1999).

——"Contested Exchange: New Microfoundations for the Political Economy of Capitalism," *Politics and Society* 18: 2 (1990), pp. 165–222.

Buber, Martin, *Paths in Utopia* (Boston: Beacon Press, 1958 [1949]).

Burawoy, Michael, *Manufacturing Consent: Changes in the Labor Process Under Monopoly Capitalism* (Chicago: University of Chicago Press, 1979).

—— *The Politics of Production: Factory Regimes Under Capitalism and Socialism* (London: Verso, 1985).

Burawoy, Michael, and Erik Olin Wright, "Coercion and Consent in Contested Exchange," *Politics and Society* 18: 2 (1990), pp. 251–66.

Burawoy, Michael, and Erik Olin Wright, "Sociological Marxism," in Jonathan Turner (ed.), *Handbook of Sociological Theory* (New York: Kluwer Academic/Plenum Publishers, 2001).

Callinicos, Alex, *Making History: Agency, Structure, and Change in Social Theory* (Leiden: Brill, 2004).

Calmfors, L., and J. Driffill, "Bargaining Structure, Corporatism and Macroeconomic Performance," *Economic Policy* 6 (1988), pp. 13–61.

Chavez, Daniel, and B. Goldfrank, *The Left in the City: Participatory Local Governments in Latin America* (London: Latin America Bureau, 2004).

Cheney, George, *Values at Work: Employee Participation Meets Market Pressures at Mondragón* (Ithaca: ILR Press, 1999).

Cohen, G. A., *Karl Marx's Theory of History: A Defense* (Princeton: Princeton University Press, 1978).

—— *History, Labour and Freedom: Themes From Marx* (Oxford: Clarendon Press, 1988).

—— "Back to Socialist Basics," *New Left Review* 207, September–October 1994, pp. 3-16.

Cohen, Jean L., and Andrew Arato, *Civil Society and Political Theory* (Cambridge, MA: MIT Press, 1994).

Cohen, Joshua, and Joel Rogers, *On Democracy* (New York: Penguin Books, 1983).

—— *Associations and Democracy* (London: Verso, 1995).

Crosby, N., and D. Nethercutt, "Citizens Juries Creating a Trustworthy Voice of the People," in J. Gastil and P. Levine (eds), *The Deliberative Democracy Handbook* (San Francisco: Jossey-Bass, 2005).

Dahl, Robert A., *A Preface to Economic Democracy* (Berkeley and Los Angeles: University of California Press, 1985).

Dorf, Michael C. and Charles F. Sabel, "A Constitution of Democratic Experimentalism," *Columbia Law Review* 98: 2 (1998), pp. 267-473.

Dowie, Mark, "Pinto Madness," *Mother Jones*, September–October 1977.

Durkheim, Emile, *The Division of Labor* (New York: The Free Press, 1947).

Ebert, Justuys, "The Trial of a New Society" (IWW pamphlet: Chicago, 1913).

The Economist, "The Free-Knowledge Fundamentalist," *The Economist*, June 5, 2008.

Elster, Jon, *Making Sense of Marx* (Cambridge: Cambridge University Press, 1985).

—— "Comment on Van der Veen and Van Parijs," *Theory and Society* 15: 5 (1986), pp. 709–21.

Engelen, Ewald, "Resocializing Capital: Putting Pension Savings in the Service of 'Financial Pluralism'?," *Politics and Society* 34: 2 (2006), pp. 187–218.

Esping-Andersen, Gøsta, *Three Worlds of Welfare Capitalism* (Princeton, NJ: Princeton University Press, 1990).

Fishkin, James S., "Deliberative Polling: Toward a Better-Informed Democracy," available at http://cdd.stanford.edu.

Flecha, Ramon, *Sharing Words* (Lanham, MD: Rowman and Littlefield, 2000).

Folbre, Nancy, *The Invisible Heart: Economics and Family Values* (New York: The New Press, 2001).

Frank, Robert H., and Philip J. Cook, *The Winner-Take-All Society: Why the Few at the Top Get So Much More Than the Rest of Us* (New York: Penguin, 1996).

Fraser, Nancy, "Rethinking Recognition," *New Left Review* 3, May–June 2000, pp. 107-120.

Friedman, Milton, *Capitalism and Freedom* (Chicago: University of Chicago Press, 2002 [1962]).

Friedman, Milton, and Rose Friedman, *Free to Choose* (New York: Harcourt, 1980).

Fukuyama, Francis, *The End of History and the Last Man* (New York: The Free Press, 1992).

Fung, Archon, and Erik Olin Wright, *Deepening Democracy: Innovations in Empowered Participatory Governance* (London: Verso, 2003).

Fung, Archon, and Joshua Cohen, "Radical Democracy," *Swiss Journal of Political Science* 10: 4 (2004), pp. 23–34.

Gastil, John, "Citizens Initiative Review," available at http://faculty.washington.edu.

—— *By Popular Demand: Revitalizing Representative Democracy Through Deliberative Elections* (Berkeley: University of California Press, 2000).

Gastil, John, and P. Levine (eds), *The Deliberative Democracy Handbook* (San Francisco, CA: Jossey-Bass, 2005).

Gastil, J., J. Reedy, and C. Wells, "When Good Voters Make Bad Policies: Assessing and Improving the Deliberative Quality of Initiative Elections," *University of Colorado Law Review* 78 (2007), pp. 1435–88.

Gibson-Graham, J. K., *The End of Capitalism (As We Knew It): A Feminist Critique of Political Economy* (Oxford: Blackwell, 1996).

—— "A Diverse Economy: Rethinking Economy and Economic Representation" (2003), available at http://www.communityeconomies.org.

—— *A Postcapitalist Politics* (Minneapolis: University of Minnesota Press, 2006).

Giles, Jim, "Special Report: Internet Encyclopaedias Go Head to Head," *Nature* 438, December 15, 2005, pp. 900–1.

Glynn, Andrew, "Social Democracy and Full Employment," *New Left Review* 211 (1995), pp. 33–55.

Gornick, Janet, and Marcia Meyers, *Gender Equality: Transforming Family Divisions of Labor* (London: Verso, 2009).

Gould, Stephen Jay, *The Panda's Thumb* (New York: W. W. Norton, 1980).

Gramsci, Antonio, *Selections from the Prison Notebooks*, edited and translated by Quentin Hoare and Geoffrey Nowell Smith (London: Lawrence and Wishart, 1971).

Haarmann, Claudia, Dirk Haarmann et al., "Making the Difference! The BIG in Namibia: Basic Income Grant Pilot Project Assessment Report, April 2009," available at http://www.bignam.org.

Hansmann, Henry, *The Ownership of Enterprise* (Cambridge, MA: Harvard University Press, 1996).

Hayek, Frederick A., *The Fatal Conceit: The Errors of Socialism* (Chicago: University of Chicago Press, 1991).

Healy, Kieran, *Last Best Gifts: Altruism and the Market for Human Blood and Organs* (Chicago: University of Chicago Press, 2006).

Hibbing, John R., and Elizabeth Theiss-Morse, *Stealth Democracy: Americans' Beliefs About How Government Should Work* (New York: Cambridge University Press, 2002).

Hodgson, Geoff, *Economics and Utopia: Why the Learning Economy is Not the End of History* (London: Routledge, 1999).

ILO Department of Communication, "Solidarity Fund: Labour-sponsored Solidarity Funds in Quebec are Generating Jobs," *World of Work* 50 (2004), pp. 21–2.

Jackson, Robert Max, *Destined for Equality: The Inevitable Rise of Women's Status* (Cambridge: Harvard University Press, 1998).

Jaffee, Daniel, *Brewing Justice: Fair Trade Coffee, Sustainability, and Survival* (Berkeley: University of California Press, 2007).

James, David, "The Transformation of the Southern Racial State: Class and Race Determinants of Local-State Structures," *American Sociological Review*, 53 (1988), pp. 191–208.

Kateb, George, "The Moral Distinctiveness of Representative Democracy," *Ethics* 91 (1981), pp. 357–74.

Kenworthy, Lane, "Equality and Efficiency: The Illusory Tradeoff," *European Journal of Political Research* 27: 2 (2006), pp. 225–54.

—— *Egalitarian Capitalism: Jobs, Incomes, and Growth in Affluent Countries* (New York: Russell Sage Foundation, 2007).

Lang, Amy, "But is it For Real? The British Columbia Citizens' Assembly as a Model of State-sponsored Citizen Empowerment," *Politics and Society*, 35: 1 (2007), pp. 35–70.

—— *A New Tool for Democracy? The Contours and Consequences of Citizen Deliberation in the British Columbia Citizens' Assembly on Electoral Reform* (PhD dissertation, Department of Sociology, University of Wisconsin, 2007).

Layard, Richard, *Happiness* (New York: Penguin, 2005).

Levi, Margaret, *Of Rule and Revenue* (Berkeley: University of California Press, 1989).

Lindblom, Charles E., *Politics and Markets: The World's Political Economic Systems* (New York: Basic Books, 1977).

MacDonald, Jack, *Randomocracy: A Citizens Guide to Electoral Reform in British Columbia* (Victoria, BC: PCG Publications, 2005).

Udi Manber, "Encouraging People to contribute knowledge", *The Official Google Blog*, posted December 31, 2007, http://googleblog.blogspot.com/2007/12/encouraging-people-to-contribute.html.

Mann, Michael, *The Sources of Social Power: A History of Power from the Beginning to A.D. 1760*, Vol. I (Cambridge: Cambridge University Press, 1986).

Marx, Karl, *The Eighteenth Brumaire of Louis Bonaparte* (New York: International Publishers, 1852 [1977]).

Marx, Karl, and Frederick Engels, *Selected Works in Two Volumes*, Vol. I (Moscow: Foreign Languages Publishing House, 1962).

Mendell, Marguerite, "The Social Economy in Québec: Discourses and Strategies," in Abigail Bakan and Eleanor MacDonald (eds), *Critical Political Studies: Debates From the Left* (Kingston: Queen's University Press, 2002), pp. 319–43.

—— "L'empowerment au Canada et au Québec: enjeux et opportunités," *Economie, géographie et société* 8: 1, janvier–mars 2006, pp. 63–86.

Mendell, Marguerite, Benoit Levesque, and Ralph Rouzier, "The Role of the Non-profit Sector in Local Development: New Trends," paper presented at the OECD/LEED Forum on Social Innovation, August 31, 2000.

Mendell, Marguerite, J-L. Laville, and B. Levesque, "The Social Economy: Diverse Approaches and Practices in Europe and Canada," in A. Noya and E. Clarence (eds), *The Social Economy: Building Inclusive Economies* (France: OECD Publications, 2007), pp. 155–87.

Miliband, Ralph, "The Capitalist State: Reply to Poulantzas," *New Left Review* 59, January–February 1970, pp. 53–60.

—— "Poulantzas and the Capitalist State," *New Left Review* 82, November–December 1973, pp. 83–92.

Mondragón, *Annual Report 2007* (Mondragón Corporate Center, Spain: Mondragon, 2007); available at: http://www.mcc.es.

Mouffe, Chantal, "Hegemony and Ideology in Gramsci," in Chantal Mouffe (ed.), *Gramsci and Marxist Theory* (London: Routledge and Kegan Paul, 1979), pp. 168–206.

Nakane, Chie, *Japanese Society* (London: Weidenfeld and Nicholson, 1970).

Neamtan, Nancy, "The Social Economy: Finding a Way Between the Market and the State," *Policy Options*, July/August 2005, pp. 71–6.

—— "Building The Social Economy: The Quebec Experience," presentation at a seminar organized by Euresa Institute Stockholm, Sweden, March 29–30, 2005.

Neamtan, Nancy, and Rupert Downing, "Social Economy and Community Economic Development in Canada: Next Steps for Public Policy," *Chantier de l'économie sociale* issues paper, September 19, 2005.

Nussbaum, Martha C., *Women and Human Development: The Capabilities Approach* (Cambridge: Cambridge University Press, 2000).

Offe, Claus, "Structural Problems of the Capitalist State: Class Rule and the Political System. On the Selectiveness of Political Institutions," in Klaus Von Beyme (ed.), *German Political Studies*, Vol. I (London: Sage, 1974), pp. 31–54.

—— "The Capitalist State and the Problem of Policy Formation," in Leon Lindberg et al. (eds), *Stress and Contradiction in Contemporary Capitalism* (Lexington: D. C. Heath, 1975), pp. 125–44.

—— "The Crisis of Crisis Management: Elements of a Political Crisis Theory," in Claus Offe, *Contradictions of the Welfare State* (London: Hutchinson, 1984), pp. 35–61.

Offe, Claus, and Helmut Wiesenthal, "Two Logics of Collective Action: Theoretical Notes on Social Class and Organizational Form," in Maurice Zeitlin (ed.), *Political Power and Social Theory*, Vol. 1 (Greenwich, CT: JAI Press, 1980), pp. 67–116.

Oregonwatersheds, "2007 Watershed Councils in Oregon: An Atlas of Accomplishments," available at http://www.oregonwatersheds.org

Overdevest, Christine, "Codes of Conduct and Standard Setting in the Forest Sector: Constructing Markets for Democracy?," *Relations Industrielles/Industrial Relations* 59: 1 (2004), pp. 172–97.

Piliavin, Jane A., and Peter L. Callero, *Giving Blood: The Development of an Altruistic Identity* (Baltimore: Johns Hopkins University Press, 1991).

Poe, Marshall, "The Hive," *The Atlantic Monthly*, September 2006.

Polanyi, Karl, *The Great Transformation: The Political and Economic Origins of Our Time* (Boston: Beacon Press, 2001 [1944]).

Pontusson, Jonas, *The Limits of Social Democracy* (Ithaca, NY: Cornell University Press, 1992).

—— "Sweden: After the Golden Age," in Perry Anderson and Patrick Camiller (eds), *Mapping the West European Left* (London: Verso, 1994), pp. 23–54.

—— "Between Neo-Liberalism and the German Model: Swedish Capitalism in Transition," in Colin Crouch and Wolfgang Streeck (eds), *Political Economy of Modern Capitalism: Mapping Convergence and Diversity* (Thousand Oaks, CA: Sage, 1997), pp. 50–70.

Posner, Richard, *Law, Pragmatism, and Democracy* (Cambridge, MA: Harvard University Press, 2003).

Poulantzas, Nicos, *Political Power and Social Classes* (London: New Left Books, 1975).

—— "The Problem of the Capitalist State," *New Left Review* 58, November–December 1969, pp. 67–78.

Przeworski, Adam, *Capitalism and Social Democracy* (Cambridge: Cambridge University Press, 1985).

—— "Self-enforcing Democracy," in Donald Wittman and Barry Weingast (eds), *Oxford Handbook of Political Economy* (New York: Oxford University Press, 2006).

Przeworski, Adam, and John Sprague, *Paper Stones* (Chicago: Chicago University Press, 1988).

Purdy, David, "Citizenship, Basic Income and the State," *New Left Review* 208, November–December 1994, pp. 30–48.

Quebec Federation of Labour, *Annual Report of the Solidarity Fund 2007*.

—— *Annual Report of the Solidarity Fund 2008*.

Rodriguez-Garavito, Cesar, "Global Governance and Labor Rights: Codes of Conduct and Anti-Sweatshop Struggles in Global Apparel Factories in Mexico and Guatemala," *Politics and Society* 33: 2 (2005), pp. 203–233.

Roemer, John (ed.), *Analytical Marxism* (Cambridge: Cambridge University Press, 1985).

Roemer, John, *A Future for Socialism* (Cambridge, MA: Harvard University Press, 1994).

—— *Equal Shares: Making Market Socialism Work* (London: Verso, 1996).

Rogers, Joel, "Divide and Conquer: Further 'Reflections on the Distinctive Character of American Labor Law'," *Wisconsin Law Review* 13 (1990), pp. 1–147.

Rogers, Joel, and Wolfgang Streeck, "Productive Solidarities: Economic Strategy and Left Politics," in David Miliband (ed.), *Reinventing the Left* (Cambridge: Polity Press, 1994), pp. 128–45.

Rothbart, Murray, *The Ethics of Liberty* (New York: NYU Press, 1998).

Ryan, William, *Equality* (New York: Pantheon Books, 1981).

Sánchez Aroca, Montse, "La Verneda-Sant Martí: A School Where People Dare to Dream," *Harvard Educational Review* 69: 3 (1999), pp. 320–57.

Sanger, Larry, "The Early History of Nupedia and Wikipedia: A Memoir," *Slashdot*, April 18, 2005, http://features.slashdot.org.

Santos, Boaventura de Sousa, "Participatory Budgeting in Porto Alegre: Towards a Redistributive Democracy," *Politics and Society* 26: 4 (1998), pp. 461–510.

—— (ed.), *Democratizing Democracy: Beyond the Liberal Democratic Canon* (London: Verso, 2006).

Sayer, Andrew, *The Moral Significance of Class* (Cambridge: Cambridge University Press, 2005).

Seidman, Gay, *Manufacturing Militance: Workers' Movements in Brazil and South Africa, 1970–1985* (Berkeley: University of California Press, 1994).

Seidman, Gay, *Beyond the Boycott: Labor Rights, Human Rights and Transnational Activism* (New York: Russell Sage Foundation, 2007).

Schmitter, Philippe, "Corporatism is Dead! Long Live Corporatism! Reflections on Andrew Schonfield's *Modern Capitalism*," *Government and Opposition* 24 (1988), pp. 54–73.

Schmitter, Philippe, and G. Lembruch (eds), *Trends Towards Corporatist Intermediation* (London: Sage, 1979).

Schumpeter, Joseph, *Capitalism, Socialism, and Democracy* (New York: Harper and Row, 1942).

Schor, Juliet, *The Overworked American: The Unexpected Decline of Leisure* (New York: Basic Books, 1992).

—— *The Overspent American: Upscaling, Downshifting and the New Consumer* (New York: Basic Books, 1998).

Sen, Amartya, *Development as Freedom* (Oxford: Oxford University Press, 1999).

Sintomer, Yves, Carsten Herzberg, and Anja Rocke, "Participatory Budgeting in Europe: Potentials and Challenges," *International Journal of Urban and Regional Research* 32: 1 (2008), pp. 164–78.

Siriani, Carmen, and Lewis A. Friedland, *The Civic Renewal Movement: Community Building and Democracy in the United States* (Dayton, OH: Kittering Foundation Press, 2005).

Skocpol, Theda, *States and Social Revolutions* (Cambridge: Cambridge University Press, 1979).
—— "Advocates Without Members: The Recent Transformation of American Civic Life," in Theda Skocpol and Morris P. Fiorina (eds), *Civic Engagement in American Democracy* (Washington, DC: Brookings and Russell Sage Foundation, 1999).
Sørenson, Aage B., "Toward a Sounder Basis for Class Analysis," *American Journal of Sociology* 105: 6 (2000), pp. 1523–58.
Steedman, Ian, *Marx after Sraffa* (London: New Left Books, 1977).
Steiner, Hillel, "Three Just Taxes," in Phillipe Van Parijs (ed.), *Arguing for Basic Income* (London: Verso, 1996).
Streeck, Wolfgang, "Community, Market, State and Associations? The Prospective Contribution of Interest Governance to Social Order," in Wolfgang Streeck and Philippe C. Schmitter (eds), *Private Interest Government: Beyond Market and State* (Beverley Hills and London: Sage, 1985), pp. 1–29.
—— *Social Institutions and Economic Performance: Studies of Industrial Relations in Advanced Capitalist Economies* (Newbury Park, CA: Sage, 1992).
Tapscott, Don, and Anthony D. Williams, *Wikinomics: How Mass Collaboration Changes Everything* (New York: Penguin, 2006).
Therborn, Göran, *What Does the Ruling Class Do When it Rules?* (London: NLB, 1978).
—— *The Power of Ideology and the Ideology of Power* (London: Verso, 1980).
Thomas, Craig, "Habitat Conservation Planning," in Archon Fung and Erik Olin Wright (eds), *Deepening Democracy* (London: Verso, 2003), chapter 5, pp. 144–72.
Van der Veen, Robert, and Philippe Van Parijs, "A Capitalist Road to Communism," *Theory and Society* 15: 5 (1986), pp. 635–55.
Van Parijs, Philippe, "The Second Marriage of Justice and Efficiency," in Philippe Van Parijs (ed.), *Arguing for Basic Income* (London: Verso, 1992), pp. 215–34.
—— *Real Freedom for All* (Oxford: Oxford University Press, 1997).
Ward, Colin, *Anarchy in Action* (London: Allen and Unwin, 1973).
Warren, Bill, *Imperialism: Pioneer of Capitalism* (London: Verso, 1980).
Weber, Max, "Politics as a Vocation," in Hans Gerth and C. Wright Mills (eds), *From Max Weber* (New York: Oxford University Press, 1946).
White, Stuart, "Making Anarchism Respectable? The Social Philosophy of Colin Ward," *Journal of Political Ideologies* 12: 1 (2007), pp. 12–31.
Woolhandler, Steffie, Terry Campbell, and David U. Himmelstein, "Costs of Health Care Administration in the United States and Canada," *The New England Journal of Medicine* 349 (2003), pp. 768–75.
Wright, Erik Olin, *Class, Crisis and the State* (London: Verso, 1978).
—— *Classes* (London: Verso, 1985).
—— "Why Something like Socialism is Necessary for the Transition to Something like Communism," *Theory and Society* 15: 5 (1986). Reprinted in *Interrogating Inequality* (London: Verso, 1992), pp. 157–72.
—— *The Debate on Classes* (London: Verso, 1989).
—— *Interrogating Inequality* (London: Verso, 1994).

—— *Class Counts* (Cambridge: Cambridge University Press, 1997).

—— "Working-Class Power, Capitalist-Class Interests and Class Compromise," *American Journal of Sociology* 105: 4 (2000), pp. 957–1002.

—— "The Shadow of Exploitation in Weber's Class Analysis," *American Sociological Review* 67: 6 (2002), pp. 832–53.

—— (ed.), *Approaches to Class Analysis* (Cambridge: Cambridge University Press, 2005).

—— "Compass Points: Towards a Socialist Alternative," *New Left Review* 41, September–October 2006, pp. 93–124.

Wright, Erik Olin, and Joel Rogers, *American Society: How it Really Works* (New York: W. W. Norton, 2010).

Wright, Erik Olin, and Rachel Dwyer, "Patterns of Job Expansion and Contraction in the United States, 1960s–1990s," *Socioeconomic Review* 1 (2003), pp. 289–325.

Wright, Erik Olin, Andrew Levine, and Elliott Sober, *Reconstructing Marxism: Essays on Explanation and the Theory of History* (London: Verso, 1992).

INDEX